The Alhambra and the Generalife

An Art History Guide

The Alhambra and the Generalife

An Art History Guide

M.ª Elena Díez Jorge (ed.)

TEXTS
M.ª Elena Díez Jorge
José Manuel Gómez-Moreno Calera
Pedro A. Galera Andreu

PHOTOGRAPHY
Vicente del Amo
(except those credited to José Manuel Gómez-Moreno Calera)

MAPS
Lourdes Gutiérrez Carrillo
based on the ordinance survey map
(except those credited to Antonio Orihuela Uzal)

ARABIC TERMINOLOGY
Juan Castilla Brazales

TRANSLATION INTO ENGLISH
Bryan Robinson

COVER DESIGN
AL•ER, Portada Fotocomposición, S. L. Granada.

DESIGN, LAYOUT AND PREPRINTS
Portada Fotocomposición, S. L. Granada.

PRINTED BY
Imprenta Comercial. Motril (Granada).

BOOKBINDERS
Encuadernaciones Olmedo Hnos., S. L.

DEPÓSITO LEGAL
GR.–1501/2008

I.S.B.N.
978-84-338-4864-2

Printed in Spain

Impreso en España

Index

APPENDICES

Prologue

SOME YEARS AGO, *in my former role as Director of the Alhambra and Generalife trust, (Patronato de la Alhambra y del Generalife) I commissioned a new edition of the official guidebook to the monument to replace the earlier, 1988 edition. The commission entailed significant revision and broadening of contents as well as the creation of a tool for study that would complement its specific use on a visit.*

The present work, coordinated by Elena Díez Jorge in collaboration with José Manuel Gómez-Moreno and Pedro Galera Andreu, is the result of that commission. The authors are university teachers who have conducted substantial research into the Nasrid complex. Elena Díez Jorge has studied the layering of Islamic and Christian elements from the point of view of multiculturalism, as well as having made a suggestive interpretation of the use of spaces from the perspective of the feminine and masculine in the architecture. José Manuel Gómez-Moreno has pursued his principle interest in the architectural defences and Pedro Galera Andreu, as well as being the author of a volume on the romantic image of the Alhambra, has conducted various studies of the Palacio de Carlos V. The three, as university teachers, have often followed their own paths through the complex, accompanied by their students, unravelling its qualities. Their experience of research and teaching come together to produce the present, scientifically and didactically grounded volume: something much more than a typical, run-of-the-mill guidebook.

The "guide" is a genre of artistic literature with a long, fruitful tradition. Art historians of importance have had no qualms about availing themselves of the genre in order to present the findings of their research in a concise format, succeeding in making good the enlightened ideal of popularizing knowledge. Today the genre has been somewhat devalued. Guidebooks are written in haste by people with limited knowledge, or even unconnected with the specialized field of art history, and are usually mere commercial products for the consumption of an undemanding tourist market. When they do not actually include gross errors of detail, these appear in the overall presentation: a jumble of names, dates and data mingled with anecdotes but lacking an interpretative overview that selects, structures and organizes information to offer a coherent vision of the historic meaning and aesthetic values of a city, monument or museum exhibits. When present, such an overview dignifies the genre and links it to the tradition I mentioned earlier. The authors of the present guide have fully accomplished their aim of presenting indisputable facts about the precinct in Granada within an interpretative overview: the information and structure draw on the most recent studies of the topic and state-of-the-art methodological approaches to the historiography of art.

The book is in two parts. The first, an introductory "History of the Alhambra: spaces, life and people" establishes the principle themes that are later elaborated and enlarged on in the second part. Among other topics, it deals with architecture, understood not as an index of types and purely formal elements but in relation to its practical and symbolic functions; the historic layers (the Muslim Alhambra and the Christian Alhambra), viewed not as sentimental adherence to the past but with rigorous, historic consciousness, capable of appreciating the cultural contribution and formal interrelationships. The brief section dedicated to the "Care of the Alhambra" is highly relevant as, if the monument has survived to our times this has not been due to chance or love, as one prestigious specialist in Arabic studies would have it, but to reason. At the turn of the nineteenth century a concept of modern historic knowledge was established that made the conservation of monuments a basic requirement. A requirement that, in Granada's Alhambra precinct, has been fulfilled in exemplary fashion.

The second part, "Visit to the Alhambra and the Generalife", proposes an exhaustive, documented, guided tour. Centred on the inside of the walled precinct and the almunia *of the Generalife – the Generalife estate comprising the palaces surrounded by their gardens – we are invited to follow other paths that complement and enrich our experience of the place: the wooded Bosque de Gomérez, the Dehesa, – the meadows in the Generalife – or the enticing pedestrian route via the Cuesta de los Chinos, and the indispensable view from the city.*

The text, written in a clear style, does not overdo the use of specialized terminology and, when this is unavoidable, provides precise definitions in the glossary (one of several useful, well-thought-out appendices). Likewise, the neat, up-to-date transcriptions from the Arabic, made with the advice of Juan Castilla Brazales, a researcher at Spain's national science research council School of Arabic Studies and the person responsible for the corpus of epigraphs of the Alhambra. Finally, the graphic material brilliantly completes the volume. Together with the planimetry of Lourdes Gutiérrez Carrillo and Antonio Orihuela Uzal, the photographs by Vicente del Amo, lecturer in the University of Granada's Faculty of Fine Arts, eloquently underline the formal qualities of the architecture: the relationship with the countryside, the geometry of volumes and spaces, or light as the element that gives shape to matter.

This work has come to light thanks to the University of Granada press and the Andalusian regional government department of Innovation, Science and Business in collaboration with Granada's Institute of Quantity Surveyors. It is a good example of how one objective of university publications – the social dissemination of knowledge – should be interpreted. Written by university teachers in response to visitors' desire to understand, it will also serve students of Islamic art at university level who, to date, lacked a manual that rigorously but simply helped them study the Nasrid monument.

Mateo Revilla Uceda
Senior lecturer in Art History, University of Granada
Former Director of the Alhambra and Generalife trust

Introduction

WHEN WE VISIT A MONUMENT WE WANT TO SEE, *understand and feel it. In the Alhambra we want to see the spaces, their formal elements, the countryside, the surroundings..., to see in order to understand what others saw and felt in their time. To understand in order to feel the pleasure of water, light, the gardens, and especially to feel the pleasure of being able to attain a deeper knowledge of Islam, a deeper understanding of medieval times in al-Andalus.*

Many visitors arrive here with just such a desire and we want to respond to them when they enter into these pages. So, this Guide has been created as something more than a simple descriptive tour of the rooms and spaces of the precinct. We wanted to present a collection of reflections that would guide visitors into each corner of the Alhambra and the Generalife, suggesting more than describing, so you can sense what it may have been like in times gone by.

The magnificence of the Alhambra and the Generalife is such that one visit is not enough to understand it. That is why this Guide is intended to offer you a tool you can read even if you are far away from the Alhambra, so you can continue to feel and live the Alhambra, in spite of the distance.

In these pages you will find suggestions and reflections to increase your understanding of the Alhambra and the Generalife but also – and why not? – to give free reign to your imagination as you begin a journey through time.

Essentially, the book is divided into two parts. In the opening pages we reflect on the meaning of the Alhambra as a palace city and the place it occupies in the history of architecture. Aspects treated superficially in traditional guides to the precinct are gathered together to offer not just a historic and artistic analysis of the Alhambra, but also to give you, the reader, clues as to its interpretation so you can question the monument: How did the meeting of cultures in the Alhambra take place? What was daily life in the palaces like? These are some of the topics openly analyzed in these first pages.

The second part of the book suggests tours, following different routes that gradually uncover each of the individual parts that make up the precinct. We analyze each of the spaces and rooms and their outstanding features through text and image, initially accompanied by a brief summary to help locate the period and style of the space you are visiting.

Finally, a series of annexes present key figures cited in the book because of their connections with the Alhambra and the Generalife, historic events, and a glossary of words and terms intended to help you with some of the questions that occur to you while reading these pages.

The responsibility that a book of this nature entails is, we believe, compatible with our choice of style. While maintaining the maximum scientific rigour, we hope it both stimulates and attracts the reader. As authors, we hope to transmit not only our knowledge of the Alhambra, distilled from years of work, but also the immense passion, delight and respect that the Alhambra gives us, day in and day out, never failing to surprise.

The Authors

History of the Alhambra: Spaces, life and people

The Alhambra: A palace city

The hill called La Sabīka, summit of paradise and power

THE FIRST THING THAT SURPRISES about the Alhambra is its geographical location on a hill sometimes likened to a ship with, at its bows, the walled precinct of the Alcazaba sited on the spur closest to the city. This location, without a doubt, conditions the shape and subsequent evolution of the Alhambra. The building has clearly adapted to the hilltop: as well as laying its foundations in the very materials of the hill, it draws the most out of the earth and the water of its surroundings. However, La Sabīka (al-Sabīka), the hill, and the Alhambra do not constitute an isolated space. Their varying heights facilitated the establishment of other buildings, some for private use and others for defence, that are set out like a crown around them.

To a certain extent, the geographical space conditions the siting of the three main areas the palace city can be divided into: the essentially military area, the centre of which ran from the beginning of the spur that looks out towards the city of Granada; the palace area, distributed all over the site but which in its final configuration would be grouped especially on the north side of the hill; and the area dedicated to housing and services, extending to the south.

The Alhambra's position on a high, rugged hill does not make it a palace city isolated within its walls but, rather, a city with needs that stretch out into its surroundings. The Torres Bermejas would be the defensive bastion of the Alcazaba, defending it from the Antequeruela, where the Jewish quarter (or Garnāṭat al-Yahūd); spread out; the Silla del Moro or Castillo del Moro controlled access from the River Darro valley and, especially, the arrival of water along the Acequia Real (Royal Watercourse). Near the Silla del Moro, the palace or estate, *almunia*, of Dar al-Arusa (Dār al-'Arūsa); would be constructed. The extension of a recreational space with the Generalife was completed with its vegetable gardens, a truly royal *almunia* supplying the Alhambra. In short, the Alhambra's surroundings have to be understood as a complete urban-agrarian system intended not just to fulfil their needs but also to continue extending the residential areas as the Dār al-'Arūsa palace shows.

In this outer urban area, the woods that surround and isolate the Alhambra attract your attention but, in fact, they distort the earlier image of a steep, impregnable hill, handed down through history by the travellers and painters who gazed on it. The wood has gained an upper hand over the Alhambra, making a very different impression to that it once did. The greenery has taken a leading role in our perception, replacing the bare curtain walls.

The creation of these woods many years after the Nasrid dynasty meant the fortress lost its essential defensive capacity. Although the question of whether or not a wood existed in Nasrid times has remained controversial – a hunting reserve did exist here under Christian rule – what we actually see today is largely a product of the nineteenth and twentieth centuries. Nevertheless, it has been suggested there must have been some woodlands during the Nasrid period where the Sultan could hunt, and the area close to the Generalife has been considered a possible location. However, the natural environment that surrounds the Alhambra is not solely centred on these woods as the Generalife's terraced vegetable gardens stretch out on the northern side and remnants of the walls built there can still be seen.

This privileged location, which has been compared with the Acropolis of Ancient Greece, helps reinforce both its markedly defensive nature and the majesty and omnipresence of a space where the summit of political and religious power is clearly perceived in the definitive perimeter of its walls.

However, before it attained the form that we see today, the Alhambra lived a long history. The Alhambra, Qal'at al-Ḥamrā', the Red Castle, mentioned in a ninth-century chronicle, was a castle defending a strategic location as the lookout post of Umayyad Granada. Under the Zirids, the castle was reinforced, despite being relegated to second place behind the all-important frontier hill of the Albaicín, the main enclave at the time.

The arrival of the Nasrids was to reverse roles and the Alhambra would become a great city where a wide variety of buildings would have to be constructed, needed not only for

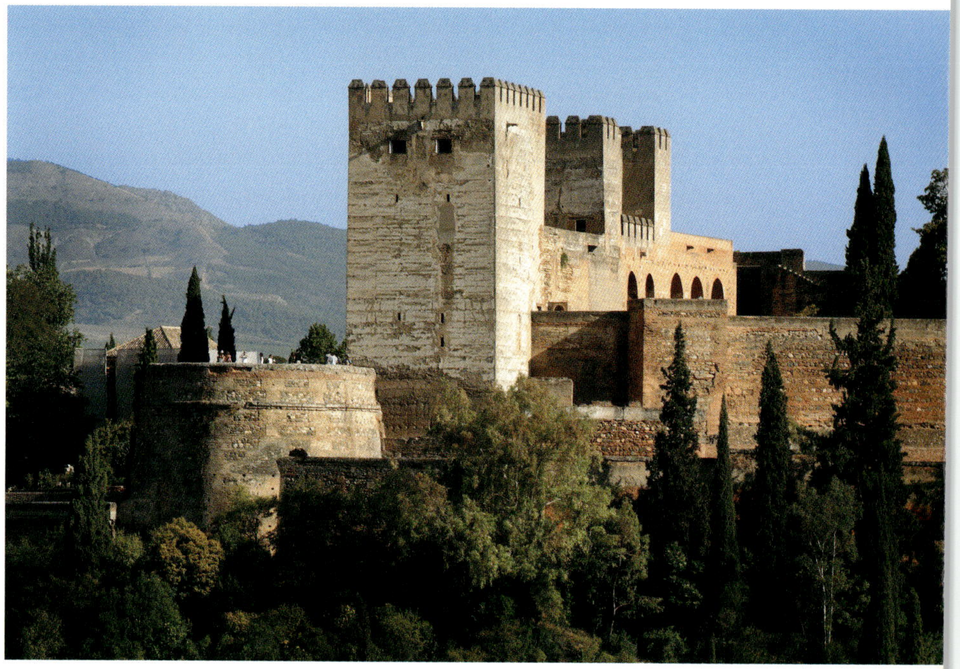

The towers of the Alhambra comprise a varied catalogue of forms and functions; together some of them constitute an important defensive structure.

physical survival, but also to express the political prestige of government. La Sabīka became the stronghold, the heart of the capital city of the recently created sultanate. In the beginning, Muḥammad I (1237-1273), or Alhamar as the founder of the Nasrid dynasty was known, would raise up the great Torre de la Vela and Torre del Homenaje entirely military constructions. But his first efforts would be surpassed in the following century with the consolidation of the palace city, converting the distorted shapes of the fortress into a regal stage, ostentatious, filled with prestige, to which the revealing structures of whimsically decorated rooms and infinite inscriptions were added.

In the Alhambra, the need for walls and their complexity is understood as a specific issue of strategy and security, given the historical circumstances in which it had to be built and its role as territorial capital. These walls, with their towers and gates, became a sophisticated system fulfilling different functions. At first sight, their essential purpose was to defend against attack from outside, but no less important was their role in controlling the comings and goings of inhabitants, visitors, numerous suppliers and all those who undertook one or another of the activities derived from the specific nature of the city. Some towers are believed to have played a role in the security and vigilance of the inside. We should also bear in mind their purely political value in representing the power of the Sultan, which can be seen in the way the towers and, above all, the palace gates evolved.

In addition to the walled precinct, the Alcazaba also contributed to the defence of the Alhambra. As headquarters of the palace city and jail too, it possesses a structural unity of its own. Initially, in the thirteenth

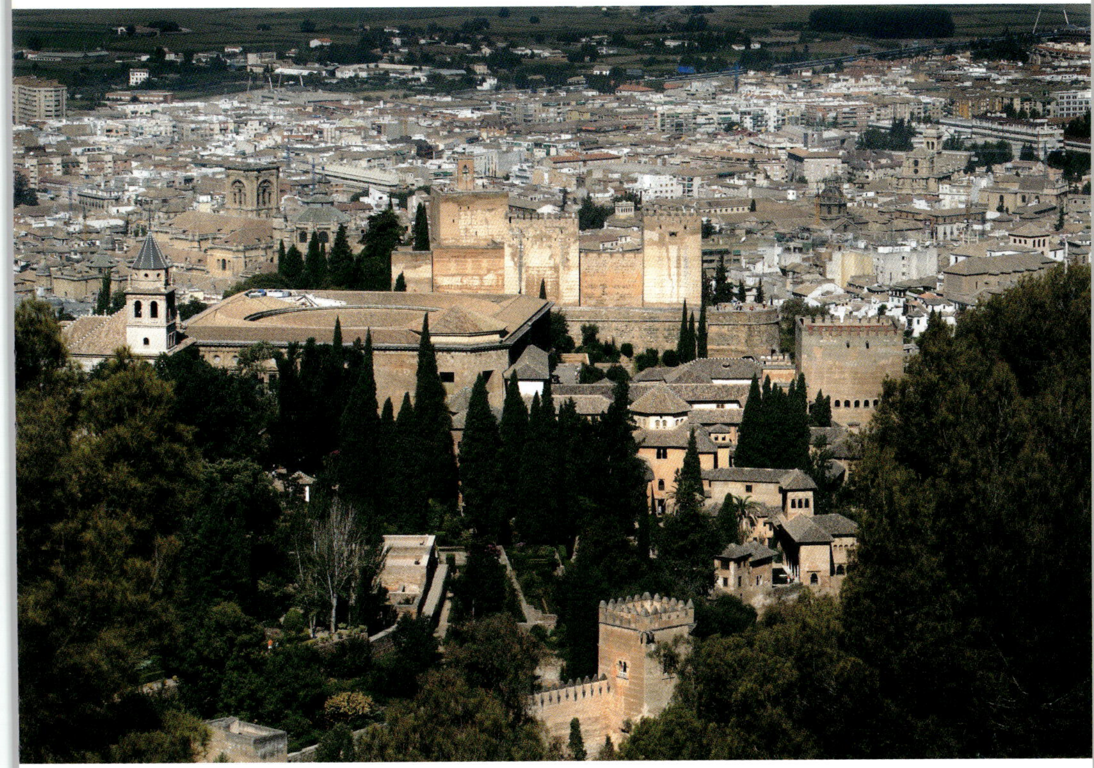

The Alhambra was built on one of the highest points of the city of Granada, the hill of La Sabīka. The site is not only a strategic defensive position but, moreover, a clear symbol of power and dominion, as portrayed in the mind of Arab poets through beautiful metaphors such as in the poem by al-Maqqarī in *Nafḥ al-ṭīb*.

"Await on La Sabīka and look from its esplanade: the city is the bride who reveals herself to the mountain, her husband"

(English version based on a translation from Arabic into Spanish by M.ª Jesús Rubiera Mata)

century, the Alcazaba and the palace city may well have been separate: the one cut off from the other as independent units with a deep pit where today we find a square known as the Plaza de los Aljibes. Originally, then, there was a defensive structure and perfectly articulated organization that only fourteenth century and, above all, Christians modifications to the palace, have hidden or distorted to some degree.

Traditionally, it has been the Alhambra's role as a fortress that has been highlighted, without integrating its defensive role with others that it might have played. But, beyond this principally defensive function, the Alhambra is first and foremost a palace city. A city first inhabited by the Nasrid sultans which, after the conquest of the city of Granada in 1492, began to be converted into a residential space for its new Christian kings.

A living space for the rulers does not mean just thinking of halls and rooms adequate for day-to-day life in the palace, as well as receptions and feasts; it also entails the entire infrastructure that a court needs for its maintenance. Consequently, artisans and food suppliers also gathered together in this place. The *medina* of the Alhambra was converted into a city created to serve the Court and filled with the life of its commerce, public baths, mosques, houses in the lower part near the Puerta del Vino, and workshops in the upper part of the city.

Architectural evolution of the Alhambra

ALTHOUGH, GIVEN ITS STRATEGIC LOCATION, the hill of La Sabīka may have been inhabited since the Romans or the Visigoths, the first recognisable remains date from the Islamic period. Some researchers consider the foundations made of a particularly hard cement that come to the surface in the lower part of the northern wall of the Alcazaba are the oldest remains.

The first written reference to the existence of a construction of some sort on the Alhambra goes back to 889 when, during the Berber and muwallad uprisings, Qal'at al-Ḥamrā' the Red Castle, is mentioned as a refuge of troops loyal to the Emir of Cordoba. In the mid-eleventh century its military value was reinforced and the first alcázar, or royal palace, was constructed by Ibn Nagrela, minister to the Zirid King Bādīs, being destroyed shortly after. In the same century, the Zirid dynasty founded Granada as the capital of one of the fifty or more, *taifas*, independent city-states resulting from the fragmentation of the caliphate, with the Albaicín hilltop at its core. Substantial remnants of walls, gates, bridges and a public baths can still be seen.

The eleventh-century Alhambra was a fortress reinforcing the defensive precinct of the city and linked to the Albaicín by a wall that crossed the River Darro at the Puerta de los Tableros, a wooden sluice gate Of this, one pillar and the beginning of an arch have been conserved. Another wall stretched from the current Alcazaba to the Torres Bermejas. The oldest remains in the Alcazaba are believed to date from this period. During the Almoravid and Almohad reigns the Alhambra continued to be a strategic outpost but other constructions dating from the period have not been found.

There can be no doubt that the Alhambra's great historic and political moment was to come when Muḥammad I (1237-1273) came to the throne, with the advent of the Nasrid dynasty. No sooner had they taken power than he decided as a political and institutional gesture, to designate the Alhambra as the citadel where he would govern. However, to understand the complex reality of the Alhambra, it is important to remember that not even at the very outset did its building follow a preconceived plan.

According to the chronicles of the time, in 1238 (AH 636) Muḥammad I moved into the spaces now occupied by the Alhambra, supplying it with water through an independent watercourse. At that time and in the years to follow the Alcazaba would be defined as the first fundamental enclave of the new palace city and except for specific renovations and extensions would become the building that most clearly represented the thirteenth-century Alhambra, predating the construction of the great palaces. Under his son and, above all, at the beginning of the fourteenth century under the third sultan Muḥammad III, the Alhambra really started to become a city and walls, towers, gates and the first palaces began to rise up, defining the Calle Real and the main mosque.

The institutional and economic consolidation of the Nasrid dynasty came in the fourteenth century coinciding with certain tensions and confrontation between the Christian and North African kingdoms. It was under Sultan Ismā'īl I (1314-1325) and, especially, Yūsuf I (1333-1354) and his son Muḥammad V (1354-1359; 1362-1391), that the Alhambra was regaled with its finest robes in the form of the spectacular palaces now conserved and visited. Ismā'īl I built a palace in the northern area and the royal baths and a pavilion with a dome in the area known as El Partal remain, along with the Puerta de las Armas, near the Alcazaba. Part of the palace was destroyed no sooner than it had been finished to make way for new buildings commissioned by Yūsuf I who, with the construction of the Comares palace ushered in the greatest period of Nasrid splendour: the Salón de Comares, Torre de la Cautiva, Puerta de las Albercas or de los Siete Suelos and the Puerta de la Explanada or de la Justicia were the buildings of greatest merit.

Under the government of Muḥammad V, the palaces of the Alhambra acquired a certain sense of unity and the decorators reached their zenith, on completing the earlier palaces with great decorative screens (Mexuar, façade, portico and Patio de Comares) and adding the most unusual and subtle of all the works in the Alhambra, namely the Palacio de los Leones, as admirable in its architectural composition and decorative virtuosity as it is enigmatic in its specific political function and symbolic meaning. At the end of the fourteenth century, the political capabilities and power of patronage of the Nasrid sultans came to an end and with this the Torre de las Infantas was built and the palace of Yūsuf III converted, which closed the cycle of great creations in the Alhambra.

The fifteenth-century Muslim governors of the Alhambra lost interest in constructing new buildings. Even the existing structure was allowed to deteriorate to such an extent that in 1492, when Granada was conquered by the Catholic Kings, contemporary sources record that they immediately had to attend to the consolidation and reinforcement of the defences and remedy the state of ruin to be found in some parts of the palaces.

From 1492 on, the Alhambra became the palace residence and seat of the Captain-General to the new Christian kings, expressing their wish to keep such a singular building standing both for its clear political significance and to use it as a royal residence. The sixteenth century saw far-reaching conversions with the careful restoration of some parts of the palaces, in harmony with the ancient Nasrid structures, and large-scale modifications to others, such as the Mexuar, the vizier's council-chamber, the Peinador de la Reina, Charles V's apartments, or the singular case of the Palacio de Carlos V. This was intended as an addition to the Islamic building for use as both residential space and for protocol and it caused an impact that even today attracts the attention of many, who perhaps fail to understand it is a building that has to be seen in its historical context and within the mindset of the period.

After the first centuries in which special sensitivity was shown along with great respect towards restoring things to their original condition, this approach was notably abandoned in the eighteenth and the first half of the nineteenth centuries. Only in more recent times has attention been returned to restoration and consolidation, not without the inevitable convulsions and conflicting opinions that affect a monument precinct as complex and problematic as the Alhambra.

Consequently, what we see today is the product of evolution in time and in architectural tastes from the eleventh century to the most recent contributions in our own century. The variety of structures responds as much to a broad chronological sequence as to different ways of understanding the occupation of territory.

The importance of the Alhambra in the history of architecture

When we approach a monument as famous as the Alhambra – the most visited monument in Spain – we must ask ourselves if its reputation is justified or is simply the product of whim and good advertising. First, we should remember that one of its principal attractions has always been the undoubted exoticism of finding a totally Islamic palace in the middle of European architectural tradition. It was the perfect manifestation of the East in the West. By a mishap of history, the visions offered by oriental tales and stories, including *The Thousand and One Nights*, became real thanks to this bewitching place. This very fact has doubtless led to it having attracted numerous travellers, poets and people of all kinds who have passed through it over the centuries.

But beyond this circumstance, it must be said that the Alhambra is one of the best conserved Middle Age, palace complexes not just in Islamic but also in Christian Europe. The oriental concept of a palace as a place destined more to create a purely ostentatious setting, in consonance with the dignity of the governor, than a comfortable space, adapted as a residence, finds its best expression in the Alhambra. The legacy of the palaces of the pharaohs' Egypt, of Mesopotamian cultures (including Assyria, Babylonia and Persia), of Hellenistic Greece or even of Imperial Rome, of which only very partial remains are left, find their continuity in the lavish courts of Sassanid Persia and in Byzantium and from them pass into Islam. But of the Umayyad and Abbasid palaces and of the different dynasties that governed in the first centuries of Islam's expansion only shapeless ruins and nostalgic evocations remain.

Consequently, the Alhambra, descending in a direct line from this long tradition, is unique and especially fortunate for its state of conservation, despite having suffered substantial restoration and the disappearance of many of the buildings that made it up.

But the Alhambra is something more. In the eyes of

educated Westerners, accustomed as we are to an art of objects and concrete figures with specific bodily existence and personality, Islamic art and ornamentation, particularly in the Alhambra, seems light, ingenious and capricious, but lacking in substance and representative value. As Leopoldo Torres Balbás said, this art is difficult to understand in the West, given that its secrets are not revealed to the hasty, distracted glance of modern man. To be able to discover its hidden messages, profound reflections and contents, we need to visit each corner, slowly; to be masters of our time and of the time when we visit the monument; to be able to sit on the floor, and thus, slowly and peacefully, follow the playful lines and linking motifs as they rise, flow and mingle with other rhythms and finally metamorphose the letters into flowers, flowers into bands and bands into a welcoming bower to cushion the symphony of forms to which colour lends the essential aroma. Only by understanding and knowing its forms can we then enter into its contents.

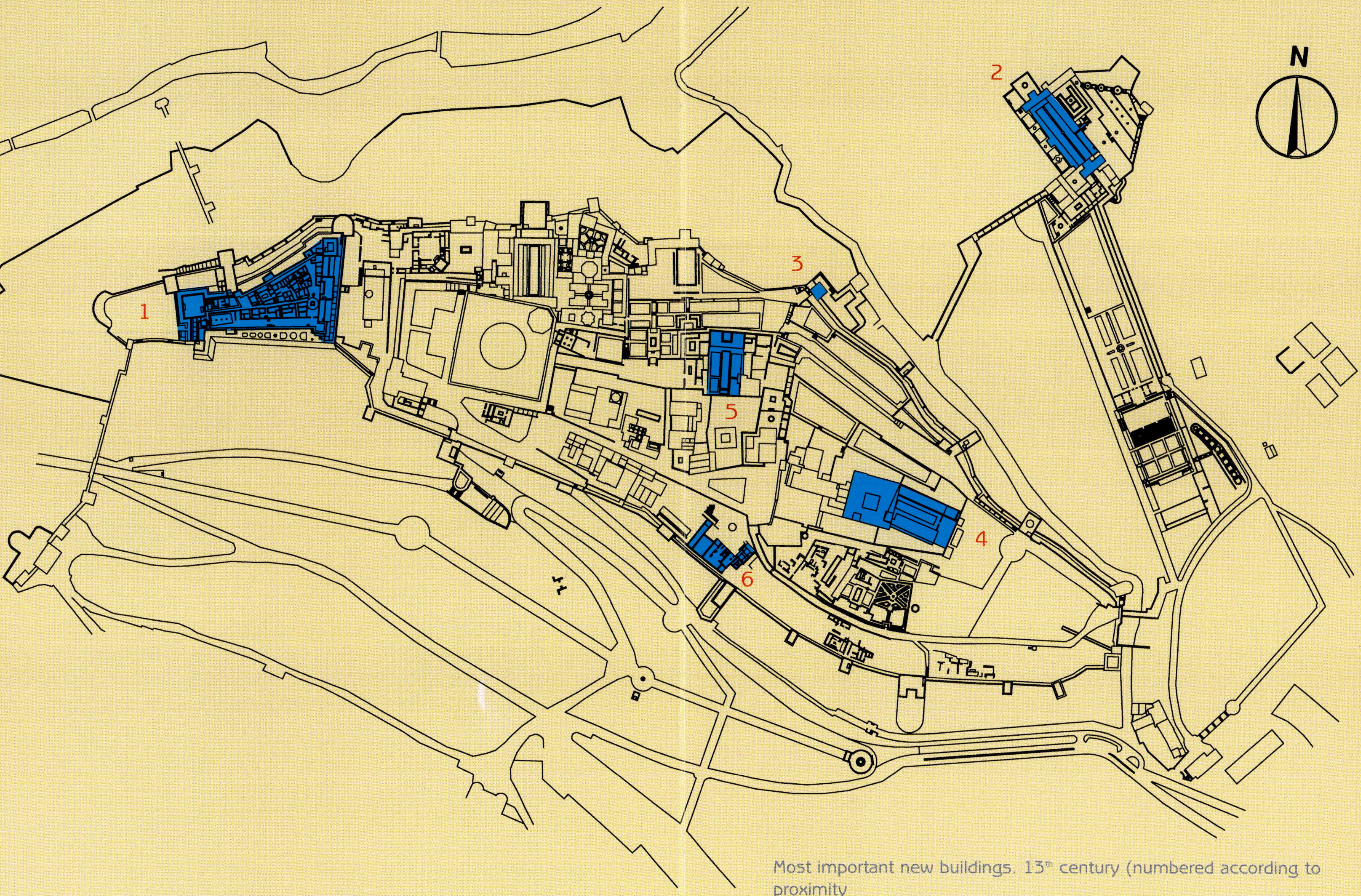

Most important new buildings. 13th century (numbered according to proximity

1. Alcazaba
2. Palacio del Generalife
3. Torre de los Picos
4. Palace in the current Parador de San Francisco
5. Palace known as the Palacio de Yūsuf III
6. Abencerrajes

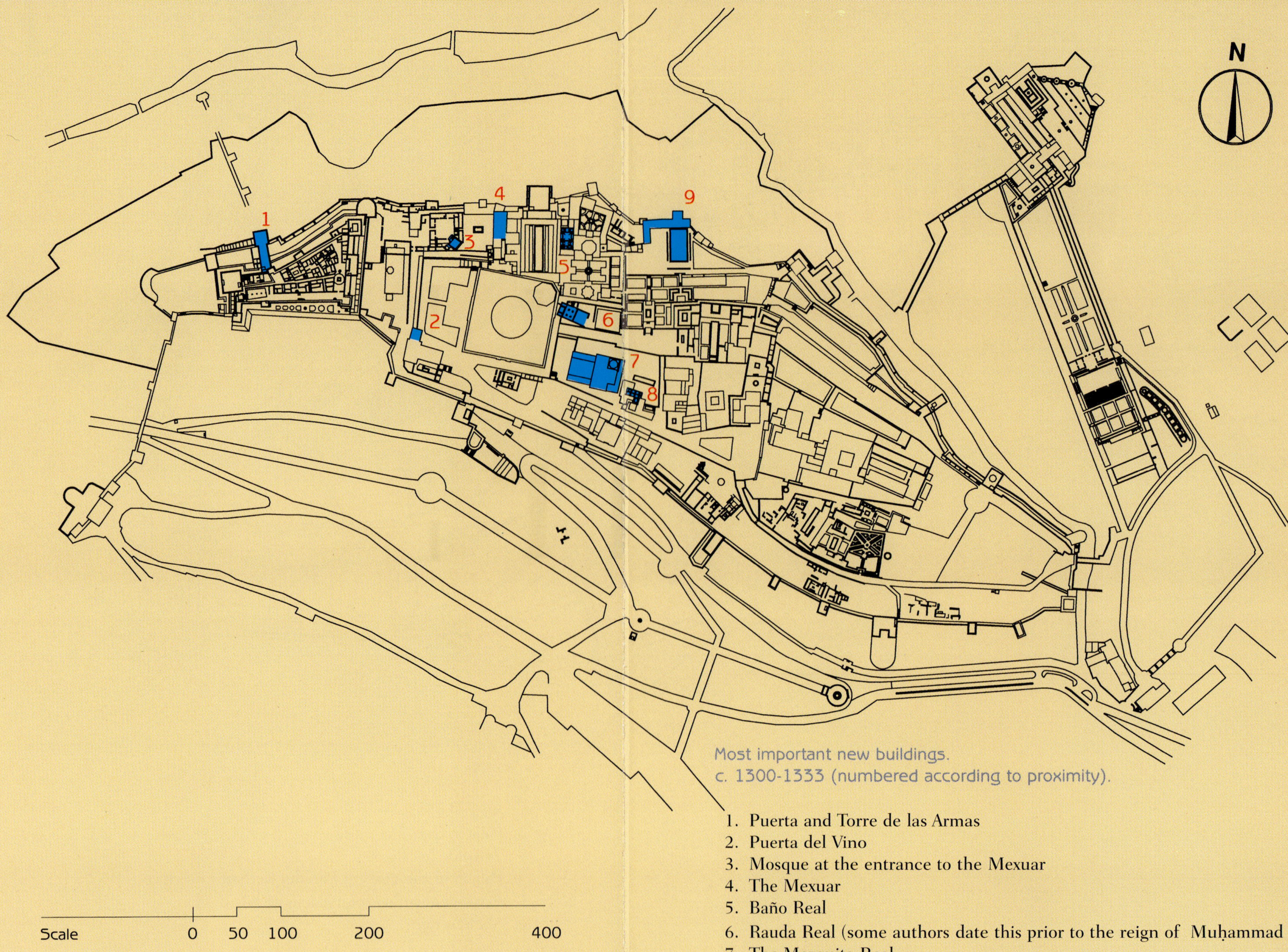

Most important new buildings.
c. 1300-1333 (numbered according to proximity).

1. Puerta and Torre de las Armas
2. Puerta del Vino
3. Mosque at the entrance to the Mexuar
4. The Mexuar
5. Baño Real
6. Rauda Real (some authors date this prior to the reign of Muḥammad
7. The Mezquita Real
8. Baño de la Mezquita
9. Palacio de El Partal

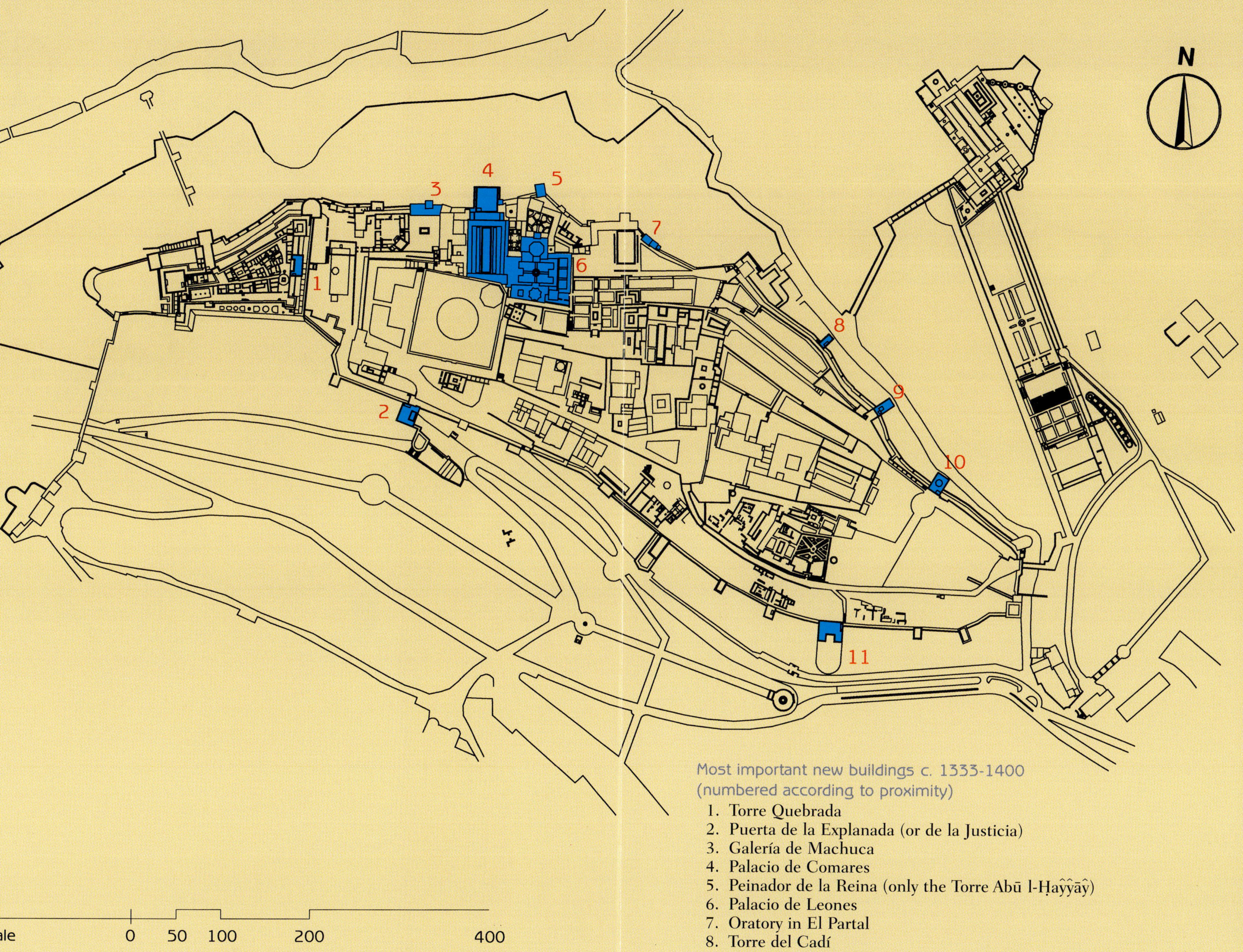

Most important new buildings c. 1333-1400
(numbered according to proximity)

1. Torre Quebrada
2. Puerta de la Explanada (or de la Justicia)
3. Galería de Machuca
4. Palacio de Comares
5. Peinador de la Reina (only the Torre Abū l-Ḥaŷŷāŷ)
6. Palacio de Leones
7. Oratory in El Partal
8. Torre del Cadí
9. Torre de la Cautiva
10. Torre de las Infantas
11. Puerta de las Albercas (or de los Siete Suelos)

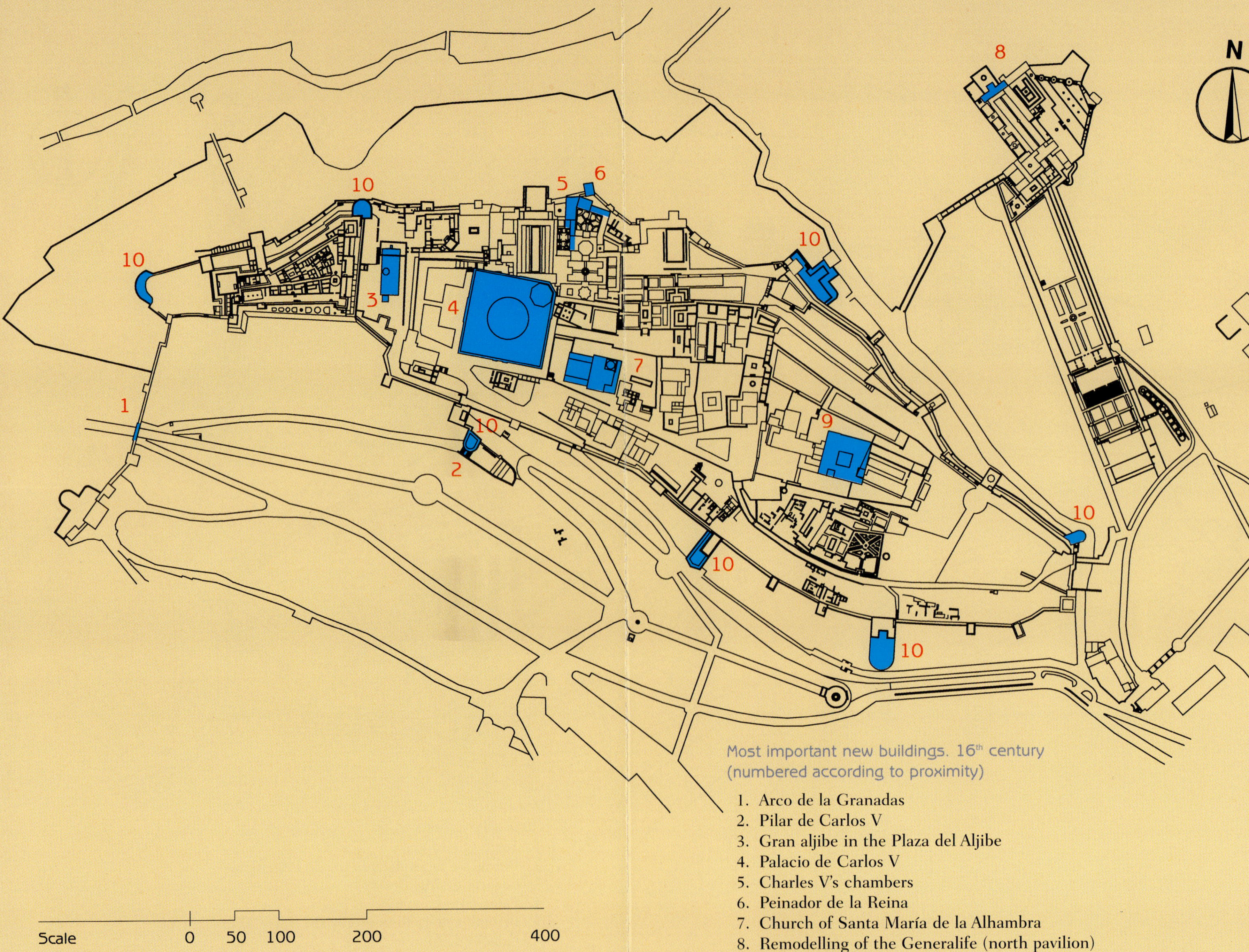

Most important new buildings. 16th century
(numbered according to proximity)

1. Arco de la Granadas
2. Pilar de Carlos V
3. Gran aljibe in the Plaza del Aljibe
4. Palacio de Carlos V
5. Charles V's chambers
6. Peinador de la Reina
7. Church of Santa María de la Alhambra
8. Remodelling of the Generalife (north pavilion)
9. Convent of San Francisco
10. Fortifications: bastions and ravelins

Life in the Alhambra: The domestic spaces

Receptions, feasts and festivals

ALTHOUGH WE HAVE COME A LONG WAY in learning about the history and heritage of the Alhambra, we have yet to shed light on many of its corners. One of these, perhaps the most important, is the secrets of its ceremonial functions. If you recall the original purpose of the palaces, you can imagine that the grand receptions – enthroning the new sultan, the arrival of ambassadors from other countries or territories, even funeral pomp – would be crucial moments when the palaces would be decked out to their finest, breaking the day-to-day routine. The almost total absence of information about these occasions forces us to search for references to other palaces, occasions and cultures, to try to rediscover what all the courtly paraphernalia would be like.

However, there is a second question that remains far from being answered. In the Alhambra we have identified various spaces or areas specially connected with formal ceremony, although the function and specific use of the different rooms is still not clear, neither in everyday life nor on occasion of most solemn events. Only the oratories, latrines, baths and little else enable us confidently to draw closer to their specific use. Tradition has it that the Mexuar was the semi-public space, the council chamber; the Palacio de Comares was the harem and throne room; and the Palacio or Cuarto de los Leones was dedicated to restricted use, for the greater intimacy of the sultan and chosen guests. An alterative view considers a division by seasons with Comares for the winter and Leones for the summer, but this is wholly unfounded. When visiting or trying to understand the Alhambra, we should not forget that until Muḥammad V (1354-1359; 1362-1391) unified and gave a degree of continuity and coherence to the palaces, each one had functioned independently. Despite all these limitations, we can point to some areas that seem more directly linked with acts that symbolize the exhibition of power. Such is the case of the façade of Comares, where solemn receptions supposedly took place when, from the time of Muḥammad V who had it built, the sultan would appear to a select group of visitors seated on his *jamuga* between the two doors of the façade. Similarly, the esplanade that stretched down from the gate of the same name, Puerta de la Explanada (or de la Justicia) must have witnessed solemn parades, feasts and celebrations like those held in front of other city gates in the Maghreb and western Islam. The Mexuar was also a semi-public place, where occasionally, aside from its specific use, ambassadors, ministers or even representatives of citizen groups could meet.

However, without doubt, every palace has as its place of special solemnity, riches and splendour: the throne room, which in the Alhambra was identified with the great Salón de Comares. After Muḥammad V, the Sala de Dos Hermanas - Mirador de Lindaraja could also have had the same function for certain solemn acts. These two areas remain identified as holding special preference in the palace structure and to confirm this evidence exists in the inscriptions that a space was destined for the throne in both of them. No evidence remains of the place where these receptions were held under sultans prior to Yūsuf I (1333-1354). Another special ceremonial space was the Sala de la Barca, where some researchers suppose the investiture of new sultans took place and where on the occasion of a visit of special relevance the sultan could pay tribute to his illustrious guest with the *baraka*, or blessing that may have given rise to the room's name. The Generalife too had its own royal room where, from time to time, the sultan would receive embassies and meet his ministers who were advised against excessively disturbing his rest in an inscription at the door: "Enter with composure, speak with science, be sparing with words and leave in peace" (English version based on a translation from the Arabic by Darío Cabanelas).

In the absence of specific data, we can only hazard a guess as to the ceremonial life of these rooms by drawing on one of the few stories that describes a celebration held there. The Mawlid, the Muslim feast on the birthday of the Prophet Muhammad, was celebrated in the Alhambra in 1362. The festivity was organized and presided over by Muḥammad V, shortly after he recovered the throne from which he had been deposed three years earlier. The sultan wanted to use the occasion, at which the half-finished, Mexuar was inaugurated, to consolidate his prestige and ingratiate himself with his subjects, especially those who had supported his cause. The great poet and vizier Ibn al-Jaṭīb, left us a priceless account of the celebration, published in Spanish by Emilio García Gómez.

Among other aspects of the tale, information about of the protagonists make interesting reading: Ibn al-Jaṭīb offers a detailed list of the guests. In first place, logically, stands out the involvement of the sultan. He was the first to arrive in the rooms chosen for the feast accompanied by his closest courtiers, among whom were servants, royal functionaries and his personal guard – usually a select group of "slaves" or Islamized Christians, depending directly on the sultan. The choice of guests reveals much of the influential forces and political groups in Granada at the time. García Gómez calculates as many as 500 people attended, gathered together around the sultan, the most important of them occupying favoured places near the sultan, and thus making themselves comfortable under cover with Muḥammad V in full view of all.

Customary courtly rituals in the palaces would have been much briefer than that described by García Gómez. An audience with the monarch known as the *besamanos* involved the main act, followed by speeches, meetings and festivities, with changes to the exact procedures to suit the motive behind the reception. Exceptionally long ceremonies required the celebration of prayers on three occasions: at the beginning, in the middle and at the climax. These were moments of special relevance and the dinner and dessert (called breakfast in García Gómez's tale) were accompanied by the recital of sermons and verses, concerts and spectacular dancing.

The complex, lengthy celebration ended with the burning of amber "forming clouds above the heads of all present", a shower of rose petals falling over them, perfuming their bodies and the atmosphere as a woodwind flute sounded a farewell. The tale of this celebration ends by evoking the cycle of birth, life and death and the peremptory nature of life, as it affirms: "Only God endures, He who events affect not and who remains constant! May He alone be glorified and praised!"

Daily life in the palace city

WHEN WE VISIT THE ALHAMBRA we are visiting a space that was once inhabited, a palace city where sultans, their families and the rest of the court lived. However, logically, any sense that it is inhabited has been lost with the multitudes of visitors and, especially, when you find yourself facing the architecture without no interior decoration, without the small objects that formed part of daily life there.

The public or semi-public function of the spaces in the Alhambra has been mentioned before: rooms for meetings with the viziers, halls for palace receptions or where the sultan would give feasts and banquets. But not only public receptions and festivities filled daily life. Hours of reading, rest, time to eat and converse also formed part of the Alhambra. Moreover, the Alhambra is not only the life of the courtiers but also of all the available serving staff with their workshops and houses located within the same precinct and especially nearby. The noise of the workshops or the voices of children at play, filled the streets of a hectic city.

However, in medieval spaces we find that rooms lack unique, characteristic functions, whether Christian or Islamic in al-Andalus, as they are multifunctional. A single space could be used for different purposes according to the time of day; occasionally a simple change of furniture was enough.

In the Alhambra, it is extremely interesting to study everyday life because within the same architecture we can find out about daily life in the Islamic court and about the changes made for the life of the Christian court. And we find similarities and differences when it comes to understanding the structure of the family, or the court, or the role of women.

Although talking of domestic spaces in the Middles Ages frequently means associating them with the women, as it was they who through the assignment of roles took charge of domestic chores, not all domestic spaces imply this identification as feminine rooms as they were occupied by men and women. Let us not forget that the sultan did not live alone, his brothers, children and wives also resided within the precinct, although we should not discount the possibility that members of the Nasrid family also lived in the city of Granada itself.

The Alhambra is not only the life of the courtiers but that of all the servants who had their workshops and houses located in the precinct itself and especially nearby. The *madīna* or the keep bears witness to this significant presence in the precincts of the Islamic and Christian Alhambra, in the same way that the early medieval texts document an intense life in the Alhambra, extending over a wide area including, among others, part of the Cuesta Gomérez approach or the area behind the church of San Cecilio.

So, the Alhambra was then primarily an inhabited space, a space full of life. In this sense, the palace city of the Alhambra is an open book on architecture where different ways of occupying and inhabiting spaces come together.

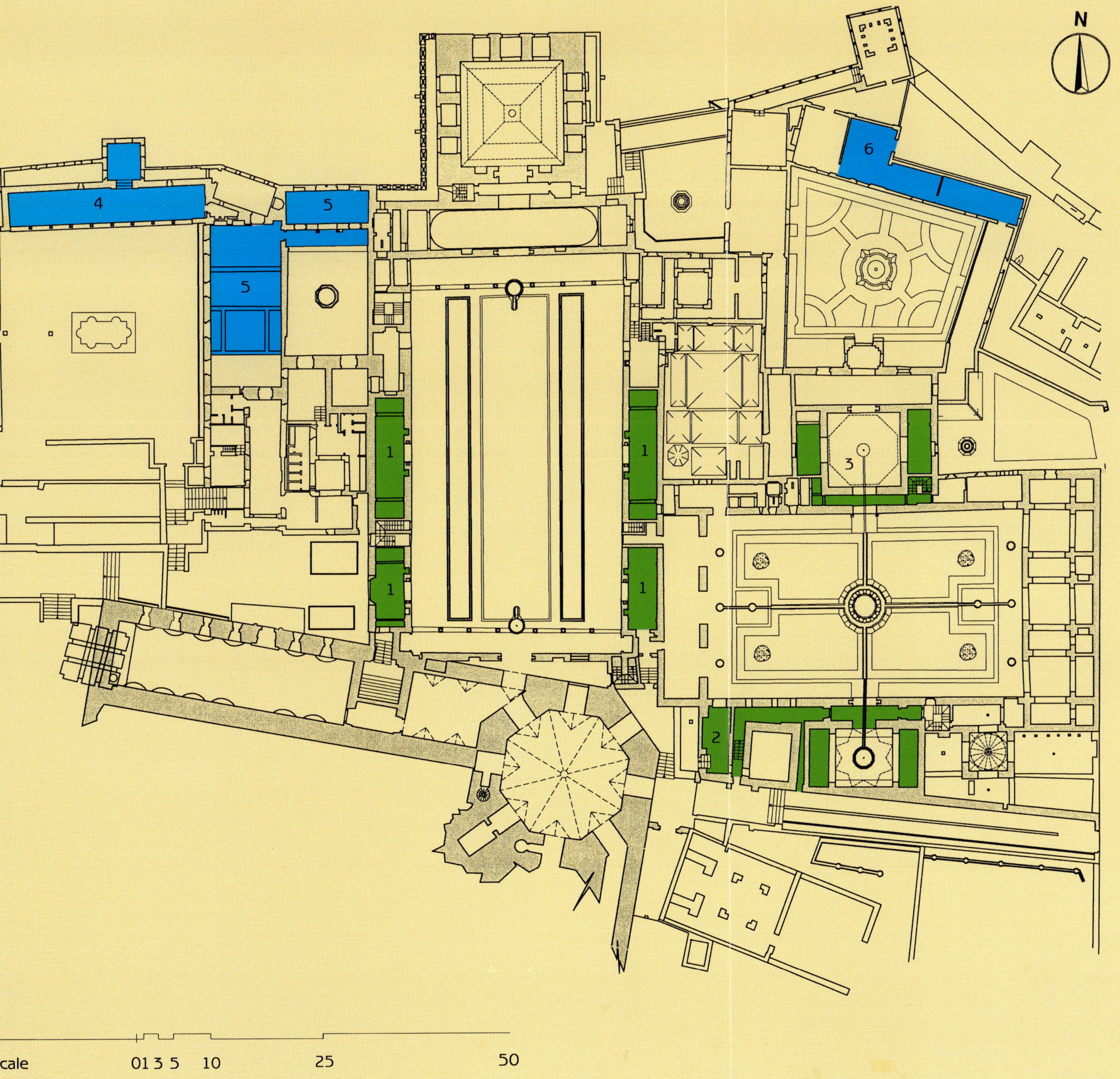

Various authors hypothetical feminine spaces in the sixteenth century

1. Side rooms in the Palacio de Comares
2. Harén. Palacio de Leones (upper floor)
3. Sala de Dos Hermanas. Palacio de los Leones (upper floor).

Various authors hypothetical feminine spaces under Christian rule

4. Galería Patio de Machuca
5. Cuarto Dorado and upper floor of the Mexuar
6. "Washington Irving's rooms"

Feminine and masculine spaces

Gender relations were present in the design of the buildings. Ancient treatises already specified the division of space by gender, generally relegating women to the domestic world due to their reproductive role, whereas men fulfilled a public role. The house was therefore converted into an eminently feminine place in as much as it was, on the whole, occupied and organized by women.

This gender division is present in the Alhambra as within both main, converging cultures, Islam and Christianity, a clear division of roles by gender existed. Significantly, the Koran and the Bible, and the sacred texts of Islam and medieval Christianity, distinguish between the public roles of men compared with the reclusion of women in the privacy of the home. This premise in the sacred texts would be interpreted very differently according to the context. The position of women in the caliph's court is not the same as in the Nasrid court, or in the court of the Trastamara family, or that of Charles V. Similarly, the more sheltered life led by the women of the Islamic or Christian court is not the same as that of women belonging to the popular classes.

The baths, mosques or churches were spaces where a clear separation between men and women was marked. This separation extended to the baths and oratories or royal chapels and therefore existed in the Alhambra, too. For example, inside the palaces we know that in al-Andalus the women did not attend the receptions until they were coming to an end. Prior to that, they withdrew to their rooms or bedchambers and from there, through wooden window screens, were able to observe the festivities.

Texts and chronicles tell us of spaces reserved for women in the palaces of the Alhambra but offer little precise detail as to the specific rooms women occupied under the Nasrids. In spite of the scarcity of data, we can neither ignore nor doubt the fact that spaces reserved for women did exist in the Alhambra: rooms were designated for women, and men who did not belong to the nuclear family would enter therein with difficulty.

In the Islamic tradition, feminine rooms should look inwards avoiding open relations with the public, and therefore predominantly masculine areas, or with the outside; few openings would appear in their construction. The patio became the thoroughfare and link between different independent rooms. The Palacio de Comares may be an example of this: rooms are distributed around a patio situating some possibly feminine spaces on the longer sides; the openings of these four rooms look exclusively inwards,

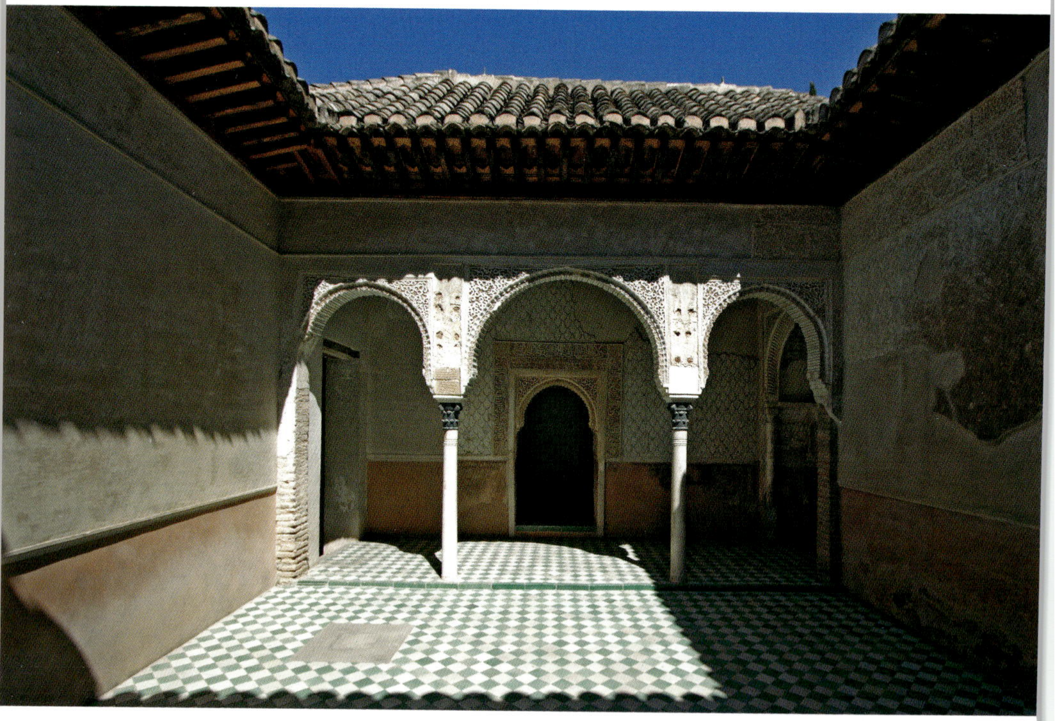

The space known as the Harem has been interpreted by some simply as a romantic name distant from reality. However, the absence of artistic novelties with a painted dado, *zócalo*, instead of the eye-catching tiles, the reuse of pieces such as the probably twelfth-century, green picrolite serpentine capitals, certain "slips" like the combination on the same side as supports of columns and semi-pilasters instead of adjacent columns, the *alfiz* in the central arch that does not match up with the sides, give the impression of a domestic space and, especially, a space possibly reserved for women. The distribution of an upper floor would enable its occupants to observe movement in the Palacio de los Leones without being seen.

distinguishing them from the throne room of Yūsuf I or the Salón de Comares, which have wide openings looking outwards. While we will have to live with the doubt as to whether or not these were feminine spaces, what we can be sure of is that they were domestic spaces.

In our search for possible feminine spaces, the different periods in the history of the Islamic Alhambra play their part. Spaces we might think were frequently used by women in the reign of Yūsuf I (1333-1354) would not necessarily coincide with those used at the time of

Muḥammad V (1354-1359; 1362-1391).

As with the Nasrids, we can establish reference points in the Christian period, which is comparatively better documented with regard to the spaces occupied by women. No functional correlation exists between gender and architecture, so the supposed Nasrid domestic spaces do not coincide fully with those of the Christians. In annotations to plans made by Pedro de Machuca in the sixteenth century are evidence that the area known as the Mexuar, possibly a public space under the Nasrids, was turned into a private space by the Christians who converted it into a chapel. The Patio de Machuca went on to be occupied by Germana de Foix, second wife to Ferdinand the Catholic, whereas the Cuarto Dorado was destined for the Empress Isabel of Portugal.

It has been suggested that some of Charles V's chambers, also known as Washington Irving's rooms, may have been designed for the Empress Isabel of Portugal, although more recently this has been questioned. The suggestion was based on their location and decoration and, especially, on symbols referring to the Empress which appear in some of them. A more widely accepted hypothesis centres on the creat-ion of two façades in the Palacio de Carlos V: one looking west for the Emperor and the south wing for the Empress. Thus, the presence of the Tuscan order makes sense in the façade to be occupied by the Emperor, in contrast with the use of Ionic and Corinthian orders for the Empress, as prescribed by the ancient Roman writer, Vitruvius.

Multiculturalism in the Alhambra

The meeting of cultures

THE ALHAMBRA IS A SPACE where different cultures, Islam and Christianity, converge. This multiculturalism was characteristic of the medieval Iberian Peninsular, when continuous relationships existed between the Christian kingdoms and the Islamic kingdoms of al-Andalus. Confrontation in territorial conquests and to achieve greater power was present not only between Christians and Muslims but disputes also arose among Christians, as they did among Muslims. However, if we only think of confrontations and strife we lose sight of other realities: shared spaces or examples of social mediation in commerce or mixed marriages all formed part of living together. Far from thinking of an idyllic situation, today we recognize that coexistence occurred with all of its concomitant toing and froing.

In this meeting of cultures one factor is important: the recognition of otherness. And this is something that happened in the Alhambra. Since Islamic times, the Alhambra has attracted the attention of Muslim travellers from faraway lands who essentially highlight the stuccowork; in contrast, western travellers point out the roofing, especially its colourfulness, the use of materials such as marble for the floors, and singularly the water and gardens. The aspects westerners highlight are considered and recognized as typically Muslim, identifying thus a way of doing things with a culture and, what is more important, recognizing the artistic expressions in the Alhambra and their reuse. To recognize this otherness, and essentially respect it, was a basic premise for possible coexistence.

And the Alhambra is an example of coexistence. Traditionally, historians describe the Alhambra as a place of failed

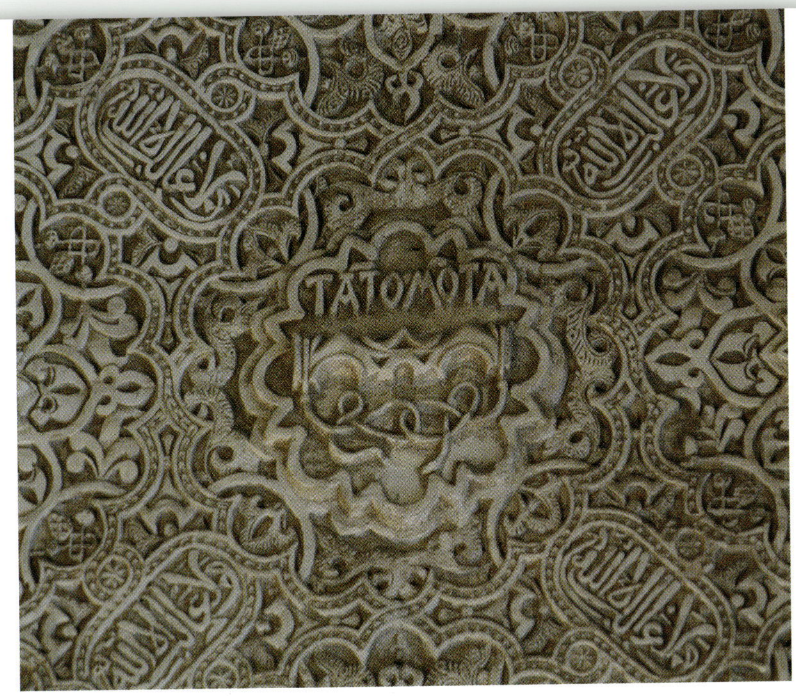

If you stop to observe the stuccowork in the Sala de los Reyes, you realize that symbols such as the yoke and arrows and other emblems associated with the Catholic Kings have been subtly integrated amid the Nasrid decoration and inscriptions.

meetings. The clearest symbol of this is the construction of the Palacio de Carlos V, interpreted as an emblem of Christian dominance over Islamic culture with, it was believed, a Nasrid palace demolished for it to be built, a theory no longer current. Effectively, the palace symbolizes power and dominance but in its design it also sought to adapt to the Nasrid palaces. Today, it has been proven that the building believed to have been destroyed was the south gallery of the Palacio de Comares and it seems almost certain that this had previously disappeared in a fire. The use of classical Ancient Roman forms in the construction of the Palacio de Carlos V clearly transmitted the message that the world stood before a new empire and a new Caesar. A new empire, triumphant in the face of Islam. So the new palace consisted of a grand façade behind which the old Nasrid royal residence remained as an integral part. This is one of the messages the Palacio de Carlos V projects. The integration of the new building in the space occupied by its Islamic surroundings was what was sought, and not the destruction of a Nasrid palace, as the eighteenth-century writer José de Hermosilla interpreted it in *Las Antigüedades árabes de España*.

To conserve the Alhambra, the new Christian monarchs had to

accept the costly investment that substantial repairs entailed. Maintenance meant both political intention and respect for the Islamic work, but conserving the Alhambra meant not only maintaining its spaces but also adapting them for its new inhabitants. In this context, we encounter similarities and differences between the two cultures.

Nasrid aesthetics in the Alhambra: Constructive sobriety and ornamental exuberance

VISITORS TO THE ALHAMBRA are struck by the contrast between the rich, refined interior of the Alhambra and its dry, naked outer appearance. Nothing on the outside seems to predict the paradise within. This is the logical result of an architecture conceived on a very human scale and sensitive to the physical medium where it stands and its historical tradition. The Alhambra was built with the materials found in its surroundings.

However, it is important to understand that these materials, with their specific properties of resistance, consistency, weight and flexibility, are almost always intentionally, wilfully employed in fixed, predetermined places. Ceramics dados, *zócalos*, appear in parts of the rooms, places likely to be rubbed and worn are thus protected. Plaster and stucco are applied to the decorative panels on the walls above the *zócalo*, using stucco so they can be sculpted individually and plaster when moulds are used. Under Muḥammad V (1354-1359; 1362-1391) this would also take on a special role in the vaulted ceilings and the stalactite-like *mocárabe* arches. Wood appears in ceilings, beams, friezes, doors, windows, eaves and wherever a certain degree of resistance is called for in combination with lightness and some flexibility. In columns, patio paving and doorjambs, marble is the material chosen to fulfil the tougher roles and be submitted to a greater degree of wear. But once all this enormous puzzle has been set out and organized and the materials chosen, exquisitely worked and integrated by specialist artisans with a highly specialized craft, the colour appears, coming to invade and integrate all the surfaces, creating this immense, sensitive, light network, that finally hides most of the original material. In the Alhambra, colour has been the great victim of time and only in the skilfully cuttiling has it been preserved with its original force.

Devoted to the inside, the Muslim aesthetic concept placed all emphasis on "dressing" the space, especially when, as in this case, it is not only a dwelling but also a space representing power. In the glazed ceramic tiles and stucco, principles of symmetry and geometric abstraction rule with a single motif on centre stage: the interlaced geometric star design or *rueda de lacería*, which in its links gives rise to an almost infinite variety of polygonal forms. Other significant motifs appearing on the wide plaster surfaces are the panels of rhomboid drawings filled with schematic plant-forms, called *ataurigues*, sometimes alternating with other natural forms as well as with the inscriptions and stalactite-like *mocárabes*. All form a continuous surface displaying a veritable "horror of emptiness".

Towards the interior, you find the patio has been closed off on the shorter sides by a light portico acting as a kind of curtain that moves forward and creates the appropriate scenery for you to pass on to the reception rooms, normally located on the ground floor and looking north to seek out the winter sunshine. A rectangular hall with bedchambers at the ends, or perhaps a square, domed hall, a *qubba*, would be at the centre of palace life, with adjoining outbuildings, which would have to have a viewing point, looking out onto the countryside through delicate, window screens. From the outside, the dwelling is hidden, lost in the countryside so you would hardly notice the existence of this sumptuous palace were it not for its form and rooftops.

If the rational use of materials corresponds to a practical purpose, the shapes and textures are aesthetically no less significant. Thus, the combination of what at first sight are oft-repeated geometric figures but in fact are sought-after derivations infinitely extending the original motif, responds to the abstract concept of a simultaneously dynamic yet static universe; a supreme order ruled by mathematical principles established by Allāh. Faced with the excellence and goodness of the Creator we have no choice but to admire His creation and eternally praise His name. Perhaps this explains the restrictions on figurative, naturalist art: it would be useless "to imitate" creation, hence the stylized abstraction of natural forms.

Christian aesthetics in the Alhambra

To think of the Alhambra is to imagine an eminently Islamic space. But without doubt a Christian Alhambra of importance does exist. To deny this would be to deny part of the history of the monument.

Occasionally, recognizing Christian aesthetics in the Alhambra is a none-too-easy task, especially when Islamic forms have been imitated and recreated. Such a cultural mix or confusion exists that when faced with certain roofing, tiled dados, or even stuccowork, we are in doubt as to whether we are dealing with a piece of Nasrid or *morisco* art-

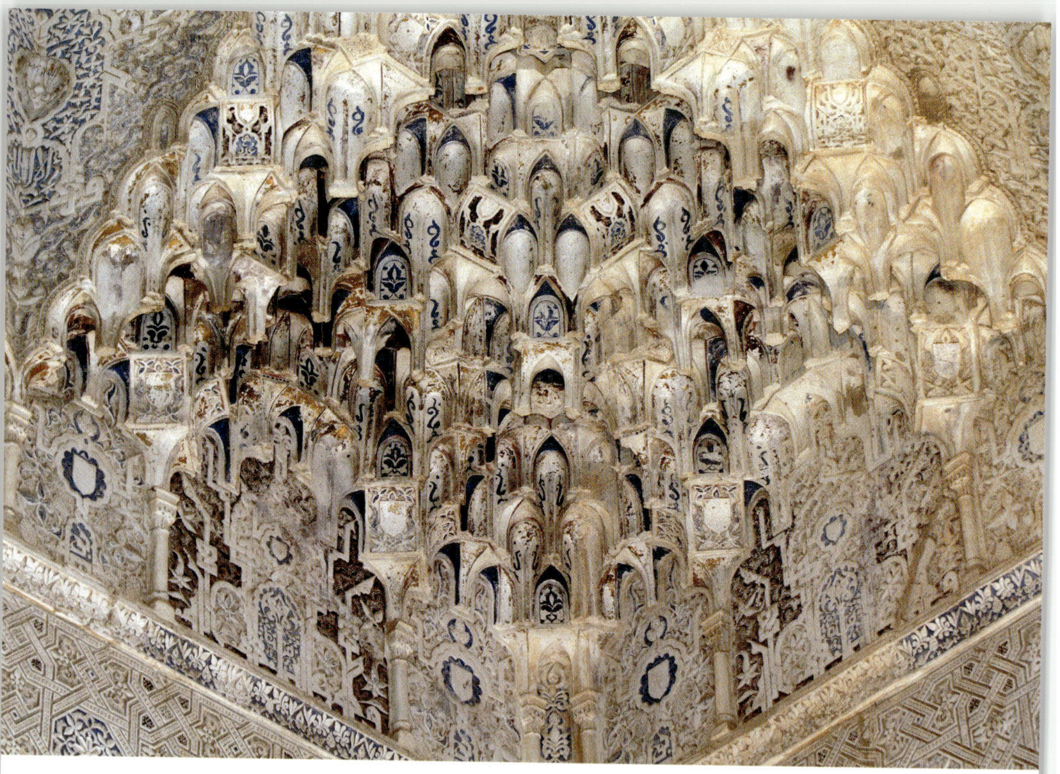

Mocárabes in the Sala de Abencerrajes

Octagonal *rueda de lazo* design

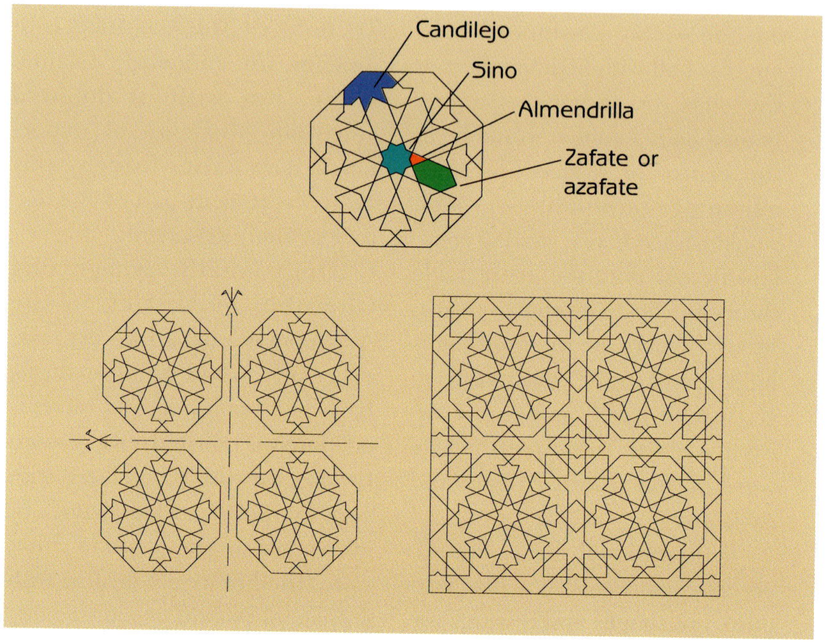

work of Muslim forced to convert to Christianity; in other cases we may be looking at Nasrid work with Christian repairs.

Starting from this beautiful difficulty, which in itself does no more than show us the extremes which the symbiosis of Islam and Christianity could go to, we continually recognize other forms introduced into the Islamic precinct although clearly Christian in origin, which distance themselves from certain aesthetic and functional premises of Nasrid art.

First, we should take note of a difference between Islamic and Christian architecture that has traditionally been pointed out and that we find in the Alhambra. If, as we have indicated, Islamic architecture tends to look inward, mistrustful of the outside, as described in the poems or materialized in the use of crooked entrance passages, or with a carefully thought out number of openings all of which protect life on the inside, Christian architecture seeks to open up to the exterior.

The Palacio de Carlos V, with the exhibition of symbolic riches and constructive forces of its façades expresses a wilfulness wholly contrary to the intimate character of the Nasrid palaces. This enormous contrast between significant spaces is a magnificent lesson on how one culture and the other feel architecture. It explains why, to the surprise of many, the main façade of the Palacio de Comares is found within a modest, interior patio.

We should point out another important difference. The house and the Islamic palace are distributed around a patio and the different rooms lead off this, all of them with a view onto the patio. In the Islamic case, the patio becomes the principal nucleus as the rooms do not communicate one with another but via the patio, in such a way that to enter or leave any of these rooms you must go through the patio. This is the case of the Palacio de Comares and the Palacio de los Leones. If we take a look at the newly-built Christian constructions in the Alhambra we realize that rooms are linked directly, as on a continuous corridor, with the patio losing its function as the only means of communication.

As well as these differences, when it comes to understanding the occupation and habitability of the spaces, on our tour of the Alhambra we clearly recognize Christian stylistic languages that, whether Renaissance or Baroque, have been introduced into the Alhambra and whose idiosyncrasies are not understood without their relationship with the Islamic palace. Christian aesthetics in the Alhambra spatially, symbolically and interpretatively depend on the Nasrid Alhambra, and this is perhaps their most characteristic note.

Nasrid words and Christian images

Traditionally, much attention has been paid to the Koran's "prohibition" on the use of images although really, more than prohibit them, what it does is limit their use to avoid falling into idolatry, a limitation also present in Judaism and, at times, in Christianity. In the religious context they are most strict, and a more permissive attitude prevails

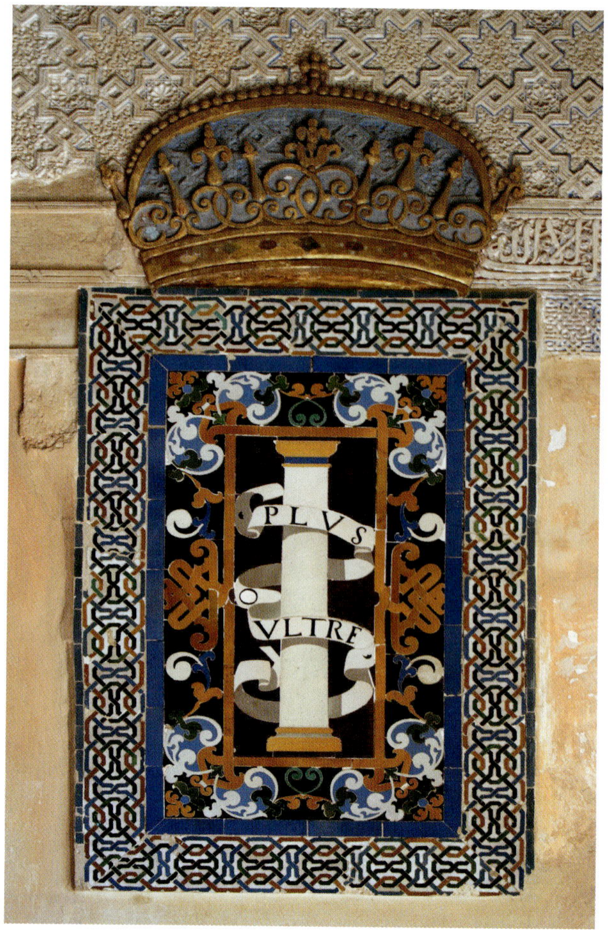

These Christian tiles are found in the Nasrid Mexuar and represent the Columns of Hercules and the motto Plus Ultra, significant emblems of Charles V. If you look carefully, you can see that motifs and colours similar to the Nasrid originals have been maintained such as the frieze that frames the panel, how-ever, the symbolism and final result tell us of a different artistic language. These panels were placed on the south wall where the altar stood and one of them is still visible today.

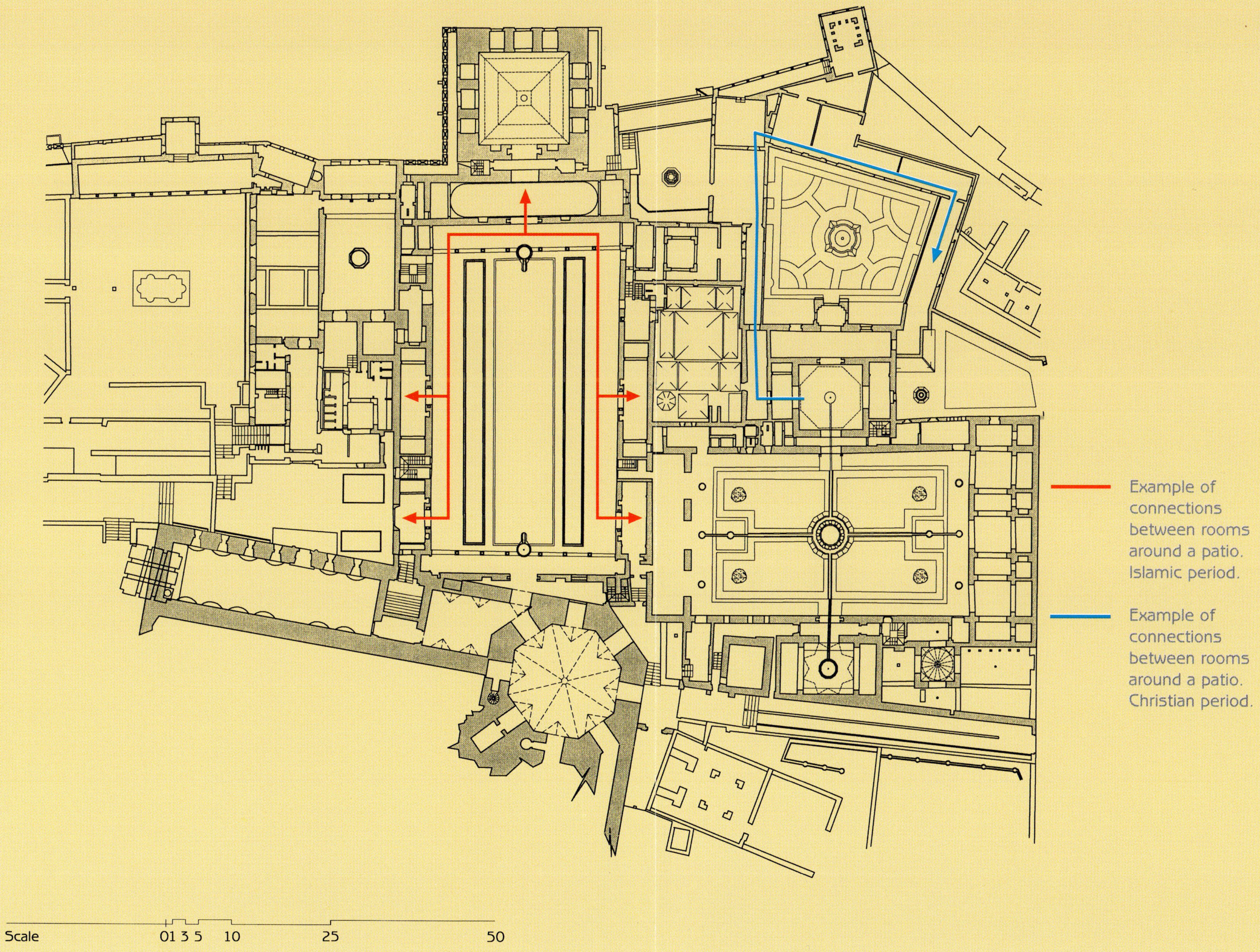
Scale
0 1 3 5 10 25 50
Example of connections between rooms around a patio. Islamic period.
Example of connections between rooms around a patio. Christian period.

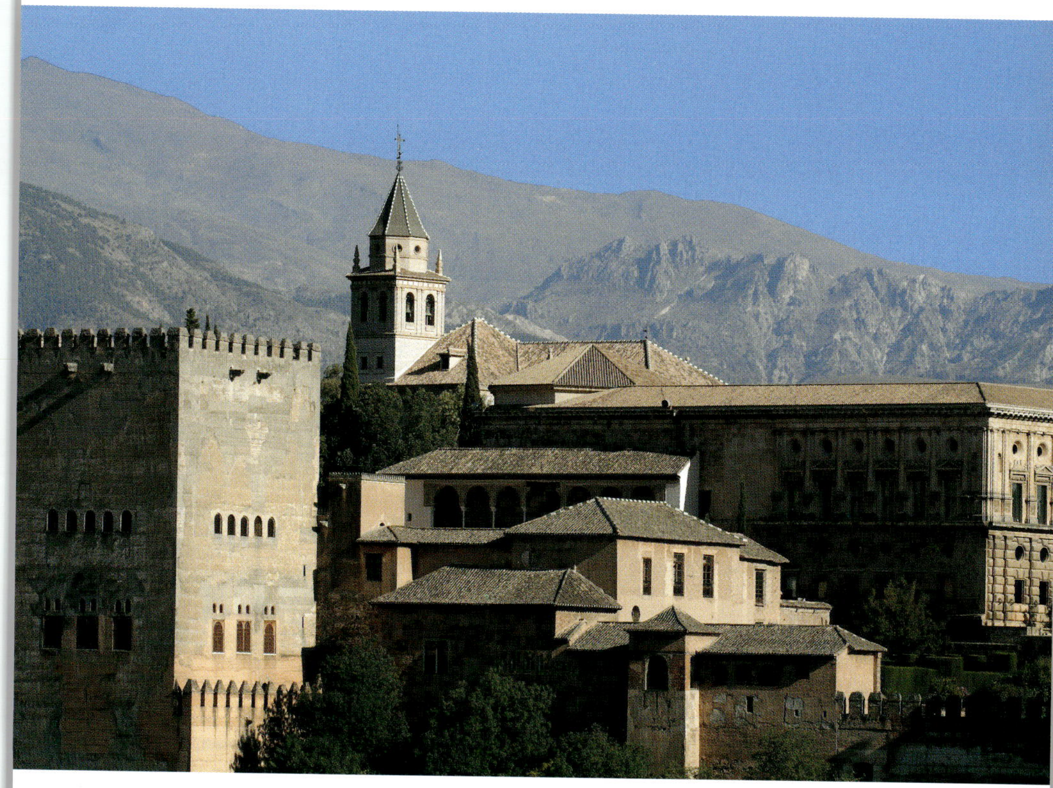

At the beginning of the seventeenth century, the image would differ little from what you see today where the Palacio de Carlos V takes up the horizontal lines of the Nasrid structures in front of the bell tower of the church of Santa María de la Alhambra, standing triumphantly erect before you.

in private palace rooms or in other more worldly contexts. In fact, exceptional examples of figurative painting are to be found in the Alhambra among which the Nasrid paintings in the Casas de El Partal stand out, although doubts have arisen about the authorship of the paintings in the Sala de los Reyes.

But more than these figurative forms, the Alhambra is images in the form of poetry. As we have said, the inscriptions in the Alhambra constitute the most luxuriously edited book of poems. These poems generally speak in first person and praise the sultan or, rather, inform us about the sultan who had the Alhambra built. Especially beautiful are those that, often through metaphor underline the significance of the architecture. Thus, in the Nasrid Alhambra, more than names of architects and sculptors it is the names of the poets that truly stand out: Ibn

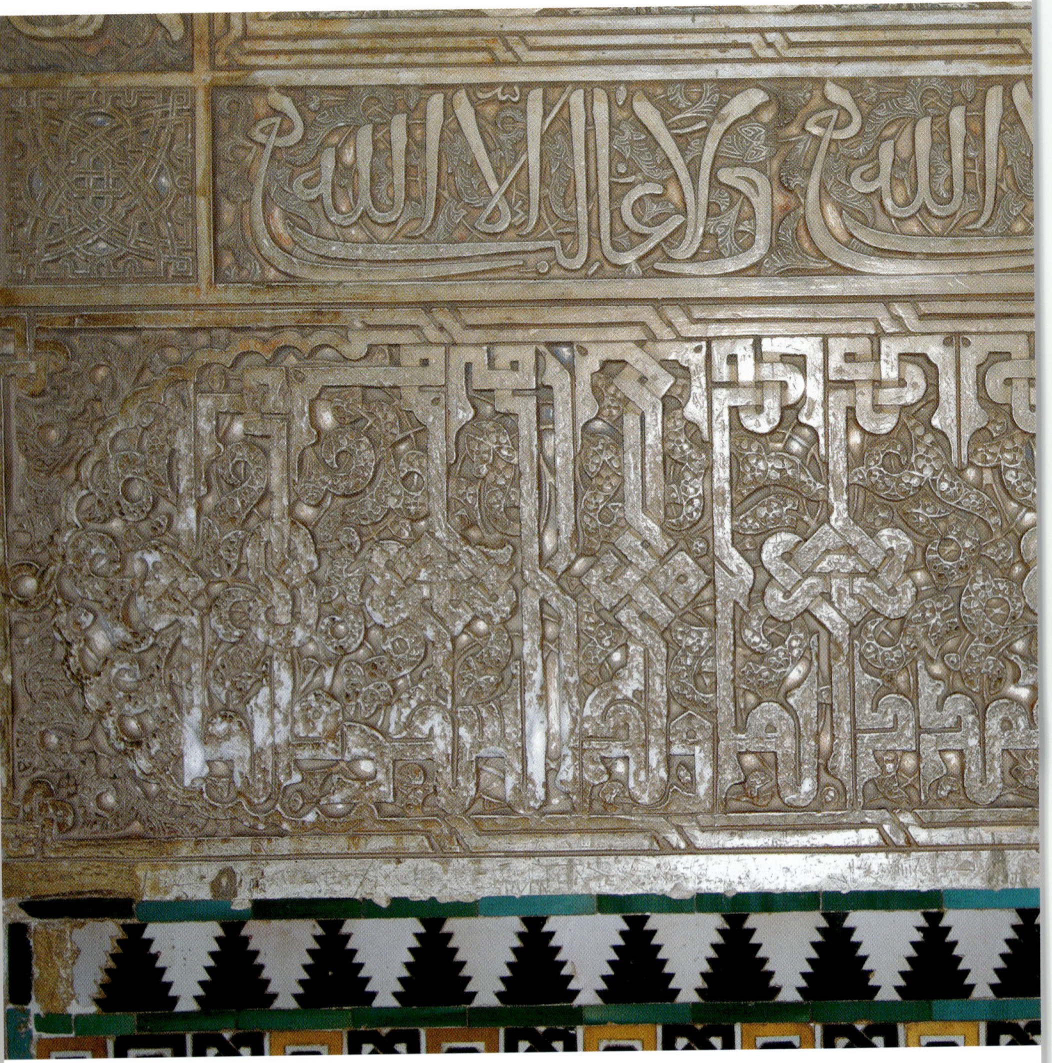

Epigraphy is the specialized term used to refer to writing or inscriptions made on hard surfaces and contrasts with the term calligraphy that is used for the art of writing on paper. Within the field of epigraphy essentially there are two distinct types of writing found in the Alhambra: Kufic script, which is angular and straight with more ornamental features and which contrasts with Naskhi script which, with its characteristic cursive features, dominates in the Alhambra.

al-Ŷayyāb, Ibn al-Jaṭīb and Ibn Zamrak.

We would never be able to understand the full aesthetic meaning of this monument without the value and use made of the inscriptions. The written word, in its dual dimensions of form and

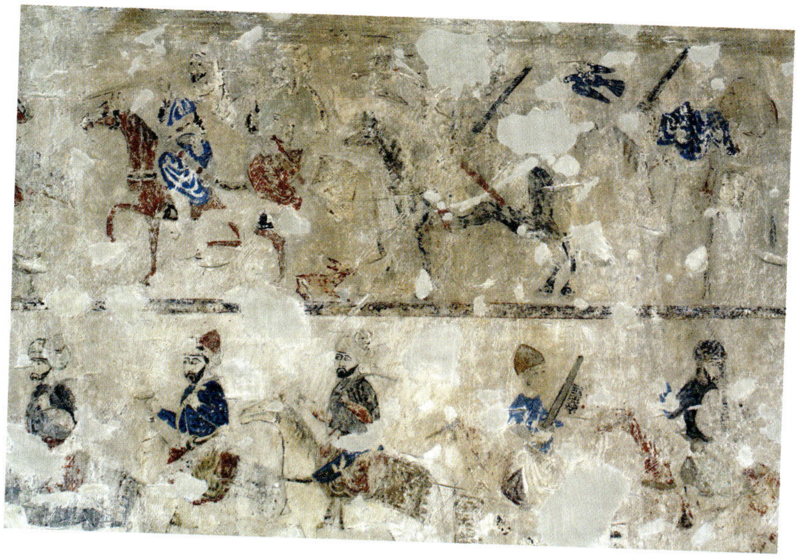

Detail of the paintings in the Casas de El Partal. Traditionally, much attention has been paid to the Koran's prohibition on the production of figurative images although Islamic art nonetheless developed the figurative image, fundamentally in non-religious contexts, as occurs in these Nasrid paintings which narrate scenes of battles and feasts.

content; the beauty of the graphics and all that they tell us, in poetic form, about the building. The value of the written word cannot be ignored for in Arabic the word is sacred as with its signs the Koran was written: "the very word of God", revealed and transcribed.

Most frequently the texts are in praise of Allāh, but most interesting are the poems that sing the praises of the spaces in first person as if the architecture itself were animate and wished to reveal to us the ultimate reason for its essence, even though it always does so through somewhat obscure metaphors. The authors were poets and courtiers of different rank, among whom Ibn Zamrak stands out in the palaces of Comares and Leones, and they combine the descriptive canticle with the *loa* in praise of the sultan of the time. Ibn Zamrak wrote of Muḥammad V (1354-1359; 1362-1391) and at the same time provided some of the few clues available that help us date specific interventions in the buildings and offers us some meanings for spaces and ornamentation in the Alhambra.

Faced with the abstraction of Nature and the use of writing, the Christian culture was to show its preferences for the figurative

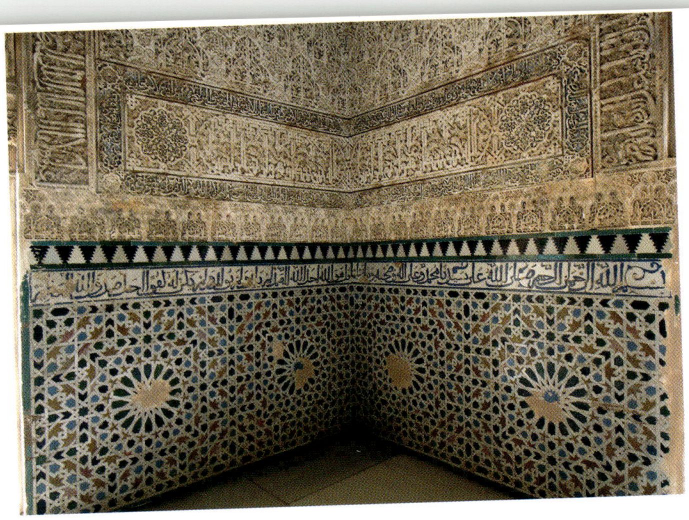

Fragment of a poem in the Torre de la Cautiva. In the Alhambra, the inscriptions, like this poem in stuccowork, were covered in gold leaf and shades of blue and other colours but little of this remains today. The poet writes of the symbolic role of the Torre de la Cautiva.

This work has come to adorn the Alhambra;
it is a dwelling for peace lovers and warriors;
Tower that contains a palace. Say!
that it is a fortress and at the same time a mansion for joy!
It is a palace in which splendour is given out
between its roofs, its floor and its four walls;
in the stucco and in the tiles are wonders, but the
wood carvings of its ceilings are even more extraordinary...

(English version based on a translation from Arabic into Spanish by M.ª Jesús Rubiera Mata)

image although this did not mean the destruction of Nasrid inscriptions when the Christian monarchs occupied the Alhambra. The poems would be respected; the Arab inscriptions would even be maintained in spaces such as the Mexuar or the Sala de los Reyes, both used as Christian chapels at different times. Care would be taken and repairs made where the inscriptions had deteriorated employing, as of old, gold leaf and indigo among other materials, to colour the stucco. Occasionally, unconnected fragments of the Arabic inscriptions were joined together despite the incomprehension of the Arabs; a response that under Philip II would lead to their translation.

However, respect for the inscriptions did not imply an abandonment of the figurative images of Christian power. Under Christian rule, the Alhambra was gradually filled with new icons like the image of Our Lady at the Puerta de la Explanada (or de la Justicia); the mythological and allegorical figures on the façade of the Palacio de Carlos V; the figurative decoration in the Peinador de la Reina; and the paintings on Christian themes, documented in some accounts, and which decorated former Islamic spaces in the Christian Alhambra.

The care of the Alhambra

Restoration and conservation in the Alhambra

The Alhambra constitutes the best-conserved palace precinct in western Islam and the only existing medieval complex of its kind. Moreover, as a living monument it is testimony to the value of the Islamic inheritance. Its continued use and the vicissitudes of history have left marks that are difficult to evaluate but which demand multiple readings and interpretations. While many additions and some interventions have broken with its Islamic essence, it is absolutely certain that, as the Alhambra has remained a living building, its purpose as a royal residence has, since its earliest days, meant that such fragile, delicate structures, created for ephemeral, immediate pleasure, have been kept standing.

Such documentary evidence about maintenance under Christian rule as has been conserved indicates substantial sums of money were invested in keeping and repairing the Alhambra, employing skilled Muslim craftsmen of renowned prestige. In purely economic terms it would have been more profitable to build a new residence but political issues and a respect and admiration for the work encouraged a single option: to maintain and care for the Alhambra.

Sixteenth-century interventions range from the introduction of new elements to the recreation of Nasrid forms. Such tasks of repair and maintenance diminished with the seventeenth century. The expulsion of the Moriscos and the lack of money, as well as a certain disinterest on the part of some of the Alhambra's governors, saw the onset of a period of comparative decline with less investment: the works undertaken were minor remodelling, above all on the occasion of visits by ruling monarchs. At the end of the eighteenth century, the Alhambra suffered serious deterioration when it became the residence of the governors and their families and some of the decorative pieces were sold off.

In 1810, Napoleon's troops reached Granada, converting the Alhambra into a military barracks. While this use brought with it severe damage for the monument, after their departure things did not improve as part of the Alhambra was inhabited, creating conditions that little favoured its conservation. After 1829, the situation gradually changed and especially from 1840, under the regency of María Cristina, a progressive advance towards its conservation began.

Among nineteenth-century conservationists, an outstanding though controversial figure is that of Rafael Contreras, some of whose interventions corresponded to criteria based on the recreation of *morisco* spaces and atmospheres which sharply contrast with today's conservationist trend. Noteworthy in the early twentieth century was the appointment of Modesto Cendoya as new architect of the Alhambra. He is to be thanked for important interventions in conservation and the underground drainage system.

The rigorous, archive–documented studies published in the late nineteenth century by Manuel Gómez Moreno in his *Guía de Granada* as well as the arrival in 1923 of the architect Leopoldo Torres Balbás as curator of the Alhambra, would introduce a new policy based on the utmost possible respect for the original buildings, solely intervening in cases of emergency. Leopoldo Torres Balbás's stated intention was to conserve the buildings exactly as they had been committed to his care, preventing them from falling into ruin, consolidating them, but never completing or remaking existing structures. His rigor and scientific knowledge led him to leave written records of all interventions in works dairies. In addition, we have access to the valuable documentation of plans that he left, for example, in the case of one of his greatest projects: the 1923 intervention in the space known as the Patio del Harén. One of his most controversial interventions was in the eastern temple in the Palacio de los Leones, where he eliminated the dome of glazed tiles built in 1859 by the architect Juan Pugnaire. Torres Balbás substituted the dome with a roof, basing his decision on scientific studies concluding that a roof, rather than a dome, was the most realistic covering for this type of temple.

Perhaps one event in which we can most clearly appreciate the slowly growing interest in the conservation of the Alhambra precinct was the delimitation and protection of its surroundings. The Alhambra was first declared a National Historic and Artistic Monument in 1870. This led to

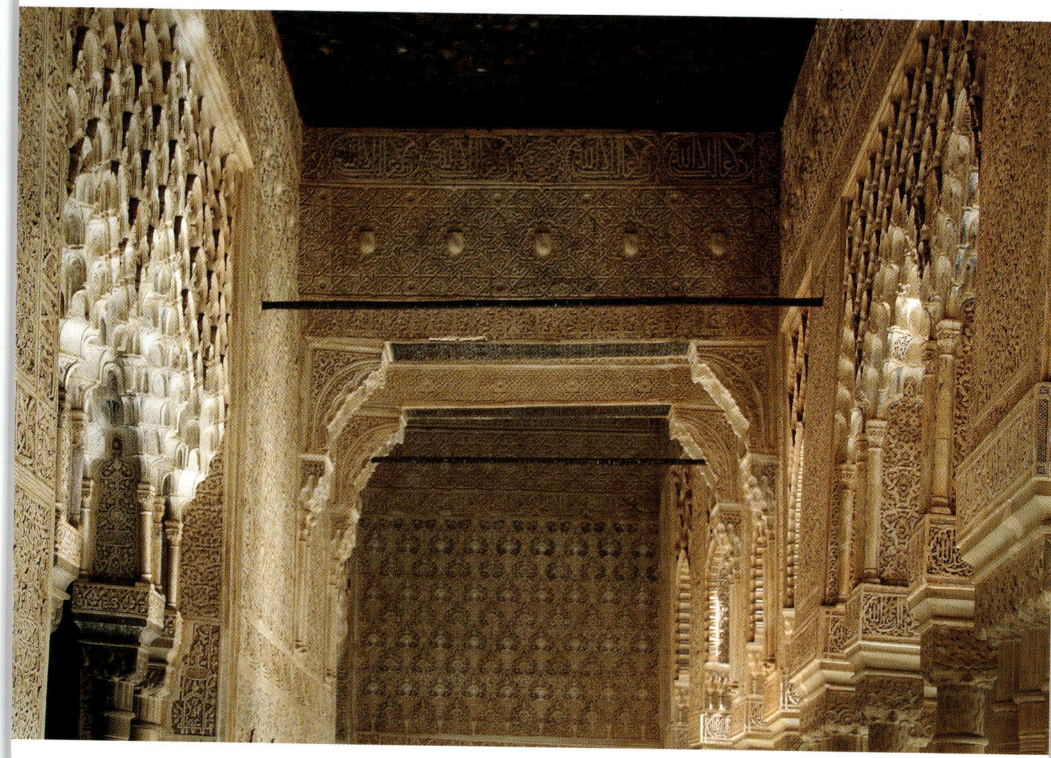

In the mid-sixteenth century, the Count of Tendilla gave written instructions that the stucco of the Palacio de los Leones should be maintained exactly as it had been made: "Firstly, repairs should be made to all the stucco from the four corridors to all the inscriptions and pieces that are missing and some panels that are missing and all the indentations should be covered and returned, restoring them in the manner in which the work shows that they had been made". (Work in the Cuarto de los Leones, 1552. A.Alh., L-5-23).

a redefining of the boundaries of the Alhambra precinct and with it the compulsory purchase of private properties, the most important of which was the Generalife acquired by the Spanish state in 1921 but not integrated into the complex until 1979. In 1943, all the Alhambra and Generalife gardens were declared of historic interest. But it was in 1979 when the process of determining the boundaries of the precinct took a considerable step forward. The area was extended to include the Palacio del Generalife, as previously mentioned, as well as the archaeological remains in the complex situated around the Cerro del Sol hilltop.

In 1984, the Alhambra and the Generalife were included in the UNESCO World Heritage

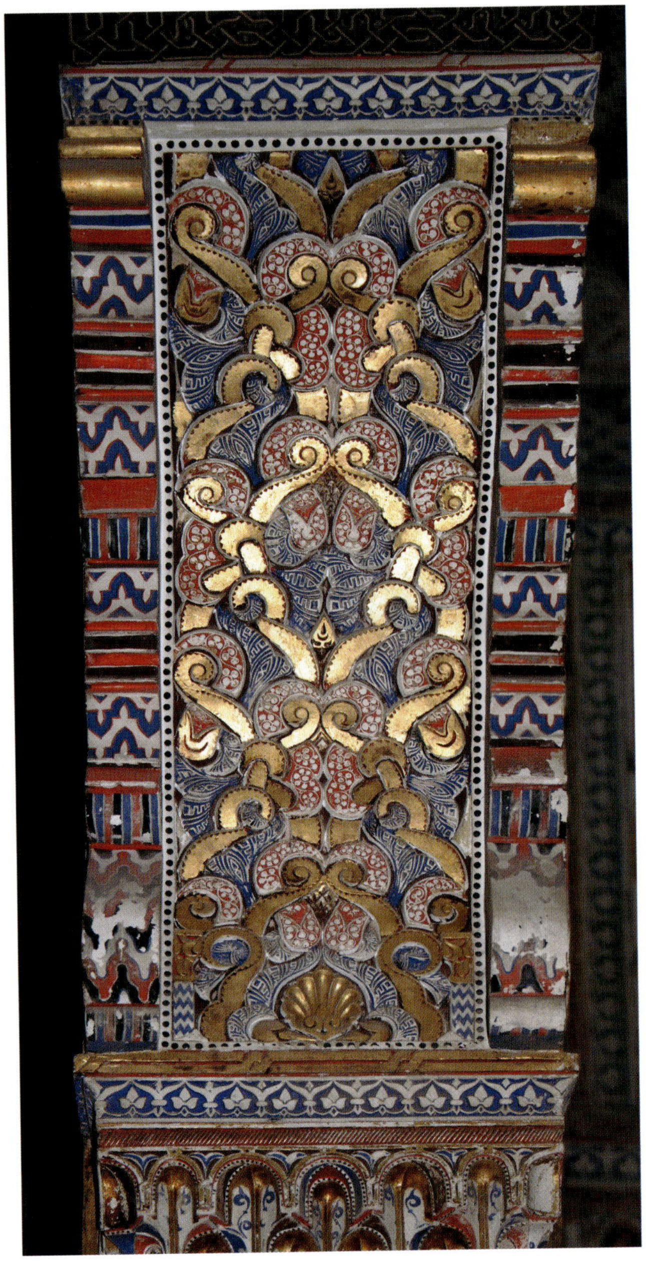

Detail of stucco in the Sala de las Camas in the Baño Real de Comares. In this space, the greatest intervention of the architect Rafael Contreras took place between 1848 and 1866, rebuilding a large part of the hall and conserving only the columns, flooring and part of the tiling of the original. This type of intervention meant that the hall should be seen more as a piece of nineteenth-century historicism than a Nasrid construction.

list. In 1989, by resolution of the Andalusian autonomous regional government's general directorate for cultural heritage, new limits were established for the perimeter of the Alhambra and the legal process was begun to declare the monument an historic complex, within the category of sites of cultural interest established by the Spanish national heritage act of 1985. In 1991, a special protection plan was published in fulfilment of the regional parliament's historic heritage act. Finally, in 2002 the limits of the protective perimeter of the precinct were fixed with a substantial extension in terms of significant architecture and countryside being newly considered part of the site.

From romantic legends to scientific research

WE CANNOT DENY THAT INTERNATIONAL recognition of the Alhambra came thanks to the Romantics. The literature, drawings and reflections they lavished on its palatial scenery contributed to the building of a myth of the Alhambra as a bewitching realm of pleasure. This imaginary Alhambra, full of the exotic and oriental much beloved by nineteenth-century Romantics, also forms part of our knowledge of the monument precinct. If you want to learn about the Alhambra, you have to recognize part of the imaginary world that has gradually been built up around it.

The first reflections and legends led to the creation of stereotypes, some of which have lasted to the present. One such enduring idea held to by historians was that which José de Hermosilla defended in *Las Antigüedades árabes de España*, published in Madrid in the late eighteenth century: in his drawings and plans he recorded the existence of a palace similar to the Palacio de los Leones and supposedly destroyed when the Palacio de Carlos V was built. Another idea that gained currency among historians was the belief that the Palacio de Comares constituted a summer palace while the more sheltered Palacio de los Leones, was for winters. The same idea had appeared earlier in the writings of sixteenth-century travellers and seventeenth-century scholars and was to gain followers until the Romantic period. These ideas, form part of the construction of an imaginary Alhambra and today have been rejected.

Among the literary Romantics we should first mention François-René de Chateaubriand with his *Les aventures du dernier Abencérage*, published in 1826, and Washington Irving whose *Tales of the Alhambra*, created the image of the Alhambra, of Granada, and to a certain extent, of Spain, which the Romantics would take from his book.

The list of Romantics who chose to set for their stories, legends and drawings in the Alhambra is lengthy. First, came Henry Swinburne who would make the Alhambra fashionable in England and France, followed by his successors: David Roberts, John Frederick Levis, Richard Ford and Théophile Gautier among others. However, without doubt, three books visually immortalize the Alhambra of the Romantics: James Cavanah Murphy's *The Arabian Antiquites in Spain*; Girault de Prangey's *Souvenirs de Grenade et de l'Alhambra*; and Owen Jones and Jule Goury's *Plans, elevations, sections and details from the Alhambra*).

Each one of the corners and spaces of the Alhambra can draw on its own legend which, well-forged by popular tradition, sixteenth-century Christian travellers or even nineteenth-century Romantics, has contributed to create an imaginary Alhambra full of romantic, oriental touches. Thus, the name Puerta del Vino, is believed to come from the fact that wine was sold there in the sixteenth century, although it has been suggested that it is the result of a misinterpretation of *al-ḥamrā'*, (the red) as *al-jamra* (the wine). Similarly, the Torre de Comares is also known as Torre de Embajadores, the Tower of Ambassadors, in the belief that it was here that the council meeting was held when it was agreed to hand over Granada to the Christians. Also, the pact between the Catholic Kings and Columbus for the "discovery" of America was believed to have been sealed on the same site.

The work of Manuel Gómez-Moreno González and Manuel Gómez-Moreno Martínez, in the late nineteenth and early twentieth centuries, are basic instruments from which we can confirm a change in the perception of the Alhambra. A change occurred converting Romantic legends and architects' exotic, decorative excesses into scientific rigor with substantial data collected by the Gómez Morenos and especially with the work of Leopoldo Torres Balbás, architect-curator of the Alhambra from 1923. In the more recent past, the figure of Jesús Bermúdez Pareja, director of the Museum of the Alhambra, was an indispensable support to the understanding, dissemination and approach of new generations to the values of the Alhambra, the complexity of its historic sequences, and the need to respect it.

Their work, with that of others, permitted and offered a new Alhambra where, starting with specialists in Arab studies, archaeologists, architects, art historians, mathematicians and restorers among others, have scientifically informed on their reflections and views of the Alhambra. Moreover, researchers have particularly drawn on the help of the Library and Archive, significantly located in one of the "New Museum" buildings to the east of the Generalife's tree-lined avenues.

The Library was founded in 1909 with the legacy of the Count of Romanones and specializes in art history, especially "hispano-muslim" art monographs, but also includes the Renaissance, historic garden monographs, and an important collection of prints of the Alhambra by Romantics from overseas. Interestingly, the Archive was originally established when the Catholic Kings located their headquarters in the Alhambra and since then its collections have grown continually. Although several inventories of the documentation have been made since the eighteenth century, it was in 1886 under Manuel Gómez-Moreno González that the first inventory was compiled and in 1956 that it was revised and the catalogue begun under the supervision of M.ª Angustias Moreno Olmedo. The Archive consists of documents dating from the fifteenth century, related to the history of the kingdom of Granada following its conquest, as well as others referring to the building works and conservation of the monument. It also includes a valuable collection of photographs.

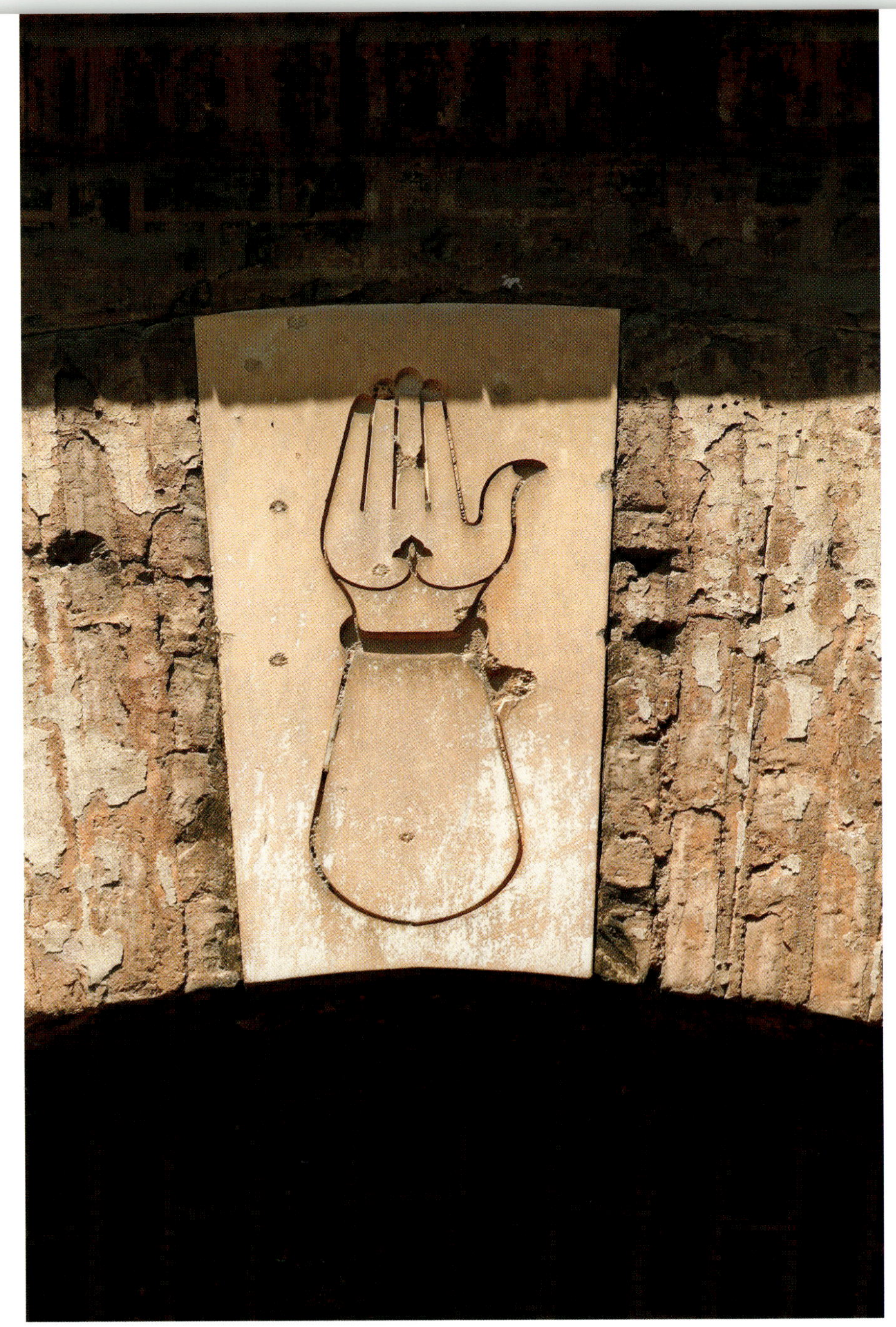

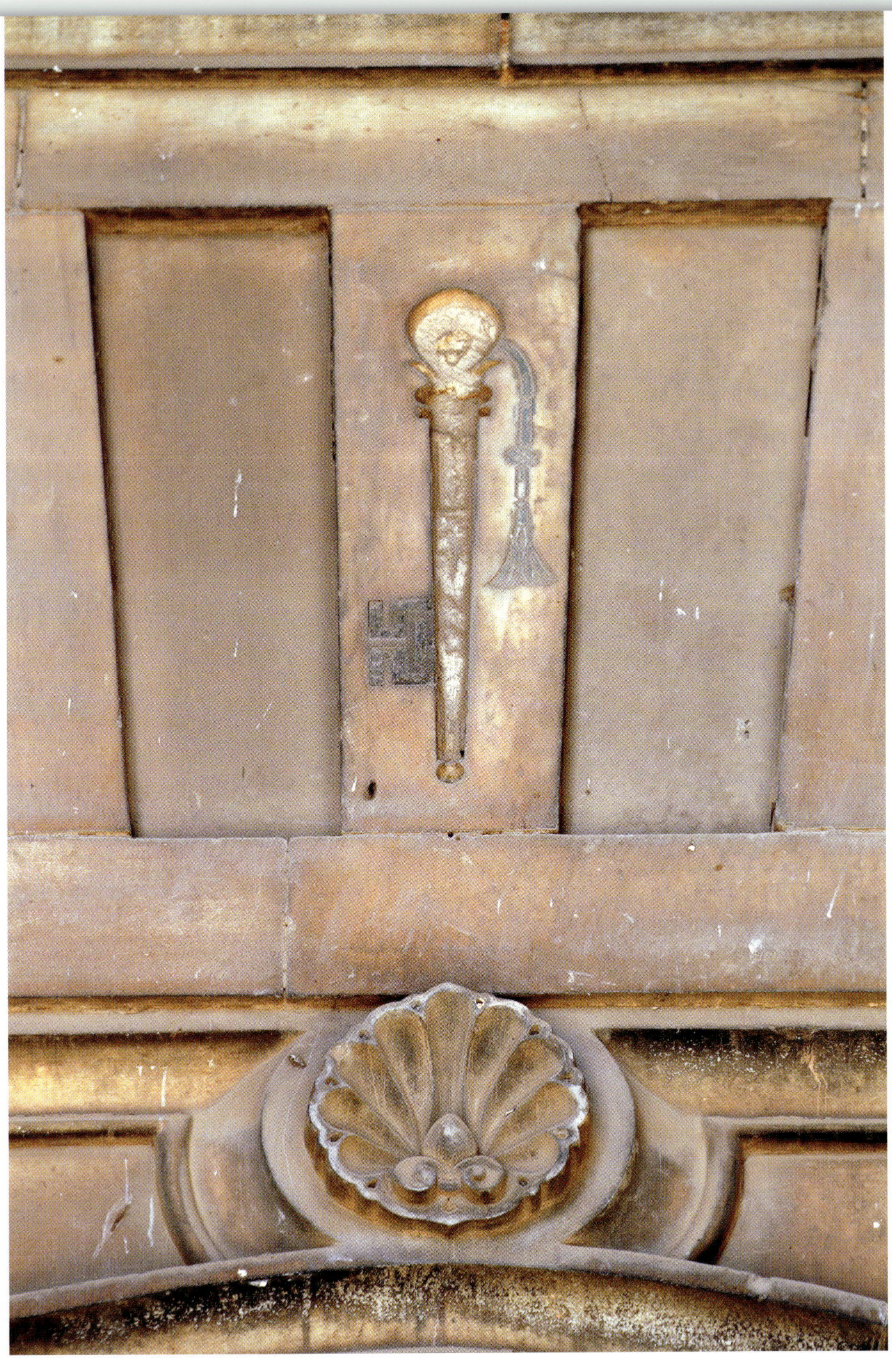

Legends. Since the sixteenth century, people have believed that the Puerta de la Justicia, Bāb al-Šarī'a, was where laws were handed down. However, today the name, Puerta de la Explanada, is used. Popular tradition points to the destruction of the Alhambra if ever the hand should grasp the key that appears on the *clave*, the keystone in the arch.

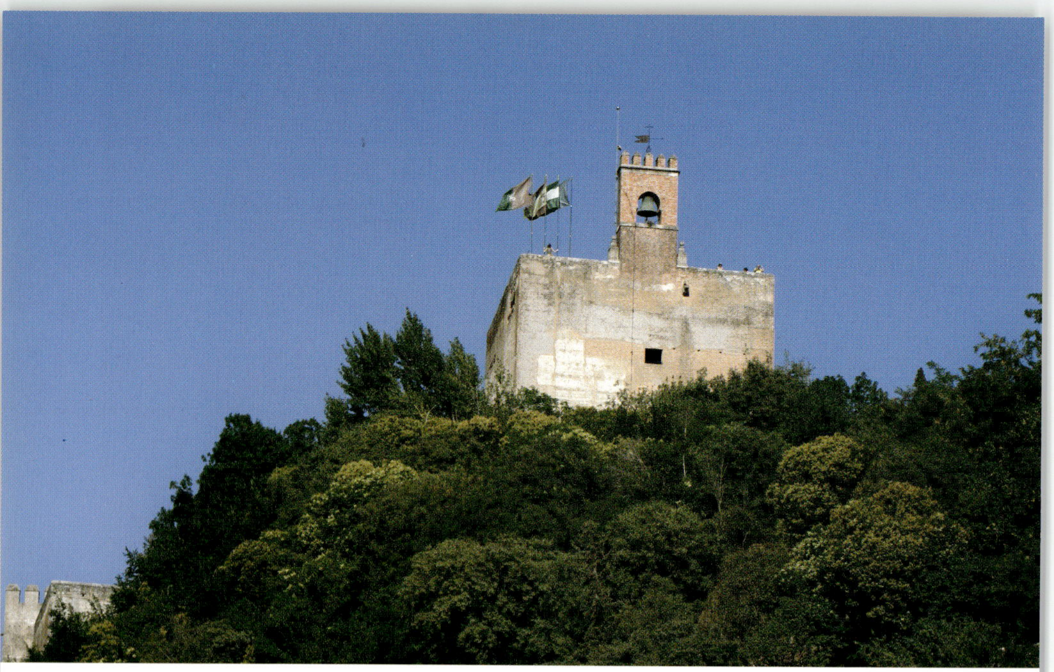

Legends. The Torre de la Vela, also known as the Torre de la Campana or Torre del Sol, is associated with the popular tradition that the women of Granada who ring the bell on 2 January will be married before the year's end.

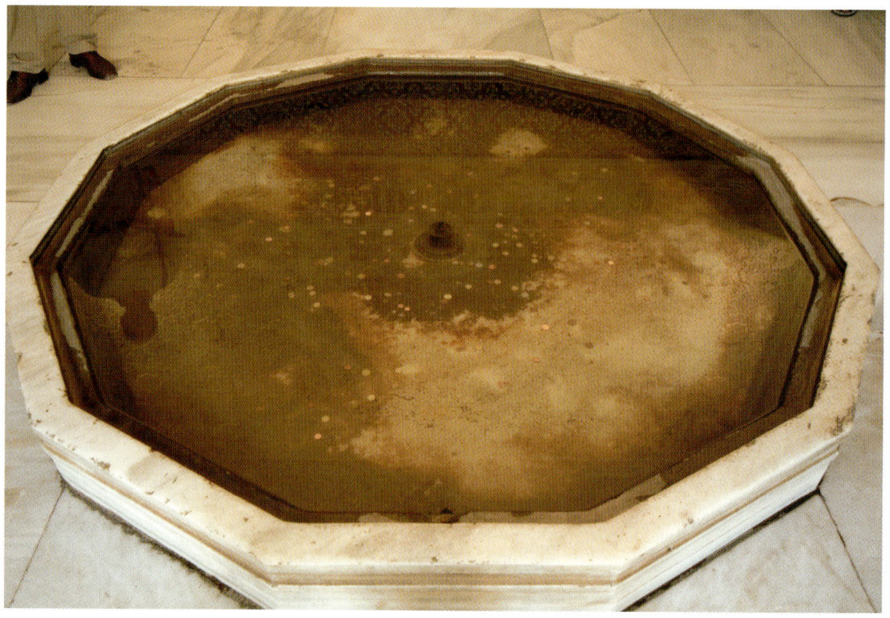

Legends. The stains on the fountain in the Sala de Abencerrajes were interpreted by commoners as traces of the blood of the Abencerrajes knights who had their throats cut there.

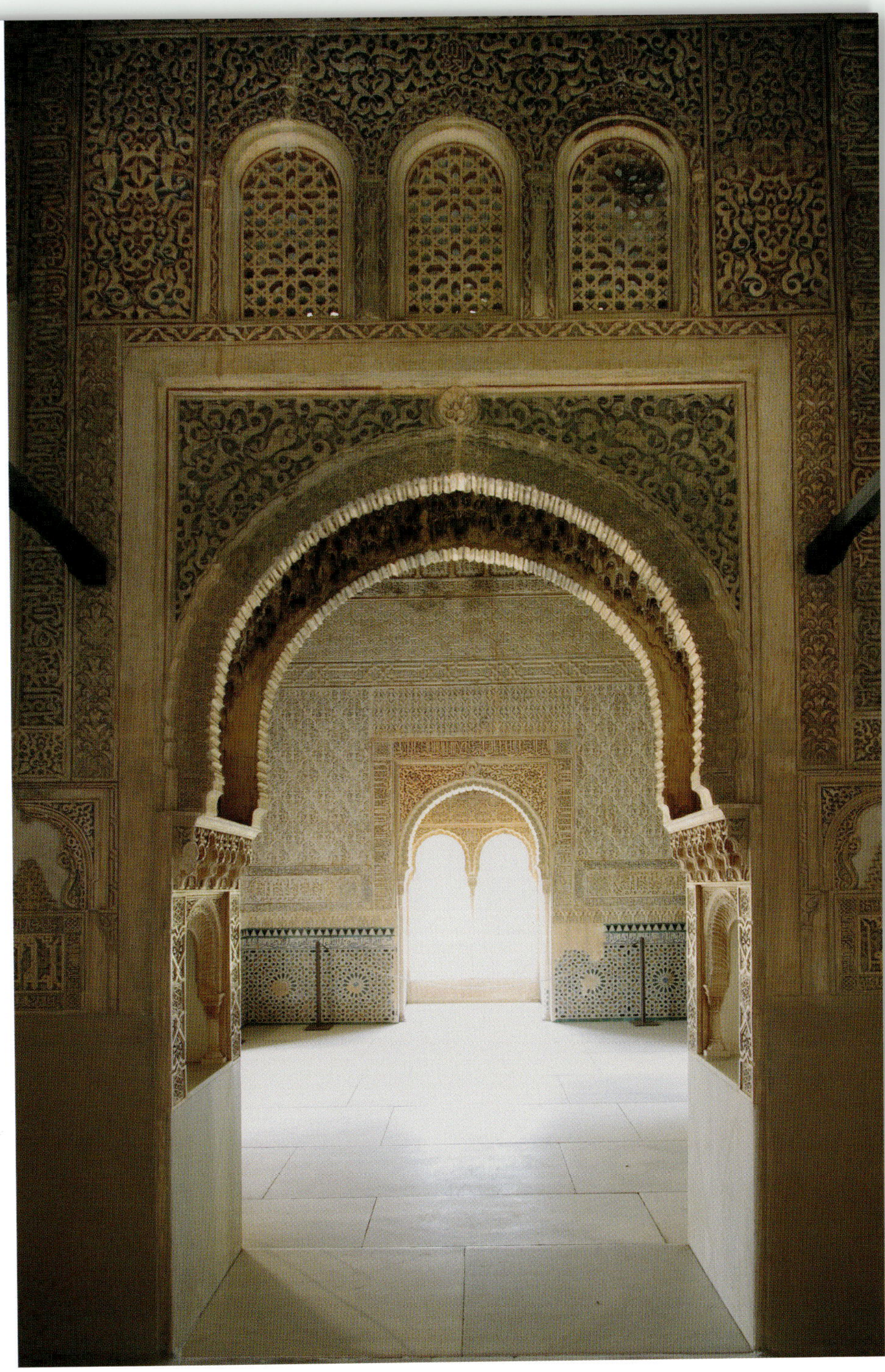

Legends. The name Torre de la Cautiva has been used since the nineteenth century and comes from the romantic belief that it was here that Dª Isabel de Solís, later to become the Sultana Zoraya, was held prisoner. From the sixteenth century, it was known as the Torre de la Ladrona or Torre de la Sultana.

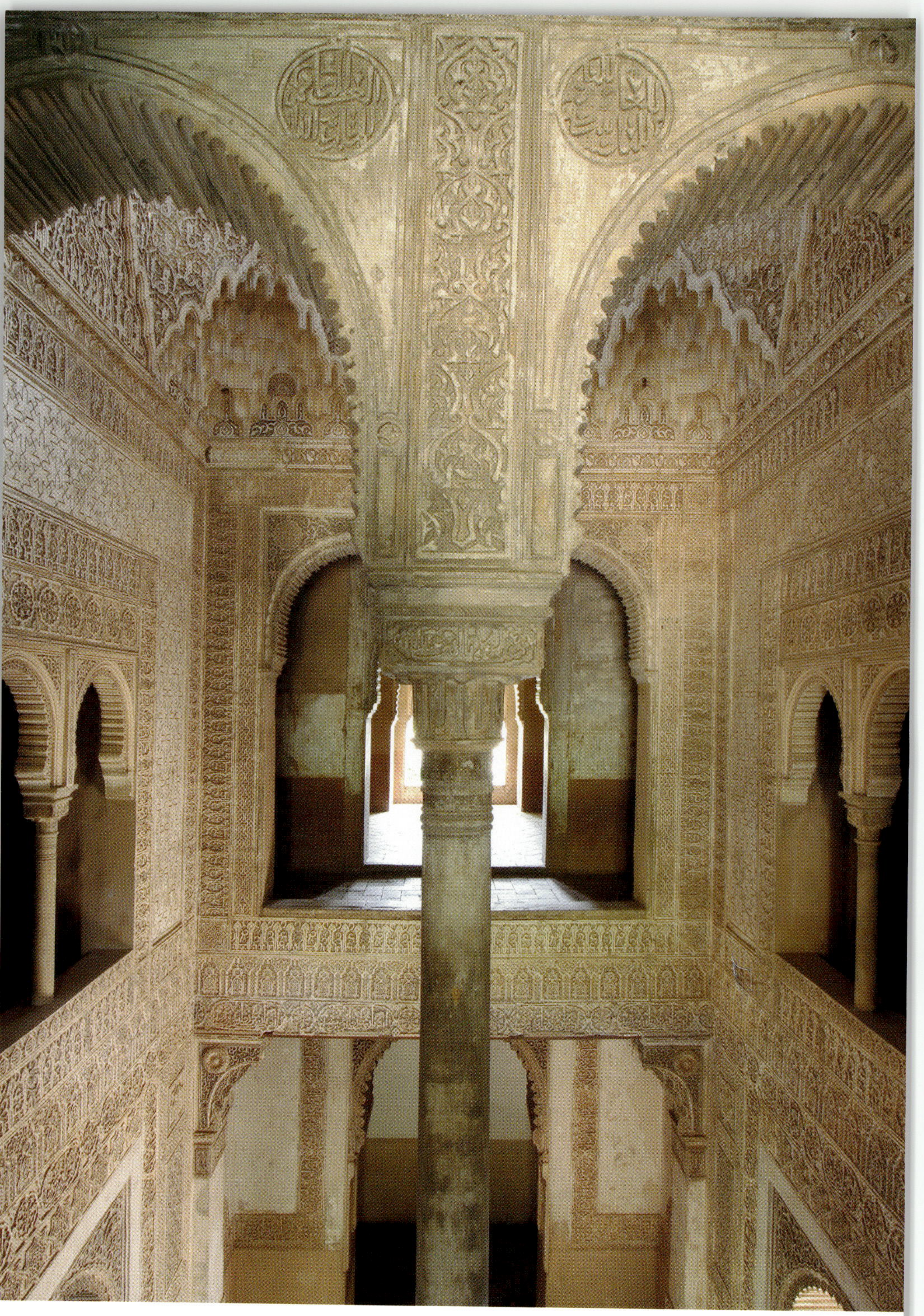

Legends. The Torre de las Infantas is linked to the legend of the three princesses, Zaida, Zoraida and Zorahaida, included in Washington Irving's *Tales of the Alhambra*.

Visit to the Alhambra and the Generalife

Introduction

THERE ARE MANY DIFFERENT *routes you can follow on a visit to the Alhambra. This guidebook suggests a few of them. The one we recommend is easy to follow and is based on proximity of location. Beginning at the entrance/exit pavilion and crossing a cypress-lined avenue, you reach the* medina *– the city inside the Alhambra – and the street named Calle Real, to finally enter the Alcazaba – the defensive, walled precinct. Once you have seen the Alcazaba, the closest building is the Palacio de Carlos V and from there you can enter the Nasrid palaces: the Palacio de Comares and the Palacio de los Leones. From the Palacio de los Leones, you approach the Emperor's rooms to later, from El Partal, begin a route along the avenue of the towers, Paseo de las Torres. Once you reach the end of this, you approach the Generalife to leave once more through the entrance/exit pavilion.*

This suggested route does not follow elements in chronological or historical order. If you wanted to follow a chronological path you would have to begin with the Alcazaba, considered the oldest part and dated from the thirteenth century, continue with the late-thirteenth and early-fourteenth-century Generalife, return to the Nasrid palaces, fundamentally built in the fourteenth century, and end with the sixteenth-century Palacio de Carlos V. If you think about it, this route would involve crossing the entire Alhambra several times.

Another interesting alternative is to walk from the entrance/exit pavilion and around the perimeter to the Puerta de la Explanada (de la Justicia), which allows you to appreciate what one access to the precinct would have been like under the Nasrid dynasty. On the way there, you see the different towers that advance considerably towards the woods to protect the foot of the wall. In front of the Washington Irving Hotel, you can admire the outpost that the Puerta de las

Albercas or Puerta de los Siete Suelos has defended since the late fifteenth century, a very important supply entrance to the city and quite spectacular despite its partial destruction at the time of the Napoleonic invasion. Following the wall along the purpose-built pedestrian footpath, you reach the Torre de las Cabezas, a prison or prisons, defended at its base by another outpost formed by a pointed spur, with embrasures for artillery pieces and muskets. From here you can climb the street that leads to the Puerta de los Carros, an entrance for vehicles constructed in the sixteenth century to allow stone to be brought into the precinct when the Palacio de Carlos V was under construction. However, we recommend continuing from the Torre de las Cabezas down to reach the most noteworthy of all the gates, the last to be built: the Puerta de la Explanada (or de la Justicia).

As we said, the Alhambra can be viewed from a multitude of perspectives and never fails to surprise you, just like our other suggested tours through the gardens, water features, or hiking paths, among others. They invite you to visit the Alhambra on more than one occasion. Similarly, you never fail to wonder at the different perceptions of the monument revealed by visiting it by day or by night.

ITINERARY

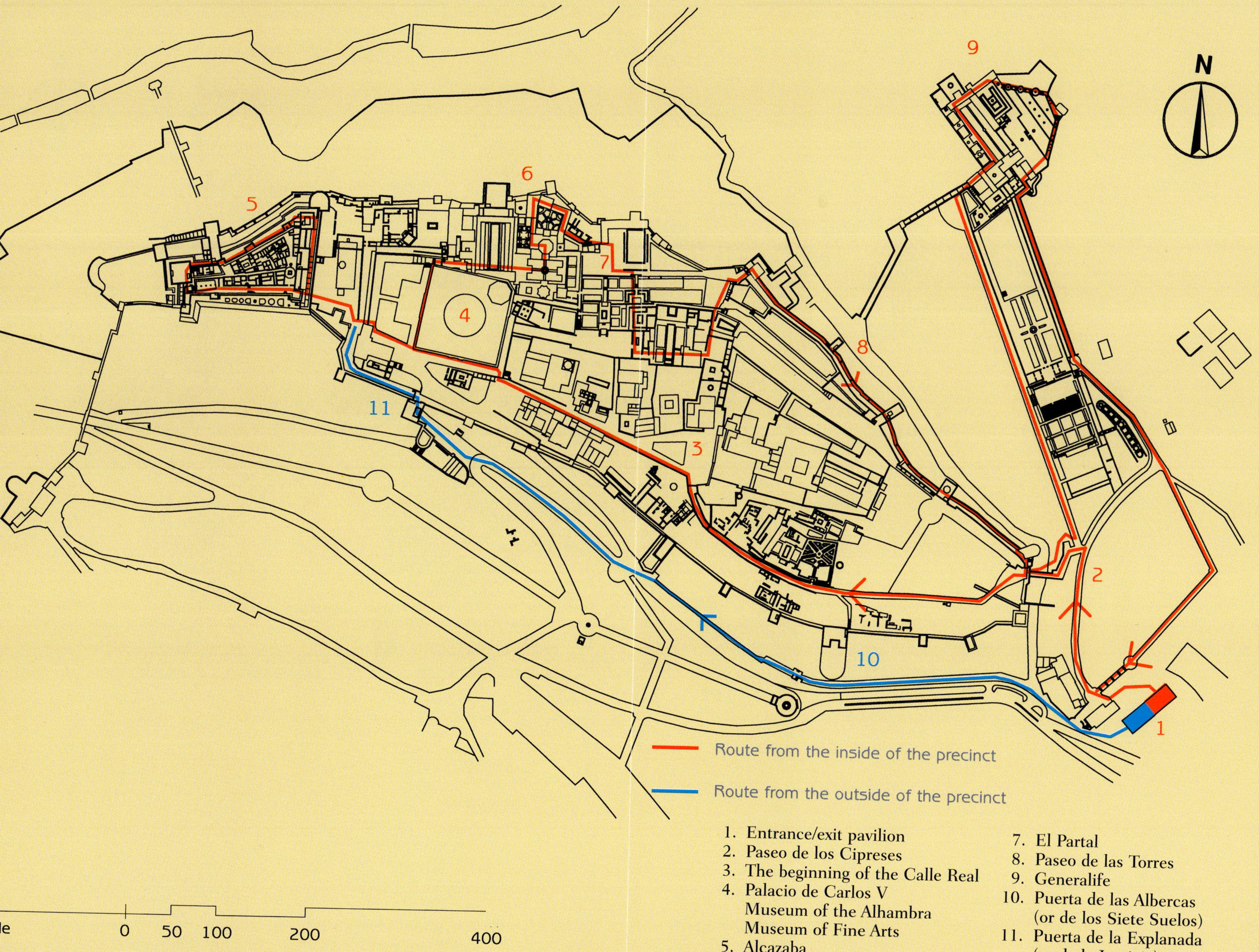

1. Entrance/exit pavilion
2. Paseo de los Cipreses
3. The beginning of the Calle Real
4. Palacio de Carlos V
   Museum of the Alhambra
   Museum of Fine Arts
5. Alcazaba
6. Nasrid palaces
7. El Partal
8. Paseo de las Torres
9. Generalife
10. Puerta de las Albercas
    (or de los Siete Suelos)
11. Puerta de la Explanada
    (or de la Justicia)

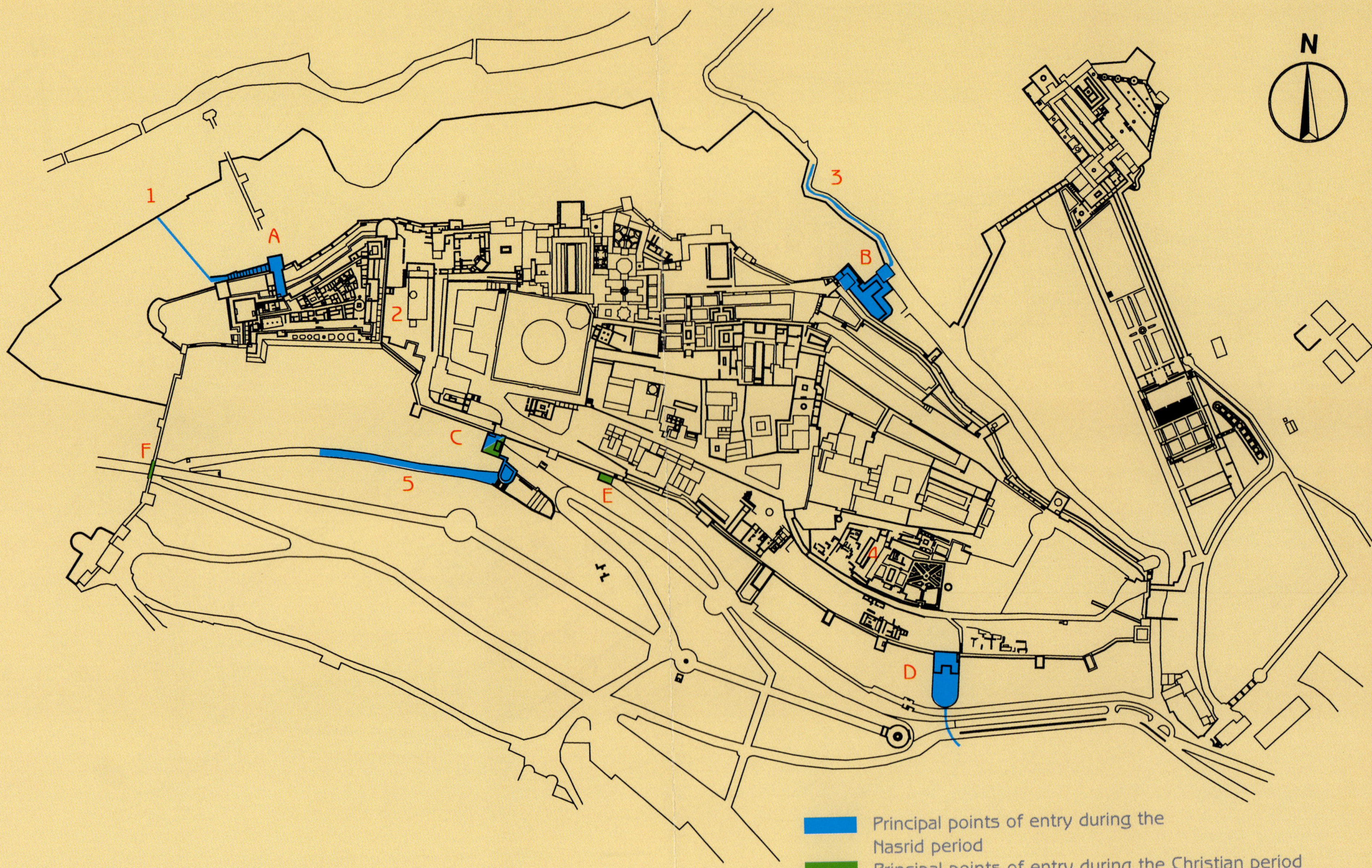

Principal points of entry during the Nasrid period

Principal points of entry during the Christian period

Scale 0 50 100 200 400

A. Puerta de las Armas
B. Puerta del Arrabal
C. Puerta de la Explanada (or de la Justicia)
D. Puerta de las Albercas (or de los Siete Suelos)
E. Puerta de los Carros
F. Puerta de las Granadas
1. Bosque de San Pedro
2. Plaza de los Aljibes
3. Cuesta de los Chinos
4. *Medina* Alta
5. Bosque de Gomérez

Entrance/exit pavilion

In Nasrid times, there were several different ways to reach the palace city. The oldest route, which linked the city of Granada to the Alhambra, started from close to the ancient aljama Almanzora mosque, today the parish church of Santa Ana in the Plaza Nueva, where you took a path through the wood, to first walk around the Torre de la Vela. Later, in the thirteenth century, you could go as far as the Puerta de las Armas, in the Alcazaba. Once you had passed through the gate, following the Camino de Ronda, you arrived at square today known as the Plaza del Aljibe, now on the inside of the precinct. Another Nasrid access started close to the Rey Chico ravine, climbing what in the twentieth century would come to be known as the Cuesta de los Chinos, and led to the Puerta del Arrabal gate beneath the Torre de los Picos. Thus, it linked the districts of Sacromonte and the Albaicín with the Alhambra. As well as these two entrances, during the reign of Yūsuf I (1333-1354) two magnificent gates were constructed: the Puerta de la Explanada (or de la Justicia) and the Puerta de las Albercas (or de los Siete Suelos). The first formed part of an access frequently used at the time, which connected the city and the precinct via the Cuesta de Gomérez. Once you passed through the Puerta de la Explanada you could reach the Puerta del Vino, which gave access to the lower *medina*. On the other hand, the splendid Puerta de las Albercas gave direct access to the upper *medina*.

The Nasrid entrances to the Alhambra changed with the Christian conquest of the city. In the years immediately following the conquest, entry was via the Antequeruela district, given the degree of mistrust that sight of the Christian monarchs and their troops crossing the city to occupy the Alhambra, might have raised. However, without a doubt, the greatest change came with Charles V when the Cuesta de Gomérez was lengthened, making it one of the main streets leading to the Puerta de la Explanada (or de la Justicia) and from there to the inside of the precinct. The transformation of this new access included the Arco de las Granadas as well as the fountain of Charles V, both very clearly in Renaissance style. The change was important because in the relationship between the city and the Alhambra its creation served to highlight the new axis that symbolically connected the Chancillería Real in Plaza Nueva with the Palacio de Carlos V in contrast with the Nasrid access that began further north at the aljama Almanzora mosque. Another point of entry during the imperial period was the Puerta de los Carros (currently used by official vehicles only), which was built to facilitate the entry of materials for work on the palace of Charles V and is located between the Torre de las Cabezas and the Puerta de la Explanada (or de la Justicia).

Today's ticket office and official entrance to the precinct were a response to the need to protect the surroundings. In 1986, a special plan to protect and reform the Alhambra and Alijares brought about the creation of a new access for vehicles which in 1988 became the objective of an international competition. The winning project proposed access by vehicle should be via the outer road network to the surroundings of the Alhambra, close to of the current cemetery, thus eliminating the harmful transit of vehicles that usually entered via the Cuesta de Gomérez. The project proposed building car parking facilities as well as the ticket office and official entrance. Significantly, the car park and pavilion initially caused intense debate centred on the integration of these new buildings into the surroundings of the Alhambra and the Generalife.

The façade of the entrance pavilion displays a map showing the route of the visit. Close by are three, bronze, scale models each of which analyzes the Alhambra from a different point of view: the Alhambra and the Islamic city of Granada, the historic evolution of the Alhambra, and the palace city of the Alhambra and its surroundings.

Once you pass through the ticket office and entrance pavilion, you reach the start of an avenue of cypresses and, some 100 metres later, the path divides in three: the right-hand fork takes us to the exit and the Generalife, the central path leads to the palace of the Generalife and its gardens (we recommend you leave this until the very end of your visit) and the left-hand path leads to the *medina*, the area known as El Secano, and into the Alhambra precinct.

The *medina:* Workshops and infrastructure at the service of the Court

El Secano

Name: The first space you enter is known as the dry land, El Secano, although vegetation planted in the first half of the twentieth century contradicts the name. It was first called El Secano during the Christian period. In the sixteenth century, the scarcity of water in this part of the Alhambra was already evident, although remnants of numerous Nasrid *albercas* and *atarjeas* show that in Islamic times the presence of water had been important here.

Date: Different periods starting in the reign of Muḥammad II (1273-1302) with a palace in the current Parador of San Francisco.

In the Middles Ages, the whole area was occupied by the houses and workshops of workers in the service of the Alhambra. Tanneries, where animal hides were cured and ovens for ceramics (still in use in the sixteenth and seventeenth centuries) are clearly identifiable. In the absence of systematic archaeological excavations, we assume that other craftsmen's workshops and the Mint, or House of Coins, also stood in this area.

If you choose the left-hand path on leaving the entrance pavilion, you pass over a modern bridge that crosses the pit surrounding the Alhambra, although originally there was no direct link between the Generalife, which lies to your right, and the Alhambra precinct you are now entering.

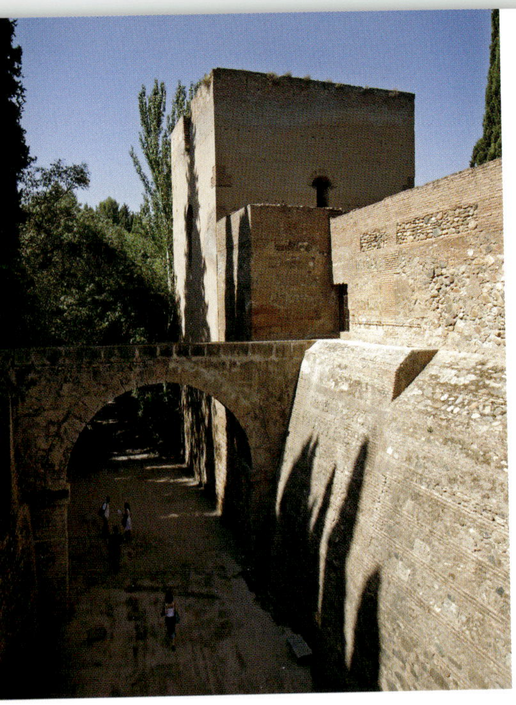

Water was an essential element in the Alhambra. Water supplies arrived via an aqueduct, tower and network of water-courses that distributed it throughout the complex. The Torre del Agua formed a part of this.

Once you cross the bridge, the tower known as the Torre del Agua and the nearby remains of the channel of the Acequia Real, which supplied water to the inhabitants of the *medina*, come into sight on the lower slopes of the path. Continuing west, you see the walled precinct and towers, all much re-built, and arrive at the Puerta de las Albercas (Bāb al-Gudur), known popularly as the Puerta de los Siete Suelos. Nearby, is the Camino de Ronda and the ruins of some

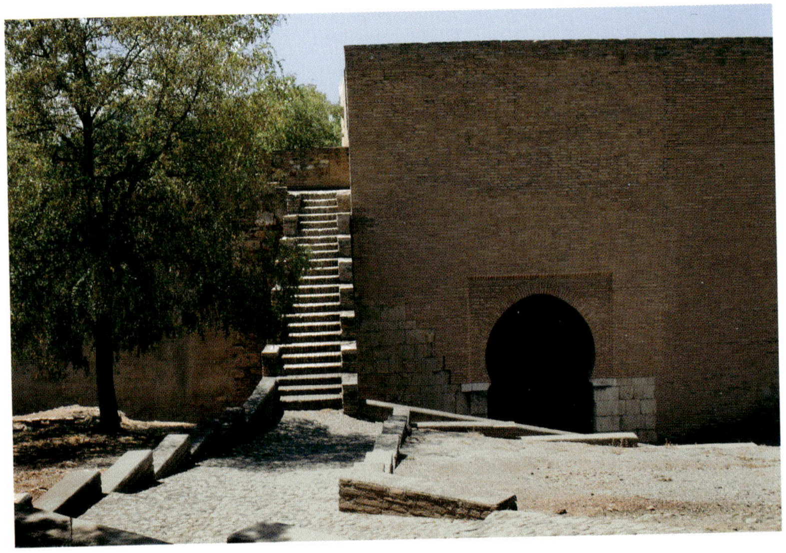

Puerta de las Albercas (or de los Siete Suelos), seen from the in-side of the *medina*.

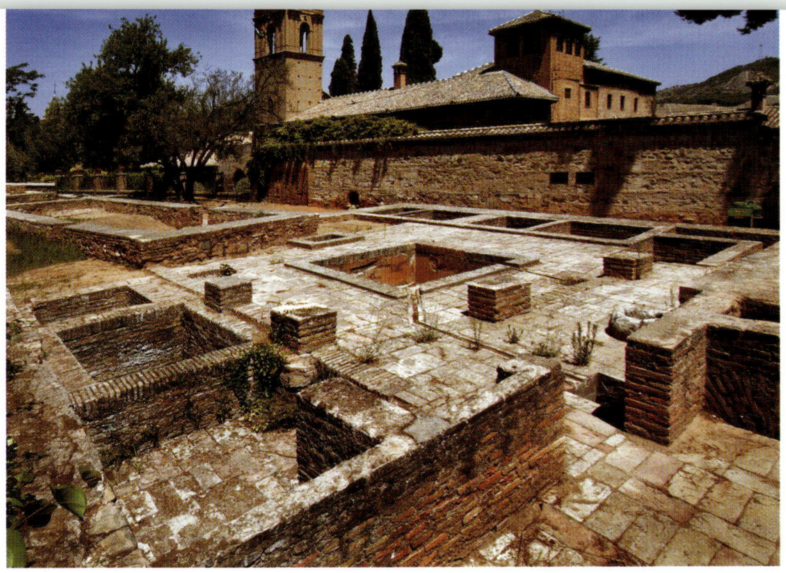

Remains of the tanneries where animal hides were cured

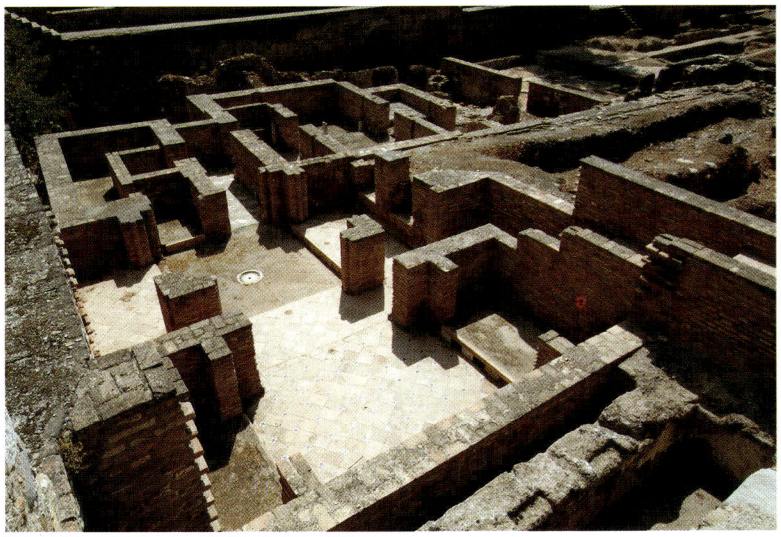

Baths in the Palacio de Abencerrajes

houses that enable you to see that the present-day garden is wholly out of place in what would have been an intricate district of houses, workshops and palaces.

To the right, at the start of an avenue of cypresses forming archways overhead, is the garden of San Francisco, created in the 1930s on the site of archaeological remains, where an underground grain silo has been

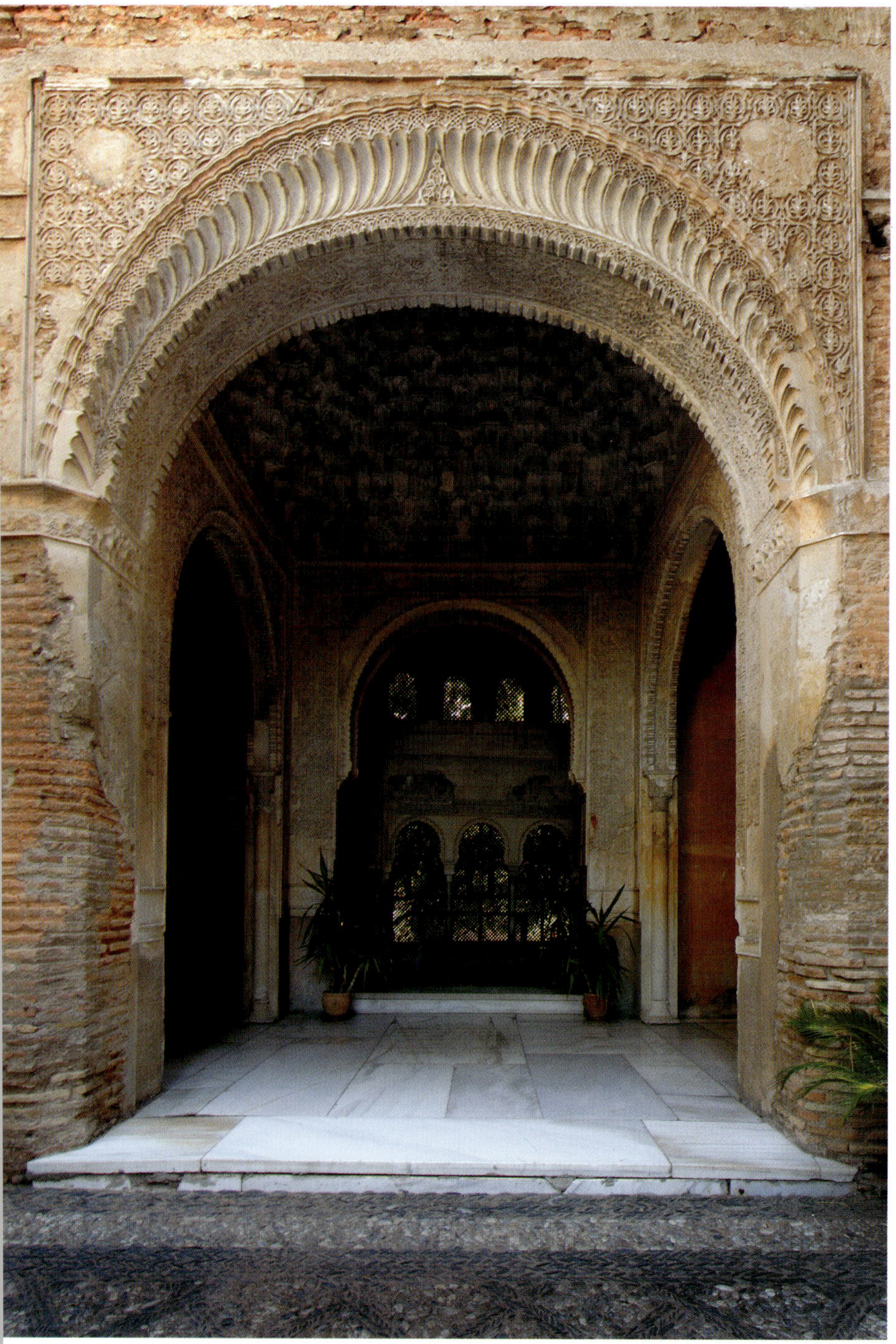

Qubba of the Nasrid palace inside the current Parador de San Francisco hotel. This was the main chapel of the convent of San Francisco and provisional burial place of Queen Isabella I of Castile.

conserved. To the north, the remains of some tanneries have been preserved; in an area dedicated to workshops or warehouses that has survived to the present day, is evidence of numerous pools, although only the central *alberca* has an entrance for water and drainage.

Near these tanneries you can see a single large *alberca* that must have been part of the patio of an important Nasrid palace. At the back of the pool stands the ancient convent of San Francisco, where the remains of a Nasrid palace have been conserved.

Moving west from the tanneries, you rejoin the avenue of cypresses. Before leaving through the iron gate that closes off the street, below and to the left stand what is left of the Palacio de Abencerrajes. Successive excavations have identified different rooms in what is assumed to be one of the oldest, most important palaces in the Alhambra. The most clearly visible parts belong to two bathrooms with their patios and typical chambers.

Through the railings and past a checkpoint, you move on into a wide, square with gardens, where the Alhambra and Generalife trust offices are located and which gives access to a hotel. The prestigious Parador de San Francisco was installed in a former Franciscan convent, founded by the Catholic Kings. Like other convents in Granada, it was founded on the site of a older Nasrid palace constructed by Muḥammad II, one of the oldest identified palaces in the Alhambra. Later, in the reign of Muḥammad V, some rooms were renovated and redecorated. Of the original palace, the hall that was converted into the main chapel of the sixteenth-century convent church is recognizable today. Its splendid Mozarabic vaulted ceiling can still be seen. On the floor, a simple marble plaque commemorates the provisional burial place of Queen Isabella "the Catholic" (Isabella I of Castile) before her remains were finally transferred to the Capilla Real, the Royal Chapel in Granada cathedral. Below and to the north of this hall lie the ruins of the original baths, with the remains of some interesting glazed ceramic tiles. A watercourse, the ancient *acequia* that ran through the centre of the palace has been partly opened up in what was once the main patio of the convent and is now that of the hotel.

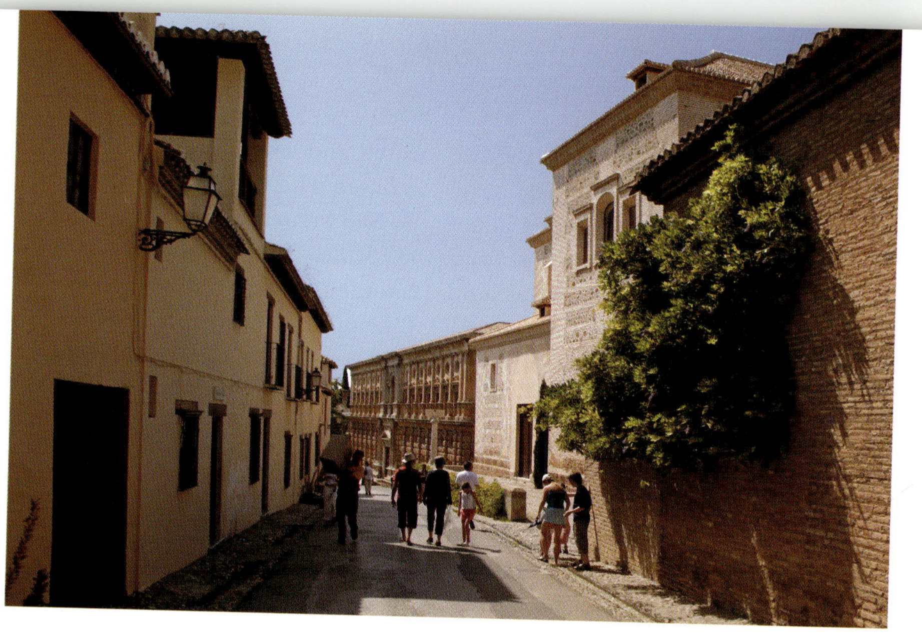

Calle Real

A street called Calle Real Alta

Name: The name Calle Real Alta was given to this street to distinguish it from the Calle Real Baja that linked the Palacio de Comares and the Palacio de los Leones. When the Palacio de Carlos V was built it cut the street in two.
Date: The Calle Real follows a path laid down during Nasrid rule although the buildings you see along it are from very different periods.
Note: This street ran into and formed part of the city, the *medina* of the Nasrid Alhambra.

When you pass through the checkpoint, you have a better view of the Calle Real Alta as it follows its ancient route as the principal thoroughfare through the *medina* and leads you towards the Puerta del Vino.

As you walk along the Calle Real, you find different, modern but nonetheless picturesque houses. Interestingly, the street called Callejón del Guindo follows the line of a side street off which the internal communication in the Alhambra led.

In Calle Real, stands a remarkable Nasrid building displaying the intimate character of the typical Granada house. It is known as the Baño de la

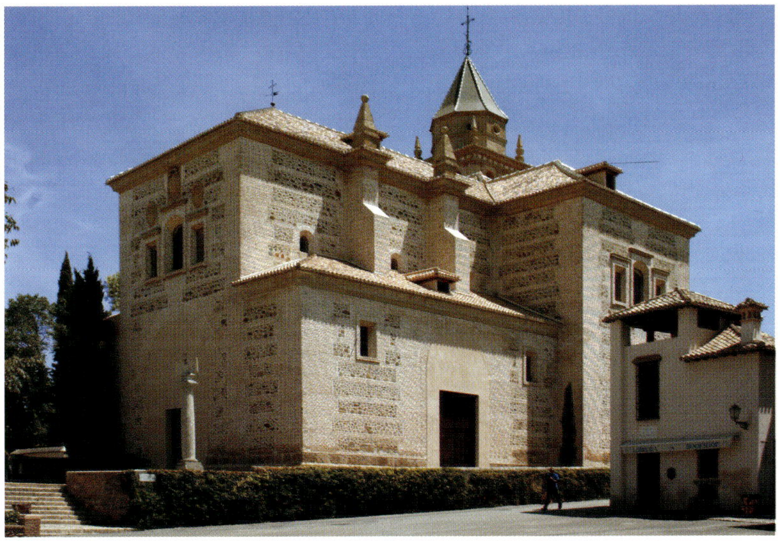

The church of Santa María de la Alhambra

Mezquita and is today home to the Ángel Barrios Museum, open to visitors at specific times only. The museum is dedicated to Ángel Barrios, a local musician and guitarist who died in 1964, and contains a variety of images and documents that recall the intellectual atmosphere of early twentieth-century Granada.

The baths, called the Baño de la Mezquita due to its proximity to the temple as is common in Islamic cities, was built in the reign of Muḥammad III (1302-1309) to provide financial support for the main mosque, also erected by this same sultan at the beginning of the fourteenth century. Although it was much altered in the nineteenth century to be used in part as what was then known as La casa del Polinario, the house of El Polinario, the nickname given to Antonio Barrios, father of Ángel. Most of the house was rebuilt in the twentieth century, helping to recover the traditional rooms associated with the rituals of Islamic baths.

One peculiarity of these baths is that the different rooms are not laid out in parallel as is normal in Nasrid baths. The dressing room, or *bayt al-maslaj*, is of the same type as that found in the royal baths of Comares, with a central lantern. The cold room, or *al-bayt al- bārid*, has a vaulted ceiling; the hot room, or *al-bayt al-sajūn*, is rectangular and has rooms off at the side and currently there is a single immersion pool although there would probably have been another on the other side, where today there is a small water basin. The space for the boiler, or *al-burma*, is found between the two immersion pools.

In front of the baths, you can still see the remains of a door, currently with wrought-iron railings, that would have been one of the connecting passages that formed part of the urban layout of the Alhambra.

Separated from the baths by a narrow alleyway, stands the church of Santa María de la Alhambra. On the same site stood the original, main mosque of the Alhambra, a temple that was praised for its sumptuousness despite its modest proportions. It had three naves separated by wood-clad arches set on marble columns. Demolished due to its ruinous state in 1576, the decision was taken to construct a new temple. This became an ambitious project for Juan de Herrera, architect of El Escorial near Madrid, but finally turned into no more than the quite modest church that you see today, completed in 1618. The structure, however, is the first of its kind in Granada, as the parish church adopted the counter-reformation and not the *Mudéjar* style. On the inside, where the layout takes the form of a Latin cross with side chapels, you find excellent altarpieces and various paintings and sculptures. Pride of place goes to a noteworthy Baroque altarpiece, carved between 1667 and 1671, that houses a beautiful image of Our Lady de las Angustias (1750-1760), the work of local sculptor Torcuato Ruiz del Peral. Its pious expressiveness is patent when it is borne in procession in Holy Week. It is truly a spectacular sight when it leaves the Puerta de la Explanada (or de la Justicia) under a shower of flower petals and parades towards Granada through the Gomérez woods. The Calle Real broadens out in this area to leave space for a wide esplanade that was to be constructed to complement the Palacio de Carlos V, offering a magnificent view. In front of this, in the direction of the Puerta del Vino just visible at the end of the street, are the remains of a Nasrid house, with a patio, a small pool and rooms, one of many such houses that were to be found all over this area. It is well worth stopping here as this is one of the best examples of traditional Nasrid houses and careful study of it helps you understand what houses of the period were like. Behind this, the higher street lets you lean over onto the upper part of the Puerta de la Explanada (or de la Justicia) and note its strategic position. In front of the southwest corner of the Palacio de Carlos V on the way towards the Puerta del Vino, stands a Visitor Centre providing tourist information and washroom facilities.

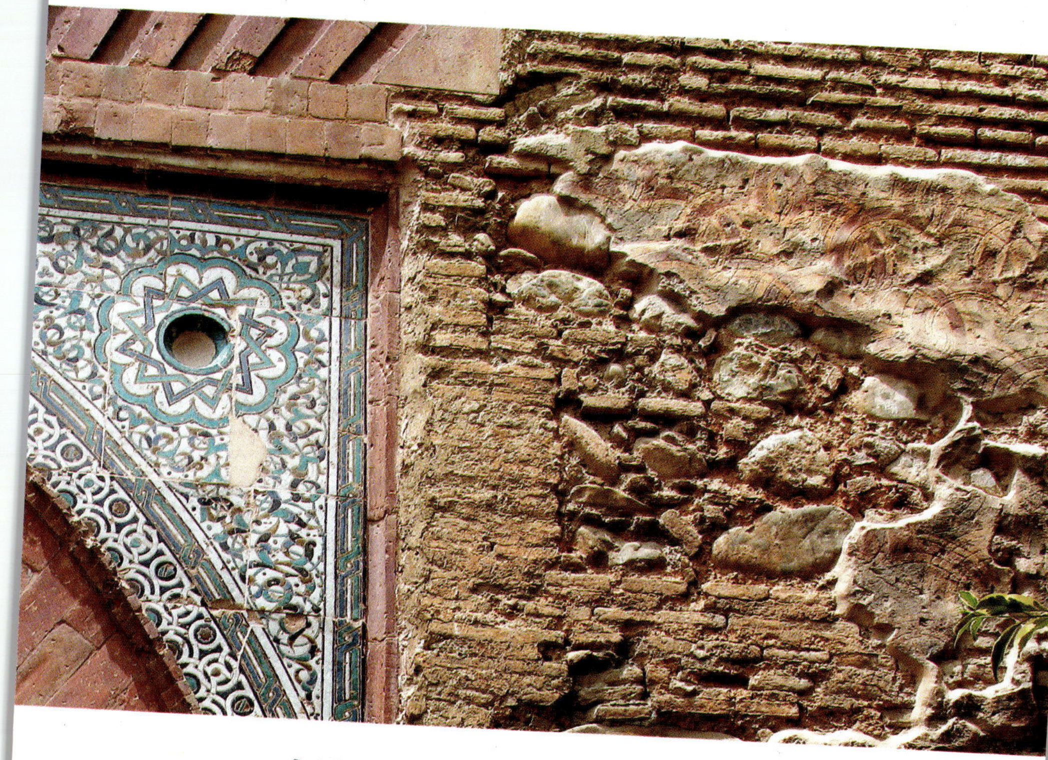

Detail of the inner face of the Puerta del Vino where you can appreciate the "dry cord", *cuerda seca*, ceramics in the pediments and remnants of the painted plaster. (Photograph by José Manuel Gómez-Moreno Calera).

Puerta del Vino, the Wine Gate

Name: Some say that the Puerta del Vino takes its name from the fact that wine was sold here in the Christian period. Others suggest it arose as a corruption of Bāb al-Jamra, Wine Gate, into Bāb al-Ḥamrā' (Red Gate).
Date: Early 14th cent.; renovated 1350-1400.
Sultanate: Muḥammad III (1302-1309) and Muḥammad V (1354-1359; 1362-1391).
Note: The gate closed off access to the Calle Real Alta in the *medina* of the Alhambra. It was initially built as an element of urban control but was later renovated by Muḥammad V and the remarkable ceramic panels of the inner arch were added along with other elements that gave it a more ornamental, commemorative nature.

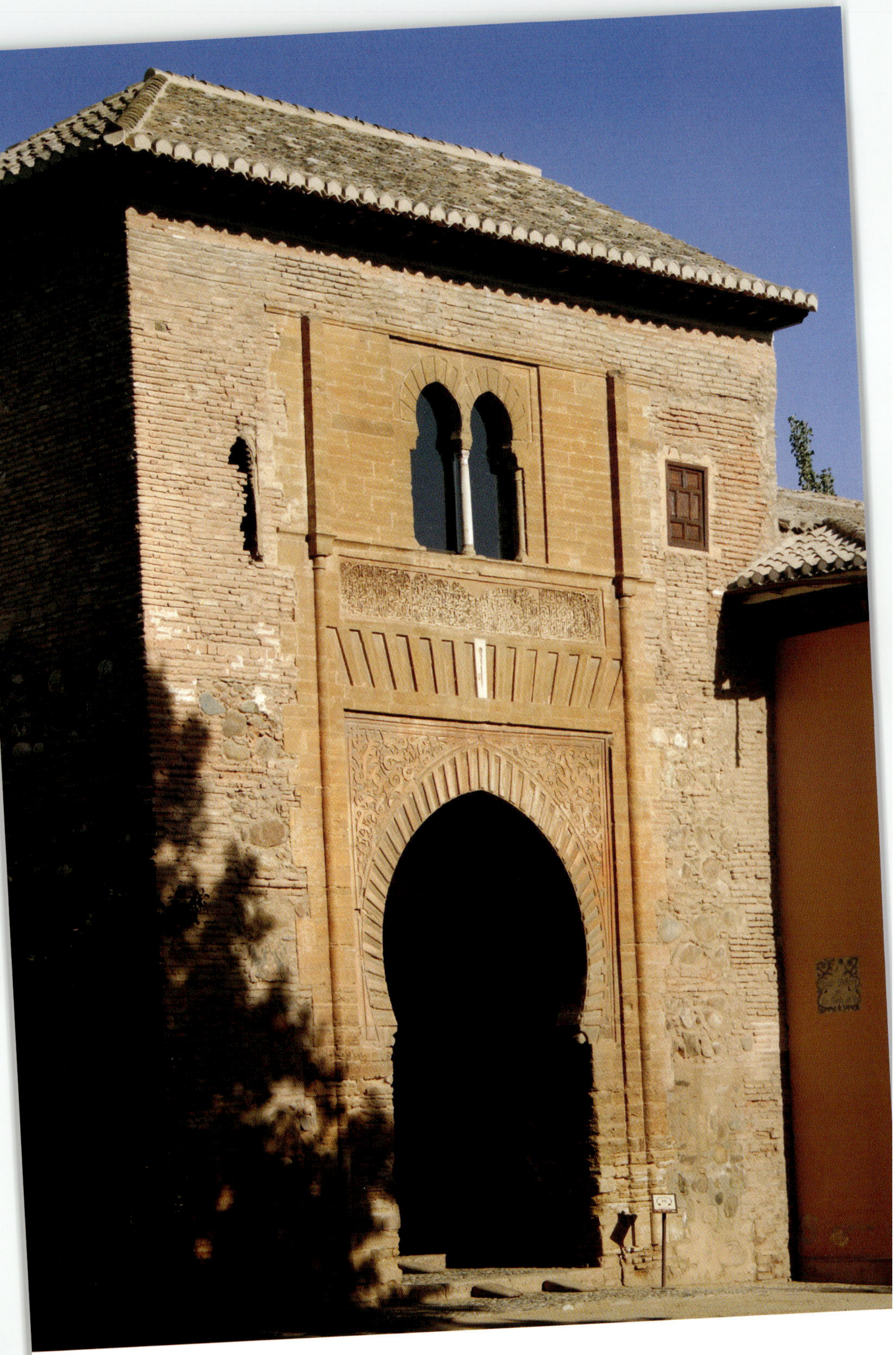

Outer face of the Puerta del Vino

Today, the Puerta del Vino remains isolated from the other medieval buildings but originally the gate enabled you to pass from the principle entry points of the Puerta de la Explanada (or de la Justicia) and the Puerta de las Armas to the Calle Real of the *medina* of the Alhambra.

The oldest parts of the Puerta del Vino suggest it was built during the sultanate of Muḥammad III, when the Calle Real finally took shape, and solemnly marked its beginning. It was renovated and redecorated in the reign of Muḥammad V.

First, you find yourself facing the inner arch. This is of sculpted brick and is completed with a delicate "dry cord", *cuerda seca*, ceramic motif in cold colours, beautifully adorned with ribbon motifs. This is the only place where this technique is used in wall decoration. To prevent colours from mixing, dry cord marks the outlines of different motifs, separated by fine lines of lead-coloured, manganese oxide, prior to firing the ceramics. The decoration of the arch and the ceramic panels in the more or less triangular pediments, or *albanegas*, that surround it, are from the reign of Muḥammad V. As an urban gate, the upper floor lacks any defensive elements and consists of a house with open windows and double arches.

On passing through the gate, you find that on the inside, the layout is in a straight line and does not incorporate a crooked entry – a single right-angled turning that left attackers at a severe disadvantage as the other gates do. This is only logical as it is an inner gate with a clearly urban purpose. In the inner corridor, you can see the doorjambs of the original wooden gates and benches to rest on in the central room. In the upper part of the tunnel vault you can see the remains of simple geometric motifs painted in the plaster.

The exterior of the gate is in stone quarried in La Malahá (Granada), with voussoirs – wedge-shaped stones alternately jutting out and set back – and decorations in the very rough *albanegas* of plant motifs, *ataurigues*, and archaic pointing. Above you can see the typical *dintel adovelado*, a lintel constructed from wedge-shaped stone blocks. The marble *clave*, or keystone, with the key and the decorative, inscribed cartouche of the outer arch dates from the reign of Muḥammad V.

Once you pass through the Puerta del Vino you have two alternatives: if you walk down the street on the left you draw close enough to look at the Puerta de la Explanada (or de la Justicia); if you continue to the right you reach the Alcazaba.

Puerta de la Explanada,
popularly known as Puerta de la Justicia

Name: Puerta de la Explanada or Bāb al-Šarī'a (Puerta de la Justicia)
Date: June 1348 (foundation stone laid)
Sultanate: Yūsuf I (1333-1354)
Note: Entrance gate to the palace city. It was the last and structurally most complex of the gates built in the Alhambra. An admirable fusion of purely defensive and ornamental elements that come together in an unusually impressive manner in the walls, with marble in the entrance arch, the magnificent inscription, and the broad ceramic panel.

ONCE YOU LEAVE FROM the Puerta del Vino and take the path on the left, you arrive at the inner face of the Puerta de la Explanada popularly known as the Puerta de la Justicia, which you need to walk through in order to understand from its original entrance its symbolic and architectural importance.

This is the only entrance gate in continuous use as an access to the Alhambra precinct since medieval times. Without doubt, it is one of the most notable works of Andalusian architecture and clearly demonstrates the Nasrid architects were not only virtuoso decorators but great builders too. It has, in its own right, a considerable span and seems to grow in height located as it is, as a backcloth to a ramp, creating a ceremonial opening that has captivated everyone who has set eyes on it since ancient times. The ramp is formed by the rear of the Pilar de Carlos V, a circular bastion raised up at the end of the fifteenth century to position

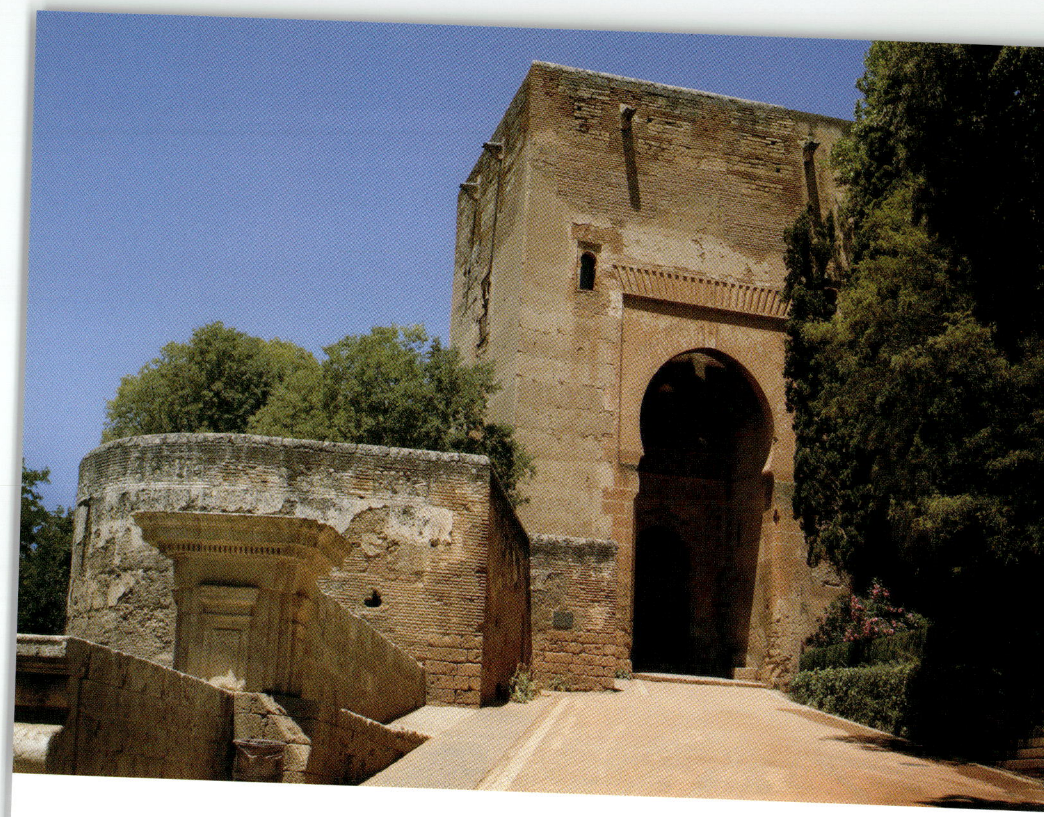

Puerta de la Justicia

firearms, in front of a curtain of cypresses masking the wall.

The Puerta de la Explanada (or de la Justicia) – one of the few buildings in the Alhambra it is easy to date precisely – is the work of Yūsuf I and was raised up in 1348, according to the beautiful cursive script inscription carved and painted on an enormous marble plaque above the main door. The gate is exceptional in many ways, but perhaps most of all because it integrates a cast-iron, structural layout, intended for defence, with the contrasting ornate nature of the two façades, intended to highlight the importance of the city you are about to enter.

The ashlars – rectangular blocks of hewn stone that reinforce the corners of the threshold to the gate – join together in alternating succession in each main wall and continue in the *alfiz,* the upper brick surround. The presence of different materials, the integration of decorative inscriptions and symbols, like the hand and the key, turn it into the richest, most complex architectural structure in the walls of the Alhambra. Above the main entrance door a grand, slightly pointed, ceremonial horseshoe arch stands out. The keystone depicts an open hand, the meaning of which is unclear although it has been granted the value of a protective talisman or sign of divine blessing. This lobed arch is

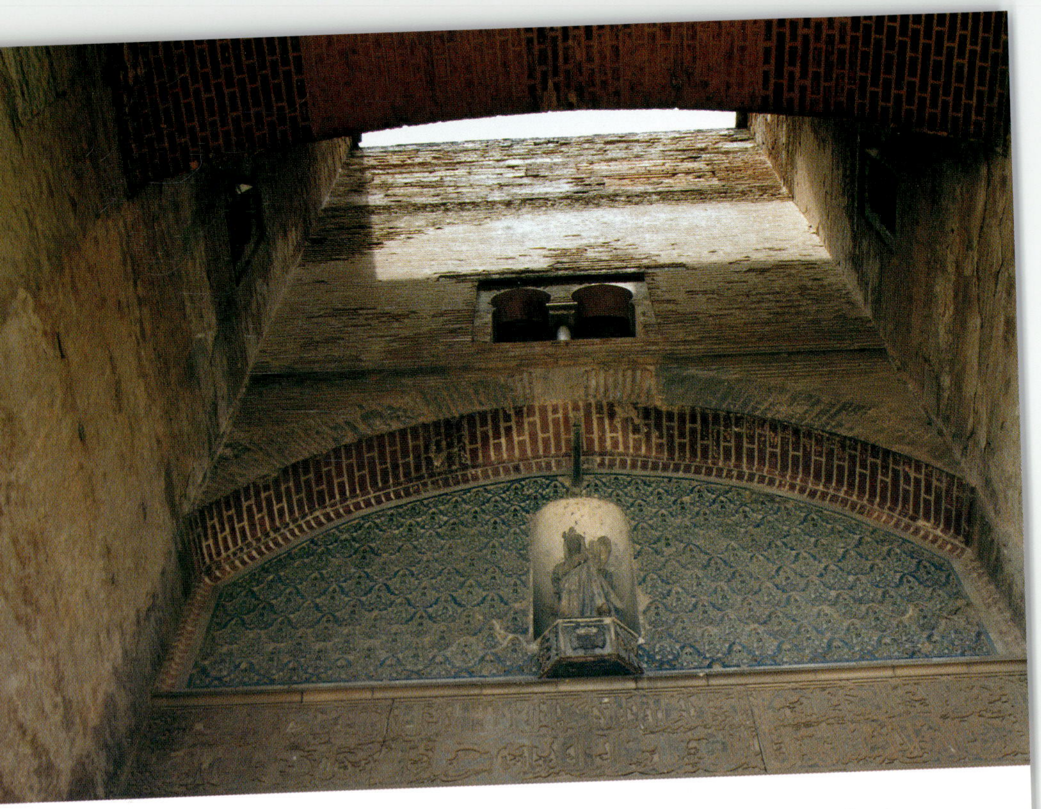

Detail of the entrance arch to the Puerta de la Explanada (or de la Justicia) with the defensive opening, *buharda*, and the image of the Virgin and Child.

admirable, and its magnificent development is contrasted by the delicacy in the use of brickwork in the arch and pediments. Above the arch, is a typical *dintel adovelado*, the lintel constructed from wedge-shaped stone blocks common in the architecture of the Islamic gates in Granada and seen on other gates in the Alhambra itself. Behind this arch is an upper opening, a *buhedera*, improving the defences by enabling those above to harass possible attackers and converting itself into a focus of overhead light that enlivens the decorative inscriptions and glazed ceramic tiles that embellish the gate. The entrance arch is marble, topped by another *dintel adovelado*, and simply decorated with scallop shells in the pediments; the keystone is inscribed with the Nasrid key as the gate symbolizes the city.

Exceptionally large and expressive is the inscribed cartouche above the arch, mentioned earlier. In addition to the date and name of its patron, the text ends with an invocation to God to protect the gate: "Make of it a defensive force and record it among pious and immortal deeds". Constructed of painted marble it linked it to the virtuoso panel of rhombus shapes, *sebka*, and the glazed ceramic *ataurique* which serves it as a worthy crown, making a unique combination.

During the reign of the Catholic Kings, and given the political and symbolic value of the gate, a Gothic statue of the Virgin was added. The original statue was deposited in Granada's Museum of Fine Arts (in the Palacio de Carlos V), and a replica substitutes it here.

Moving on to the inside, you encounter a crooked entrance passage with a double bend in it which, as well as improving defence (complicating entry by making a direct route into the city impossible) became an element of mystery and surprise. Here you can see benches where the guards could sit, protected by splendid arches, perches for their pikes or ancient lances, and a layout of vaulting covering each stretch – groin vaults, vaults with a flat keystone, with successive groins – a variety of solutions used constantly in the gates and towers of the Alhambra. The upper walls and some of the vaulting conserve traces of the plaster that assiduously decorated Islamic works, simulating regular lobes of brick with red-coloured bonding. It is also worth taking a careful look at the door that closes the entrance arch, minutely plated and nailed to avoiding its burning and to hold off any foreseeable intrusion for as long as possible, as well as the magnificent three-bolt lock that constitutes a worthy complement to the door.

Towards the end of the passageway you can see a chapel and Renaissance altarpiece (usually closed to the public) built by public subscription in the neighbourhood of the Alhambra in 1588, and at its side a Gothic script plaque, with a long eulogy to the Catholic Kings, to commemorate the completion of the *aljibe*, the cistern, built in front of the entrance to the Alcazaba. When you leave, the gate is a pointed horseshoe arch and it conserves much-deteriorated remnants of its original ceramic decorations. Closed to the public and with an entrance from the upper street, although originally it would have been from the covered parapet walk along the top of the walls, the *adarve*, the upper floor of the tower remains. Usually this served as accommodation for the gate keeper, with different rooms and access to the terrace, and a variety of vaulted ceilings. Looking at it from the outside, you can see the highest parts of the tower, which have been repaired, and the great gargoyles that drain water from the terrace.

In the eyes of the visitor, this gate bestowed on the palace city of the Alhambra the image of prestige that suited the political discourse dictated by Yūsuf I. The wide esplanade that precedes it, with the Alhambra cemetery not far away, became the space where, on certain dates, military parades and religious feasts were celebrated.

It is, finally, the building that introduces the architectural treasures you can find on the inside of the city.

Leaving from the Puerta de la Explanada (or de la Justicia) you find a street that goes up in search of the entrance to the palaces and of the urban area, leaving to the right the beginning of the Camino de Ronda and ruins of medieval houses and others constructed in the Christian period to lodge soldiers. The wall that goes up, closing off the left side, displays the remains of tombstones used to rebuild it in the early sixteenth century, some adorned with geometric shapes and inscriptions. Returning by the path that led you to the Puerta de la Esplanada, you can go back towards the Alcazaba.

The Alcazaba: A palace space and military precinct

Name: Alcazaba (al-Qaṣba)
Date: 11th and 13th cent. Extended 14th cent.; Further renovated and extended at later dates.
Sultanate: Zirid period (11th cent.), Muḥammad I (1237-1273) and other later sultans.
Note: Principal defensive centre and lookout for the Alhambra. It is the oldest construction in the precinct. The presence of the great keep stands out for its novelty, along with the earlier barbican or walls and the existence of a barracks to house the garrison with dungeon-silos, an *aljibe*, cistern, and baths.

Heading towards the walled precinct that is the Alcazaba, you find a wide esplanade called the Plaza de los Aljibes. Its name comes from the existence of an enormous underground cistern, an *aljibe*, built during the reign of the Catholic Kings shortly after the conquest of the city to guarantee an adequate supply of water in case of a rebellion. Remember that the Alhambra was the only wholly Christian space, and the military and civil headquarters of the recently taken city.

Between this square, which extends forward to the Palacio de Carlos V, leads a ramp or street that originally had access from a lower esplanade and organized the urban network on the inside of the palace city, especially the beginning of Calle Real Baja, running close to the outer walls of the Nasrid palaces, as well as Calle Real Alta, going up towards the Puerta del Vino, and giving visitors and residents of the Alhambra access to the upper part of the *medina*.

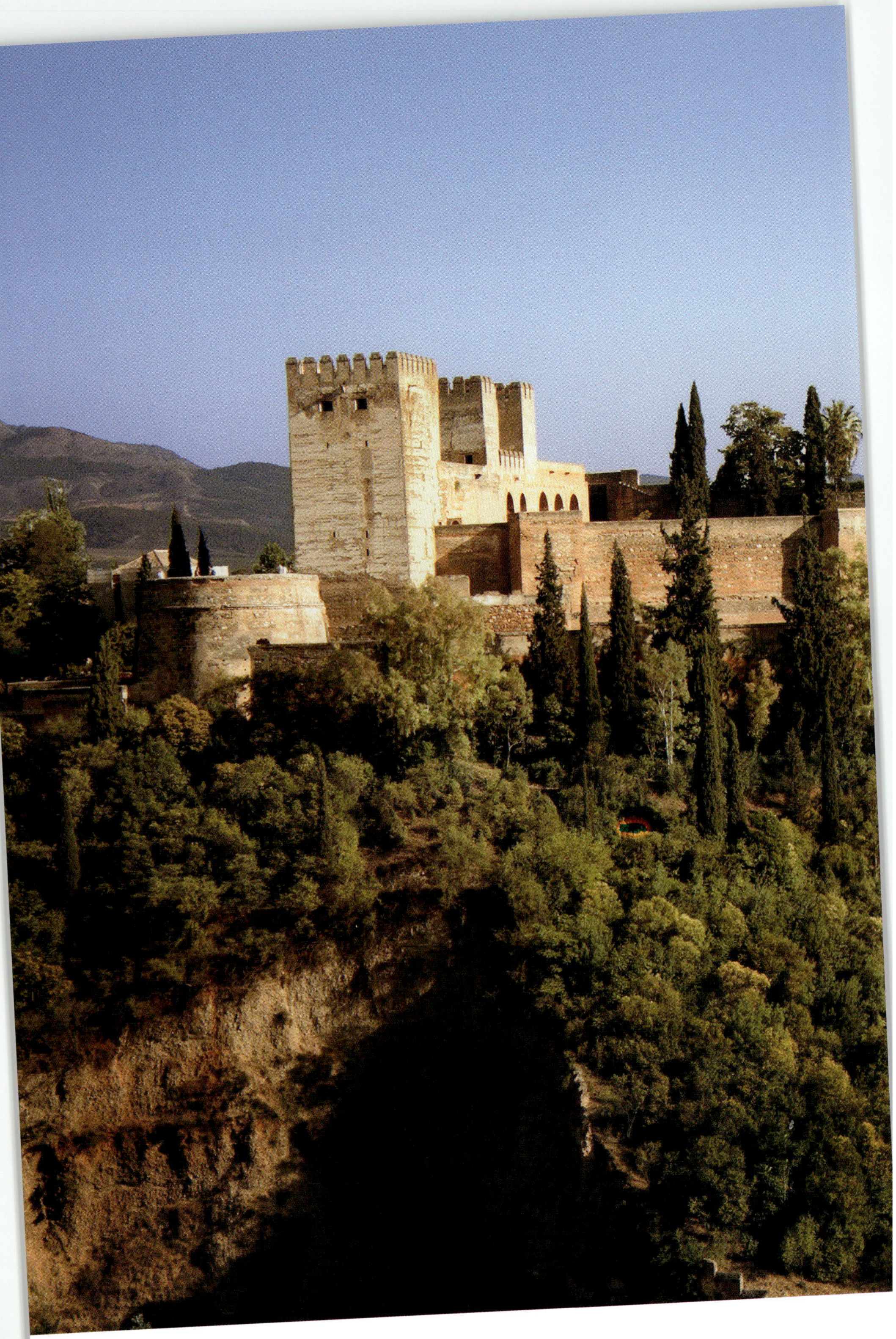

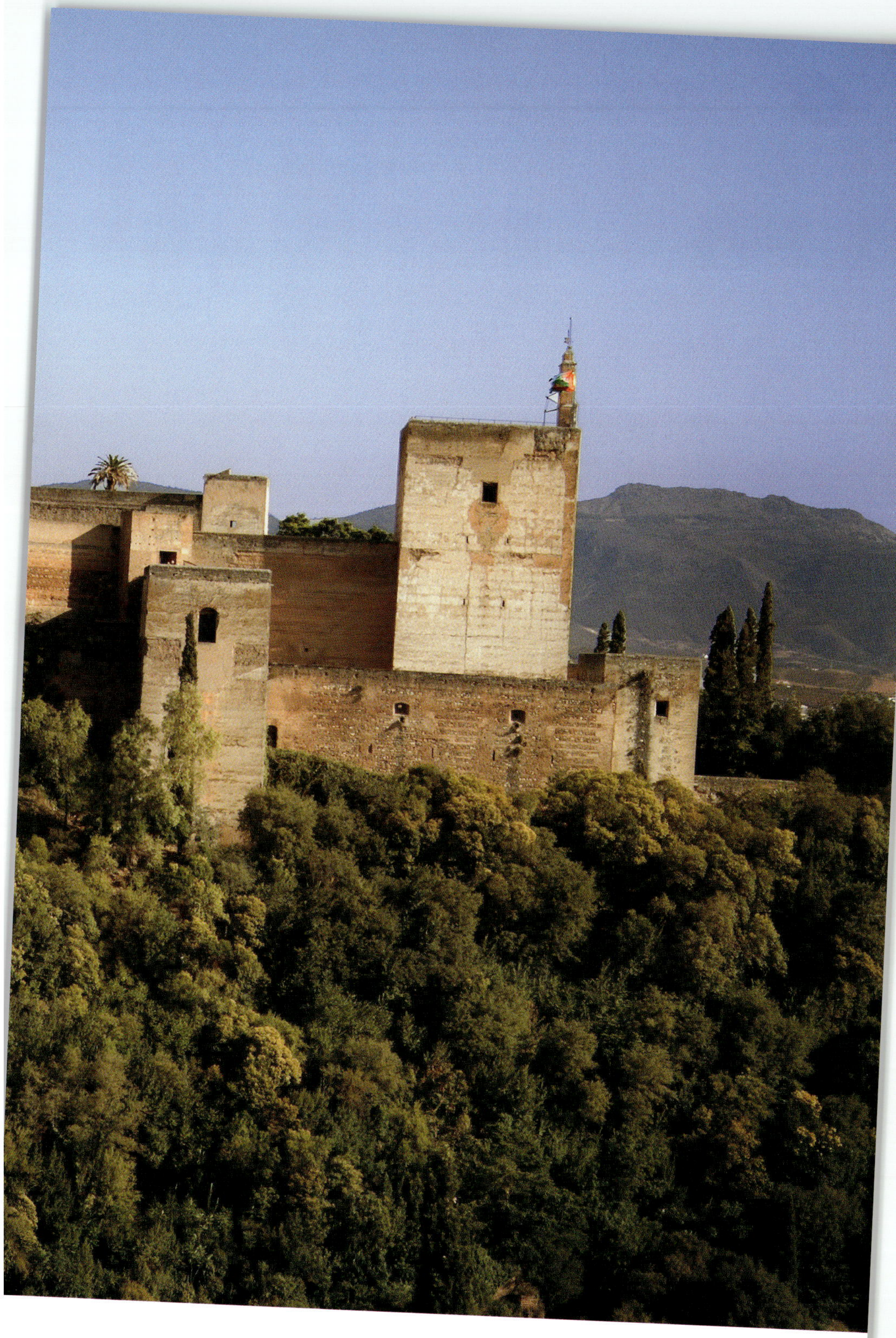

The Alcazaba

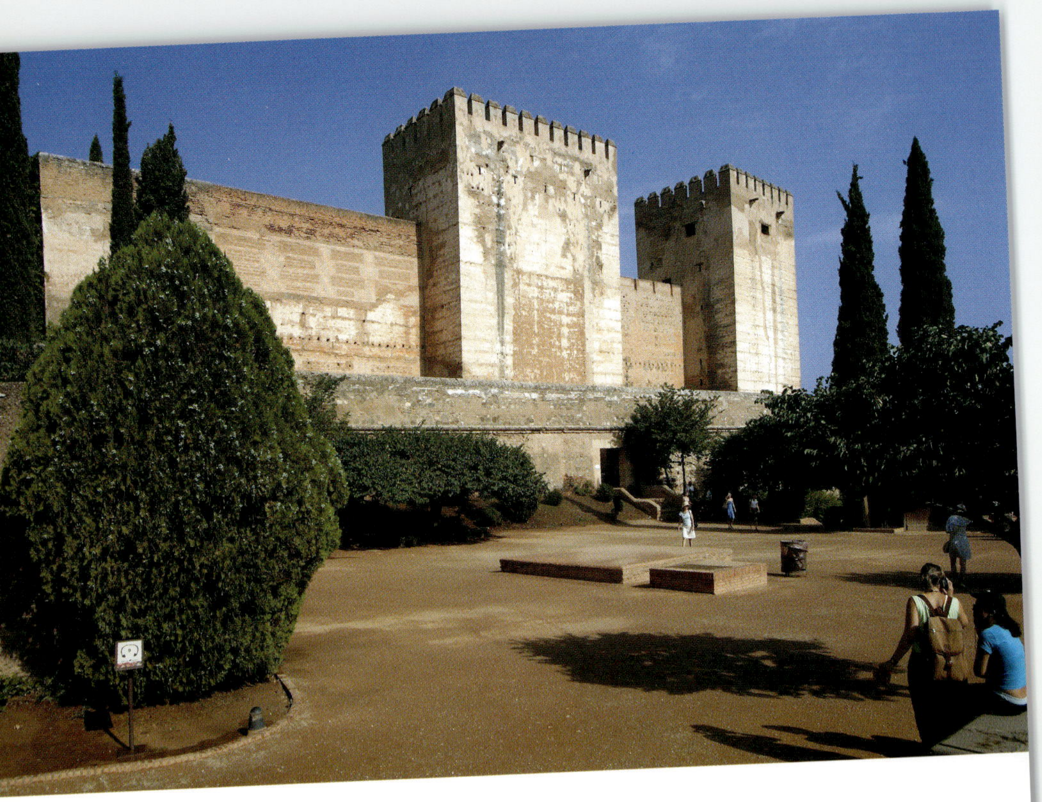

Detail of the Alcazaba from the Plaza de los Aljibes

Although some authors argue that the whole of the Alhambra was itself a single *alcazaba*, a walled precinct or citadel, the name has specifically been given to the area located on the westernmost spur of the hill of La Sabīka.

The Alcazaba has to be considered the bridge, commanding the entire city from the headquarters, although its limitations of size suggest that a large part of the army and guard would be have had to be housed in other buildings and towers, especially those who defended the gates and other strategic places. The Alcazaba was home to the Keeper, the *alcaide* of the Alhambra, and in the early days the founder of the Nasrid dynasty would have lived here. The presence of dungeon-silos and literary references reveal it was also used as a secure, royal prison. One stretch of wall running along the north flank and linking up with the Albaicín – crossing the River Darro by a bridge of which part remains to this day – and another to the south connecting with the Torres Bermejas, permitted the establishment of a complex, wide-ranging defensive network to protect the palace city and Granada itself.

The recognizable elements of the Alcazaba make it the oldest building in the Alhambra. In fact, as early as the ninth century, records tell of a first castle located here and named Qal'at al-

Ḥamrā', the red castle, the name that was later consolidated as synonymous with the very royal Nasrid city: Madīnat al-Ḥamrā'. According to the chronicles, the building goes back to the Umayyad period and some believe a more distant Roman or Visigoth construction may have existed although the oldest identified remains are eleventh century. In 1238, on the site of this original castle, the first Nasrid sultan (Muḥammad I), ordered the construction of another fortress, reinforcing its walls, raising up high towers and supplying it with water. This is considered the authentic act of founding the palace city. The main part of the complex belongs to the thirteenth century with some earlier elements and later restoration, and the work can be attributed to the initiative of the first two sultans, Muḥammad I and Muḥammad II, with its construction preceding that of the great palaces, showing extreme sobriety and strength.

On entering the Alcazaba from the Plaza de los Aljibes you can see the earlier barbican, reconstructed in 1557, behind which, from right to left, proudly stand three towers: the Torre del Homenaje, Torre Quebrada and Torre del Adarguero, forming the eastern flank of the fortress. Their location on the flattest part of the hill requires greater defence; at the same time converting them into a defiant screen facing up to any attempted revolt or conspiracy. Without a doubt, the breadth and interior architectural complexity of these towers – in contrast with their exquisite symmetry – is the most important novelty of the Alcazaba.

Crossing a large modern door, opened up in the barbican, you come to the lists or pit, a passage set out between important precincts and leading towards the inside of the fortress, enabling you to observe different kinds of wall bond that show the substantial alterations and restoration the building has undergone. At the end of this stretch of the pit you can go up to the Cubo, a semicircular tower assumed to have been built in 1586 on the site of an earlier Islamic gate, known at the beginning of the sixteenth century as the Puerta de la Tahona and which controlled one of the streets giving access to the palaces. The Cubo, empty on the inside in the twentieth century, has a layout that would have made it suitable for use by artillery and is today a privileged terrace where you can contemplate the unequalled countryside of the River Darro valley and the Albaicín.

Going down from the Torre del Cubo and following the pit north we find a zigzag climb towards a narrow pass adapted to give access to the inside of the precinct.

Torre del Homenaje

Name: Torre del Homenaje
Date: 1238-1273
Sultanate: Muḥammad I (1237-1273)
Note: A keep and warehouse and perhaps residence of the *alcaides*, the keepers of the Alhambra. Its sobriety and smooth outer appearance mean you would never suspect it housed a variety of vaulted ceilings covering its six floors. The first of these has a completely closed, dark dungeon-silo and the last, a residential area around an interior patio, suggesting that it was one of the first palace spaces.

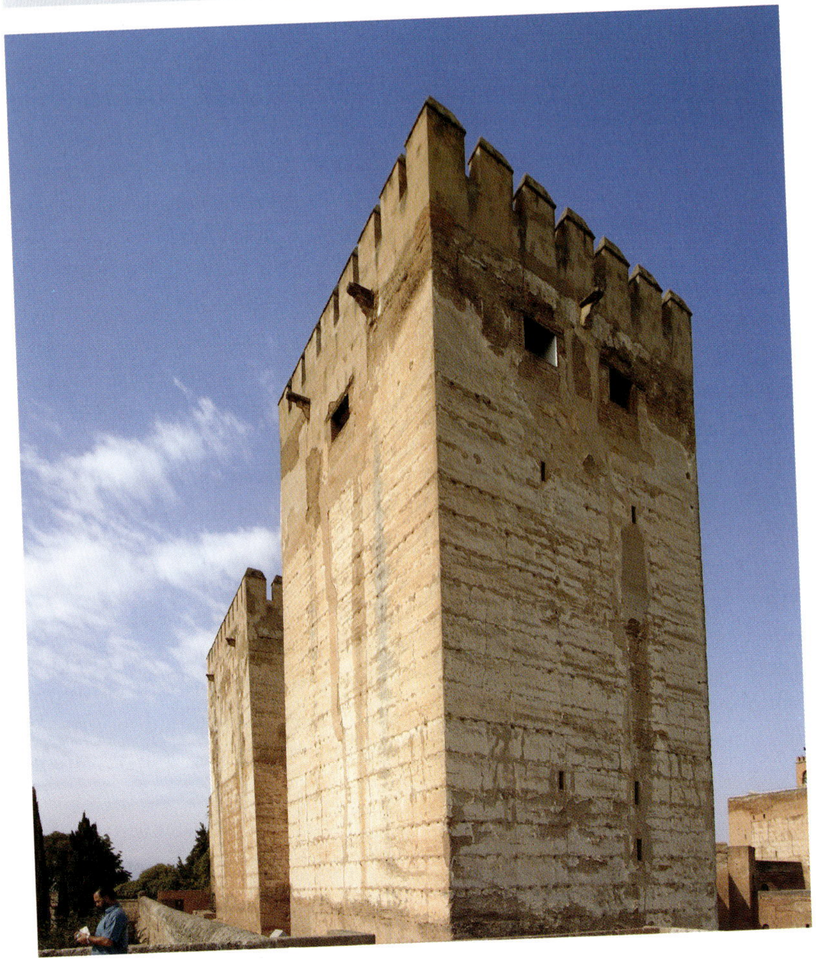

In the foreground stands the Torre del Homenaje in the Alcazaba

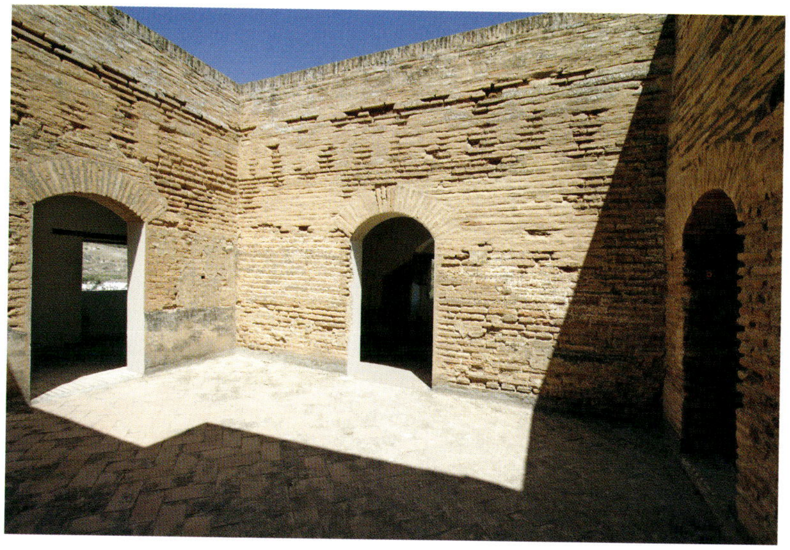

Raised patio in the Torre del Homenaje in the Alcazaba

ONCE ON THE INSIDE OF THE PRECINCT, you can admire the lofty heights of the Torre del Homenaje, rising up at the highest point of the fortress; a quite original work in its interior layout and fundamentally of strategic value. In its little more than 22 metres height it houses a dungeon in the cellars, and above has five floors with a variety of vaulted ceilings and domes. The last of these has been converted into accommodation around a small interior patio which, together with that of the so-called Harén constitute the only two raised patios in all of the Alhambra. The residential area might have been used by Muḥammad I and later by the keepers of the Alhambra as the nerve centre and bridge of command to organize defence. From the heights of this tower and of its companion, the Torre Quebrada – on the inside apparently lightened by wide arches that guard ancient stone projectiles – the whole palace city precinct could be observed. Such a varied combination of functions (warehouse, prison, meeting rooms, housing and lookout post) occurs nowhere else in the military architecture of al-Andalus.

Today, the tower remains closed to normal visits on account of the layout and the narrowness of the stairs although it is opened on certain occasions during the year. However, you can climb up to the *adarve*, the covered parapet walk, and enjoy a magnificent view of the parade-ground that helps you understand the strategic value of the tower.

Barrio castrense

Name: Barrio castrense.
Date: From 13th cent.
Sultanate: Muḥammad I (1232-1273) and other later sultans
Note: Remains of foundations and walls of houses in the military quarter largely maintain the layout of one of the first inhabited areas of the Nasrid Alhambra.

THE MILITARY QUARTER WAS THE RESIDENTIAL area of the fortress that lacked what you might call the parade-ground, typical of medieval fortresses. In this case, on the inside stood a concentrated series of houses and other buildings to ensure the survival of a limited number of families.

Before coming into the main street, you can see excavations of an underground dungeon-silo. Buildings like this were conical, like the neck of a bottle, with access through the mouth at the top so that you went down to the stores or prison. In the latter case, simply withdrawing the ladder or rope made any attempt to escape impossible.

The main street divided the district into two. To the north, the right-hand side as you move up the street, the main houses are situated. In spite of their modest size, some have staircases indicating the existence of an upper floor; others have a patio and a latrine visible next to the door. The most spacious house is found almost at the end of the military quarter and could have been the palace of the first sultan with its patio and *alberca* and the main room with benches at the top. Rooms in houses on the other side of the street may have provided lodgings for troops and warehouses for stores.

The final stretch of the street is flanked by an *aljibe* and a bath. Of the bath, you can now only see part of its structure as the original vaulted ceiling has disappeared; the *aljibe*, however, to store water to attend to the needs of the inhabitants of the fortress, is hidden below a terrace. The street forks on reaching the Torre de la Vela, leaving the original door giving access to the Alcazaba, and the most ancient door in the Alhambra, outside of the visit.

One element strangely missing in this Alcazaba is the mosque. A suggested explanation for this absence is the existence of a first open-air oratory (*muṣallà,*) next to the Puerta de la Explanada (or de la Justicia).

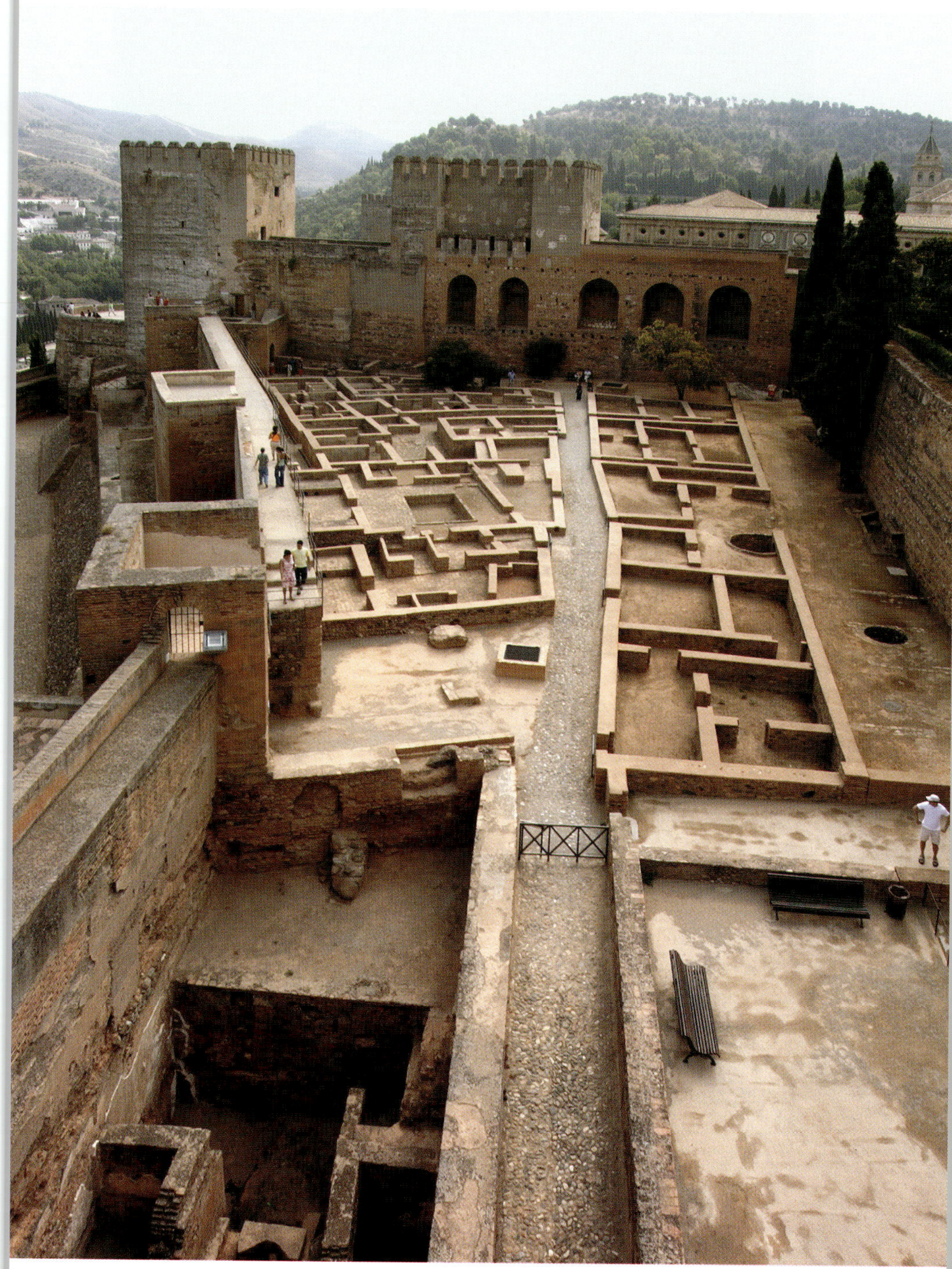

The military quarter in the Alcazaba

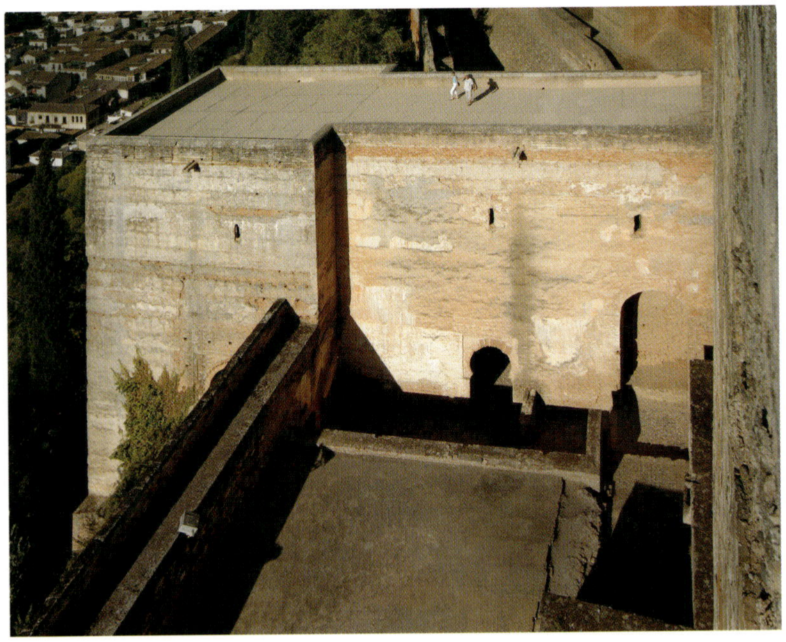

Torre de las Armas and Puerta de las Armas

Torre de las Armas

Name: Torre de las Armas
Date: c. 1400-1433
Sultanate: Ismāʿīl I (1314-1325)

NEAR TO THE REMAINS of the Alcazaba baths you can continue to the upper part of the tower that protects what already in 1470 was called the Puerta de las Armas (la Bāb al-Silāḥ). This gate, today not generally open to visitors, was one of four outer gates to the Alhambra and was added to the precinct in the reign of Ismāʿīl (1314-1325). It is not linked to the Alcazaba and should really be considered an independent unit.

From the upper part of the Torre de las Armas you can see how, on the eastern side, an unusually wide, cobbled street leads towards the palaces, crossing the Puerta de la Tahona covered over by the sixteenth-century Cubo. On the opposite side, soldiers returning from their rounds or other activities, passed through a patio and a passage that bent its way around the base of the Torre de la Vela to the Alcazaba.

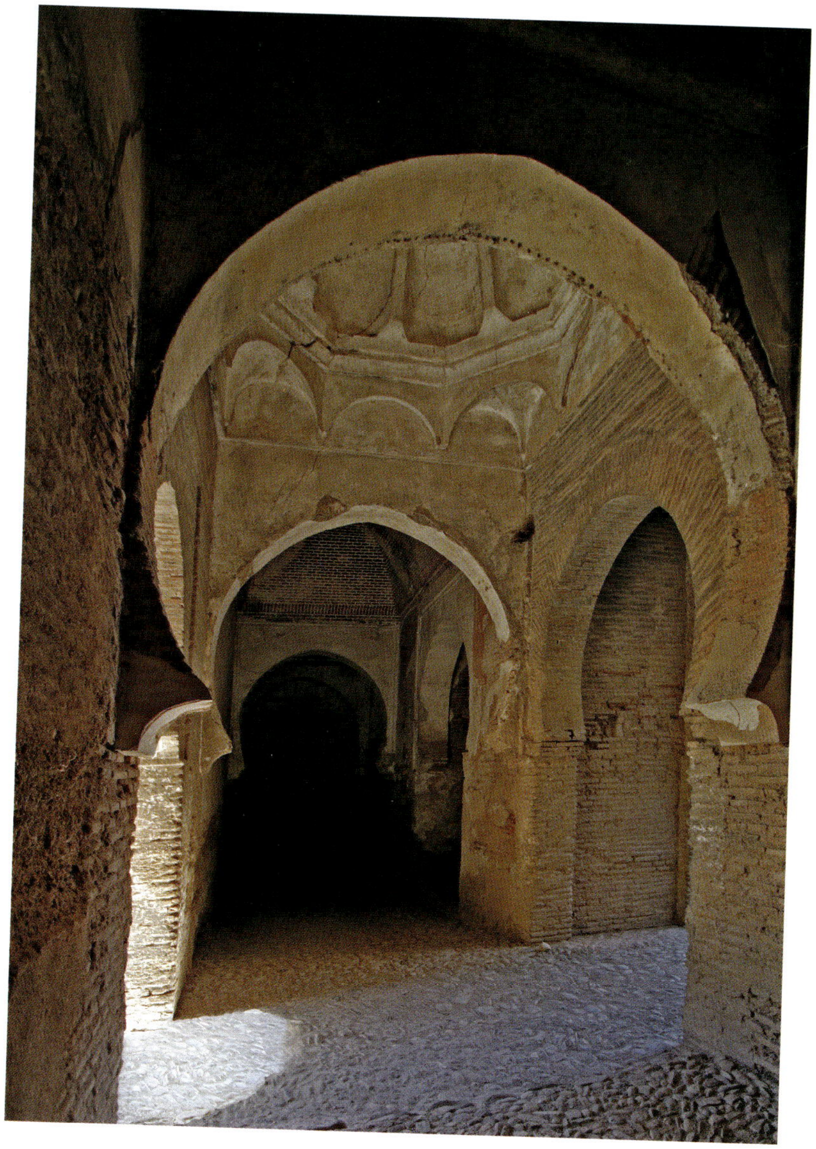

Inside the Puerta de las Armas

The inside of the gate is only open to visits on special dates, but here you can admire an arch similar to that at the exit from the Puerta de la Explanada (or de la Justicia). On the inside, you will be surprised by the presence of two umbrella domes, a cloister dome and a sail dome, sumptuously painted to imitate the regular brick lobes, to great effect and related with the Moroccan Almohad gates. At this door, the box through which the portcillis was lowered to defend the entrance, has been conserved.

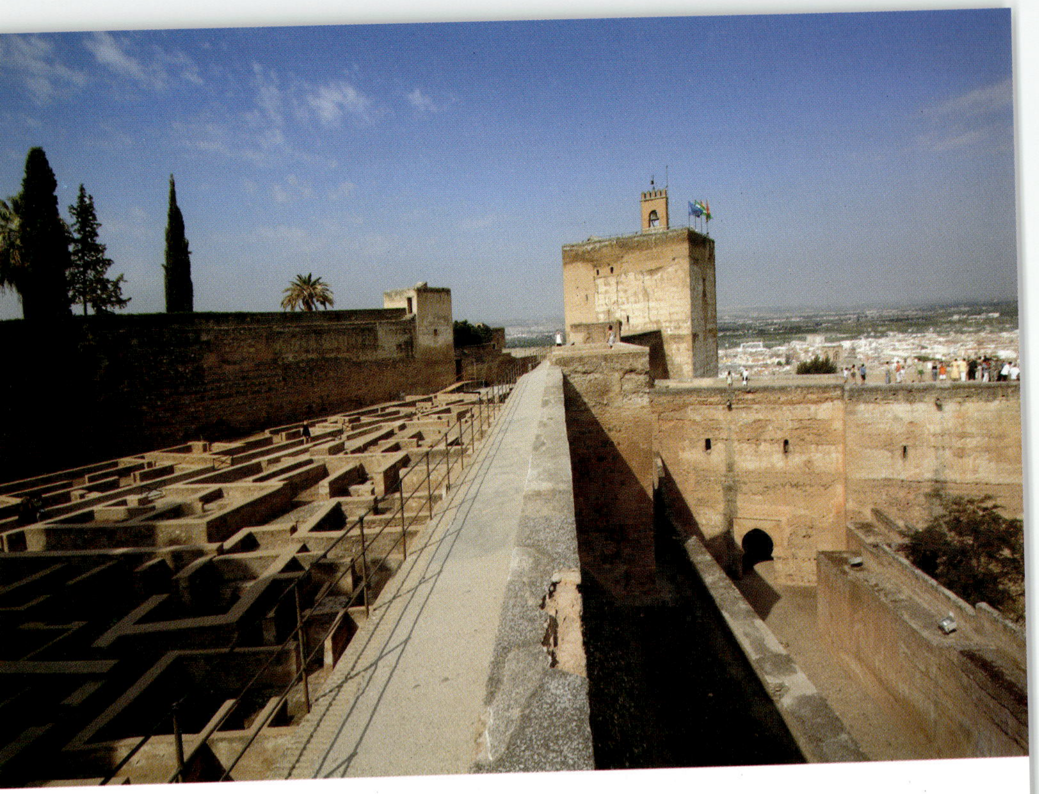

Torre de la Vela in the background with the barbican and wall of the Alcazaba in the foreground

Torre de la Vela

Name: Torre de la Vela, del Sol, de la Campana (its medieval name is unknown)
Date: 1238-1273
Sultanate: Muḥammad I (1237-1273)
Note: Keep-cum-warehouse that defended the western spur of the Alcazaba. To a certain extent, this tower constitutes one of the most characteristic emblems of Granada. The width of the structure permitted a complex, functional, interior layout, while the terrace offers privileged views of Granada's beautiful countryside.

On the westernmost edge of the Alcazaba stands one of the most historically significant of the towers, the inspiration for the greatest legends of the Alhambra, of great strategic importance, and highly original in its structure. To understand how much restoration it has undergone it is enough to think that all the outer walls were once of mud bricks, so the patches of brickwork that we see today are the products of later repairs.

Entry to the tower is on the second floor, and the first floor and the dungeon that lies below it are closed to visitors. The staircase was built in the Christian period and is much wider than the Nasrid staircase would have been. The layout of the floors was very original, with one wider room in the centre, covered with vaulting, surrounded by a double corridor of pillars and brickwork arches.

Today, the terrace offers one of the most remarkable views of Granada. From here, you begin to understand the strategic value of the location as you gaze at the natural and urban surroundings unequalled despite the mutilations they have suffered in modern times. From the Sierra Nevada mountains in the southeast (or Sierra del Sol, the Mountains of the Sun as the Nasrids called them), to the Sierra Elvira range, named thus because at its feet stood the original provincial capital of Granada, Medina Elvira (Madīnat Ilbīra), a whole, broad panorama of mountains and the splendid fertile plain, the *vega*, stretches out at your feet. Closer, you can see the country houses of Granada, the beauty of its historical districts, where new buildings fail to silence the powerful monuments of church and convent towers, with the Cathedral, head and shoulders above the rest. From this terrace you can also see the ravelin, the outworks pointing out from the edge of the hilltop like the prow of a hypothetical boat, where artillery was located in the late fourteenth or early fifteenth century.

For centuries the bell, hanging from a bell-tower reconstructed in the late nineteenth century, regulated irrigation in the *vega* until not long ago, through a complicated tolling of bells that went on into the early hours of the morning. This is the role that meant the name de la Vela, which means to watch over or night time vigilance, should have imposed itself over the sixteenth century names such as de la Campana and del Sol and other earlier ones. Every year, on January 2, the day when Granada was conquered by the Catholic Kings and the standard of Castile was flown for the first time, the people of Granada go up to ring the bell following an ancient tradition.

Torre de la Pólvora and Jardín de los Adarves

Name: Torre de la Pólvora and Paseo de los Adarves
Date: 13th cent.; remodelled (converted) 17th cent.
Sultanate and Monarchy: Muḥammad I (1237-1273), Philip IV (1621-1665), other periods
Note: A watchtower and early access to the *adarve*, the covered parapet walk over the southern barbican, the outer fortification of the city. This area has been greatly modified by hollowing out the tower to make a gateway and, in the seventeenth century, converting the ancient *adarve* and barbican into a garden and viewing point on the initiative of the Count of Tendilla, governor of the Alhambra.

Leaving by the Torre de la Vela, you reach the Torre de la Pólvora, today much spoiled. Its function was to keep watch to the extreme south of the fortress. From here you can appreciate the wall that descends along the wooded ravine and, passing through the Puerta de las Granadas, joins the Alhambra to the Torres Bermejas, another military building dated from the early Muslim period in Granada and constituting a strategic bastion to keep watch over the city.

Next comes the Jardín de los Adarves, one of the oldest gardens in the precinct. Located between the main wall of the Alcazaba and its barbican or forward wall, it is a pleasant, leafy space: a place of rest created in the seventeenth century when the fortress lost part of its military value. The garden creation was one of the Count of Tendilla's whims. For whatever reason, in 1628 he commissioned the making of the two Mannerist pillars that stand at each end of the garden and created a belvedere or wide balcony, clearly in the Italian tradition, which predates the character of the *cármenes* of Granada, the typical houses that usually feature a space open to the countryside just like this. Here the beautiful Nasrid lusterware vases were located as decorative complements – one of them is on display in the Museum of the Alhambra. The fountain with a jet of water in the centre was originally in the Fuente de los Leones fountain and although it may belong to a long-gone Nasrid room, was removed from the fountain as it constituted a Christian addition passing to this garden in 1624. The presence of flowering plants, together with bay trees, ivy, myrtle, privet and other species, enlivens the space that constitutes one of the many corners for rest

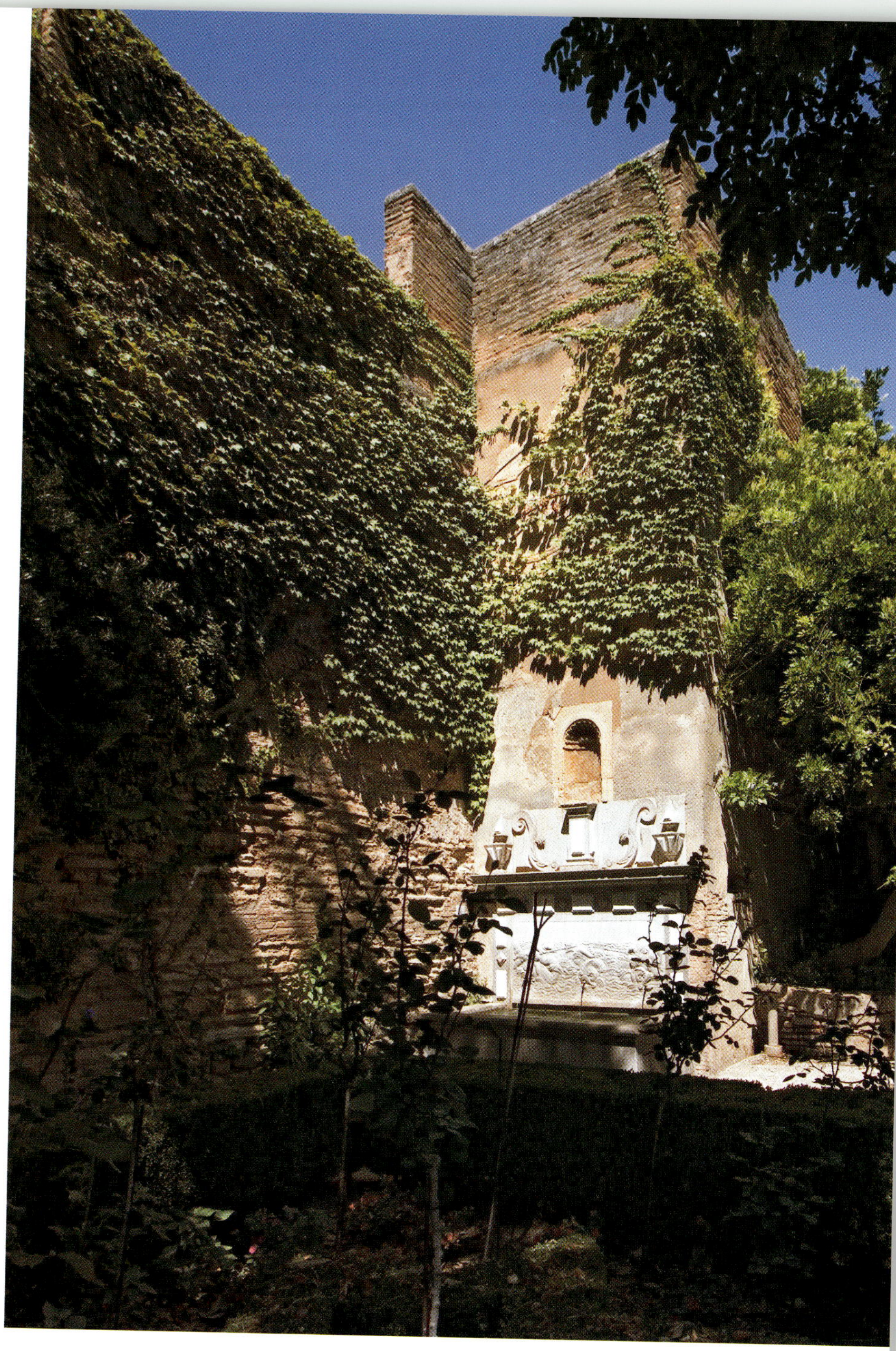

Jardín de los Adarves with the walls of the Alcazaba in the background

and contemplation in the Alhambra.

When you leave the Alcazaba, you have before you the imposing main façade of the Palacio de Carlos V.

The Palacio de Carlos V, imperial residence

Palacio de Carlos V

Name: Palacio de Carlos V. The Palacio de Carlos V was named as such because it was built to be the residence of the Emperor, although he never actualy lived there. In Court circles it was known as the "Casa Real Nueva", the new royal palace in the Alhambra.
Date: Most building work took place in the sixteenth century; only the staircases and roof of the south hallway and the northern hall now called the Sala de Presentación are seventeenth century. The structure was completed with reinforced floors, roofing and a staircase on the right-hand side, in the twentieth century.
Note: The exterior, especially the western and southern façades and the circular interior patio.

STANDING SIDE BY SIDE WITH the Nasrid Palacio de Comares, it surprises and to a certain extent shocks visitors with its bulk and volume and the concept of space and style that differs so much from Islamic architecture. The sharp contrast has often drawn fierce criticism of the building, despite its singularity within what is understood as Renaissance architecture in Spain. Such is the extent of this criticism that it has forged a fateful legend about its final destiny as an unfinished work, never to house a Spanish king. This has happened not only because it was considered to wound sensitivities, being built so close to the magic Islamic palaces but, moreover, because it was largely financed with taxes paid by the Moriscos, who stayed in Granada after the Christian

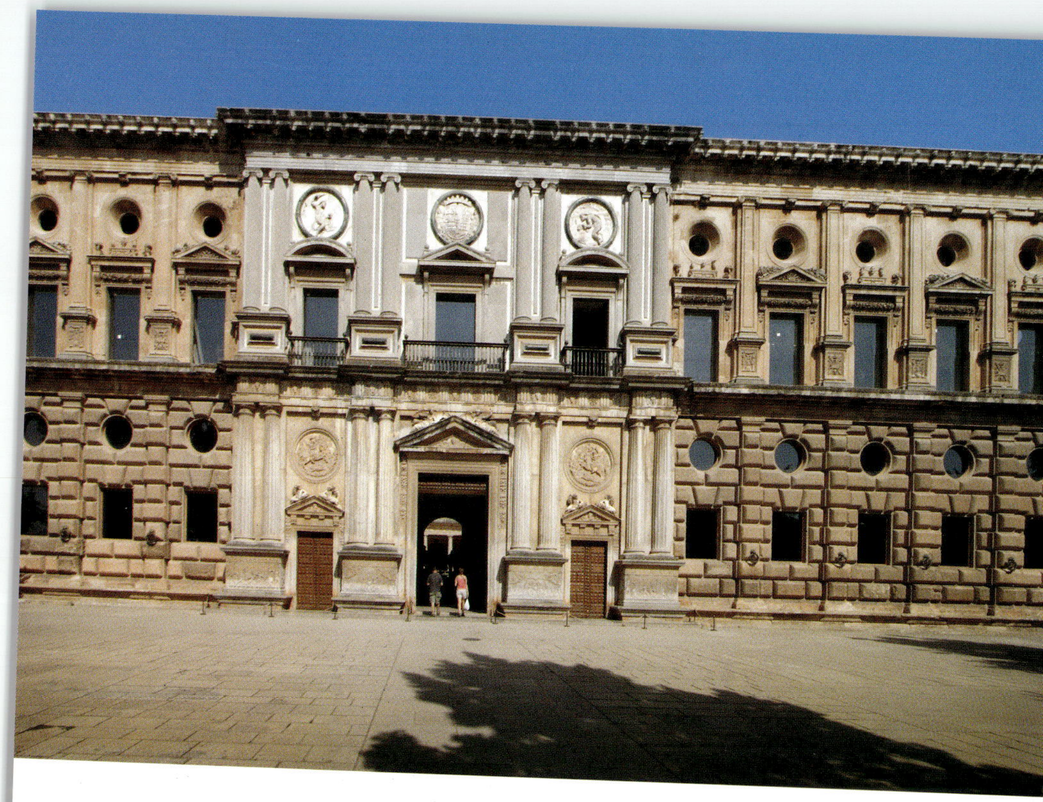

Western façade of the Palacio de Carlos V

conquest in order to continue to maintain certain traditions and customs. When they rebelled in 1568, building work, which was going well, was abruptly halted, languished for some time and finally stopped altogether in the first third of the seventeenth century. So, with the walls built but scarcely any roofing except that over the two hallways and the lower gallery of the patio, it reached the twentieth century as a ghostly ruin, finally roofed and renovated to fulfil its role as a museum.

Intended as the imperial residence following Charles V's marriage to Isabel of Portugal in 1526, after staying in the Alhambra for several months the Emperor, impressed by the palace, left the construction work in the hands of the *alcaide* and governor Íñigo López de Mendoza, later to be succeeded by his son, Luis Hurtado de Mendoza. It was they who were really responsible for the building. Charles V's only interest was that it should stand alongside the Nasrid palace, for which he had a profound admiration, to form the royal household in the Alhambra, the "Casa Real de la Alhambra", although later the old household was distinguished from the new one, which would become the official reception area. As the new palace could not be built exactly parallel to the Nasrid constructions, partly so as not to impinge on the site of the nearby church of Santa

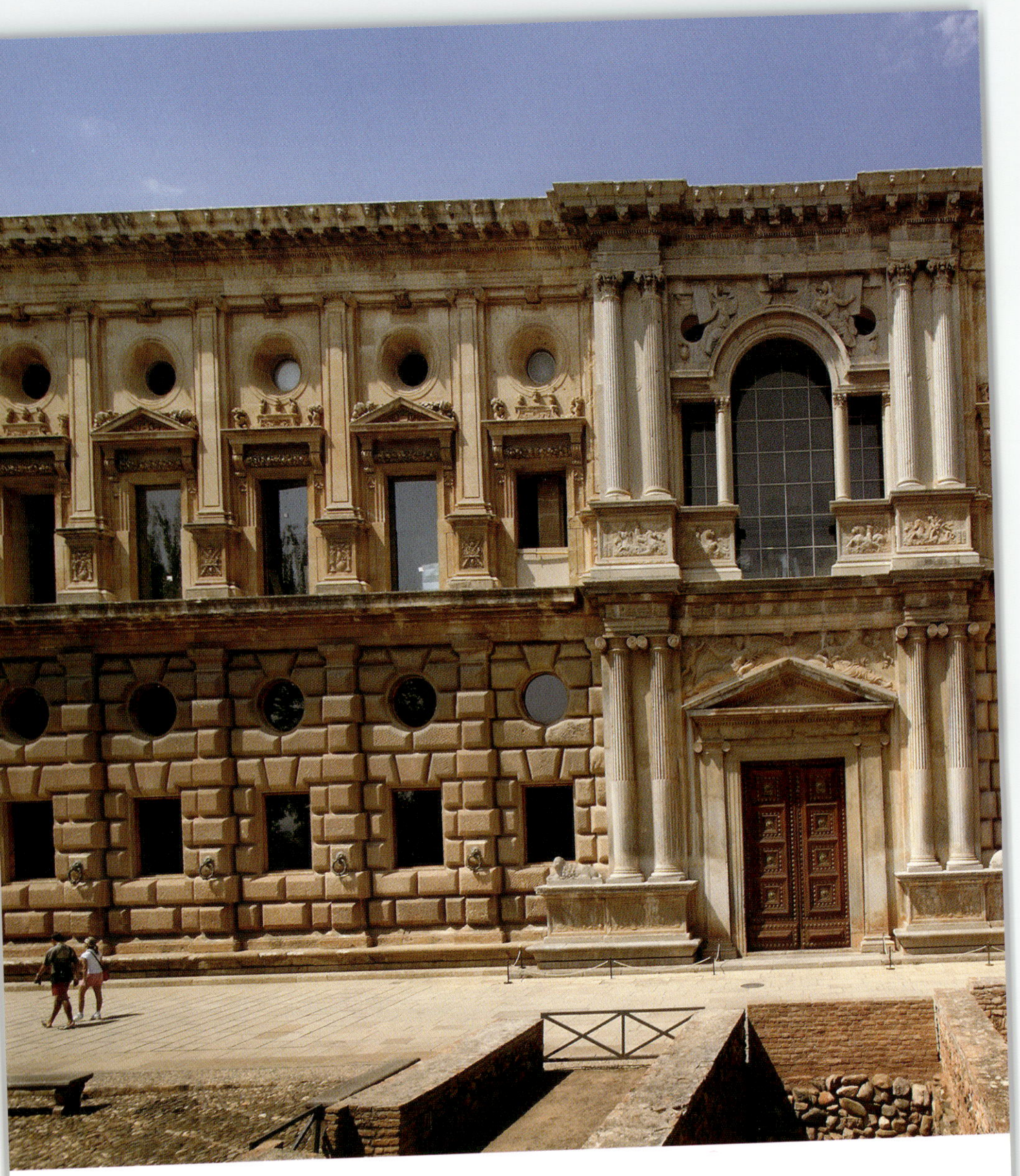

Southern façade of the Palacio de Carlos V

María de la Alhambra and partly to accommodate the two projected squares in front of it – though only the western square was actually drawn out – it was set at an oblique angle tangential to the Palacio de Comares. Thus a link between the two residences was assured and, turned at an angle as it is, and never to be used for accommodation, underlines its apparent function as the grand vestibule to the Casa Real. An exceptional vestibule, accompanied by two squares in front of the two main façades, to the south and west, each closed off by its own gallery intended as stables, and

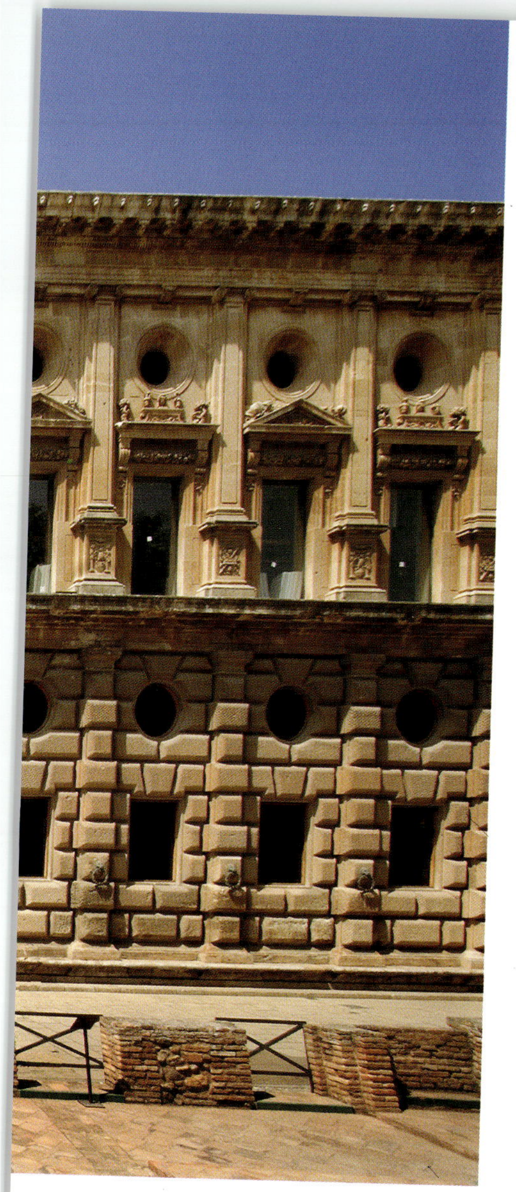

joined by an arch of which the base on the southern side remains near the corner of the other façade. Moreover, the project included a banqueting hall on the north side in front of what is today the Patio de Machuca, and the corresponding kitchens, next to the Rauda, or cemetery.

Building began in 1531 and the project underwent several modifications during the following decade. From the outset it was in the hands of the painter and architect Pedro Machuca, a squire to the *alcaide* and fully in his confidence. Machuca had worked in Rome, above all as a painter in the circle of Rafael, so he had first-hand knowledge of Italian, High Renaissance style. On his death in 1550, he was succeeded by his son, Luis Machuca, and later by his son-in-law, Juan de Orea. However, although Pedro Machuca was considered a Renaissance artist, the design, or rather, designs of the palace may well not have been entirely his own. The Italianate shapes of the façades and even the circle inscribed in a square that gives it its ground plan, are very likely to have come directly from an Italian master (Giulio Romano or someone close to Baldassare Peruzzi have been suggested).

That the two main façades should have been finished and, moreover, built swiftly (the other two are only partially finished and the façades are much more modest), indicates the extent to which the imperial ideal was expressed through the decoration, particularly of the façades, which were modified after building had begun. The structure consists of two floors and a mezzanine, separated by a cornice that divides the upper floor accentuating its horizontal lines in a manner characteristic of formal Renaissance composition. The lower part is more "rustic" with pillow-shaped stone blocks, typical of the entry spaces, guard rooms, and "offices", while on the upper or noble floor, destined for halls and bed chambers, the architectural order is based on alternating pilasters and windows. However, the most significant aspect of both façades is, without doubt, the portals.

The portal of the southern façade, which adopts the Ionic order in the lower body and the Corinthian in the upper one where it is accompanied by reliefs portraying mythological scenes of Neptune and Amphitrite, has been associated by a dominance of the feminine, with the presence of the Empress in this southern part of the palace. However, the remains of arms and other military motifs referring to peace and war appear in the pedestals and can only be intended to represent imperial power, in this case over the seas – the conquest of Tunis was very recent (1535) – and signified the definitive triumph of "Plus Ultra" as the imperial motto, which extended around both façades alternating with other emblems. So, imperial triumph and its inherent virtue was made wholly obvious, culminating in the elegant Serlian window or balcony at the portal – named after the Renaissance architect and writer Serlio who popularised the design – or the composition of a central arch with two recesses with lintels, among the first in Spain, and inspired by a significant triumphal motif originating with the Roman emperors of the Early Empire.

In two bodies, the western façades present two very different designs. The lower one forms part of the original plans and is in Doric order. In the company of the predominant reliefs and allegories of the pedestals and gates referring to war and peace, it sets a virile tone that identifies this entrance and all the façade with the presence of the Emperor. The second body, in Ionic order, as dictated by the general order, repeats the same number of panels as gates, three, but these are now more sober balconies, very different in style and typical of their author, Juan de Herrera, and of the 1580s. The reliefs on this upper floor represent the Labours of Hercules and also refer to the Emperor, although in their making much has been lost of the delicacy of execution displayed in the reliefs and figures on the lower floor.

Inside, the ground plan is of a single square floor with four spaces between supporting walls of which only the main walls and some rather unfortunate dividing walls were built; they were to remain unroofed for some time. The simple schema was enriched, however, with small spaces within the bays that take on different

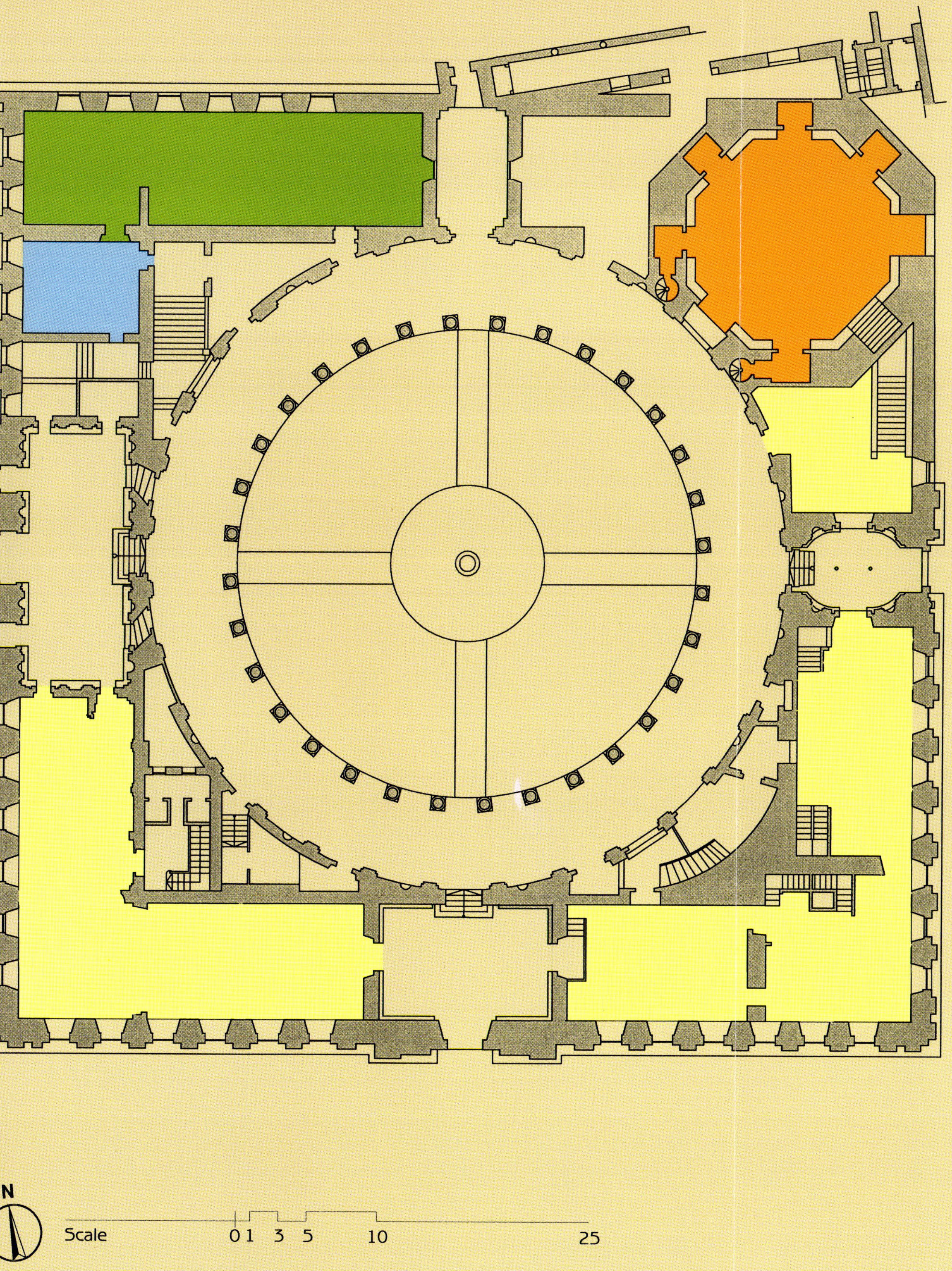

Current use, ground floor of the Palacio de Carlos V

Museum of the Alhambra

Conference room

Ancient chapel

Bookshop

geometric forms, like the octagon of the chapel floor in the north-eastern corner, or the pseudo-elliptical shape of the eastern hall. These animate the rectangular simplicity of the bays and play with the impact of the surprising circular patio. Of all these, Charles V only placed importance on the chapel, stressing that it should take pride of place. In fact, its location, in a corner that looks onto both the Palacio de los Leones and the Palacio de Comares, points moreover to a diagonal axis of great compositional interest as it is like the line that joins two slopes, one formed by the east and south bays and the other by the north and west bays. If the first is identified with the Empress and the second with the Emperor, both parties, with their respective entourage, would join together in the chapel, which in effect is open with empty spaces on both floors for each of the bays. Furthermore, at the other end of this diagonal, south-western corner, a spiral staircase was planned, perhaps for servants.

In the centre, the patio is the most striking element: the authentic heart of the palace to which all entrances and main staircases lead. At a height above the level of the outer entrances, the patio has raised many questions about its purpose or meaning. With certainty, we only know there must have been a fountain in the centre as an underground gallery exists decreasing in size until reaching this point. Further speculation has focussed on the meaning of such a perfect circle inscribed within a square. Whatever the truth may be, as it stands open to the skies, at the very least it must have some cosmologic significance, to counterbalance the other great, enclosed circular space, erected at the same time in Granada: the Cathedral main chapel. Initially intended as a royal pantheon for the Emperor himself, this would complete a whole programme destined to express Charles V's dream of a single "Universitas Cristiana" ruled from Granada.

In its Doric severity, the patio is a source of admiration for the sober, solemn rhythm of the columns. The form chosen with the magnificent barrel vault that runs around the entire ground floor approximates it more than any other model to that of Hadrian's Villa in Tivoli; a prodigy of the Spanish stone masons' art. It is constructed with stone from Toba which, apart from being lighter, has a beautiful irregular surface of small fossilized hollows that combine with the granite from Santa Pudia used in the columns: a mixture of various minerals and limestone, which tones in better than the compulsory white marbles, present in Tivoli, and also considered for use here at one point. The second body uses the Ionic order with the same type of columns, though smaller in height and

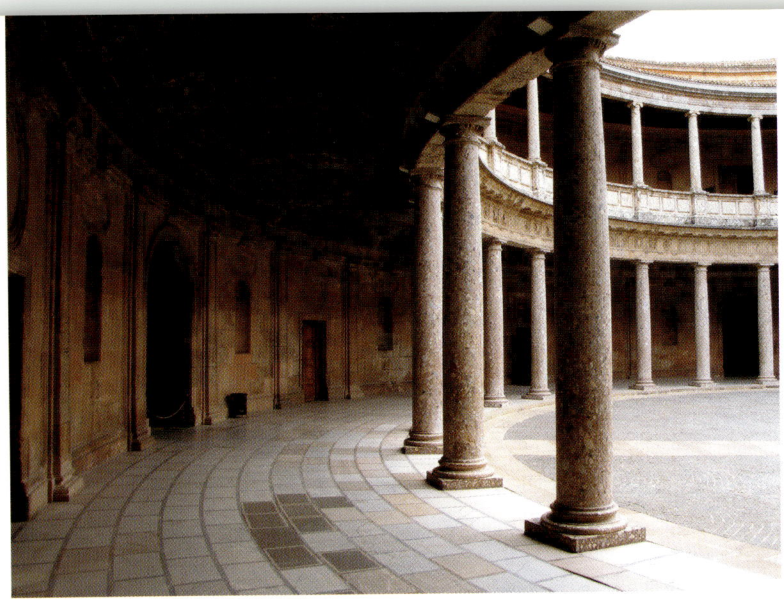

The interior patio of the Palacio de Carlos V

diameter, but this gallery remained unroofed, not being completed until recently, around 1970, using timber roofing.

This type of princely residence had been the model proposed by Italian writers since the end of the fifteenth century and would continue to be so during the following century. The evocation of the famous Villa Tivoli, built at the command of Hadrian, the Roman Emperor of Spanish origins, is patently obvious in the circular patio, which so recalls that of the well-known Villa's Teatro Marítimo. A few years earlier, Pope Leo X had had another villa built (Villa Madama), with a similarly round patio, on the outskirts of Rome. In the outer façades, structured on two floors with a mezzanine, there is a clear parallel with the series of elegant palaces designed by Rafael for Vatican dignitaries or the tiny Villa Doria which the famous navigator had built in Genoa and where Charles V had been lodged in 1529.

Three staircases give onto the patio: two connect it to the upper floor. The left-hand side stairs, built *c.*1630, are the oldest. In contrast, the beautiful spiral stairway on the opposite side is the work of contemporary architect Francisco Prieto Moreno. The third stair, descending towards the Palacio de Comares through the opening in the north hall, was planned by Juan de Herrera and Juan de Minjares in 1585 with some later modifications. It was roofed over in the 1950s to convert the space into the vestibule of the Museum of the Alhambra, installed by then in the upper bay of Comares. In 2000, it was re-roofed as part of a restoration programme for the palace begun in 1992.

As for the rest, the southern and western halls are larger in

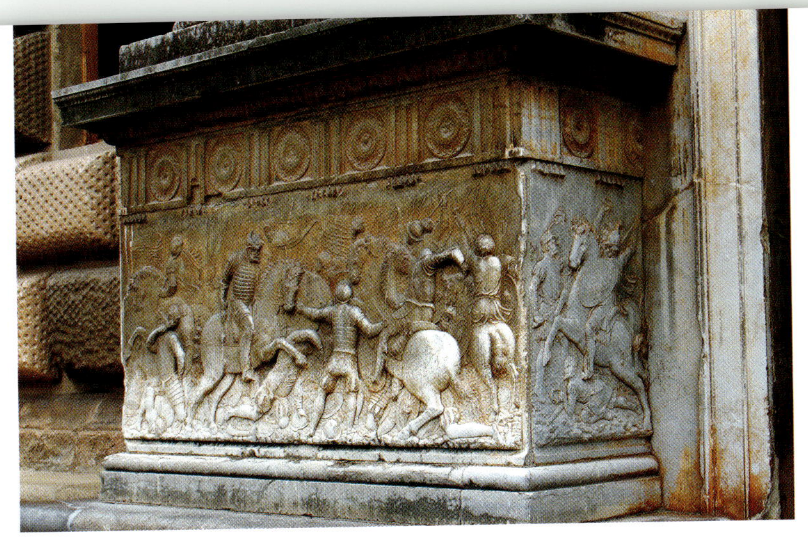

Detail of left stylobate of the western façade. (Photograph José Manuel Gómez-Moreno Calera).

keeping with their importance, mentioned earlier. In spaciousness and name they respond to a definitively Hispanic concept in contrast to the narrower vestibule, typical of the Italian palace. The rectangular western hall was redesigned around 1580, and was originally even lower than the patio you can see today, raised one metre by the architect Torres Balbás. The southern hall was roofed over in the early seventeenth century. And as for the eastern hallway, intended first to have an elliptical floor plan and later designed with a semicircle at one extreme joined by straight sections, as we see today, it was roofed in modern times by the architect Leopoldo Torres Balbás.

Leopoldo Torres Balbás is the architect responsible for the first and fundamental campaign to restore the palace, following the plan drawn up earlier by Velázquez Bosco, laying down the structure and dividing up the halls on both floors. This work was continued after the 1936 war by the then architect-curator of the Alhambra, Francisco Prieto Moreno, who apart from the elements mentioned introduced a broad adaptation for administrative and museum services that modified the original structure and distribution. Finally, after 1992 a new, restoration programme was initiated destined to restore the original structure as faithfully as possible, suppressing the administrative functions and promoting its function as a museum on installing the Museum of the Alhambra on the ground floor. The author of this plan is Juan Pablo Rodríguez Frade.

If you go on again towards the western hall, you find yourself in one of the side passages with the entrance to the Museum of the Alhambra, a compulsory visit that helps you understand more of life in al-Andalus and, specifically, in the Nasrid period.

The Museum of the Alhambra

Name: Museum of the Alhambra
Location: Palacio de Carlos V
Note: Pieces such as the wooden door to the Sala Dos Hermanas and the Jarrón de las Gacelas, especially enable you to learn about the interior decoration of the Alhambra and therefore bring you closer to life in the palaces.

In 1994, the Museum of the Alhambra was founded by the Spanish Ministry of Culture replacing a frustrated project for a National Museum of Hispano-Muslim Art. It was to be located within the Palacio de Carlos V which was to be recovered for that purpose. This had been proposed as early as 1885 by the learned archaeologist from Granada Manuel Gómez-Moreno González for the creation of an "Arabic-Spanish" museum, and four years later, in 1889, the eastern part of the Palace was designated by Royal Decree for use as the Museum of Fine Arts and Archaeology. The idea of a Museum of the Alhambra is however, earlier. It dates from 1870, when the Alhambra was declared a National Monument, and was initially installed in what were known as the houses of the Governor, a space to be found between the Mexuar and the Palacio de Comares. Curiously, it returned to this site in 1943 when the architect Leopoldo Torres Balbás began to restore and renovate the Palacio de Carlos V for it to house the museum.

In 1994, the last restoration project commissioned under architect Juan Pablo Rodríguez Frade, saw the building restored to a state closer to the original, eliminating the distribution of administrative offices in place since 1940 that had altered the original layout. The original purpose of a museum on the ground floor has been recovered in as much as the Museum of Fine Arts has been retained on the upper floor. Among works deposited in the Museum of Fine Arts are sculptures and paintings of or connected with Granada from the fifteenth to the twentieth centuries. Notable items are the Limoges enamel ware, *The Burial of Christ*, by Jacobo Florentino, *Still life with thistle* by Fr. Juan Sánchez Cotán, Alonso Cano's great religious sculptures of St. Joseph and St. Didacus of Alcalá, as well as some of his canvases and others belonging to disciples like Bocanegra, Juan de Sevilla and Risueño, and the recently acquired *La Madraza* by Mariano Fortuny.

The Museum of the Alhambra was first located in the south

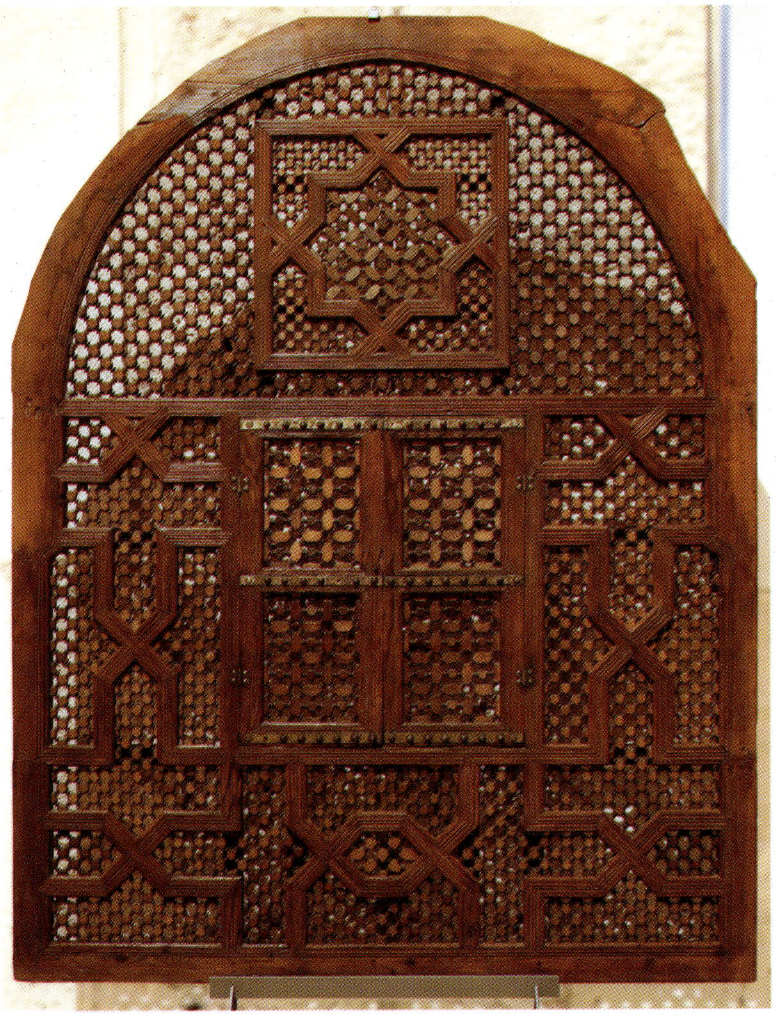

Window screen originally in the Sala de Dos Hermanas. Museum of the Alhambra.

bay and in part of the western and eastern bays, but always with a view to its extending to the rest of the floor. The pieces selected for the Museum from among the more that 10,000 items that make up its current stock, together with some deposits and donations, are exhibited to meet the demands of a modern museum, ordered by theme and chronology. The architectural intervention, in which priority is given to the recuperation of all the original bays, is accompanied by the equally primitive maintenance of the walls, altered only by the minimal presence of structures of modern materials, indispensable for the installations, separated moreover from the walls to indicate their temporary nature.

A fragment of marble-faced wall at the entrance serves to separate the reception from the rest and to indicate the existence of part of a wall that appears in the first plans of the palace, we assume erroneously, abutted to a window!

The tour begins in Room I with a collection of coins that includes some pieces minted in the Alhambra itself. As is typical of Islamic coins, they carry details of the date and mint where they were coined. In the emirate and caliphate silver coins dominated and to a lesser degree coins made of gold, and from the Nasrids comes an excellent series of dinars with dynastic emblems, which is part of the selection on display.

In Room II, a fragment of a Nasrid cobbled street, the Calle Real Alta of the *medina*, has been uncovered in the subsoil of the palace. The pieces on display here are fundamentally a collection of items related to the first years of Islamic presence in the Iberian Peninsular, during the emirate and caliphate. In this context, the exhibition of pieces showing the evolution of the capital during the emirate and caliphate and its derivation of the classical Corinthian capital is of special interest. Also of note here is the tenth-century carved stone basin dating from the period of the Caliphate in Córdoba that enables us to prove as well as the importance of water in al-Andalus, the continuity of the classical legacy in its decorative themes. Tenth-century braziers and oil lamps from the period of the emirate and caliphate complete the repertory.

The following room, Room III, runs chronologically from the period of the caliphate until the start of the Nasrid reign, that is from the tenth to the thirteenth centuries. In the first display is an example, the tenth-century carved stone basin coming from a palace in Almanzor in what was then the Caliphate of Córdoba and fruit of its sacking by the Zirid king of Granada Bādīs in the eleventh century. He had it brought to his fortress in the Albaicín and later, under Muḥammad III, it was taken to the Alhambra and placed in the entrance to the military quarters, near the Torre de la Vela. Worked on all four sides, it is of unquestionable iconographic interest with the theme of the lions attacking deer face-to-face around a "hom" or tree of life, an old eastern theme often repeated in al-Andalus, occupying the longitudinal fronts, and open-winged eagles on the sides, but moreover with an epigraphic legend on one of the carved fronts in Nasrid times that informs about the vicissitudes of the basin.

The second display brings together clearly Almohad pieces.

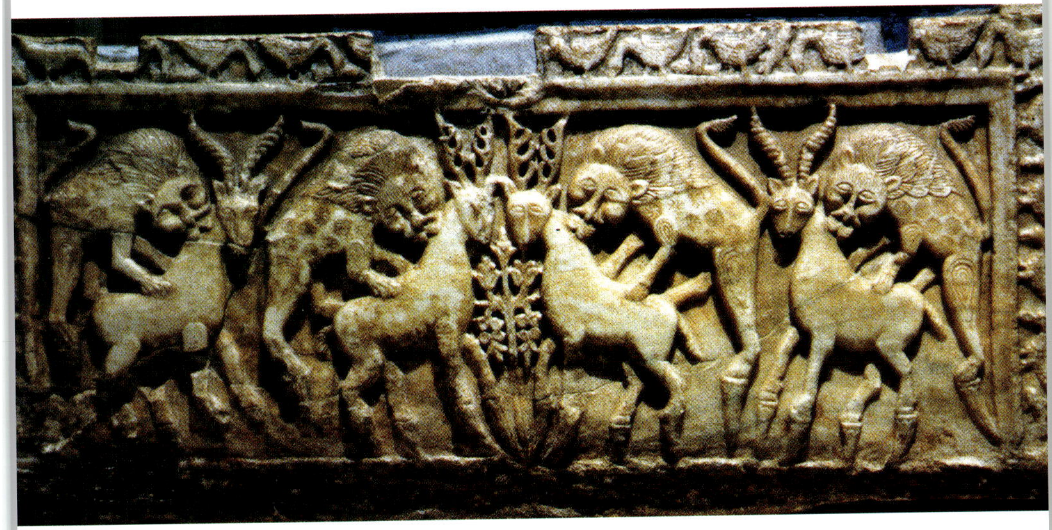

Carved stone basin. Tenth-century caliphate. Museum of the Alhambra. (Photograph José Manuel Gómez-Moreno Calera).

You can see Corinthian capitals and an example of what is known as a "handle-" or "ear-" capital, so-called because the volutes fall and detach themselves from the body of the capital forming authentic handles. A good example of these is conserved in the Cuarto Dorado, although the one on display here comes from the upper floor of the Baño de Comares. The large, Almohad, earthenware jars (twelfth to thirteenth century) are of interest. They are modelled in red clay and were used to transport foodstuffs. In the centre is a *yamur* or bronze adornment from a minaret belonging to the Almanzora mosque in Granada.

Room IV corresponds architecturally with the south hall of the Palacio de Carlos V, opting for the transparency of glass to maintain the volumes and aesthetics of the original space. Also on display here are items coming from buildings in the Granada of the period. The upper doorjambs from the fourteenth-century Casa de la Chapiz house and a superb, fourteenth-century Nasrid fountain from the main Alhambra mosque, later reused in the church of Santa María de la Alhambra. Of special value are the two lions: fourteenth-century marble fountains from Granada's Maristán, the hospital for the mentally ill, and its foundation stone dated 1367.

After Room V, the rest of the museum tour places special interest on furniture from the Alhambra itself. When you visit the Alhambra, you see it without

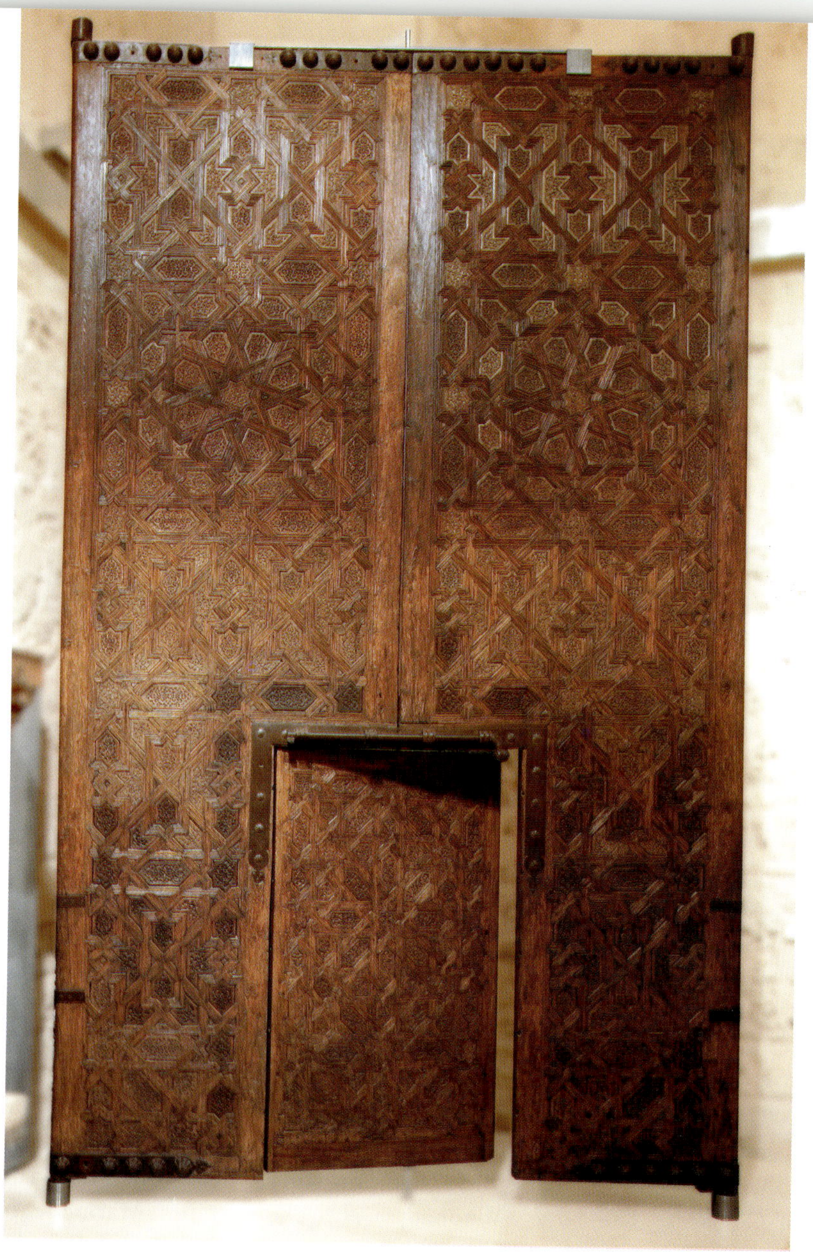

The leaves of the gates to the Nasrid Alhambra combine perfection in the search for the maximum use and care in their technical execution with beauty in their decoration. These gates, originally in the Sala de Dos Hermanas, today in the Museum of the Alhambra, are exemplary. Lower doorjambs are usually stone as they have to support the weight exerted by the rotation of the door whereas upper doorjambs can be wooden, and occasionally they have beautiful *mocárabes* or plant decorations. Generally only a small door in the gate was opened, maintaining intimacy, and holding in the warmth or coolness of the room.

the inner life it sustained in its day. Today the sensations of the music, smells from perfume burners, colours, or even the murmuring of the fountains timidly breaking the silence, are absent. It is impossible to recreate these atmospheres, not only because you are merely visiting but because the objects that formed part of its interior require specially conditioned places to display and preserve them. Also, particularly, because it is easy to fall into a lack of scientific rigour. We strongly recommend you complement your visit to the Alhambra with a tour of the Museum as this can bring you a little closer to knowing what the inner life of these palaces was like.

This first display contains some window screens from the Nasrid palaces where they were used as a visual separation, covering windows and hiding the gaze of the Islamic inhabitants and their Christian counterparts. Through the window screen you could see without being seen; a part of the constant search to maintain intimacy that characterizes Islamic architecture. Nasrid window screens are normally jointed and turned in complicated structures without any type of nails and with a decoration based on painted bands. The best example of a window screen is the fourteenth-century piece conserved in the Museum of the Alhambra. It comes from the Sala de Dos Hermanas, where it remained above the Mirador de Lindaraja viening-point until it was transferred to the Museum in 1962. It is a half-point lancet arch with a basic jointed structure and turned timber on the inside.

Also in this room are the outstanding fourteenth or fifteenth-century, marble and glazed ceramic Nasrid fountain from the Palacio de Dār al-'Arūsa, and the remains of ceramic paving from the Alhambra.

The second display captivates your attention with what is indisputably the most excellent piece in the Museum: the Jarrón de las Gacelas vase, considered one of the finest items in the entire history of ceramics. From the Nasrid period and dated in the sixteenth century, it is large, at 1.35 metres high, and remarkably slender, characteristic of these vases, with a very narrow base that broadens out as a large earthenware jar would to compensate in the upper third for the elongated neck and two flat handles. Above all, it is the lustre technique that has been used, with shades of gold and cobalt-blue on a base of tin, which earns it the universal acclaim it enjoys. In its day, it was recognized as a luxury item, adapted to the ornamental beauty of the inscriptions, plant or animal motifs, in this case gazelles standing face-to-face before the tree of life, stylized to fit the shape of the vase itself and widely popularized

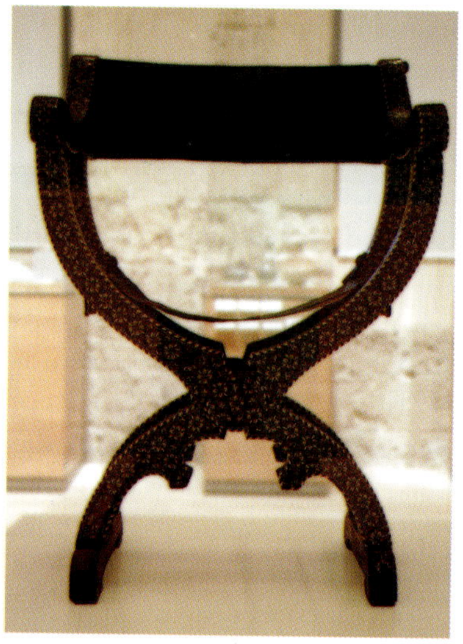

Nasrid *jamuga* in the Museum of the Alhambra

through the orientalising tastes of Romanticism that managed to convert it into an authentic "emblem" of the Alhambra.

In the same room, you can also see one of the best conserved gates of the Alhambra. The gates' function as a means of isolating spaces does not prevent them from being decorated with interlacing *rueda de lazo* designs where the sculpted borders scarcely conserve remains of the black, blue and red paint that once decorated them. The decoration of these gates floods even the smallest detail like the stone doorjambs decorated with plain leaves and the wooden upper doorjambs where plant decorations combine with *mocárabes*. An outstanding example is the door to the Sala de Dos Hermanas, dated around 1380. It has two leaves and a smaller gate or door used preferentially in winter. The two leaves are decorated all over and on both sides with fine assembled woodwork that depicts different but similar geometric figures on each side, in the inside of which are framed panels with *ataurique*s and seed-shaped motifs similar to those employed in the stucco. Remains of the original paintwork were brought to light after restoration.

In Room VI, you should really take the trouble of contemplating the working of the *jamuga* chair on display there. The *jamuga* was one of the items of furnishing that formed part of the interior decoration of the palaces and is supposed to have had a ceremonial use. It takes the form of a double-scissored chair, foldable, with a leather seat and backrest. The chair in question is Nasrid and dates from the fourteenth or fifteenth centuries. It displays some delicate marquetry in various materials such as silver, ivory and different woods. The leather backrest has been embossed with a shield.

Also on display here are headstones from the Rauda, the royal cemetery of the Alhambra; a copy of the 1305 lamp from the main mosque of the Alhambra; and two copies of the Koran, one of Almohad origin (late twelfth and early thirteenth centuries) and the other either

Marinid or Nasrid (fourteenth to fifteenth century).

The first display in Room VII highlights some roofing the origin and date (fifteenth to eight-eenth centuries) of which are unknown. In the second, as well as a low fourteenth-century Nasrid shaped-umbrella fountain, glass pieces that are also Nasrid, and fragments that show us the original colour decoration of the walls of the Generalife, is a surprising, magnificent fourteenth-century Nasrid piece: the golden vase, the Vaso de Fortuny-Simonetti, known as such because it once belonged to the painter.

Moving on to the eastern hall of the Palacio de Carlos V and coming closer to what was the crypt, you reach the last room in the Museum, which centres especially on textiles. The multiple uses that a single room in the palaces might have makes the absence of more or less fixed furnishings, such as wardrobes, understandable. Rooms might be used as bed chambers or even as meeting rooms, so pieces of furniture that were easy to transport held sway in the interior decoration of the palace. Sometimes, a hanging cloth used as a curtain was an adequate separation. Moreover, to combat the cold they would use textiles such as wool or silk to cover the walls while the floors were covered with rugs.

Especially outstanding is the rug traditionally identified with the Generalife although in fact its original location is unknown, though it may have belonged in the Nasrid palaces. From the Mamluk period, dated around 1448-1482, and originally from Cairo (Egypt), the rug must have been a present to the Nasrid dynasty. It is made from wool with a Persian knot and restoration work began in 1996 with it finally being put on display in this room in 2003.

Once you have visited the Museum and before heading towards the Nasrid palaces you should visit the Sala de Presentación, in the north façade of the palace of Charles V, where panels, materials, models and an audiovisual presentation are available which will contribute to your understanding and seeing the Alhambra.

The Nasrid palaces

WITHIN THE COMPLEXITY OF THE ISLAMIC precinct of the Alhambra and Generalife, it must be said that the current layout and distribution is the product of buildings that from the thirteenth to the fifteenth centuries were not built according to a specific ground plan. Logically, if the heart of the precinct was the Alcazaba, construction would extend from there progressively. However, in chronological order, documentation shows that after the Alcazaba came the Generalife, physically quite far away, followed judging by the date of construction by the Palacio de Abencerrajes and El Partal and finally with the Nasrid palaces (what we currently know as the Nasrid Palaces refers to the complex formed by the Palacio de Comares and the Palacio de los Leones and corresponds to constructions dating from different parts of the fourteenth century).

Apparently, as early as the thirteenth century, the desire to endow this side of the fortress with the greatest symbolic significance was plain. It was to be a showpiece of power in the face of the Albaicín, the hill that had always been a stronghold at odds with the sultans. Moreover, from the Alhambra the *medina* of the Albaicín had always been considered an exemplary cradle of genuine, Islamic Granada.

Following the first constructions, begun in the thirteenth century, the will to concentrate the palace keeps on the north side became more marked. This should not be taken solely as a consequence of the tradition or need to locate them on this side to ensure the greatest possible isolation from the south, but as a proud gesture of grand ostentation in addition to the relationship of shared views that continues to form a cultural bond between Granada's two, historic, Islamic cities: the Alhambra and the Albaicín. The two hills admire

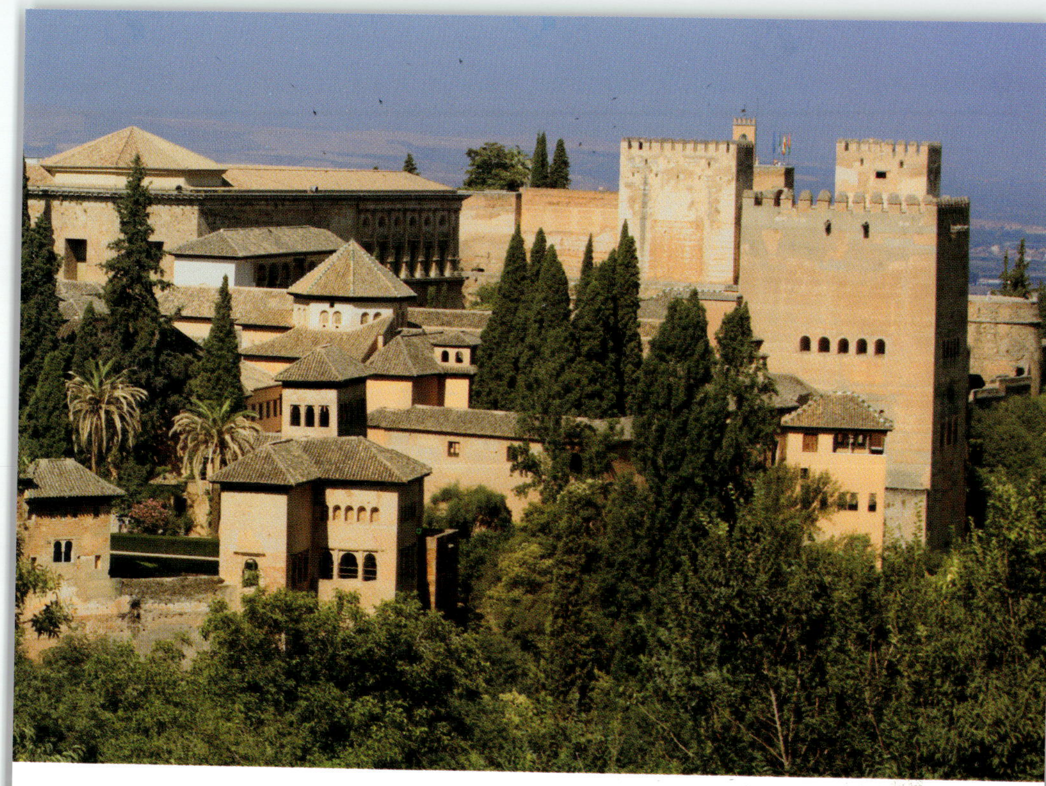

The Nasrid palaces with the Alcazaba in the background

and, at the same time, fear each other and this mutual contemplation is a challenge, defended from behind their window screens, *ajimeces*, and viewing points.

If, in the thirteenth century the Alcazaba was the military precinct and possibly the palace of Muḥammad I, at the end of the century and in the years that followed the move to the urban area began and the first palaces were built. But also then, when the Palacio de los Leones was still missing, all the administrative functions, of court and protocol, of withdrawal and private enjoyment, took place in the built part. Once the Palacio de los Leones was finished, functions would be redistributed again. Consequently, it is only right to talk of a continuous evolution in the organization and use of the different structures in the Alhambra and, therefore, of the palaces of Comares and de los Leones.

From the moment of the Christian conquest, the two palaces were traditionally seen as a single clear unit, especially when construction of the Palacio de Carlos V began in 1531, and the new building was referred to as the new royal palace, Casa Real Nueva, in contrast with its predecessor, the Casa Real Vieja, that is, the Palacio de Comares and the Palacio de los Leones. Sixteenth-century travellers and visitors perceived the Casa Real

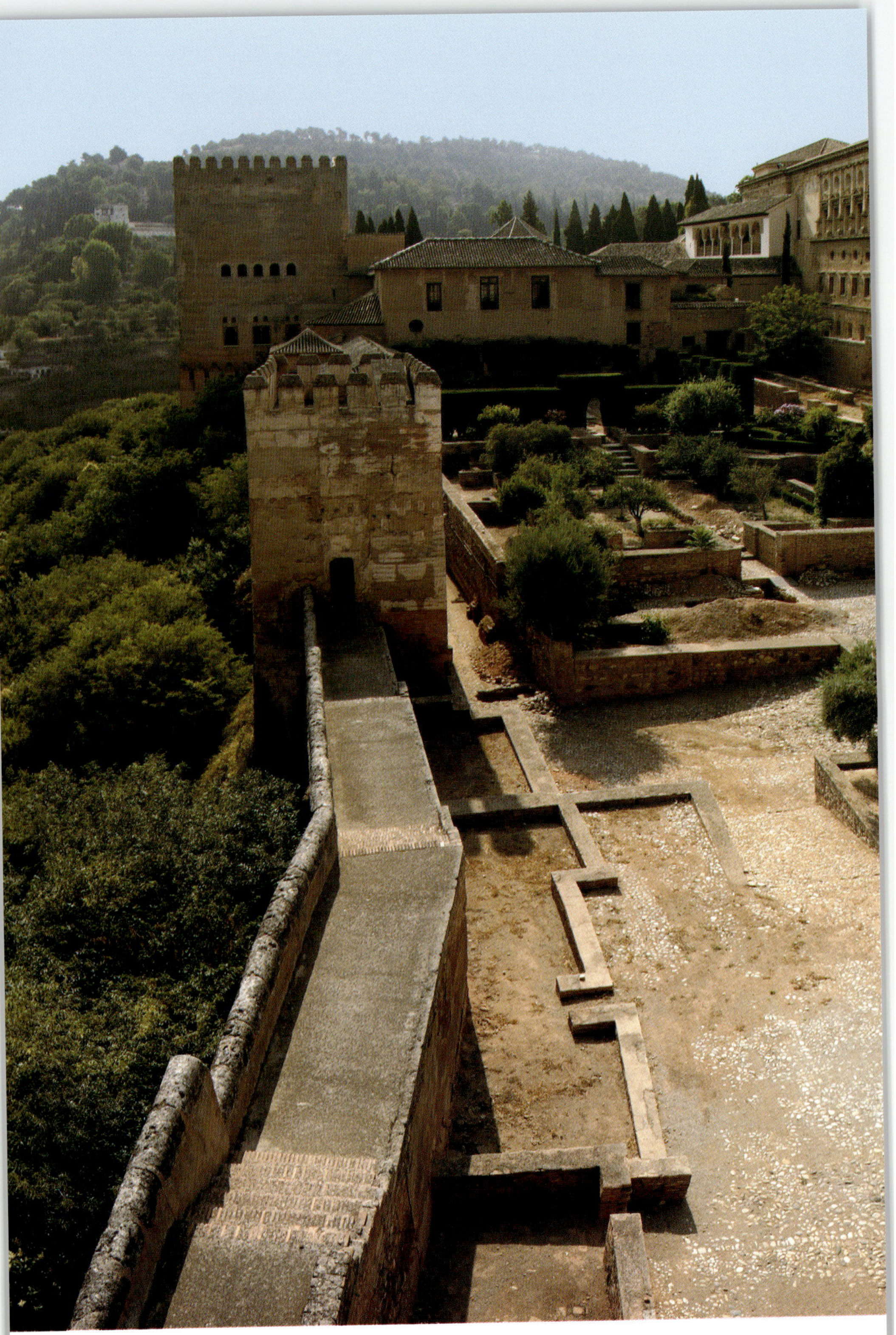

Tower of Muḥammad I

Vieja, the old royal palace, as the residential area, distinguishing between a summer palace, Comares, and a winter palace, de los Leones; an idea current research rejects.

Fruit of this "unreal" idea of unity was that forged during the eighteenth century, when some authors wanted to seek symmetry in the structure of the residential area and to do so they pointed to the existence of another palace, supposedly destroyed in order to construct the Palacio de Carlos V. In the face of this idea, excavations and written documentation show another palace can never possibly have existed, thus undermining the theory. In broad terms, the interrelationship of the layout of the Palacio de Comares with that of the Palacio de los Leones represents a right angle. What today we are able to confirm is the creation of a first palace area, Comares, to which later would be added the other palace area, the Palacio de los Leones.

Before you enter the Nasrid palaces, below the terrace that stretches out in front of the Palacio de Carlos V, you see the remains of some earlier constructions attributed by some authors to Muḥammad III and by others to Ismā'īl I. First, you see a stone-paved square which gave access to, and off which led the main street in this area. Next, at a slightly different height, stands the base of the walls of an ancient mosque (marked by a square privet hedge), various rooms apparently destined for administrative use and a patio close to the Mexuar. In the background stands the tower of Muḥammad I, apparently modest but of special strategic importance as from here you could observe the movement of the guards along the parapet walk, *adarve*, the start of the Camino de Ronda, and the flood of people entering the palaces and city.

The centre of the patio is occupied by a small *alberca*, a pond with an original shape; in the background we see a portal with columns that shelters and precedes the small viewing point built on instructions from Yūsuf I. From the sixteenth century, this patio was given the name Patio de Machuca as it here that the architect who built the Palacio de Carlos V had his studio.

Mexuar

Name: The Mexuar (al-Măswár or al-Măswara).
Date: c. 1314-1325
Sultanate: Ismāʿīl I (1314-1325)
Note: It underwent many alterations both in Islamic times – Ismāʿīl I, (1333-1353), and Muḥammad V (1354-1359; 1362-1391) intervened here – and in the Christian period – one of the Islamic spaces that underwent most alterations under Christian rule, although the conversion into a chapel employed Nasrid techniques to some extent – making it difficult to imagine a possible, original layout.

THE MEXUAR is supposed to have been the residential palace of Ismāʿīl I; later, Muḥammad V converted it into the throne room at the feast of the Mawlid (birth of the prophet) in 1362. This same sultan later focussed his attention on building the Palacio de los Leones and left this area as the Mexuar, the high court of justice and seat of the sultan's administration, where the counsel of viziers, or ministers, met; a space commonly found in medieval Islamic palaces.

The portal you see today on entering the Mexuar was originally thought to date from the Nasrid period and it was believed to have been placed here in the

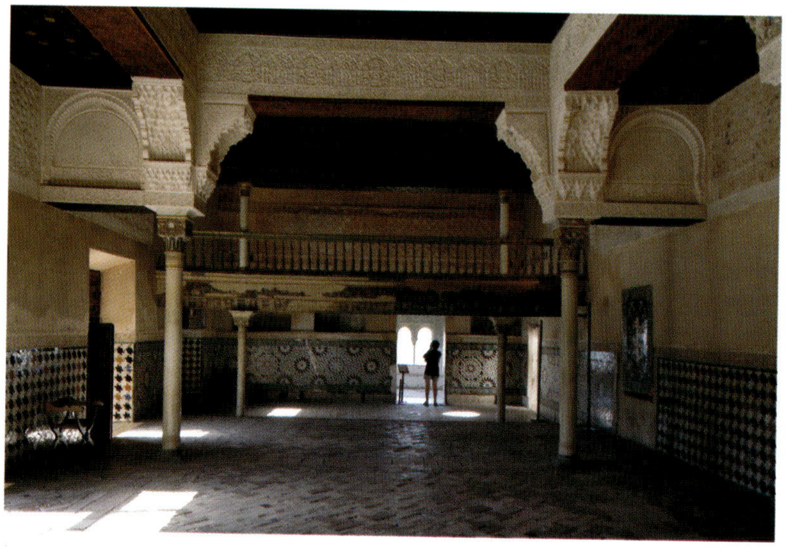

General view of the Mexuar

reign of Muḥammad V, when he renovated the Mexuar. However, currently the possibility that it comes from the Christian period and has been made from re-used Nasrid elements is being studied. Whatever the case may be, it has the typical characteristics of Nasrid art, with stucco adornments running around the door drawing on plants, geometry and inscriptions, above panels that divide up and order all this capricious decoration. Above the door hangs an eave on wooden corbela and bases at the ends that serve to mark the visual limits of these portals and protect them from the effects of the rain.

In Islamic times, the Mexuar had a different layout, consisting of a central lantern of two floors and upper body of windows, supported by the four columns that we now see and surrounding recesses that limit the four rectangular secondary rooms. The stylized columns are outstanding as is the delicacy of the cubic capitals, typical in Nasrid architecture; the paintwork has been brought back to life following its restoration. The plaster cantilever set on the capitals gradually increases the visual weight of the architecture and portrays beautiful wooden panels nailed onto the beams that support a supposed gallery. The roofing that now covers the central room is modern but with a single enormous well-made *rueda de lazos*, the typical interlaced geometric star design. This type of room, where its centred, vertical character takes precedence, is found elsewhere in the Alhambra, too, in the Sala de las Camas (Baño de Comares), ancient Torre del Peinador, Baño de la Mezquita, among others. In the area where there is a banister on a wooden beam at mid-height, a sort of balcony, in Islamic times stood a wall that closed off the room on this side and behind opened up a corridor that gave access to the patio of the Mexuar and separated this room from the oratory that can now be seen in the background. The step in the paving also serves to mark the two levels and functions of this room. With the Christian alterations, the room changed from being a centralized space with a clear vertical structure to become an elongated room with a definite horizontal projection.

In the sixteenth century it was to be converted into the palace's Christian chapel, which would represent a complete change in function. This is something that was to characterize the Christian alterations: the reuse of spaces does not necessarily imply their use for the same function. Therefore, in the Christian period, from being a political, administrative room it became a private, religious space. A logical change, if you recall that while in the Islamic period this area was public, in the Christian period it acquired a private, intimate meaning

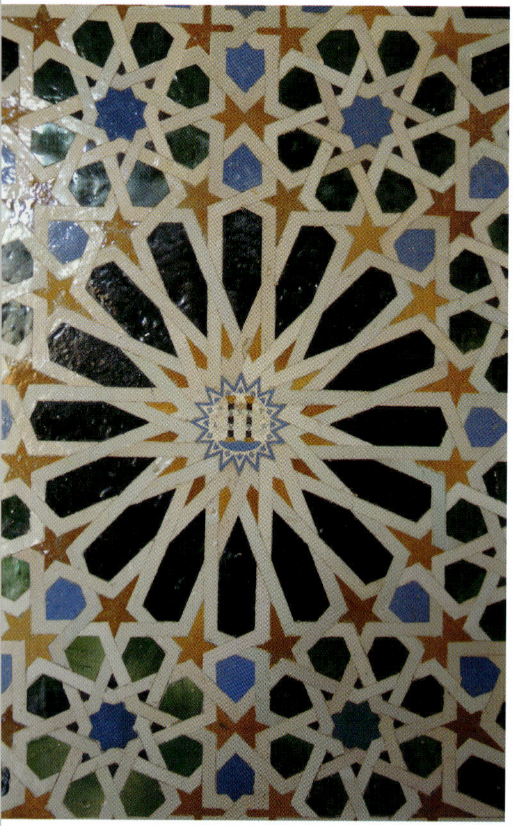

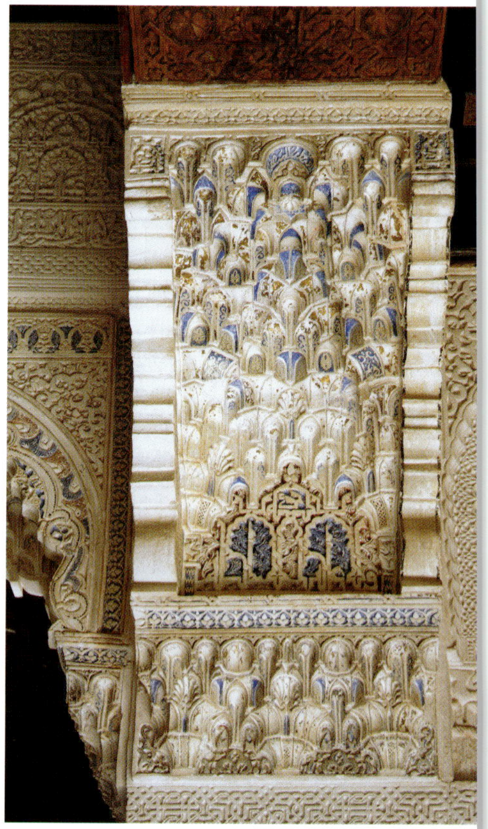

In the tiling in the Mexuar you can appreciate Islamic techniques were maintained but Christian symbols were introduced in the sixteenth century. This is clear in the symbiosis of the *rueda de lazos*, the interlaced geometric star design in which the central tiles display the columns and "Plus Ultra" emblem of Charles V.

Nasrid stucco was generally produced by chiselling out moisture-absorbing plaster, which could easily be dampened, although moulding was also used, without doubt a less complicated technique. In the Christian period, the use of moulds become generalized for the stucco. Blue and yellow, among other colours, filled the stucco that, together with the remains of original paintwork which can be found and have been recovered in the Nasrid capitals of the marble columns, tell us of an explosion of sharply contrasting colours, distant from the homogeneous vision that you see nowadays.

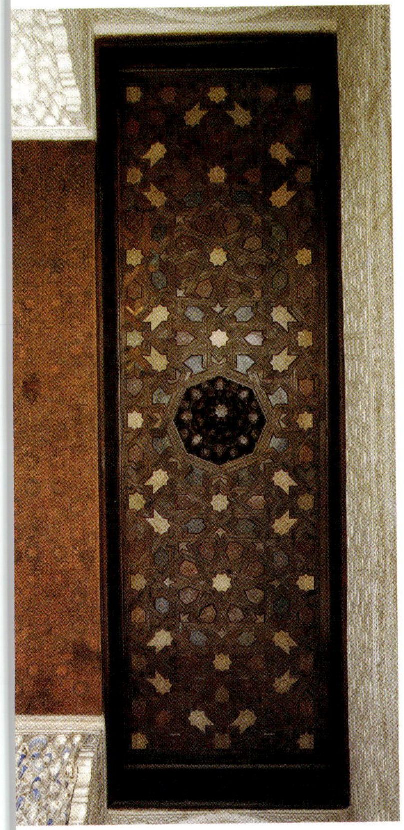

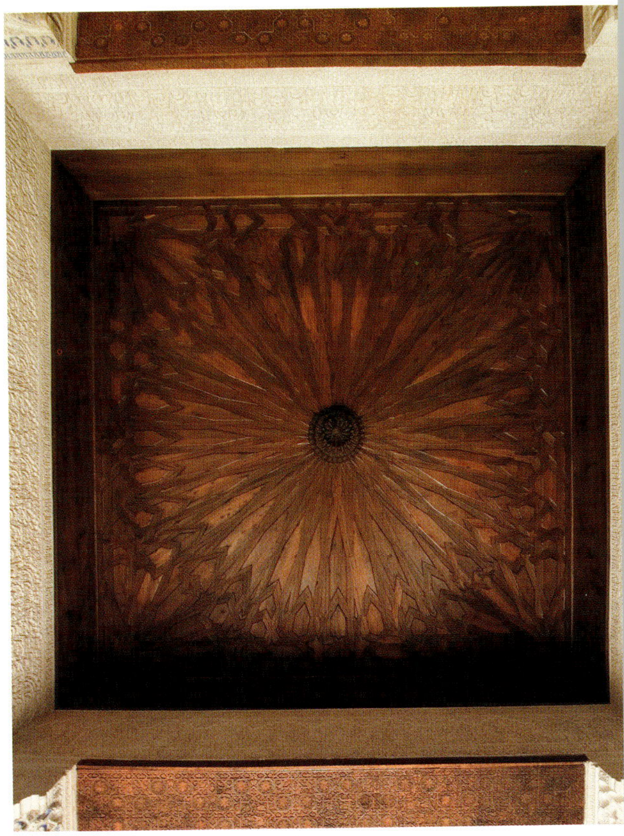

The wooden roofing constitutes another element documented as having been the work of craftsmen in the Christian period. Most of the roofing you see in the Mexuar is Christian and later, although Nasrid materials have sometimes been reused. These ceilings take as their central motif the *rueda de lazos*, the interlaced geometric star design, and the octagonal motifs that were so frequent in the Nasrid period. On the left, a Nasrid wooden panel. On the right, the central panel in the Christian Mexuar.

as close to the Mexuar a space was prepared for Germana de Foix, the second wife of Ferdinand the Catholic, in what today is known as the Patio de Machuca, while later the nearby Cuarto Dorado was prepared for the Empress Isabel of Portugal.

So, during the sixteenth century, and especially before 1550, the intense activity of artisans has been documented. Under Christian patronage, they not only altered but repaired this space. In their interventions they maintained the Arab inscriptions in the stucco and repaired the Nasrid tiling, as these represented no obstacle to Christian use of the space. Such was the level of integration that elements of other rooms were relocated, such as the frieze of inscriptions that runs above the tiled dado and that possibly came from the Patio de Machuca to be located here in the sixteenth century, or the tiling that probably originated in the destroyed southern hall of Comares.

In the Mexuar you find some of the artistic expressions you are going to see often throughout your tour of the Nasrid palaces, for example, the use of tiling in the dado. These tiles include Nasrid pieces although there are also Christian interventions and pieces and sometimes on first sight it is difficult to distinguish the one from the other. These are cut pieces of glazed ceramic and are set out as if in a puzzle according to an initial design or drawing. The tiles principally use white, black, blue, yellow and green. Forms and colours enhance the decorative motifs, among which the interlaced designs that create many-pointed stars are exceptional. In the centre of some of these interlaced geometric star designs in the tiled dado, you see the symbols of the Nasrid dynasty, the shield with the band, as well as Christian emblems like the two-headed eagle or the columns of Hercules, a reference to Charles V.

If you pass under the banister, along what in Nasrid times would have been a corridor open to the sky, you come to a small oratory with its *mihrab*. Originally, this would have been independent as access was from the western side and from the north portal of the Patio de Machuca. The oratory is set at an angle to the wall in the direction of prayer towards Mecca. The decoration today is the product of several interventions undergone in the sixteenth and twentieth centuries.

The patio or open corridor that in Islamic times would have linked the Mexuar and the oratory probably permitted access to the Palacio de Comares avoiding the need to cross the Mexuar.

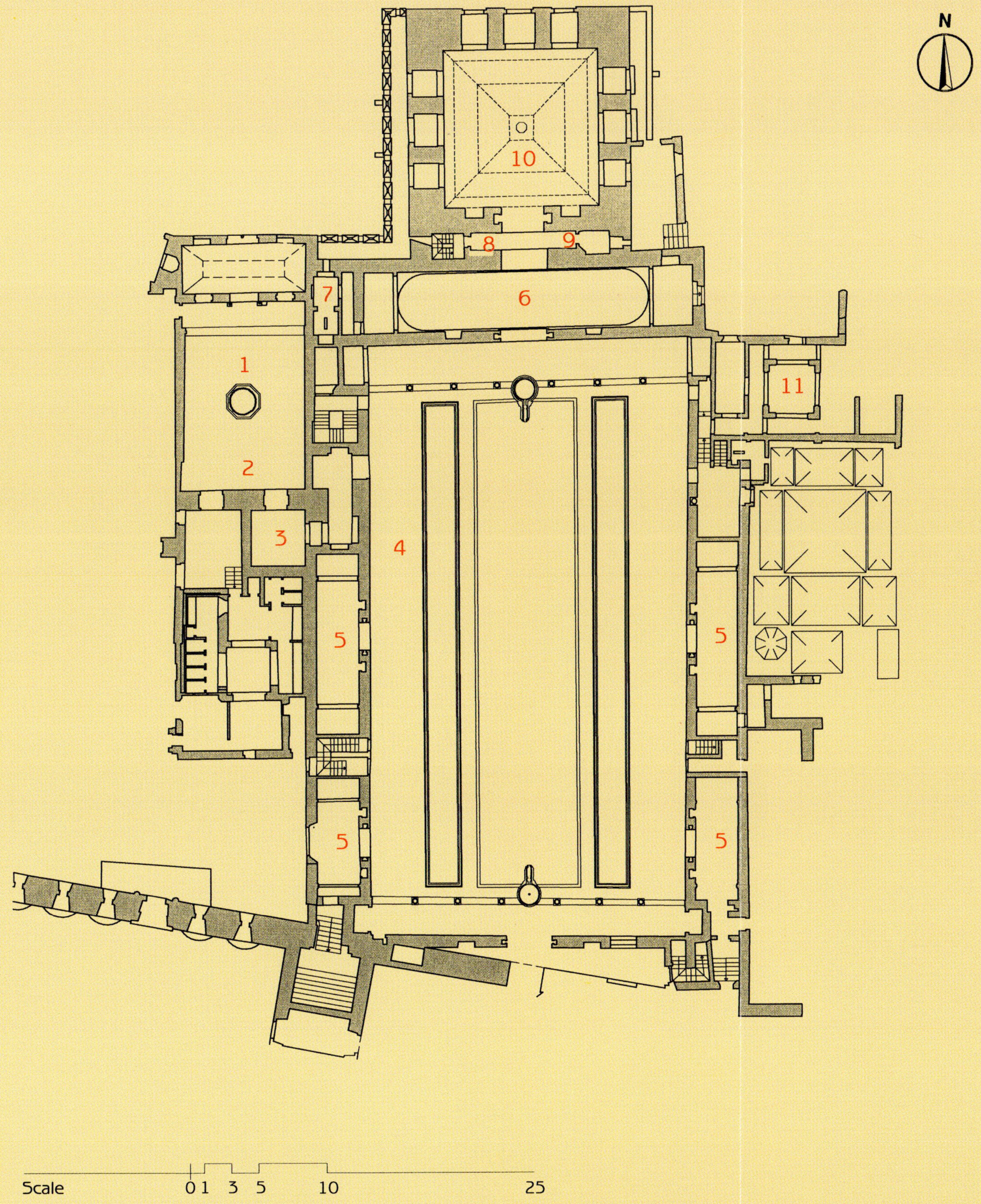

Palacio de Comares

1. Patio of the Cuarto Dorado
   Access to the Palacio de Comares
2. Façade of the Palacio de Comares
3. Hall
4. Court of Comares or Arrayanes
5. Side rooms
6. Sala de la Barca
7. Lavatory or latrine
8. Raised staircase
9. Oratory
10. Salón de Comares
11. Baño de Comares

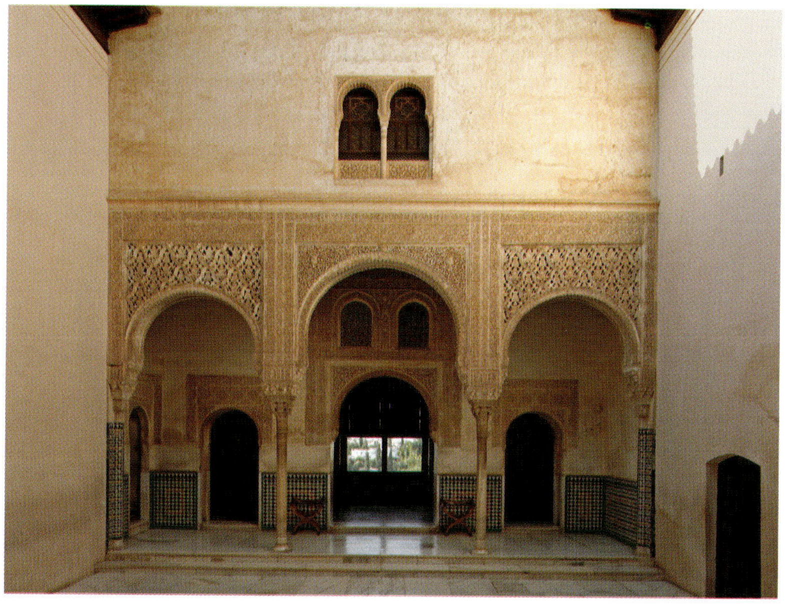

The Cuarto Dorado

Cuarto Dorado

Name: Cuarto Dorado, named thus on account of the gilded ceiling
Date: Uncertain; possibly 16th cent. One alternative theory dates it at c.1369, when the façade of Comares was built.
Sultanate: What remains of the original decoration is from the reign of Muḥammad V (1354-1359;1362-1391). 16th cent. alterations (windows and painted cladding). 20th cent. repositioning of stucco and tiles.
Note: The painted ceiling is truly outstanding.

Some academics interpreted the Islamic function of this room as being a room for the women although today the hypothesis that it was a transitional space, a waiting room for those entering the Palacio de Comares is considered more likely as it is located between the administrative and residential areas. Others, bearing in mind that the sultan could hold audience against the façade, suggest it was the room where sentences were handed down and written out at his dictation.

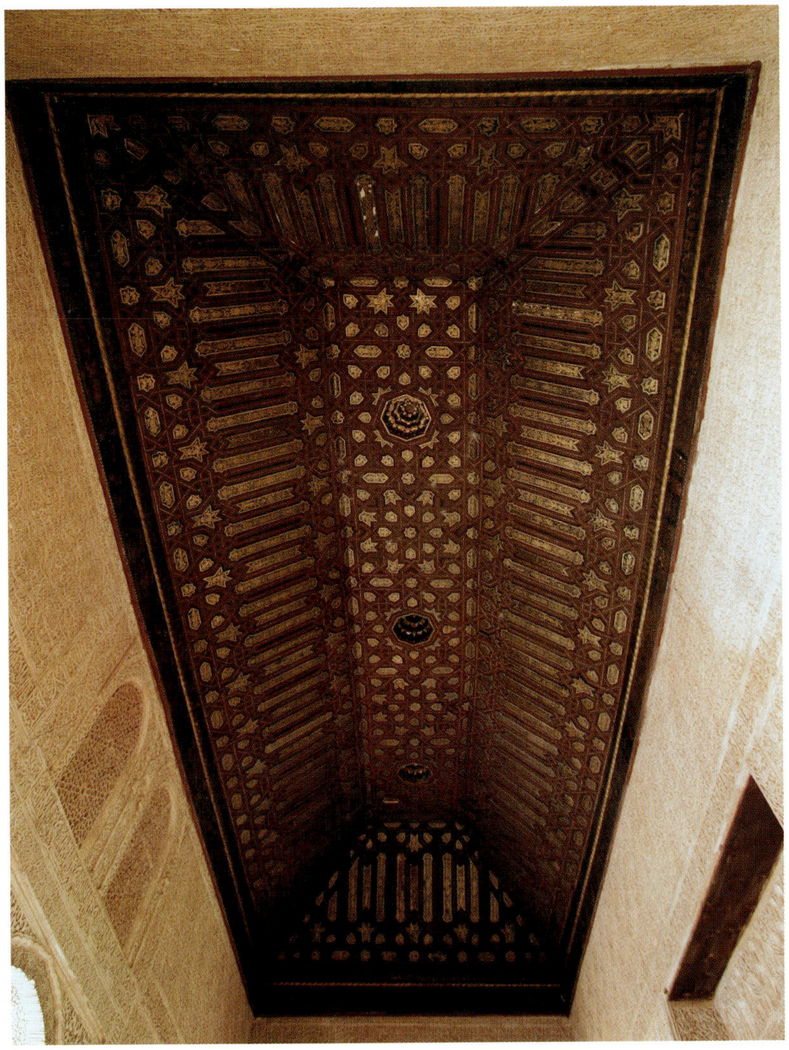

Ceiling of the Cuarto Dorado

As in the Mexuar, the room was to be altered in the Christian period, being adapted to be used by Isabel of Portugal in the sixteenth century, although finally the Empress never actually occupied this room. One result of the Christian alterations would be the construction of a wall with two arches to cover the façade of the Cuarto Dorado, which was removed in 1947. Also the rectangular window, with arches and Gothic capitals, its elevated layout and the side ledges, identify it as being made to suit Christian fashions and tastes. In the splendid façade that you see today, the capitals of its entrance arch are outstanding. They are catalogued

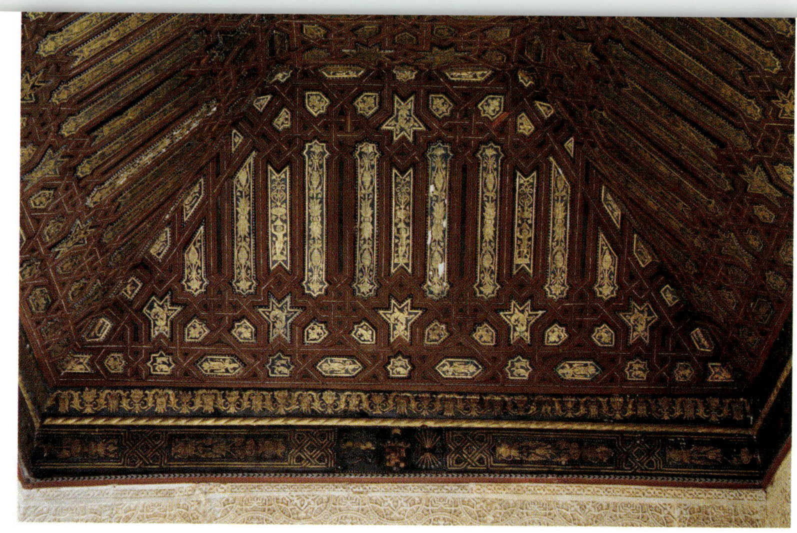

Detail of the ceiling of the Cuarto Dorado

among the oldest in the Alhambra as they date from the twelfth or thirteenth centuries, and are considered to belong to the Almohad-Nasrid transition. These are called "handle-" or "ear-" capitals because the volutes fall and detach themselves from the body of the capital forming authentic handles. It is one of the most original compositions of Islamic capitals and arouses much curiosity as very few examples of this type are known and all of them are to be found in Granada, as has been seen in the Museum.

The most outstanding features of the room are the frame structure with four base panels in the ceiling and the ensembles with the interlaced geometric star motifs, typically Hispano-Muslim, and common in *mudéjar* roofing. Your gaze is held by the painting if you stop to study the *arrocabe*, the frieze that marks the line where wall and ceiling join. Here, you can pick out the shield of the Catholic Kings with the yoke and arrows, while in the base panels putti, little angels, have been painted, in true Renaissance tradition. Despite the painting, it is not clear which tradition we should ascribe the ceiling to as it may be Christian painting on a Nasrid ceiling or an entirely Christian ceiling.

When you leave the room, you cross the patio del Cuarto Dorado in the centre of which is a 1940s copy of the fountain that was in the Jardin de Lindaraja garden, and is currently in the Museum. The patio, whose nineteenth- century uses and alterations were recorded by Romantic engravers, enables you to perceive and wonder at the solemn grandeur of the façade of the Palacio de Comares, inviting you to enter the palace residence.

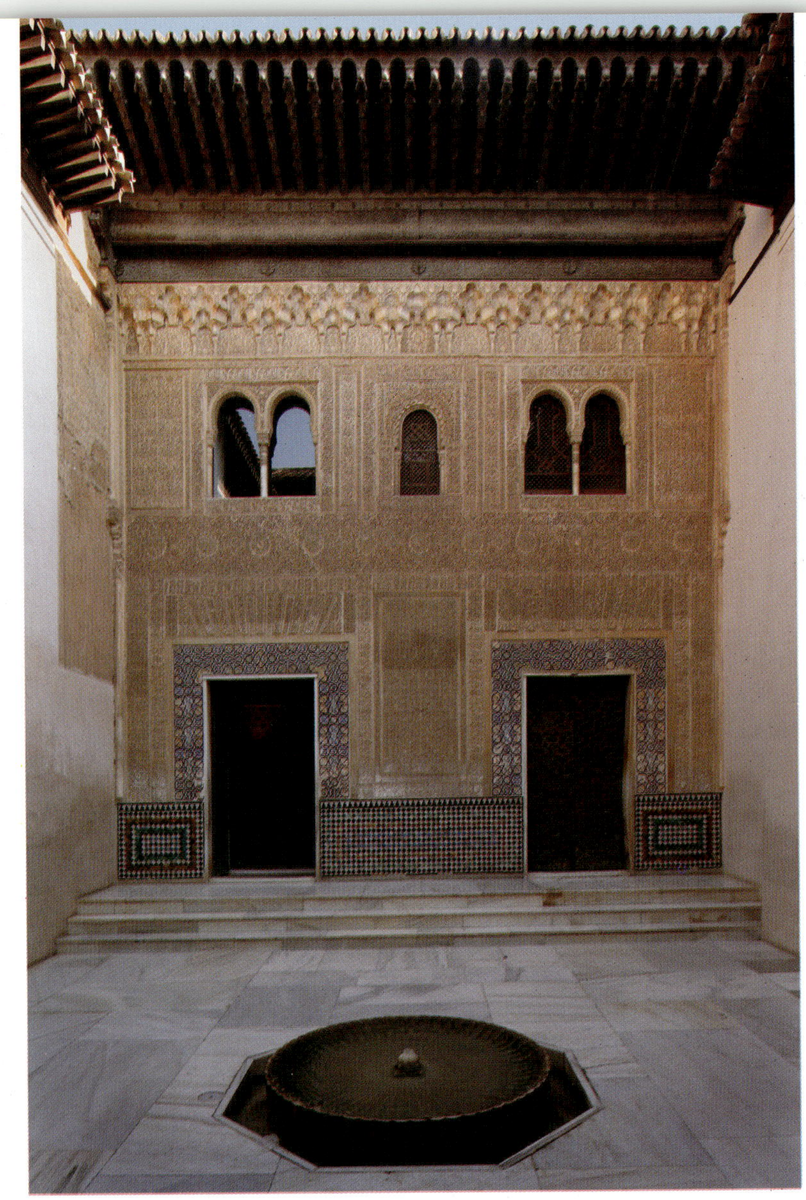

Façade of the Palacio de Comares

Palacio de Comares

FAÇADE OF THE PALACIO DE COMARES

Name: Façade of the Palacio de Comares
Date: 1369-1370
Sultanate: Muḥammad V (1354-1359; 1362-1391)
Note: The spectacular grandeur of this interior façade, the largest and richest in Nasrid architecture.

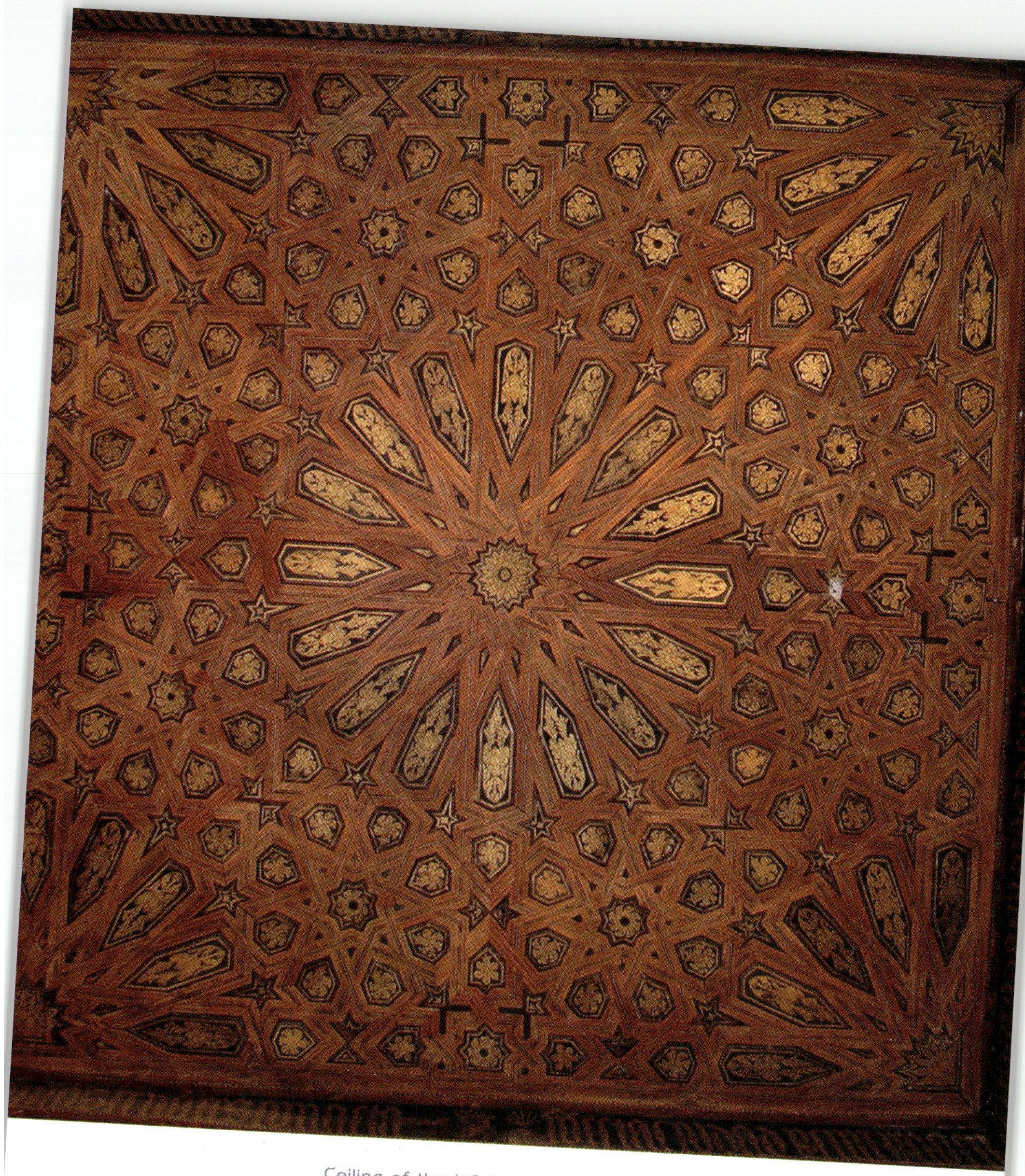

Ceiling of the left-hand entrance to the façade of Comares

The façade of the Palacio de Comares was erected at the behest of Muḥammad V. It was inaugurated in 1370 to commemorate the conquest of the city of Algeciras (1369). The three steps that precede the façade were, it is suggested, where the sultan held public audience with his subjects. What is absolutely certain is that the façade is on the inside and it gives us a taste of the interior majesty of the palace itself.

The façade has a lower body with two gates. Looking straight at it, the door to the right would lead to a service area and an upper floor or private rooms, whereas that on the left gives access to the inner patio. The five upper recesses correspond to private rooms where, through the window screens, whoever came to the palace could be observed without being seen. The façade ends with a large overhanging eave that protects and crowns it. This eave is the most original element and is one of the few that remain in the Alhambra. It is peculiar in that it is at an angle making it look like a Chinese or oriental pavilion.

In addition to the stucco with curved *lazo* motifs, an interesting aspect of this façade is the epigraphy which has served to interpret the symbolism of the door. It is a poem by Ibn Zamrak that decorates the header of the eave (marking the transition between the wall and the structure) and where the meaning of this monumental portal is described.

> *My position is that of a crown and my door opens on two paths; the West believes that in me lies the East. Al-Ganī bi-llāh has commanded me to cross the entrance to the victory that is already announced. And I await his appearance [to permit him to enter], in the same way that the horizons introduce the dawn.*
> *God, may you beautify his works, they are handsome in their appearance and their nature!*

(English version based on a translation from Arabic into Spanish by Darío Cabanelas and Antonio Fernández Puertas)

On entering the left-hand door, you pass through a crooked entrance passage with three bends in it, lined with benches for the guards, where you can admire a small ceiling area decorated with different painted motifs. The first ceiling is especially attractive: it is square, with a sixteen-pointed star, and around the header runs an inscription in Latin characters referring to the Catholic Kings.

This type of crooked entrance is common in the Islamic tradition and fulfils two needs: it is defensive and it protects the residents' intimacy. A straight entrance would enable you to appreciate the inside from outside of the building. This type of entrance protected the inner life of the palace. Thus, the entrances to the palaces are always magic thresholds that narrow and twist, seeking to effect the greatest surprise on those who enter. The crooked entry, the entrance that is always around a corner or at the side of the patio, are intended to cause the visitor a feeling of instability, of lack of balance, so that, as life itself, finding balance should be the product of a search, of a passing through the interior until once the point of symmetry, of balance, is found you take a seat and rest in order to better understand and contemplate the subtlety of its construction.

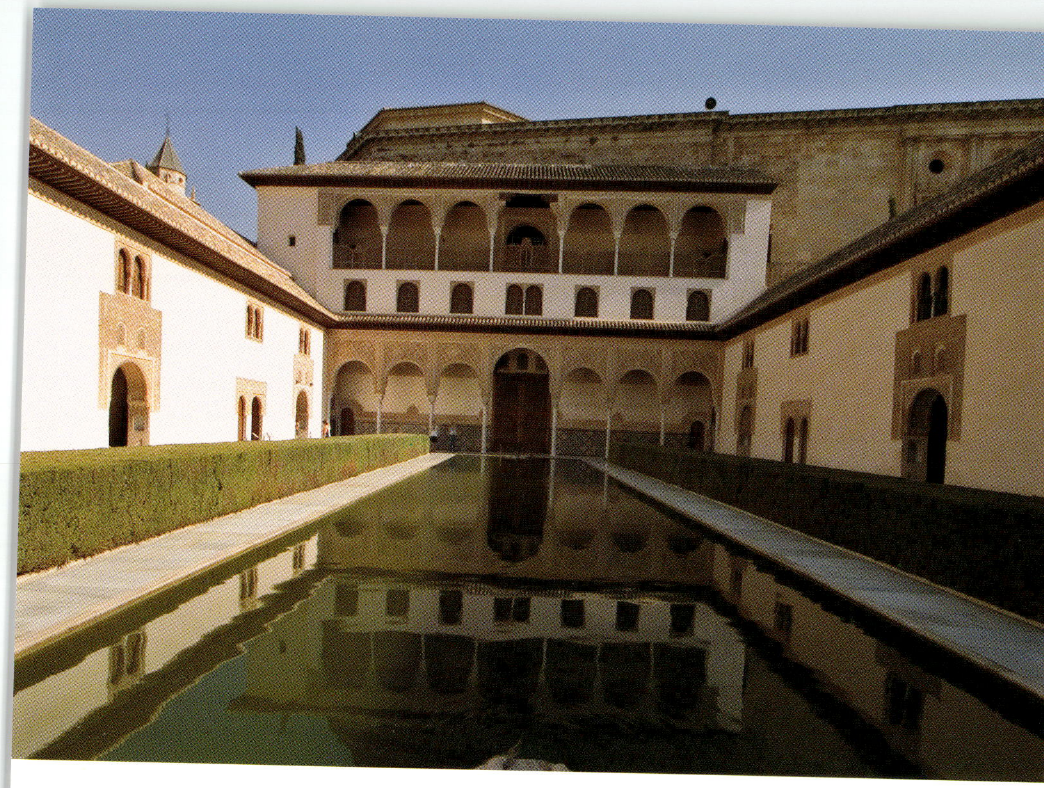

The Palacio de Comares

Patio de Comares

Name: Palacio de Comares. The etymology of Comares is unclear; some writers suggest it was named after the *qamariyya* or skylight, a technique of coloured glass that the must have been used in the Torreón de Comares tower. Others believe the word is of Berber origin and came to be translated as 'height'. It is also known as the Patio de la Alberca and the Patio de los Arrayanes after the shrubs that run along both sides of the pool and that have probably been there since the Christian period.
Date: Post-1360s to c.1400
Sultanate: It was begun during the sultanate of Yūsuf I (1333-1354) with the construction of the Torreón de Comares. The projected palace was finished by his son Muḥammad V (1354-1359; 1362-1391).
Note: The layout constitutes a clear example of the traditional type of patio with an *alberca*, or pool around which the rooms are distributed.

THE GROUND PLAN and layout of Comares corresponds to a traditional type of palace, or at least the most common one in the world of Granada, and is found on a smaller scale in some Nasrid houses. Various rooms are distributed around a rectangular patio with a pond. The patio is the true organizer of the space as well as the common element because the rooms are not interconnected so movement from one room to another must be via the patio. This characteristic of the patio is emphasized by the water that reflects back at you the architecture to the point that architecture and water blend into one and you we might well ask whether the water wants to capture the image of the architecture or the architecture wants to dominate the water. Whichever may be the case, it is a clear appropriation of the space.

The palace represents an expansive type of architecture, as the rooms extend themselves occupying quantitatively a substantial area, in contrast to the architecture of palace layout where the occupation of ground space is less and height takes preference. These are different ways of understanding the residential architecture of the palace.

The north and south porches each have an arcade of seven semicircular arches with no structural function. They are purely decorative and are decorated with panels of *sebka*, resting on the traditional narrow shaft, Nasrid columns and *mocárabe* capitals in the centre. Behind these arcades and to the sides are recessed compartments or small rooms.

These porches are a kind of decorative screen that mark the transition between the open space of the patio and the interior of the rooms. The arcades do no more than enhance this and indicate that the principle rooms are located on the north and south sides of the patio: the Torreón de Comares tower to the north, and to the south research suggests the existence of two pos-sible rooms, one above the other, for the prince and heir. The name Salas de las Elias or Helias, as it was called in the Christian period, may come from *'āliya* meaning high. However, this is mere hypothesis as whatever was on this south side was affected by a fire in the Christian period and modified on building the Renaissance Palacio de Carlos V. It must be said that the construction of the Palacio de Carlos V, despite the fact that a supposed south gallery may have been destroyed, entailed maintaining the inner harmony in the court, so that the south arcade should act like a curtain or façade, hiding the stone blocks of the new royal palace.

Four rooms lead off from the patio, two on either side, each with a grand entrance arch. A small door at the side of the main entrance arch, which can be seen to be open in two of the rooms, permits you to go up to the upper part or *algorfa* of these houses. Some writers suggest that the ground floor was used in summer and the upper floor in winter. Comparisons with other Islamic palaces, have led to the suggestion that these four rooms might have been for the four legitimate wives of the sultan, although this too is mere hypothesis as the space effectively occupied by women in the Alhambra is unknown. What is obvious is that there is a great difference between these four rooms, with simple flat, wooden ceilings, *alfarje*, and scarcely any decoration and other spaces such as the Torreón de Comares, meaning they can be classified as having a clearly domestic function.

Today these side rooms have been greatly altered as to the southwest a doorway was opened up to give access in a straight line to the interior of the palaces; to the southeast access to the upper part was closed off to join the Palacio de Comares with the Palacio de los Leones.

Doubts about the south gallery, and about the use of the side rooms, do no more than demonstrate the complexity of this space. A complexity that leaves us in doubt about whether or not marble paving was used in Islamic times, even though sources close to the time of the Christian conquest highlighted its use in flooring.

Torreón de Comares

Name: Different meanings of the word Comares have been mentioned earlier, moreover this tower has been known by other names such as the Salón de Embajadores, which was used in the belief that it was here that the council meeting took place at which it was agreed to hand over Granada to the Christians.
Date: c.1333-1366
Sultanate: Yūsuf I (1333-1354)
Note: Its dimensions and the symbolic power specially achieved through the stucco, the inscriptions and the ceiling.

Inside the Palacio de Comares, this impressive tower is outstanding. It imposes its presence on the other towers in the precinct not only through its grandeur and magnificence but also because the wide openings on each side reveal an architectural style that is more open to the outside.

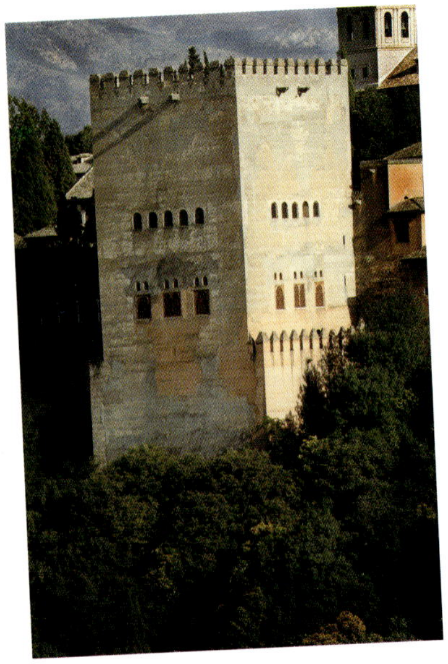

View of the outside of the Torreón de Comares

On entering the tower, you find on each side of the entrance arch the *tacas* (*ṭāqa*s), small vaulted niches so frequent in the Alhambra and to which a multitude of functions have been assigned, some without any foundation at all, such as their being used to store slippers or to hold perfume burners. But the symbolic explanation, as indicated in the poems, is that they are used to store jars of water. After all, water is an important element in Islamic architecture as a symbol of purification and as a gift of the sultan. These *tacas* at the entrance to the Torreón de Comares stand out as they are of marble and not plaster. The *taca* on the right of the entrance to the Sala de la Barca displays this poem:

With perfection and beauty
I am of a bride her dais.

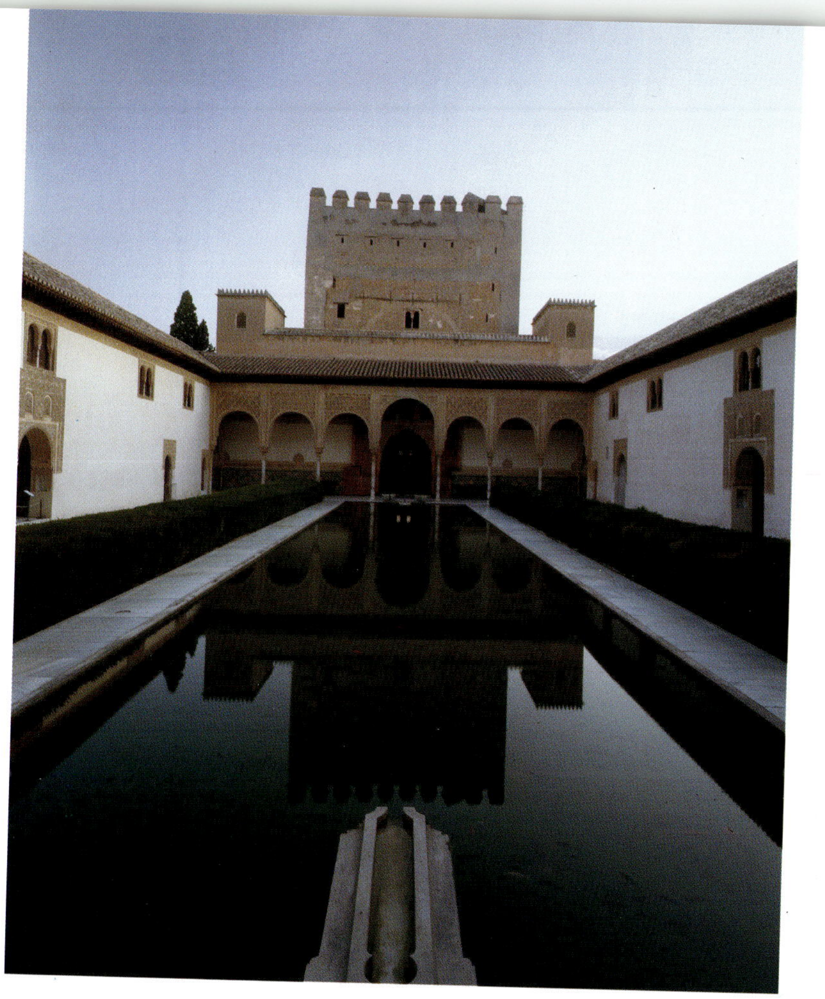

General view of the Torreón de Comares in the Patio de Comares

You know that I tell the truth
my pitcher when you look
Arches like the half moon
a Crown over me...

(English version based on a translation from Arabic into Spanish by Emilio García Gómez)

The first room that you encounter on entering the tower is the Sala de la Barca. Traditionally, it was believed that the name came from the shape of the ceiling, which looks like the keel an upside -down boat. However, the wall inscriptions do repeatedly use the word *al-baraka*, the blessing. The ceiling you see today is, in fact, a faithful copy of the original which was destroyed by fire in 1890.

Just like the other rooms in the Nasrid palaces, the Sala de la Barca is characterized by its plurifunctionality. The same room could be used as a bed chamber or as a meeting room... These

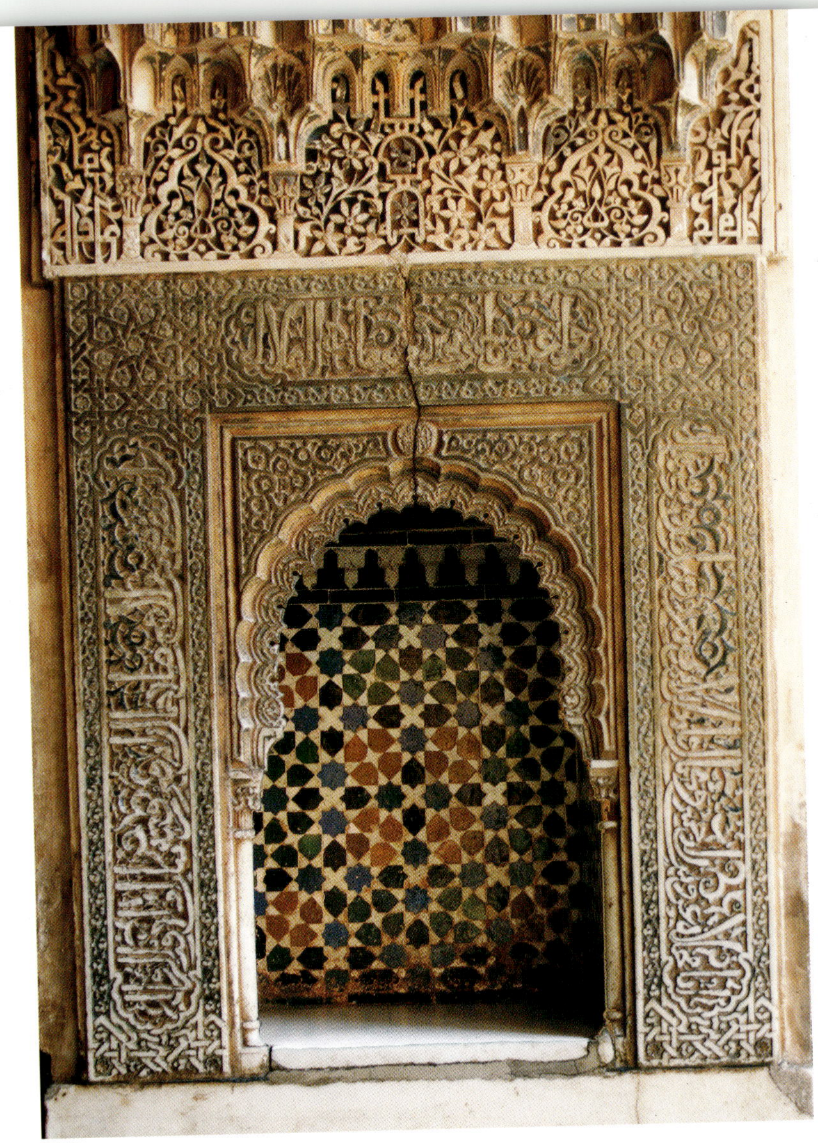

The *taca*, the vaulted niche on the right-hand side as you enter the Sala de la Barca

multiple uses make the absence of furniture, at least of typical pieces of more or less fixed furniture like cabinets, tables or chairs, all the more pointed.

Although currently closed to the public due to limitations of space, at the back of the Sala de la Barca on the left-hand side a small door leads to a latrine – a small opening in the floor, generally connected to a watercourse – where an earthen-coloured, painted dado has been conserved.

On passing from the Sala de la Barca to the inside you find on your left a door leading into the Torreón de Comares, which is on several floors. To your right,

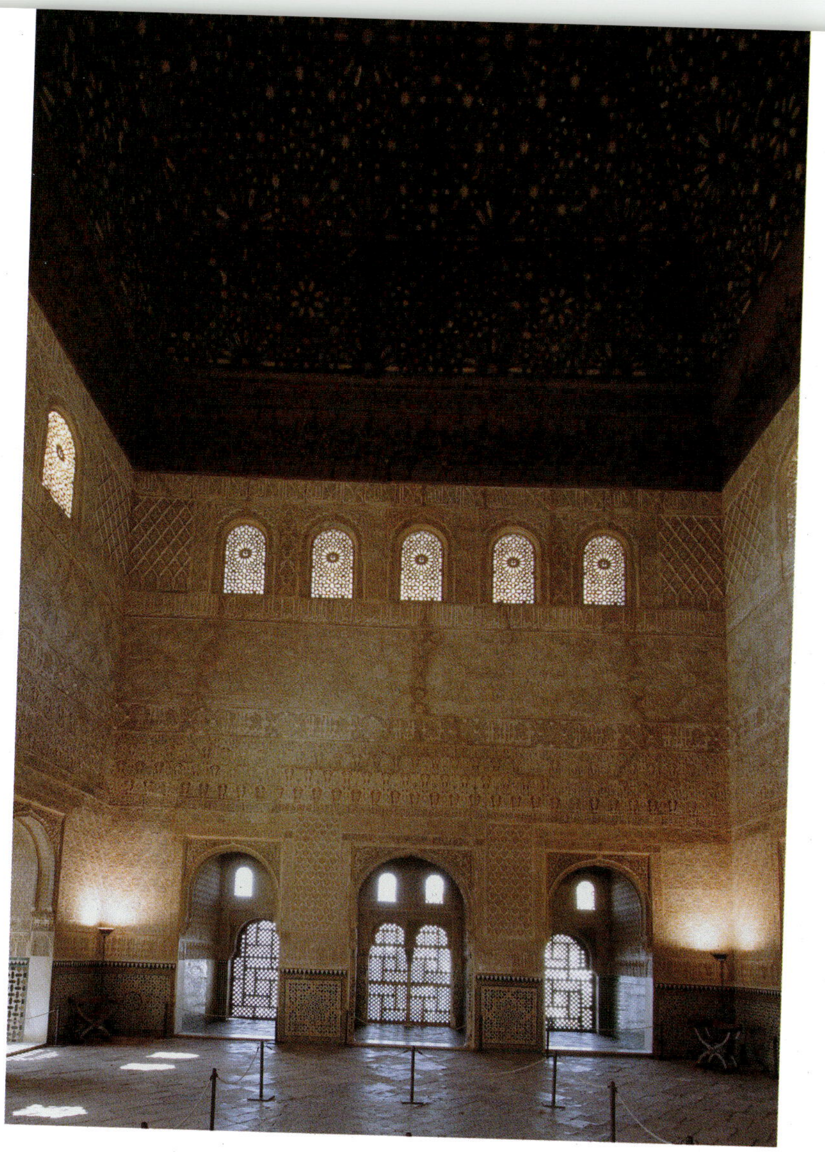

Salón de Comares

is a small oratory which is recognised as being one of the best-oriented towards Mecca in al-Andalus. Next, the thick wall has been chipped away to house two *tacas*, vaulted niches, and minute decoration dated from the reign of Yūsuf I, with inscriptions again referring to water.

When you enter the Salón de Comares, the throne room, the explosively coloured decoration startles you. The ground plan is square and the walls harbour three recesses on each side, that enable you to appreciate the great thickness of the wall itself. The central chamber on the north wall is the most elaborately decorated and where the sultan's throne would have be located, a hierarchical position that is

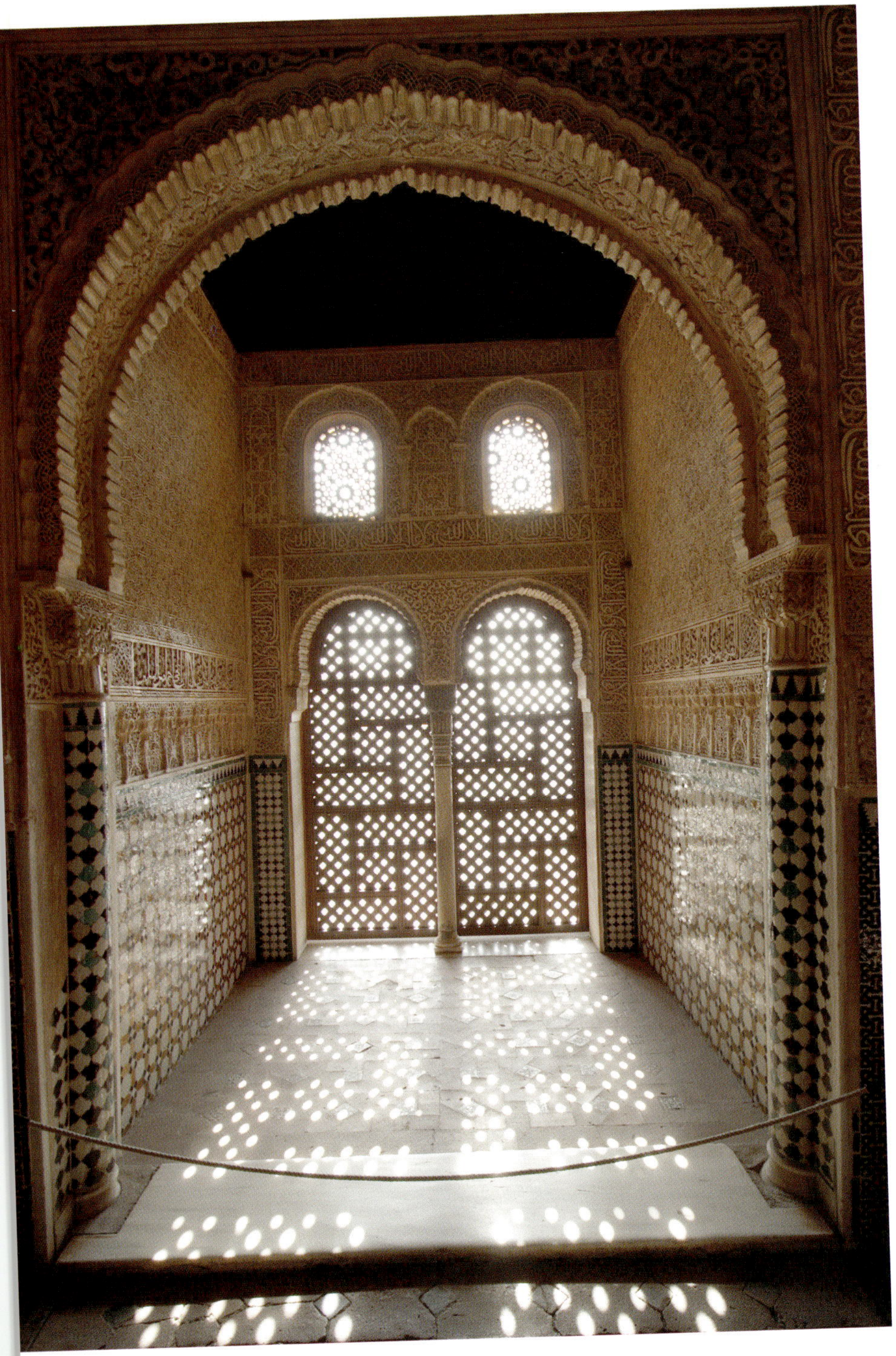

Alcove in the Salón de Comares

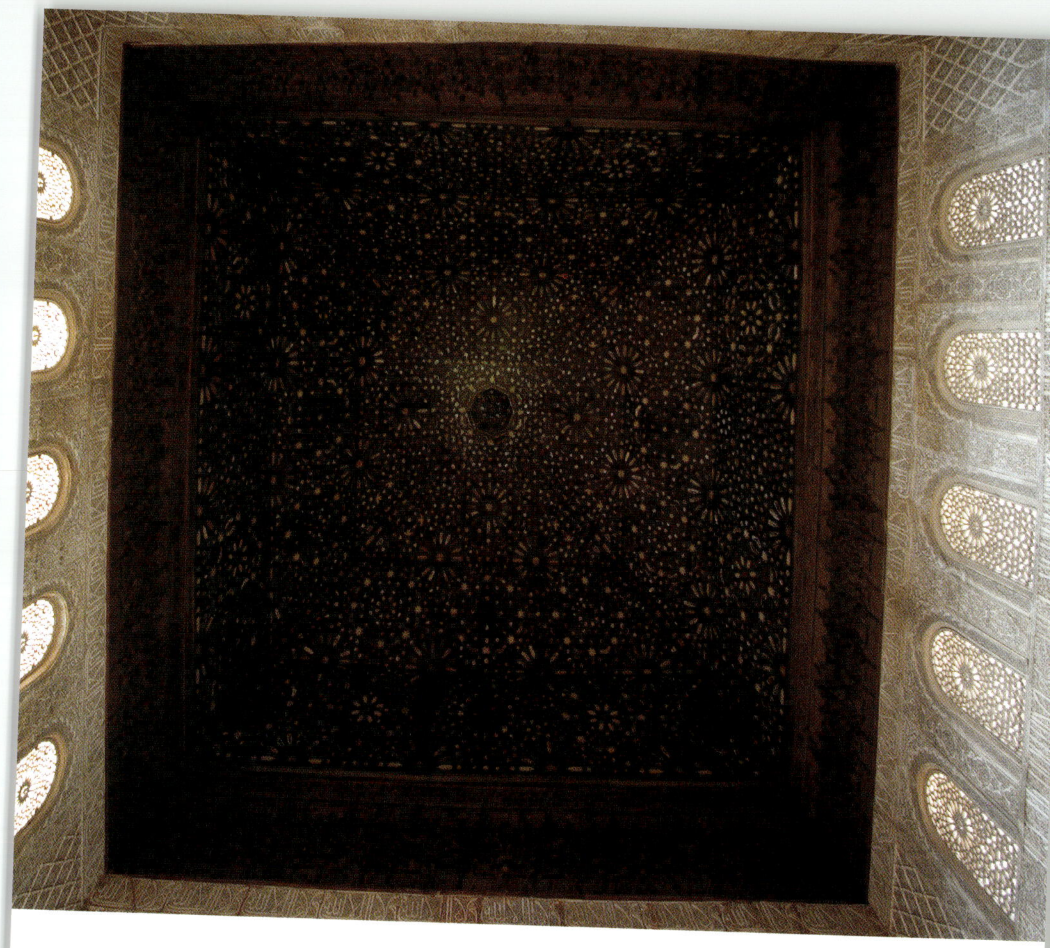

Ceiling of the Salón de Comares

recorded in the inscriptions. In the centre of the paving is a square made up of various pieces, both Nasrid and Christian, and without any pattern or Islamic design. This confirms these pieces were placed here in the Christian period, although we suspect the floor may originally have been tiled.

In the Salón de Comares, the entire dado, or *zócalo*, is tiled and tiles even cover the columns of the chamber as if it were a second skin. From the tiles up, as if it were a tapestry, stucco covers the space reaching up to the ceiling. If the stucco in the Sala de la Barca and the entrance arch to the Torreón de Comares refers to Muḥammad V, the stucco here refers to Yūsuf I. The tiled dado, stucco and ceiling, completely cover this space so that everything is decorated, showing a patent horror of empty spaces.

But, without a doubt, the most outstanding feature is the grand, magnificently-decorated ceiling; structurally complex, its symbolic meaning is even more so. The ceiling is square with four panels around the base. From right to left, there are another seven panels with an eighth in the central dome *mocárabes*. Similarly, from the dome or central *almizate* we find seven concentric rows of *ruedas de lazo*, the interlaced geometric star design, as a reference to the seven heavens of paradise, whereas the eighth would be the Throne of Allāh and the four limes in the corners, the trees of the Islamic paradise. A whole star-filled sky brimming with symbolism and colour as the ceiling is completely painting.

Under the ceiling we can read from the north a verse from the Koran:

> *Blessed be He whose hand holds sway! He, above all, is powerful.*
> *He who has created death and life to prove who among us is fitter. He is the almighty, the Indulgent One.*
> *He who created the seven heavens, one above the other... Look and see if you can find any flaws in the work of the Merciful One. Look again! Can you found any faults?*
> *Then, look again a couple of times, your sight will become tired and fatigued.*
> *We have adorned the heaven of this world with lamps, that we have placed like stones to stone the demons, for whom we have prepared the torment of fire.*
>
> (English version based on a translation from Arabic into Spanish by Darío Cabanelas)

Leaving the building and once again in the Patio de Comares, on the eastern side you walk past a door that formerly gave access to the Baño de Comares. Another more recent door, at the end of this side leads you through an entrance to the Palacio de los Leones.

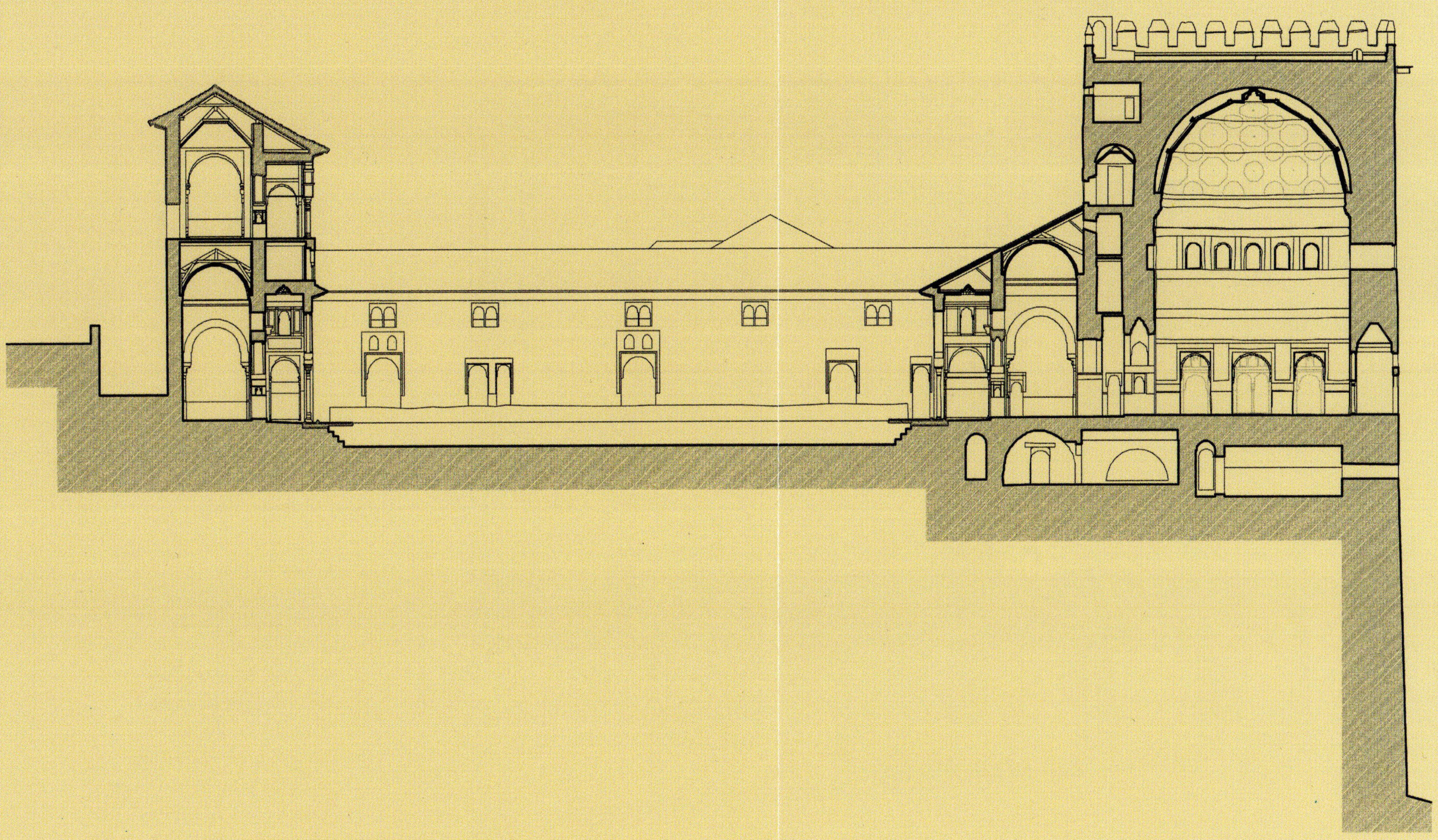

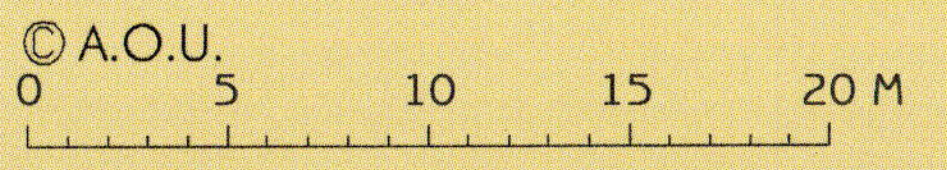

Palacio de Comares. North-South section: Hypothetical initial state (according to A. Orihuela Uzal, *Casas y Palacios Nazaríes. Siglos XIII-XV*, 1996, p. 97).

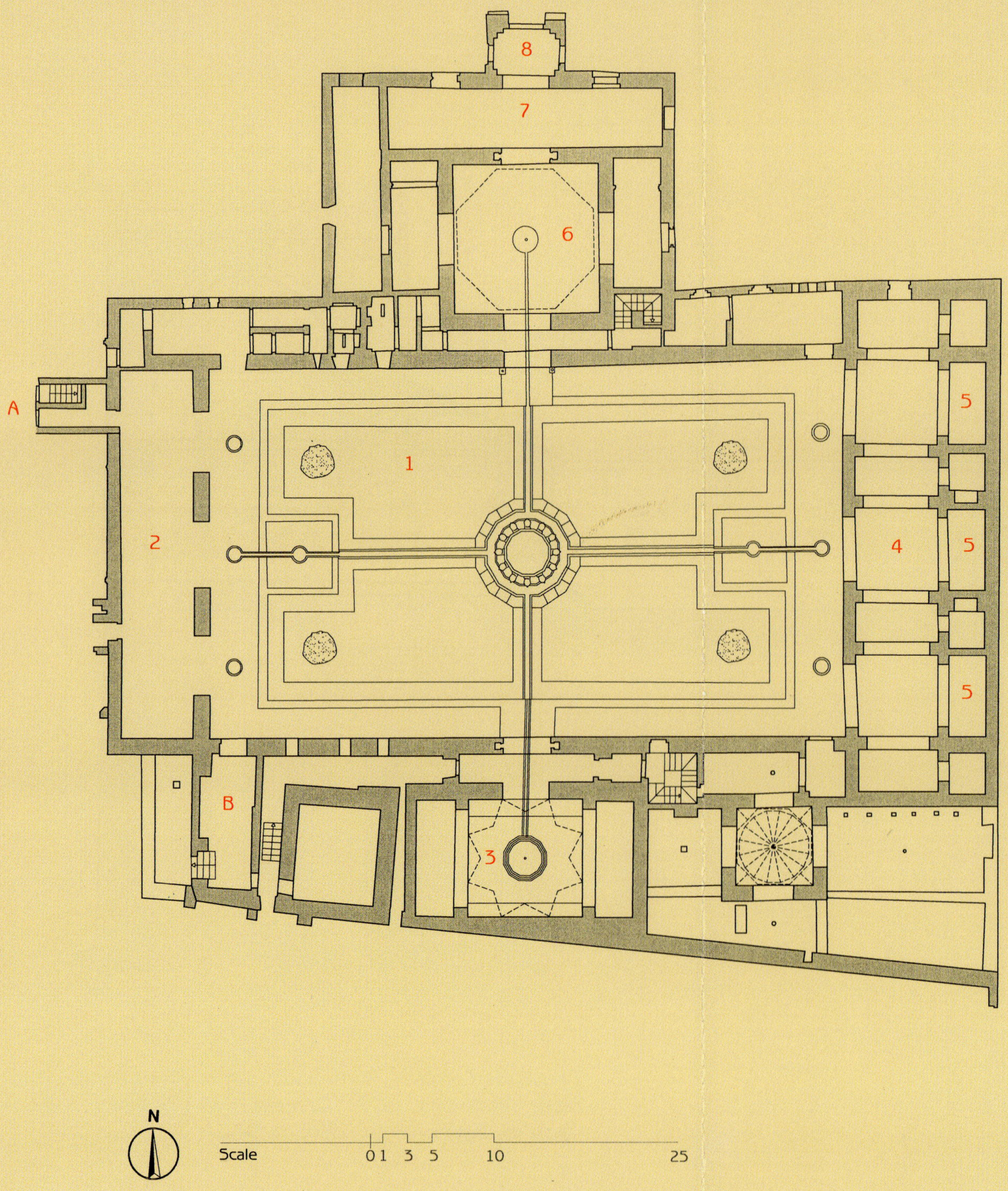

Patio de los Leones

A. Current access
B. Original access to the palace
1. Patio and Fuente de los Leones
2. Sala de Mocárabes
3. Sala de Abencerrajes
4. Sala de los Reyes
5. Alcove with paintings
6. Sala de Dos Hermanas
7. Sala de los Ajimeces
8. Mirador de Daraxa

Palacio de los Leones

Patio de los Leones

Name: Palacio de los Leones, although other possible names include the Palacio del Jardín (Qaṣr al-Riyāḍ) as before the palace was built, it seems there was a garden in this area. The term *riyāḍ*, which is actually the plural form of *rawḍa*, meaning garden, flower and fruit garden, was converted into a singular not only in the spoken language but also in writing, so, although it was a plural, it can be translated with the singular meaning of garden.

Sultanate: Muḥammad V (1354-1359; 1362-1391)

Note: The design of the palace is unusual in that it has a crossing, and is shaped like a cloister. The fountain of the Leones is remarkable.

Traditionally, writers have wanted to give a single view of the Nasrid palaces as a whole, suggesting the Palacio de Comares was a summer palace and the Palacio de los Leones was a winter palace, as it was more sheltered. Similarly, it has been said that Comares had more public functions in contrast to the greater privacy of the Palacio de los Leones. However, the Palacio de los Leones probably responds rather more to the wishes of Muḥammad V to build his own palace, having concluded his father's project for Comares. This view, that it is the palace erected by Muḥammad V as a residence for the sultan, is the most widely accepted hypothesis although other possible functions have been considered.

The architectural type is quite interesting as it show, as does the Palacio de Comares, the patio as an organizational element, but in this case it is a crossing, where two watercourses meet to form a cross and divide the patio in four parts. We do not really know what the four parts the patio is divided into would have looked like. Some authors suggest it was probably paved with marble or even tiled, others consider it may have been a garden.

Without doubt, it is an interesting example of the integration of architecture and water, as the Fuente de los Leones fountain, in the centre of the patio, distributes water all over the palace, making it a clear visual element of union between the patio and its sides. Thus, from the fountain spring forth four little channels

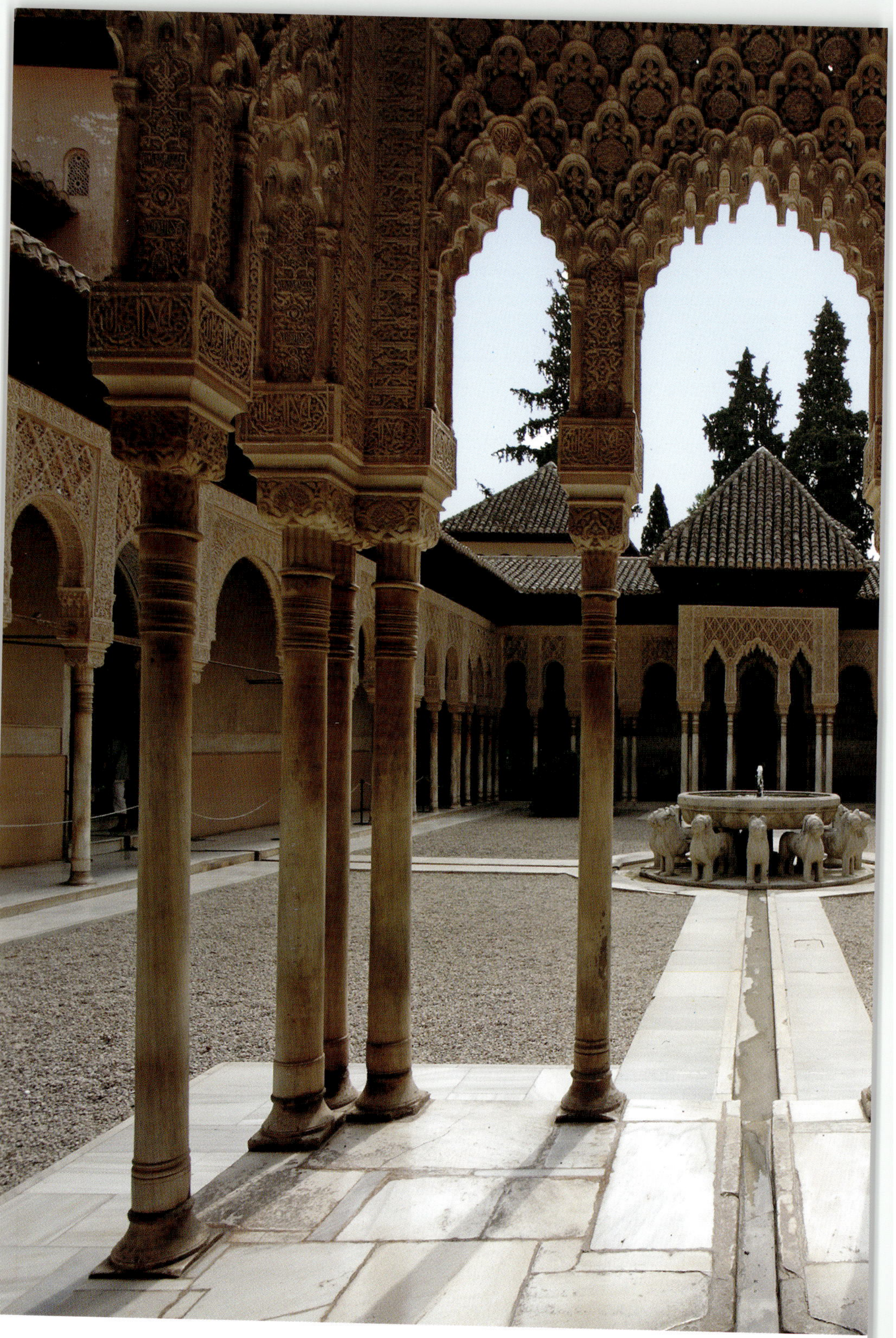

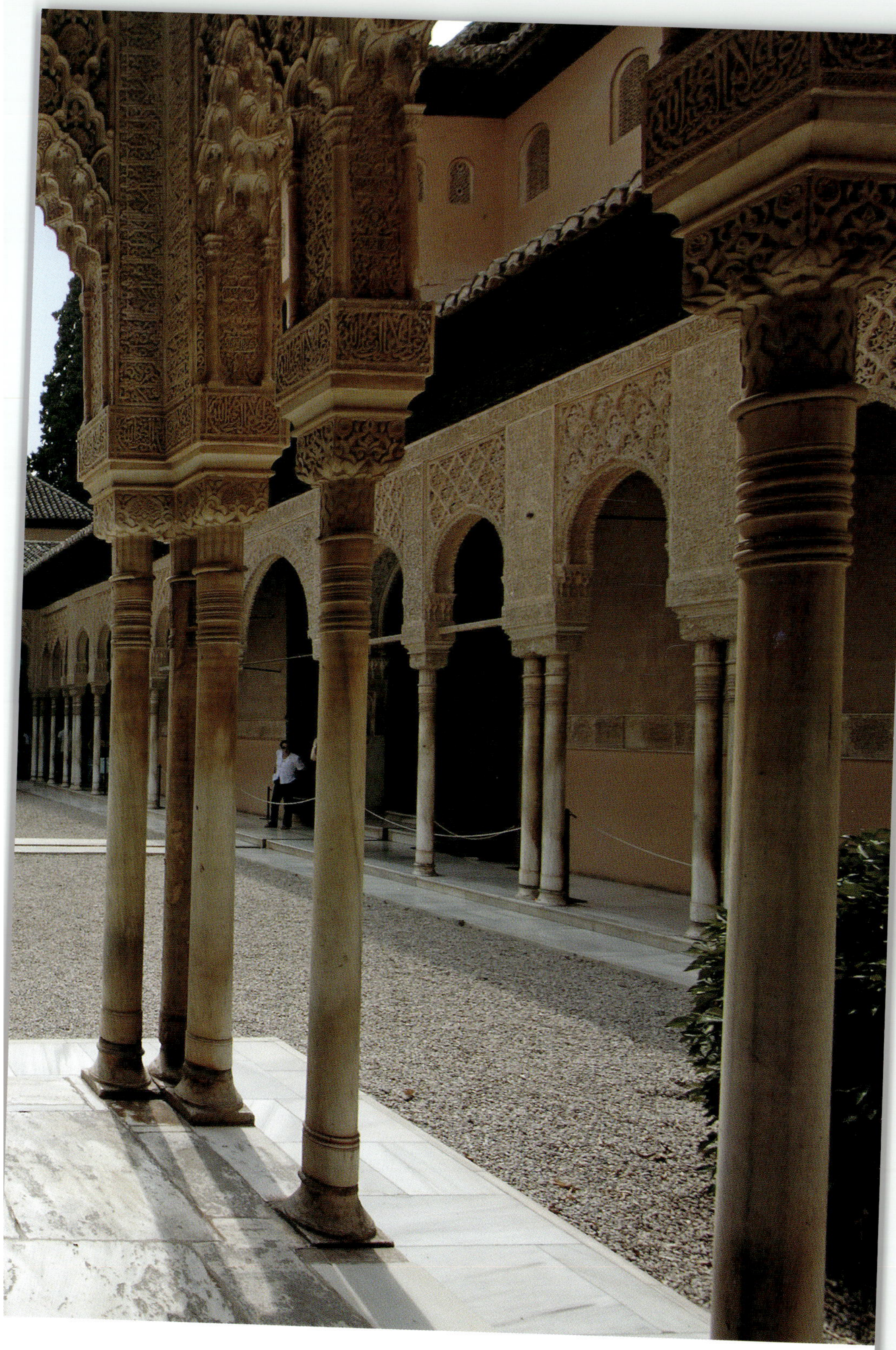

Palacio de los Leones

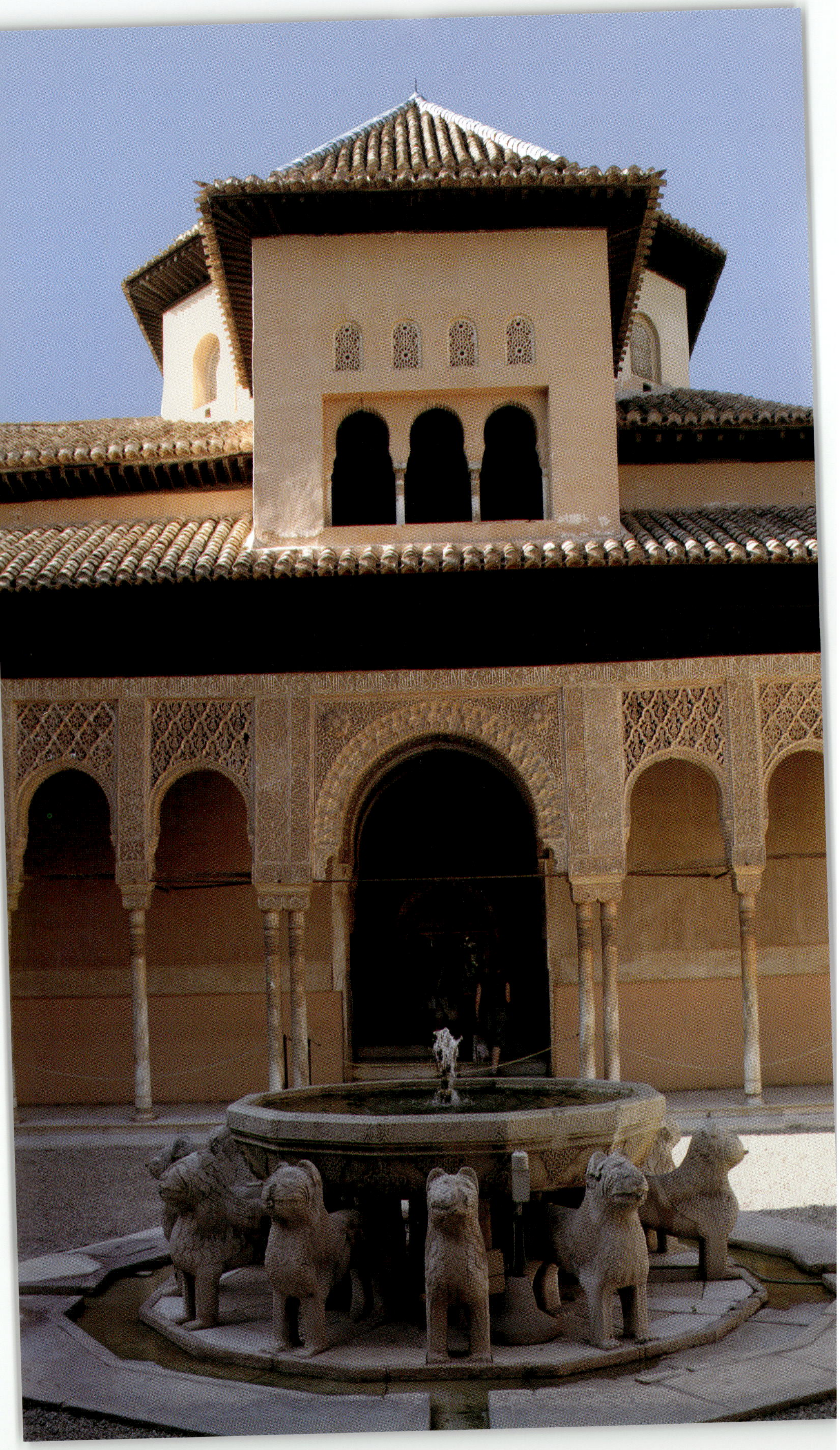

of water, which may symbolize the four rivers of paradise, each one advancing to one of the four sides of the patio, to return again to the fountain.

Around the patio are distributed the various rooms preceded by a gallery of columns reminiscent in shape of a Christian cloister. This possible Christian influence, along with that of the Marinid universities, makes it truly original in Islamic architecture. The gallery is made up of 124 Macael marble columns, displaying a great variety of decorative riches in the capitals. Columns stand both in isolation and in twos, threes and fours. The layout and number of columns has given rise to various studies of their possible symbolic value and purpose using highly complex mathematical calculations.

On the shorter sides of the patio stand two pavilions like oriental kiosks. Their restoration has caused a great deal of controversy as the eastern pavilion had a nineteenth-century glazed tile dome which was dismantled for it to be recovered with the current roofing in the first half of the twentieth century. In the western pavilion, in the stuccowork that gives onto the patio, you can appreciate Christian symbols like the two-headed eagle of Charles V, very subtly introduced into the Nasrid stucco to make the appropriation of the space visible. The outstanding feature in the centre of the patio is the Fuente de los Leones, after which the palace was named. According to tradition, the twelve marble lions, which originally were painted, may have come from an ancient, eleventh-century, Zirid palace built by the Jewish vizier Ibn Nagrela in the area of the current Alcazaba. Other writers reject this idea, dating the lions as sixteenth-century pieces. The dodecagonal basin that rests on the lions is fourteenth-century work and inscribed around its border is a poem by Ibn Zamrak explaining the symbolic meaning of the fountain. The verse tells that it is the sultan who has the gift of water – that is, the jet of water in the fountain – that he bestows on his royal guard – the lions. However, there have been many symbolic interpretations of the fountain. It has variously been associated with the twelve tribes of Israel, the twelve signs of the zodiac, or described as a sundial; other interpretations point to the traditionally symbolic nature of lions in union with power, force and justice, or suggest that they may in fact be six lions and six lionesses.

On the previous page: Palacio de los Leones with the Fuente de los Leones

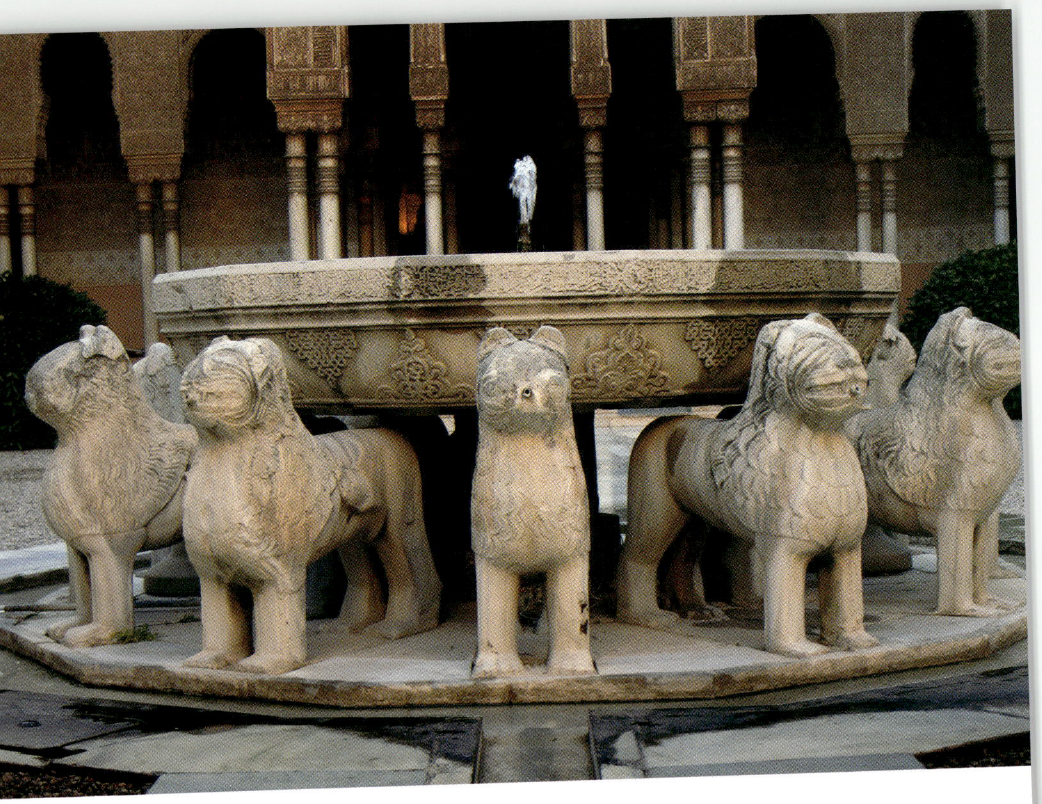

Fuente de los Leones. Around the edge of the fountain is a poem by Ibn Zamrak that explains its symbolic value:

May The One who granted the imam Muḥammad
with beautiful ideas to decorate his mansions be blessed.
For, are there not in this garden wonders
That God has made incomparable in their beauty,
and a sculpture of pearls with a transparent light,
the borders of which are trimmed with seed pearl?
Melted silver flows through the pearls,
To which it resembles in its pure, dawn beauty.
Apparently, water and marble seem as one,
Without letting us know which of them is flowing.
Don't you see how the water flows over from the basin
but its spouts hide it immediately?
It is a lover whose eyelids are brimming with tears,
tears that hide for fear of betrayal.
Is it not, in fact, like a white cloud
that pours its water channels on the lions
and seems like the hand of the caliph, who, in the morning,
grants favours to the lions of war?
Whoever gazes on the lions in a threatening attitude,
[knows that] sonly respect [for the Emir] holds back their anger
Oh descendent of the Ansares, and not through an indirect line,
heritage of nobility, who despises the fatuous:
May the peace of God be with you and may you live long and unscathed,
Multiplying your feasts and tormenting your enemies!

(English version based on a translation from Arabic into Spanish by Darío Cabanelas and Antonio Fernández Puertas)

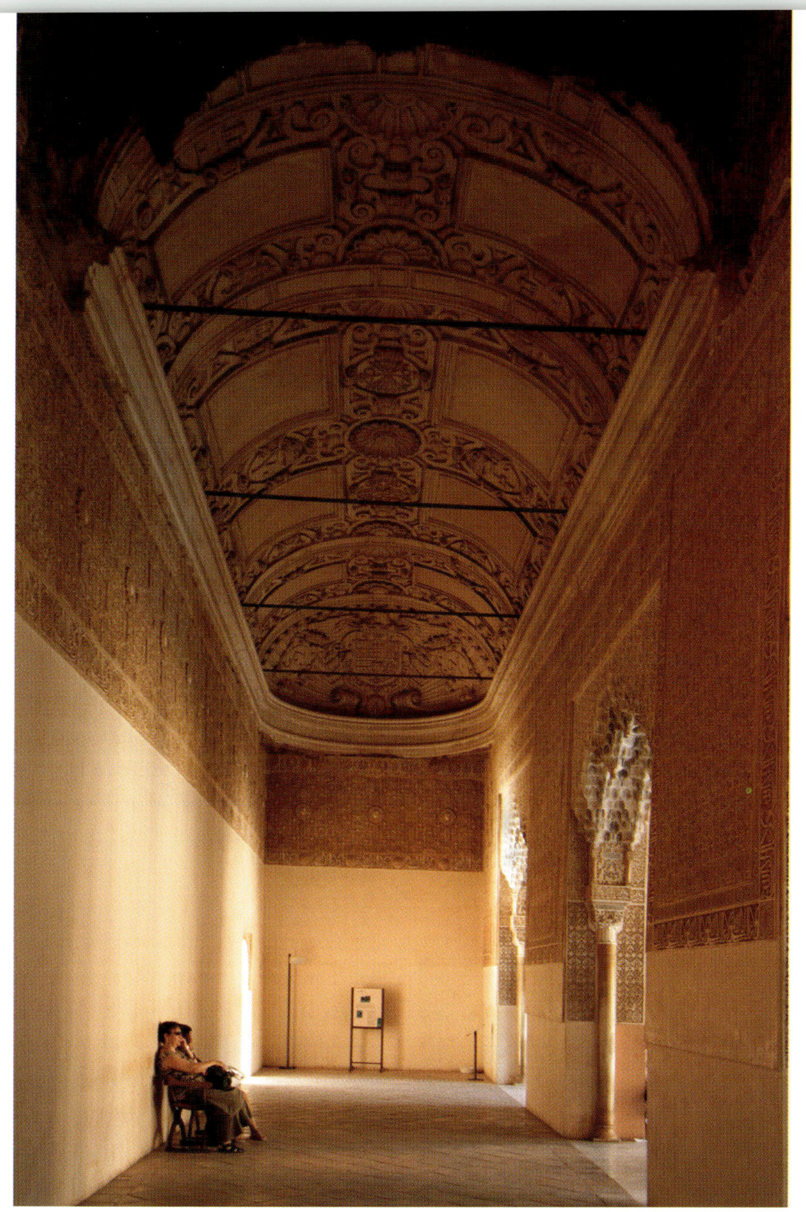

Sala de los Mocárabes

Sala de los Mocárabes

Name: Sala de Mocárabes
Date: 1350-1400
Sultanate: Muḥammad V (1354-1359; 1362-1391).
Note: The substitution of the original Nasrid vault for a seventeenth-century one.

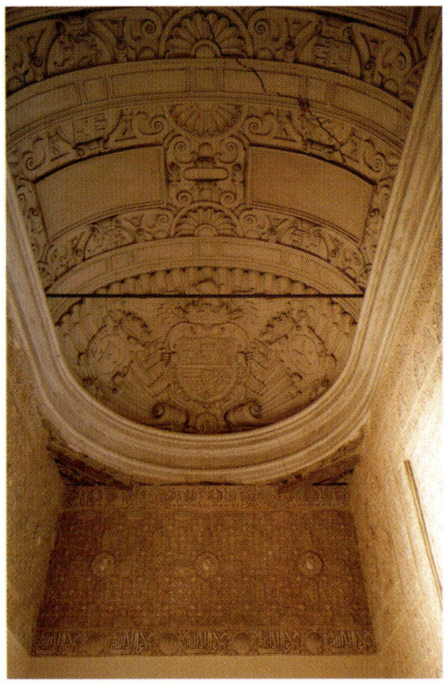

Detail of the late Renaissance vault of the Sala de Mocárabes

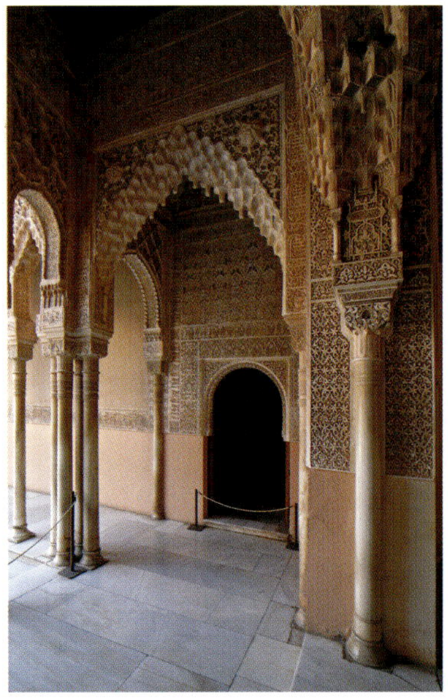

Original entrance to the Palacio de los Leones

The current link between the Palacio de Comares and the Palacio de los Leones corresponds to an intervention in the Christian period as in Nasrid times both palaces would have been independent. The original entrance to the Palacio de los Leones would have been located on the south-western side of the palace and, therefore, close to the Sala de los Mocárabes. This suggests it would probably fulfil the function of reception room, discounting its residential use given the absence of gates in the three large recesses that open onto the patio. This function of vestibule or reception room means that the decorative richness seem natural as the space is enhanced by the pavilion.

Originally all the room would be covered by a single, enormous, rich *mocárabe* vaulted ceiling of which little remains. These *mocárabe* roofs, instead of the traditional wooden structures, were a great novelty introduced by Muḥammad V or his architects. This one was damaged by the explosion of the arsenal located near to the church of San Pedro y San Pablo in 1590. When an estimate was made of the resulting damage, it was decided not to repair the vault but instead to replace it with a new one. The new covering over the Sala de Mocárabes was not planned along Nasrid lines, which had been so present in prior interventions in the Palacio de los

Leones, but according to the tastes of the period. It was not in their interest to emulate structures that had been developed in the palace but to replace what had been damaged with another vault choosing for this a plaster roof in the new artistic language of the late Renaissance. The symbols of the yoke and the arrow, that kept the memory of the Catholic Kings present, together with the shield of the Austrias, were introduced in the new vault.

Once you cross the Sala de Mocárabes, on your right you can see the original entrance to the palace straight ahead. Entry to the Palacio de los Leones was from the Calle Real Baja, giving access at the southwest corner of the palace.

Sala de Abencerrajes

Name: The Sala de Abencerrajes was given its name in the seventeenth century, after the members of the dynasty of the Abencerrajes who, legend has it, were assassinated here by order of the sultan Muḥammad IX.
Date: 1350-1400
Sultanate: Muḥammad V (1354-1359;1362-1391)
Note: The dome of *mocárabes* and impression of instability and spatial lightness, as well as the location of a fountain in an interior space.

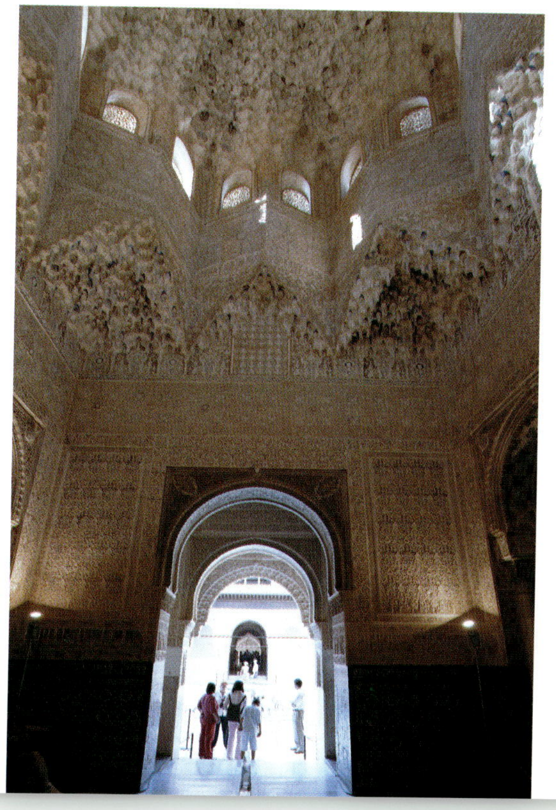

Sala de Abencerrajes

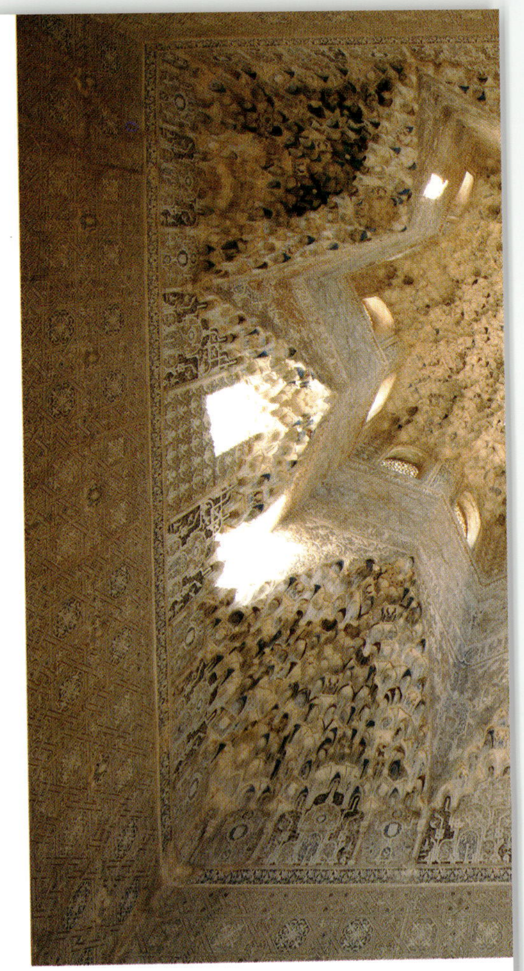

Like the rest of the rooms in the Alhambra, and specifically in the Nasrid palaces, the Sala de Abencerrajes could have been a multifunctional space, performing different functions at different times. Traditionally, it is said that feasts and banquets may have been held here, with the diners seated in the recesses at the sides.

Before you enter the hall, you should look at the admirable gates and you will immediately see two entrances, to the left and right, both closed to the public. The one on the right leads to the cistern, the *aljibe*, where a latrine may have been located; the one on the left takes you to an upper floor where you find the space known as the Harén.

The Sala de Abencerrajes is a more or less square-shaped space, with recessed alcoves in the side walls which you enter through beautiful arches with a variety of mouldings, and covered by a painted wooden roofing. Part of the room is occupied by a large, dodecagonal, marble fountain which was originally located nearer to the door, thus permitting a better use of the space in the room. All around the lower part are sixteenth-century

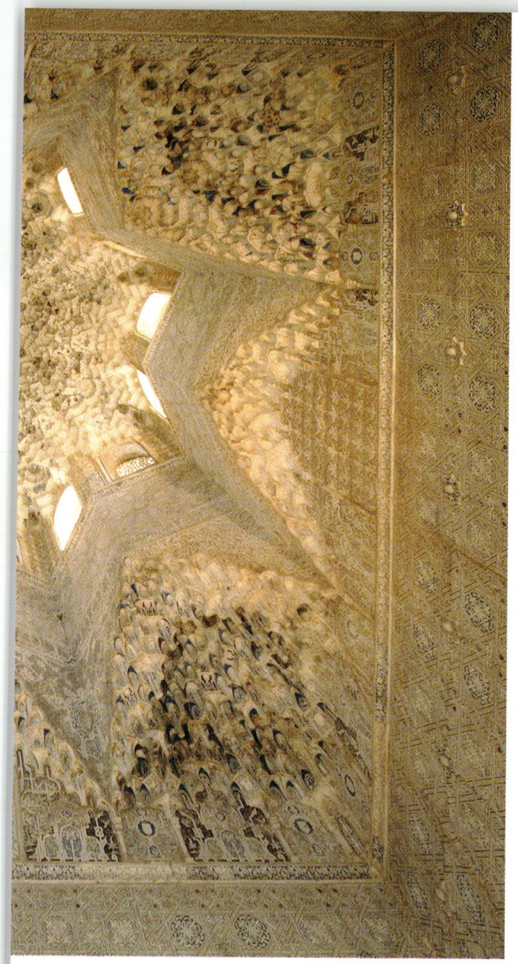

Dome of the Sala de Abencerrajes

azulejos de arista – coloured, decorative tiles – much of the stuccowork consists of modern replacements.

However, without a doubt what most forcefully attracts your attention is the immense dome of stucco *mocárabes* which covers this space. You move from a square-shaped floor in the lower part to a polygonal space in the upper part with the dome in the form of an eight-pointed star covering the room, thus moving away from the spherical roofing. This is a skylight dome, as the windows located in each one of the sixteen sides of the eight-pointed star, allow light to enter illuminating the room and at the same time creating beautiful games of light changing according to the time of day. The light comes into contact with the many facets or faces of each one of the *mocárabes*. Without a doubt, this small space encloses a handsome metaphor of the Universe, where the earthly lower floor is illuminated by the heavenly vault symbolically represented in this starry dome. To view this from below produces the illusory effect of an infinite, revolving heaven.

The "Harén"

Name: Traditionally known as the harén (*al-ḥarīm*) because some authors suggest it may have been a space reserved for women, although others believe it is simply a domestic space.
Date: 1350-1400
Sultanate: Muḥammad V (1354-1359;1362-1391)
Note: This is a clearly domestic space with the singular attraction of having a patio on the second floor.

The access to the east *harén* is located in the left-hand corridor that precedes the Sala de Abencerrajes. It is closed to the public in general partly because the layout and dimensions of the entry staircase do not favour the movement of the numbers of visitors who daily come to the Alhambra, but especially as it is one of the most difficult spaces to conserve among other reasons because of the paintings in the dado in the patio. It is opened to the public for programmed visits and for research.

Once you have climbed the staircases, you arrive at what is considered a clearly domestic space because of its layout and decoration. First, from here you can appreciate the outstanding viewing point over the Patio de los Leones, from where you have a visual command of the different rooms of the palace. But,

Detail of the tempera mural dadoes, *zócalos*, in the Patio del Harén, where geometric figures are represented in ochres and reds.

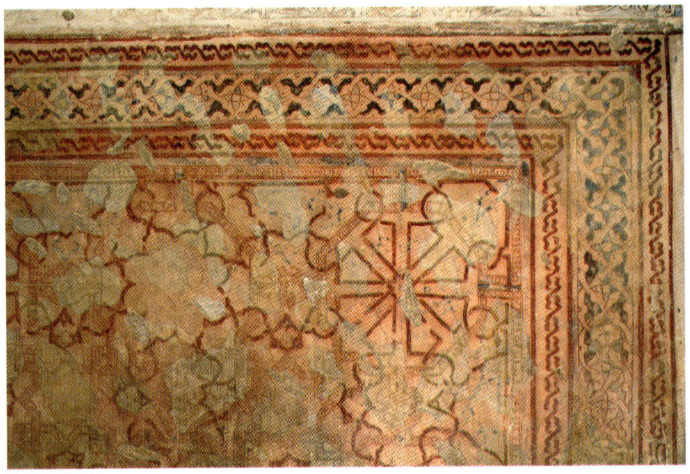

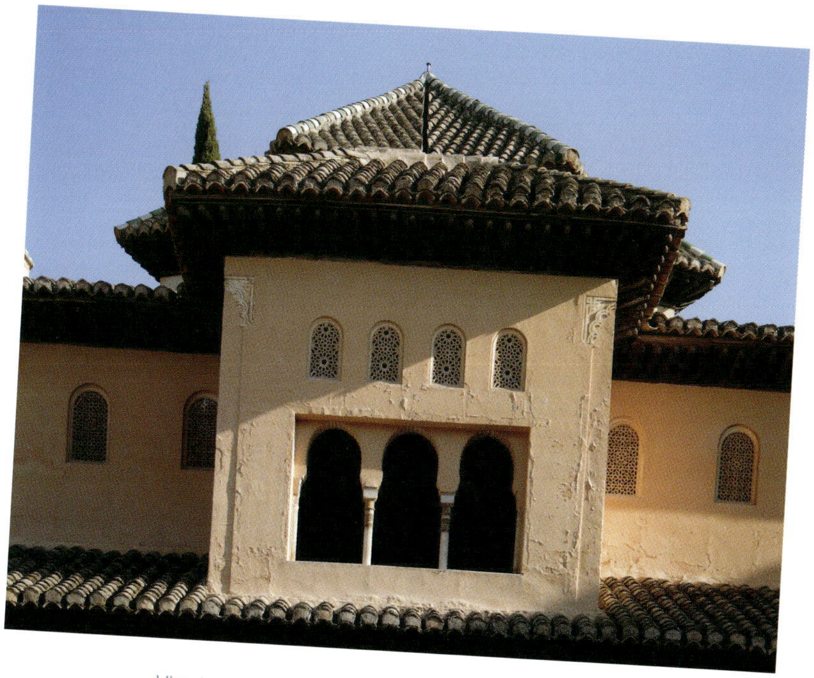

Viewing point of the Harén

without doubt, the most intimate and singular space is the patio itself, constructed on top of the cistern, and therefore functioning as an *impluvio*, an entrance for rainwater. Around this patio you find two spaces with porches; from the west porch you can see the original Islamic entrance to the Palacio de los Leones.

By comparison with the novelties in the rest of the Palacio de los Leones, this space has some archaisms. In the eastern porch you find an arcade of central columns with brick semi–pilasters at the sides, instead of the typical semi columns, and capitals of green dark, probably twelfth-century serpentine are reused in the central columns. And you even find apparent carelessness such as the uneven *alfiz*, the box shape around the central arch and the sides of the porches. Even the use of decorative paintings in the dado contrasts with that of the attractive tiling elsewhere; another detail confirming that, independently of whether or not we agree that this is a place reserved for women, it cannot be denied that it is a space with a clear domestic function.

In the Christian period, the Palacio de los Leones was one of those most appreciated by Charles V, with the Patio del Harén being used, according to the documentation, as the space where Count Henry of Nassau, counsellor to Charles V, slept.

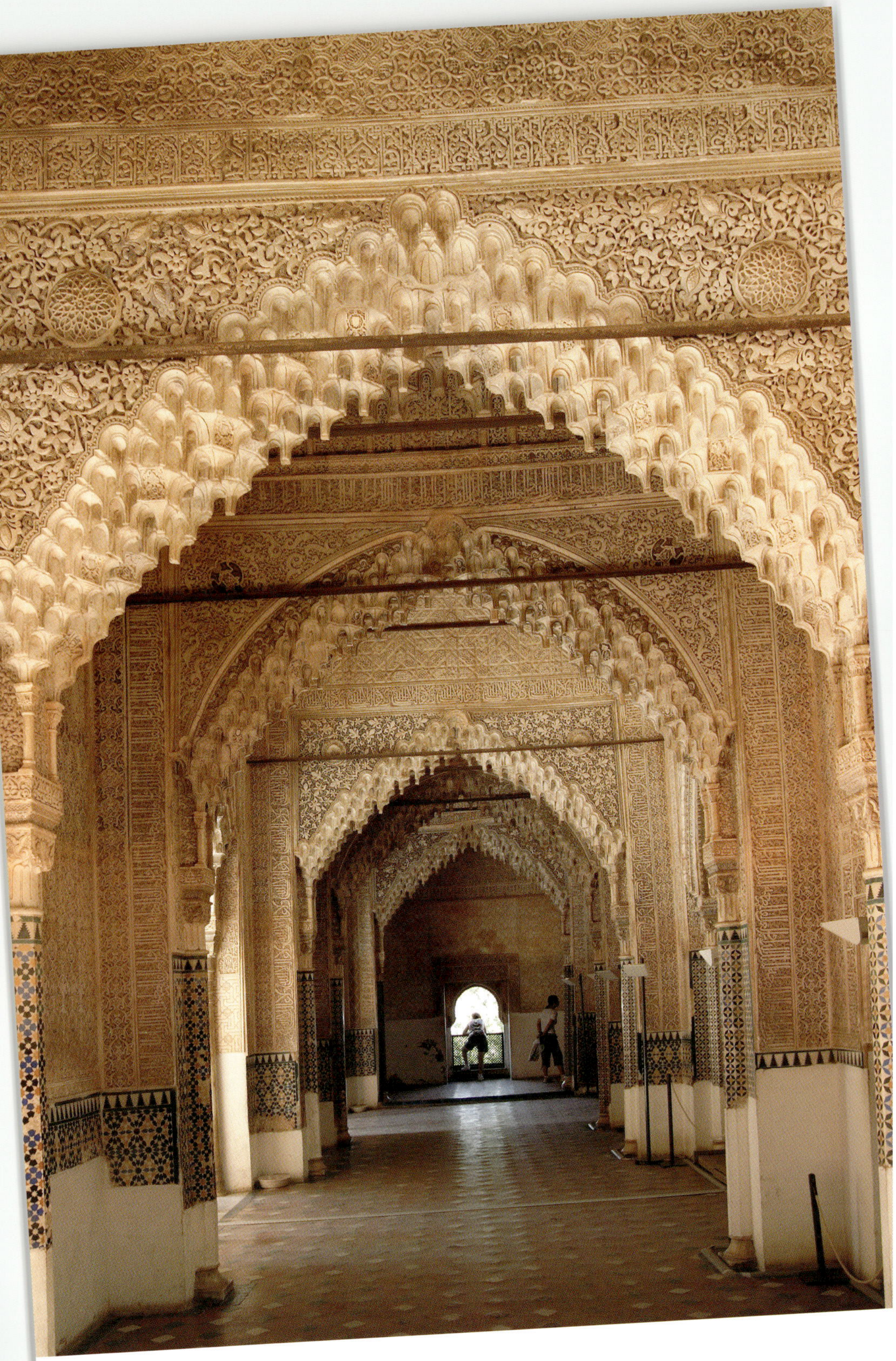

Sala de los Reyes

Sala de los Reyes

Name: Sala de los Reyes, named after the painting on the central ceiling vault in which the figures were interpreted to be kings of the Nasrid dynasty.
Date: 1350-1400
Sultanate: Muḥammad V (1354-1359;1362-1391)
Note: The highlights are the layout of three halls (or *qubbas*) and the paintings in the three vaulted ceilings.

The Sala de los Reyes is one of the most spectacular images of the Alhambra. The room is rectangular, like the Sala de Mocárabes with which it has a common boundary wall, but divided into three ports or *qubbas*, that open to the porch, alternating with the four rectangular areas that are closed on the side of the porch. The view of the room you gain from either of its extremities is of a succession of changing curtains. Its layout and the treatment of the arches recalls models found in Almohad mosques.

The internal division of the room is achieved through the use of *arcos de atajo*, arches that cut up the room perpendicularly. The intrados of the arches are lined with stalactite-like *mocárabes*, but the faces are entirely covered with stucco which some academics believe clearly shows the influence of Toledo due to its more fleshy, naturalist form. Christian symbols have been subtly included in the stucco, intermingling with Nasrid emblems. This occurs in the first *qubba* to the south-east where between the stucco of the arch that divides it from the following room in one of the circular foils you find the symbols of the yoke and the arrow inscribed; in another appears the motto "tanto monta", "we rule as equals", both from the period of the Catholic Kings.

The function of the Sala de los Reyes is unclear, as is usual in palace spaces in the Alhambra if we bear in mind the many uses that could be fulfilled by a single room. Rather than a residential use, it has frequently been suggested that its function was as a space for celebrations and banquets, so diners would be distributed around the three principle recesses while the tables of food would be located in the small corridors that separate the three rooms with vaulted ceilings. Others suggest they are small spaces reserved for maintenance. We do know something more of its function in the Christian period as documentation indicates the space was converted into a parish church while the new church of Santa María de la

Alhambra was being built at the end of the sixteenth century.

However, without a doubt, what most attracts our attention are the paintings in the three vaulted ceilings which, if we are to judge by the cladding, have been dated around 1380. The wooden vaults are covered with egg-based tempera paintings on leather. It is not clear who painted them, some believe the painting shows a clear Italian influence and have even gone so far as to point to Genoan or, rather, Gothic-Christian artists, because of the style and a mistaken idea that Muslims were forbidden from painting images. Others say these paintings were created by Mudéjar craftsmen who took advantage of the good relations between Muḥammad V, sultan of the Nasrid kingdom of Granada, and Peter "the Cruel" of Seville, by coming to the Nasrid court and creating these paintings.

Sala de Dos Hermanas

Name: The name Sala de Dos Hermanas or Sala de las Losas comes from the two large flagstones that constitute the floor of the room and that lie on either side of the small, low, central fountain. It was thought that this was a modern name, although, Ibn al-Jaṭīb referred to two sisters in one of his poems.
Date: 1350-1400
Sultanate: Muḥammad V (1354-1359;1362-1391)
Note: This space concentrates some of the most interesting creations in the Alhambra like the tiled dado, *zócalo*, the poem by Ibn Zamrak inscribed on the walls and, especially, the dome of stalactite-like *mocárabes*.

On the north side of the Palacio de los Leones you find the Sala de Dos Hermanas. The two large leaves of the monumental door to the hall were dismounted for their conservation and are currently to be found in the Museum of the Alhambra.

This space may have been the possible Mexuar of Muḥammad V when the Palacio de los Leones was under construction. An idea supported by a poem by Ibn al-Jaṭīb that was replaced by the current poem by Ibn Zamrak. You can see the poem inscribed on rectangular cartouches located in the corners of the hall above the handsome tiled dado. Other authors believe the hall was principally for residential use.

The Sala de Dos Hermanas is

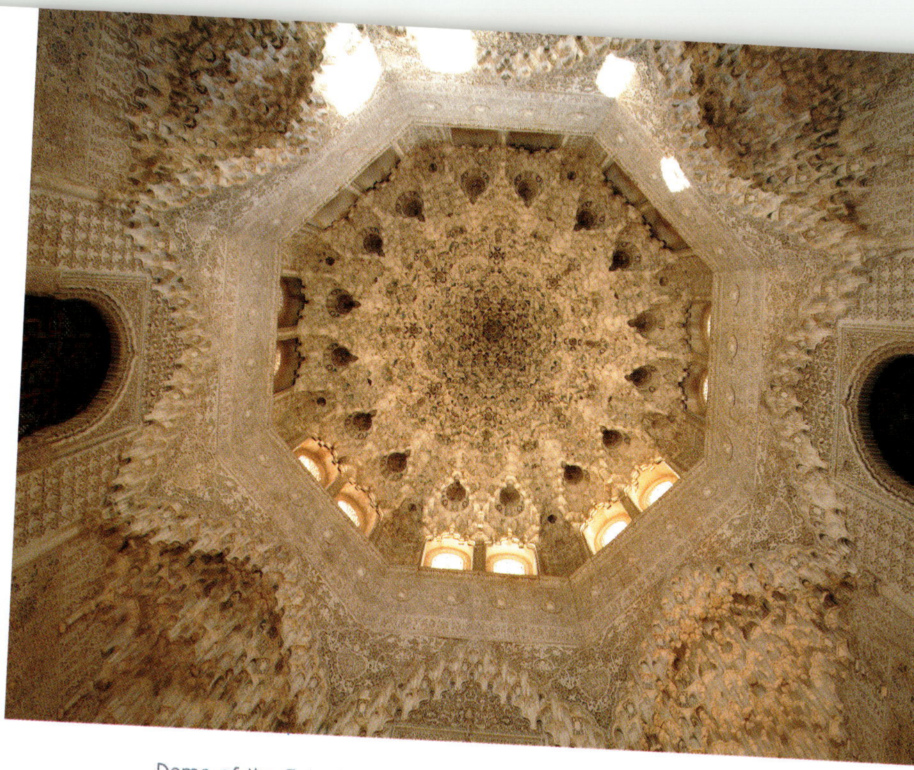

Dome of the Sala de Dos Hermanas

square-shaped and is preceded by a corridor which on the left-hand side takes you to a latrine, and on the right-hand side to the upper private rooms. This layout on a higher level recalls that of the neighbouring Sala de Abencerrajes. The highlight of these private rooms is a viewing point covered by a small wooden ceiling and open to the patio that can be appreciated from the Patio de los Leones. Unfortunately, the hall is closed to the public.

In the background, to the north of the Sala de Dos Hermanas, is the well-known Sala de los Ajimeces which precedes the Mirador de Lindaraja. To the east and west of the central hall are two roofed recesses. The one on the left was opened up under Christian rule to connect the Sala de Dos Hermanas with the rooms of Charles V, as the new Christian rooms sought to integrate the spaces with the Palacio de los Leones. In sharp contrast with this integration of spaces, is the artistic rupture with Nasrid aesthetics, perceptible when you enter the new rooms of Charles V.

Doubtless, though, your attention will be caught by the grandiose, octagonal dome of *mocárabes* that covers the square floor of the hall. The dome is considered one of the best in western Islam and some authors have pointed out that it consists of more than 5000 prisms to configure the beautiful original *mocárabes* apparently hanging from it. The inscriptions reveal its cosmic meaning, as a kind of night-time view of the constellation of the

Pleiades. It makes a worthy comparison and counterpoint to the dome over the Salón de Comares:

I am the garden that Beauty adorns:
See it, it alone, will explain to you my rank.
For Moḥámmed, my imām, on a par I place myself
with the best that may be or may have been.
Sublime is the mansion, because Fortune
ordered it should surpass all other houses.
What delight it offers to our eyes!
Always new is here the desire of the noble.
The Pleiades of night here seek asylum;
from here the mild zephyr, to the dawn, rises up.
Unequalled, a radiant dome is in it
with charms, patent and hidden.

(Fragment of the poem. English version based on a translation from Arabic into Spanish by Emilio García Gómez)

Sala de los Ajimeces and Mirador de Lindaraja

Name: The Sala de los Ajimeces may have received this name due to the *ajimeces*, the parts of the wooden balconies closed off by window screens the windows must have had, that juts out from the wall. The viewing point, or *mirador*, is known either as the Mirador de Lindaraja or Mirador de Daraxa, the Castilian adaptation of the Arabic *'ayn dār* 'Ā'iša or "Eye of the house of 'Ā'iša.

Date: 1350-1400

Sultanate: Muḥammad V (1354-1359; 1362-1391)

Note: The view you could have enjoyed from here before the construction of Charles V's appartments must have been spectacular. It is worth stopping to admire the tiling in the Mirador de Lindaraja and the original wooden and glass roofing.

From the north of the Sala de Dos Hermanas and through a large arch you pass into the Sala de los Ajimeces. The east hall is covered with stucco except for the lower third where the walls are bare, without tiles, and would probably have been covered with textiles. The vaulted *mocárabe* ceiling, with interventions from the Christian period, must be similar to the one that was in the Sala de Mocárabes.

What is undoubtedly most interesting about this space, however, is the opening that protrudes out halfway along its northern side. From here, the Mirador de Lindaraja, in Nasrid times you could glimpse some unbeatable views of the River Darro valley and of the walls of the Albaicín but these were blinded with the construction of the rooms of Charles V, giving way to the garden or closed Patio de Lindaraja.

The viewing point, it has been suggested, could have been the space occupied by the sultan's throne, if you accept the idea that the Sala de Dos Hermanas was the Mexuar. But there can be

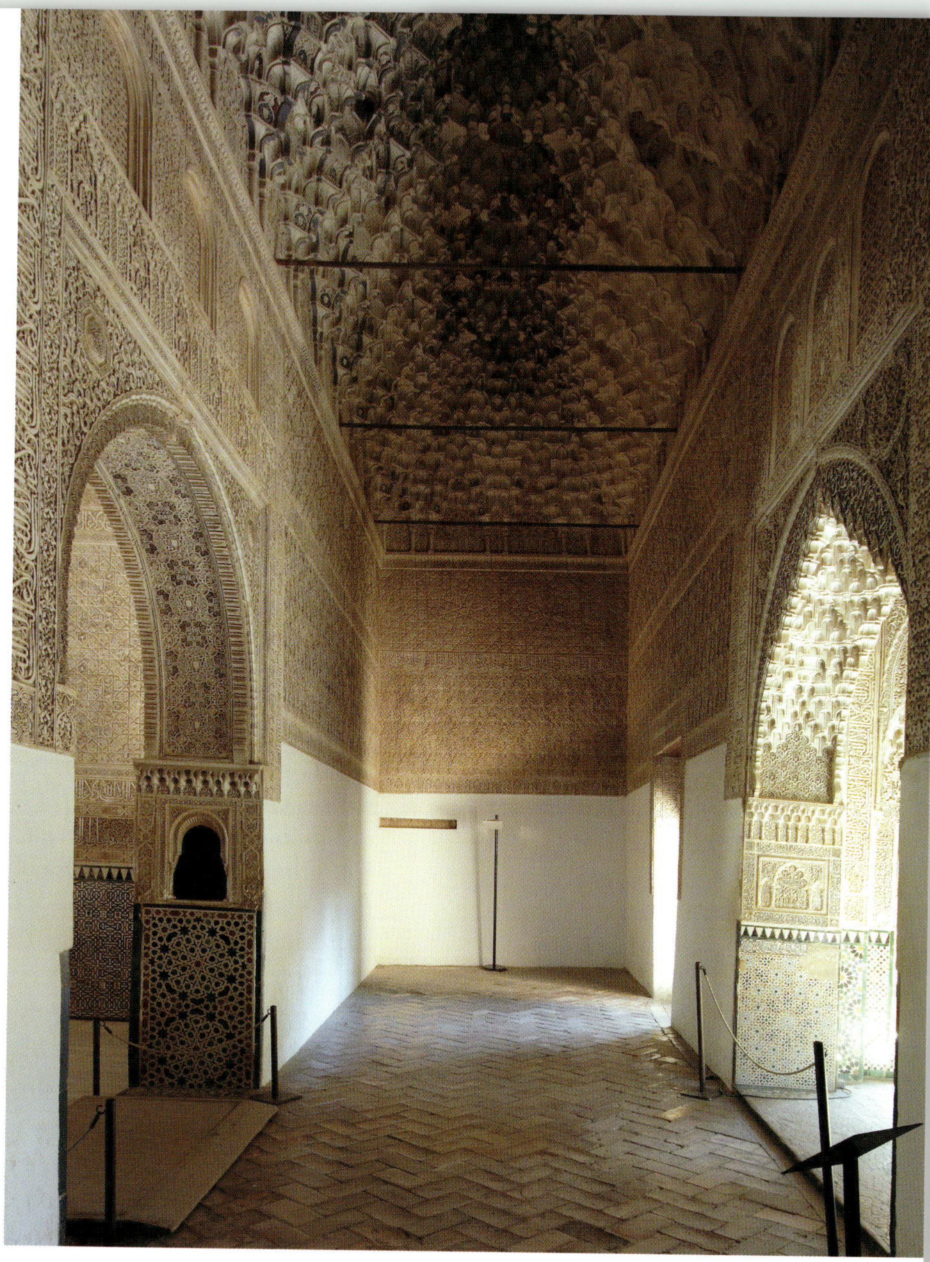

Sala de los Ajimeces

no doubt about its function as a viewing point, which the very design suggests. It is a square-shaped space that opens out with a pair of matching windows in each of the three outer sides, with a very low windowsill or lower ledge, in order to enjoy the views while seated on the floor.

The viewing point concentrates in one space much of the decoration in the entire Palacio de los Leones, so it should not seem strange that it was one of

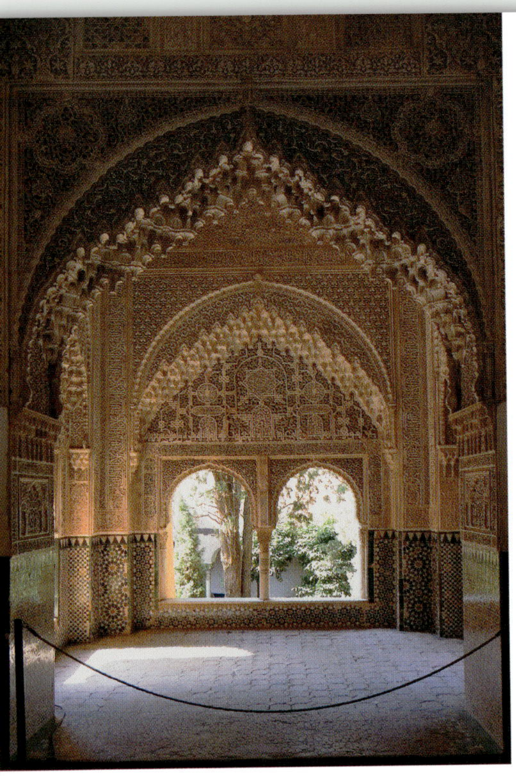

the places preferred in the times of Charles V. The roof consists of a false structure of coloured glass with a wooden frame or shell. The light that penetrates through the coloured glass proceeds from small windows between the glass structure and a more resistant upper ceiling. Although some of the glass has later been replaced there is no doubt that the glass ceiling dates from the Nasrid period, as the inscription confirms.

In the entrance to the Mirador de Lindaraja you find some of the most beautiful, original tiles in all the Alhambra. The reduced size of the pieces that form the geometric pattern imply it is technically more difficult to create. Even the inscription in praise of the sultan is made from cut-out pieces of ceramic.

Mirador de Lindaraja

Coloured glass ceiling in the Mirador de Lindaraja

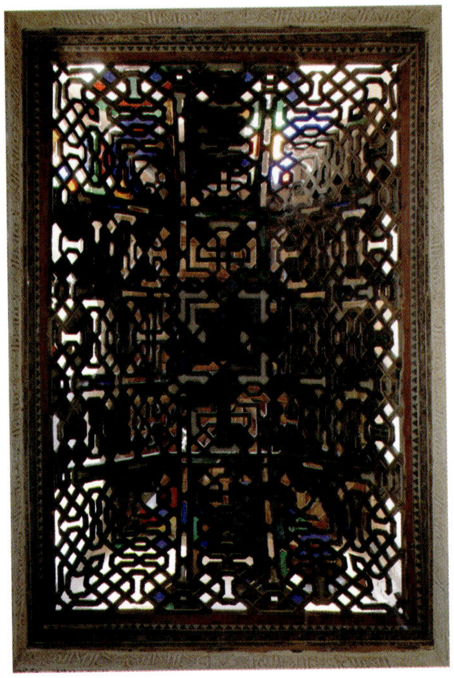

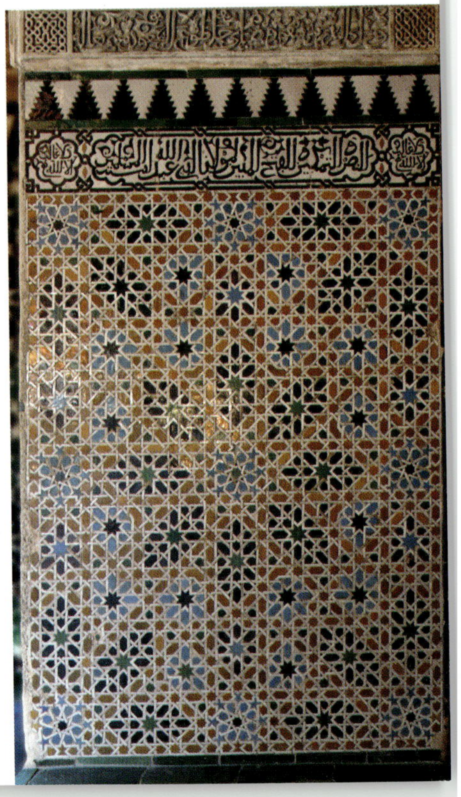

Tiling in the doorjambs of the entrance to the Mirador de Lindaraja

The Emperor's rooms

Name: Six rooms built during the reign of the Emperor Charles V receive this name; in 1829, the rooms on the north side were occupied by the American writer Washington Irving, author of the famous *Tales of the Alhambra*.
Date: 1528-1537
Monarchy: Charles V (1516-1556)
Note: The contrast in architectural and ornamental concept with respect to the Nasrid palaces. The beautiful wooden, coffered ceilings, chimneys and pictorial decorations are outstanding.

The name rooms or "chambers" of Charles V is given to a series of rooms built between 1528 and 1537 in the two bays they occupy, alongside the Palacio de los Leones, the Patio or Garden of Lindaraja on one side and the Patio de la Reja on the other. Both patios represent the Christian concept in this type of open interior space, the first is clearly cloistral; the second, more intimate and special. This intervention transformed a piece of unbuilt land behind the two Nasrid palaces, Comares and de los Leones. Under Muslim rule, it seems the land was put to military use, but soon after the conquest it was destined for residential purposes. Still, in the times of Charles V, the Patio de la Reja was called a "meadow", but on the eastern side the current slightly pointed arches of the lower gallery denote the intervention, documented in the years immediately following the fall of Granada.

It was, then, above this gallery that the series of chambers for the Emperor began, prior to starting work on the Renaissance palace, in the hope that he would return to Granada shortly and thus be able to resolve the serious problem of accommodation for the Court that existed in 1526. To do so, a corridor was opened up from a side chamber of the Sala de Dos Hermanas using the space of a window, converted into a door, and then running around the limits of the Baño de Comares, where we will halt again further on. As you advance along the corridor, on your left you see the upper chambers of "the beds", especially the chamber that may have belonged to the keeper of the baths, where you can admire the wooden ceiling. This closeting of the only baths to have endured, surrounded by modern rooms, is significant as it was used by the Emperor himself, who had a bath tub installed for him to immerse himself in, as was the fashion in refined Roman society of his time. After this view of the bath you are led out into the first of the rooms.

The first room is the most spacious of the six that form the complex. Today, with no decoration other than the chimney, you find here an outstanding relief of birds metamorphosed into plants and a winged head, all identified with the fantastic sculptures of the circle of the Renaissance sculptor and architect Diego de Siloé. Of greatest interest is the ceiling of wide Italianate caissons, ornamental panels sunken in the ceiling, which feature repetitions of the imperial motto PLUS OULTRE, adopted at this time, and the anagram K and Y (K for Charles and Y for Isabel). A rigorously classical inscription runs around the frieze in the room: IMPERATOR CAESAR KAROLUS V HISPANIARUM REX SEMPER AUGUSTUS PIUS FOELIX INVICTISSIMUS (Emperor Caesar Charles V King of Hispania Always August Pius Happy Undefeated) which has given rise to the view that this chamber was used exclusively by the Emperor for public acts.

The link with the adjoining hall is through a door set in one side of the wall and in line with the entrance, as is common in Renaissance palaces, but it also had a passage, later lost, in the same corner, that connected it directly with another room in the north bay, without having to pass through the first adjacent room that functioned as a kind of junction. The square-shaped hall is also covered with a Renaissance wooden ceiling and Doric frieze. The series of rooms in the north bay is known generically as "Washington Irving's Rooms", because the famous North American writer and diplomat lived in them. They are also known as the Salas de las Frutas, Halls of the Fruit, in reference to the painted decoration used in the last two rooms. These rooms are generally closed although they are opened for scientific visits or as the "space of the month".

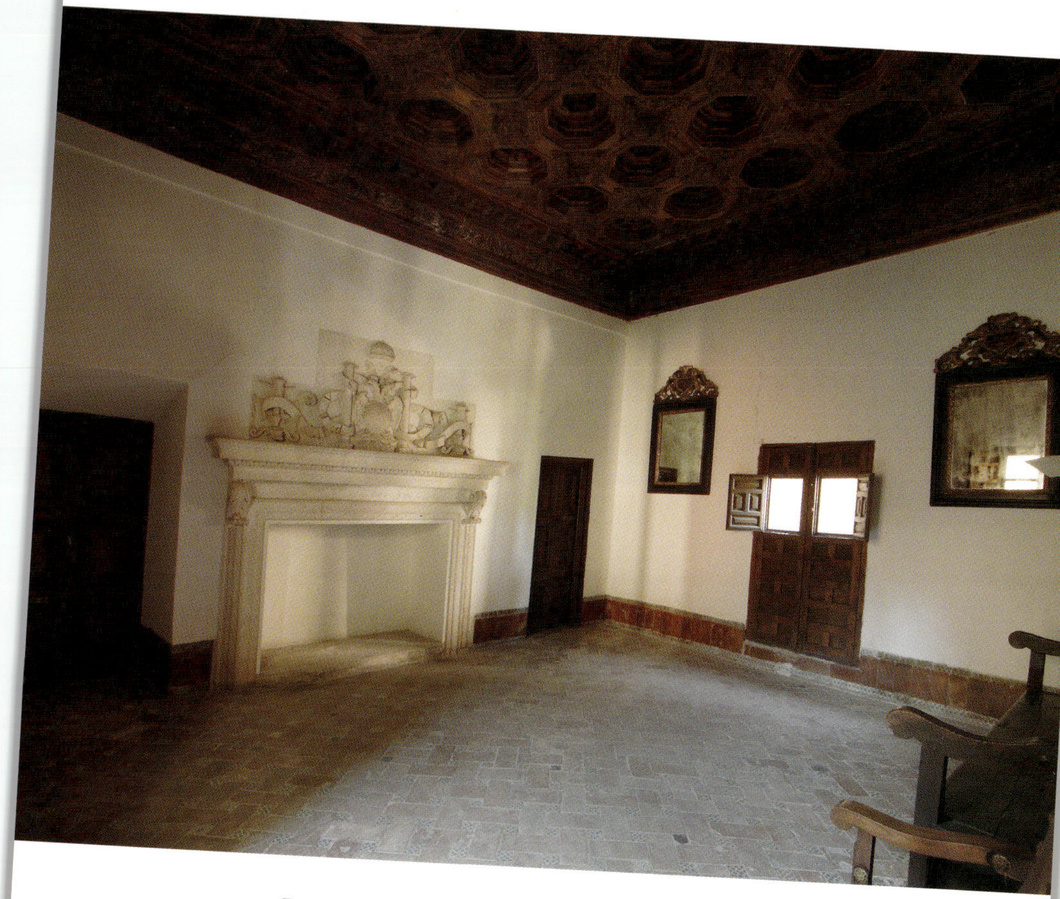

Perhaps this was Charles V's bed chamber. (It is traditionally known as one of Washington Irving's rooms.)

The first, a four-sided room, is identified as a chamber and also as a royal bed chamber, connected in principle by the passageway that we mentioned earlier for strictly private use. Here the outstanding ornamental chimney gives meaning to the space accompanied as it is by the imperial shield and a two-headed eagle holding up the globe of the Earth in a very clear demonstration of the overseas possessions of Spain and Portugal, by the columns of Hercules and the motto PLUS OULTRE, together with two winches with a thick, coiled rope, referring to the Emperor's domination of the seas, enhanced by his marriage to Isabel of Portugal. Also outstanding is the ceiling of hexagonal caissons with several ornamental motifs in the interior. The second room, conventionally identified as "the Empress's bed chamber" possesses another valuable wooden ceiling that displays star-

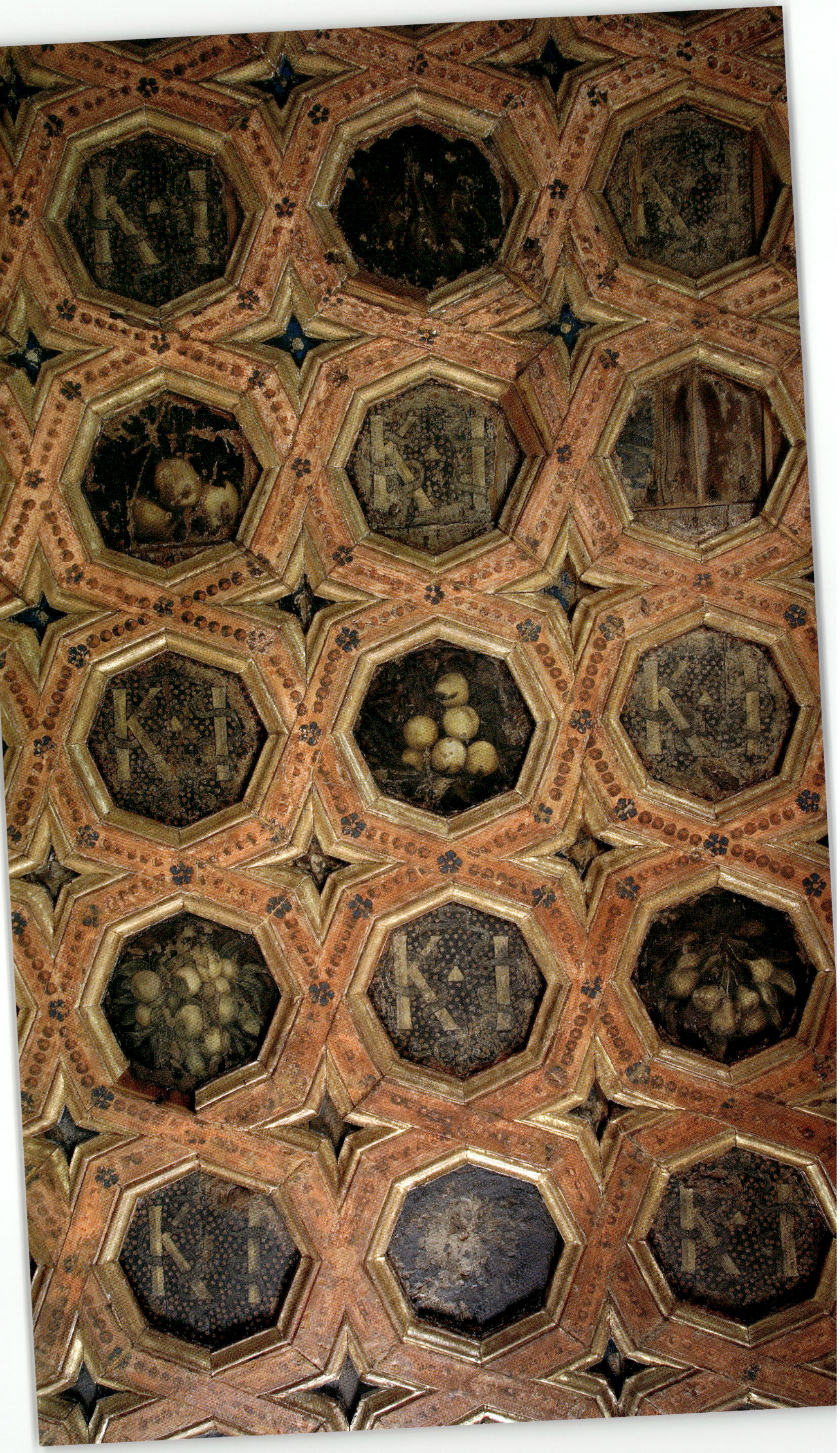

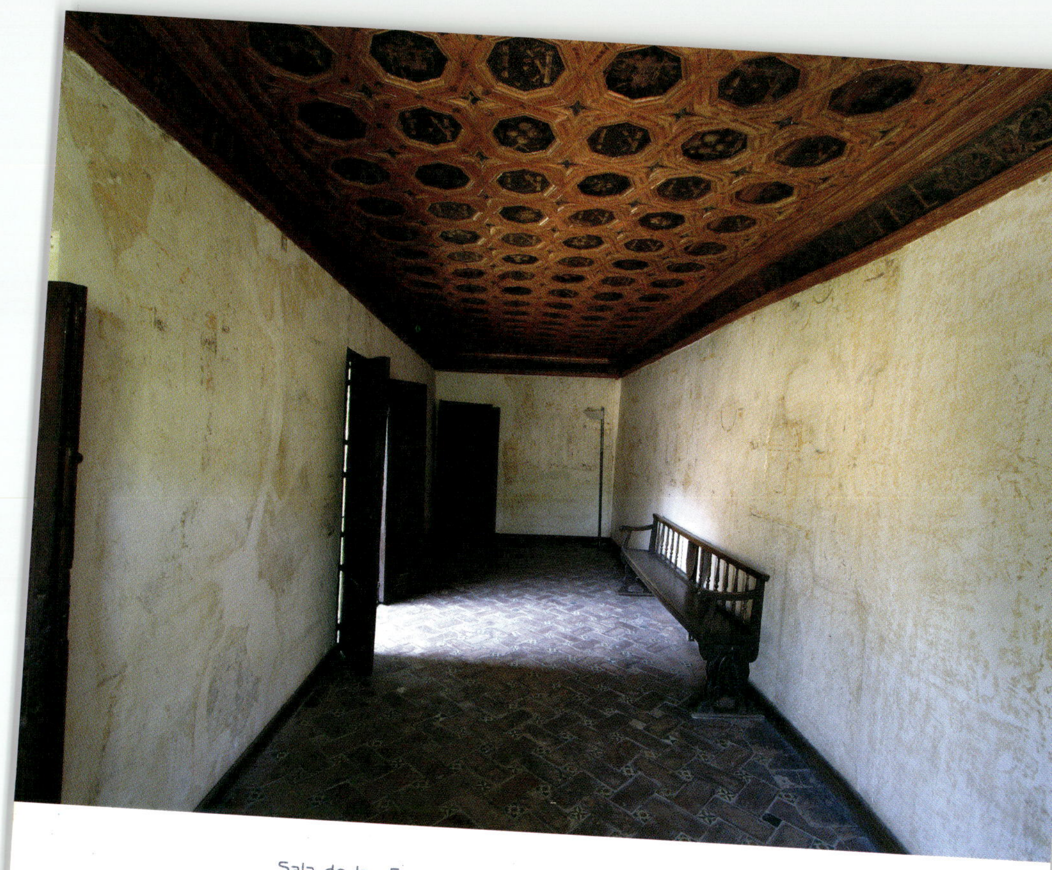

Sala de las Frutas

like and hexagonal shapes. The wooden frieze that runs below the ceiling alternates the emblems of the PLUS OULTRE and the winch, the latter motif clearly ascribable to the Portuguese royal house.

Two long, narrow rooms with lower ceilings follow these. The most attractive thing about them are the ceilings of flat hexagonal caissons with the background filled with bunches of fruit, which alternate with others that display the "K" and "I" anagram joined by interlaced ribbons. Some writers say that the letter "I" refers to Isabel of Burgundy, while others consider it should be interpreted as "Imperator". Moreover, the last of these rooms conserves remains of decorative painted murals with grotesques and Roman-style chandeliers introduced to the Alhambra by painters in the circle of Rafael, Julio Aquilis and Alejandro Mayner, who painted the chamber in 1537. From this point there are connections with the upper gallery that closes off the Patio de Lindaraja on the eastern side, via a gallery of lowered arches.

Previous page, a detail of the ceiling in one of the Salas de las Frutas.

Peinador de la Reina

Name: This has been identified as the Tower of Abū l-Ḥaŷŷāŷ, but in the Christian period the upper part of the tower came to be known as the Peinador de la Reina.
Date: 14th-16th cent.
Sultanate and Monarchy: Yūsuf I (1333-1354), Muḥammad V (1354-1359;1362-1391); Muḥammad VII (1392-1408); Charles V (1516-1556)
Note: In Islamic times this was a pavilion for recreation or meditation; under Christian rule, the upper part became a private chamber to which the king could withdraw. One of the most original structures in the Nasrid Alhambra, it was initially isolated and dominated its surroundings. The sixteenth-century conversion into a private chamber and the decoration of the upper floor in Roman style, is one of the most interesting of the Christian interventions in the Alhambra.

From the last hall that you can visit in the rooms of Charles V, and before entering the viewing gallery of the Patio de la Reja, you find access to the Peinador de la Reina. Nowadays, the space is closed due to the difficulty of managing the large numbers of daily visitors.

The Peinador de la Reina is part of the complex of imperial rooms even though it is separated from them as it occupies the upper part of the Tower of Abū l-Ḥaŷŷāŷ, the Nasrid tower and viewing point over the wall jutting out over the River Darro valley.

What you could call the lower Peinador constitutes the ancient tower, built on the wall and isolated from the other palace constructions in Nasrid times.

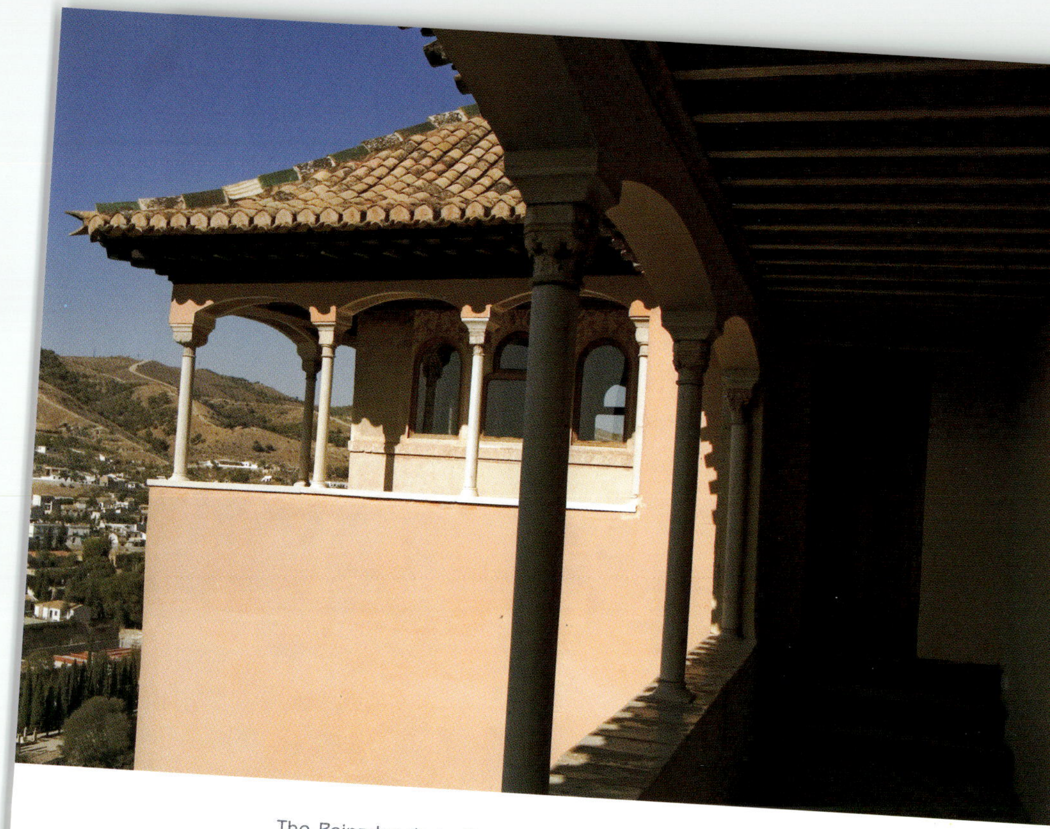

The Peinador de la Reina

Originally it was a pavilion open to the countryside, which suggests it was used as a spiritual or profane retreat. The interior structure consists of a central hall with a lantern raised on four marble columns over some narrow side passages. The whole chamber is open on the four sides through very low arched windows, a typical design enabling the occupants to contemplate the surrounding landscape while seated on the floor. The wide windows give an especially diaphanous lightness to the room. Novelty features that enhance the room include elements such as the paving tiles with figures and coats of arms, the painted dado with geometric motifs, and the *aliceres*, the glazed ceramic surrounds to the windows, some of the few original ones that have been conserved in the Alhambra.

The area that we might call the upper Peinador is considered by some authors to have been a "dressing room" for a queen, possible when occupied by Isabel de Farnesio and Philip V in 1729. In fact, inside the tower, you find the anagrams of the royal couple together with eighteenth-century decoration. However, originally this reformed body of the tower was known as "the Stove", as at one end there was a marble flagstone with holes in it through which rose the smoke or perhaps the vapours from a perfume burner. It could clearly have been the

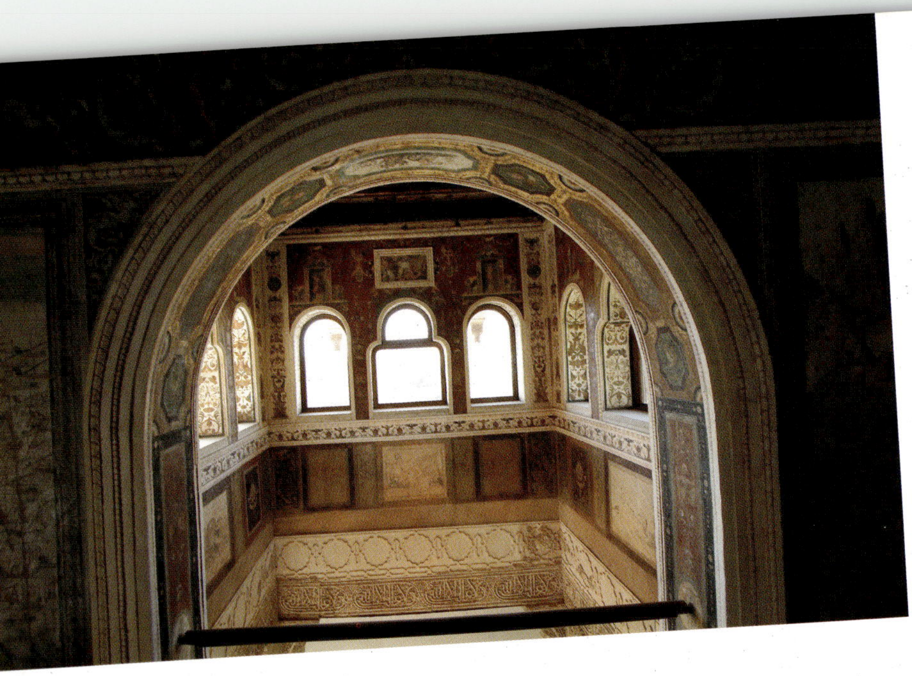

Inside the Peinador de la Reina

Detail of the mural with scenes from the conquest of Tunis in the Peinador de la Reina

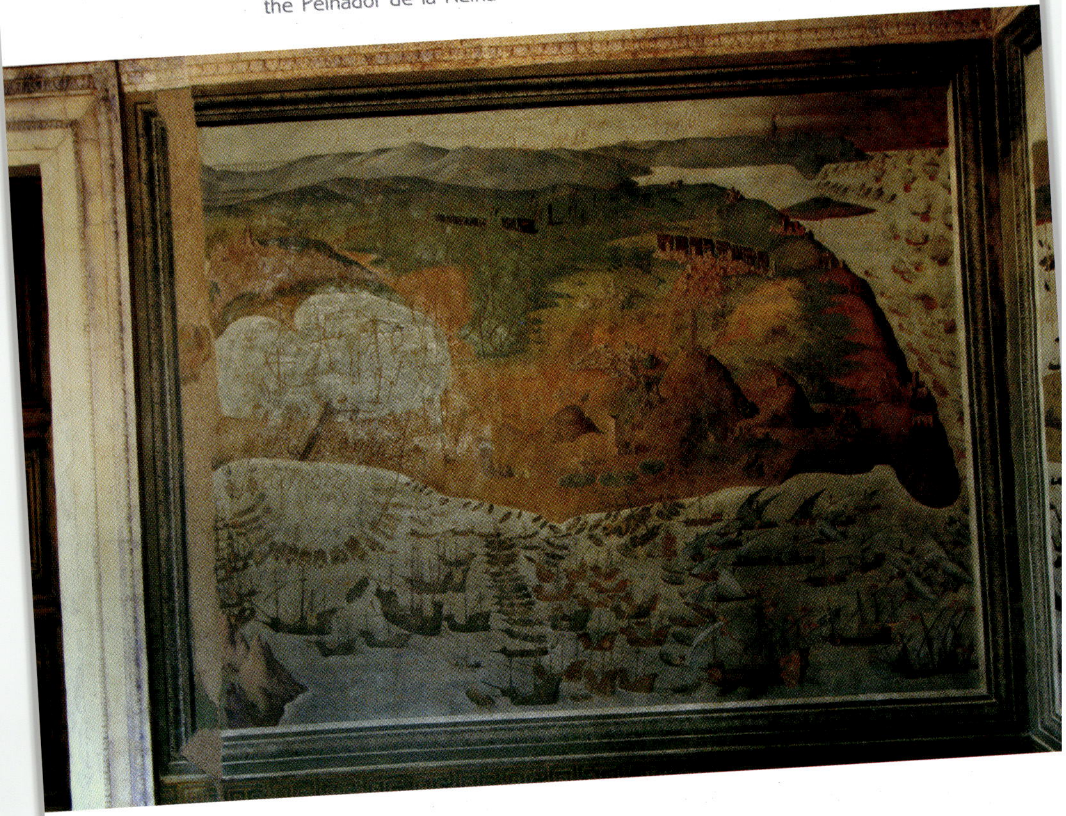

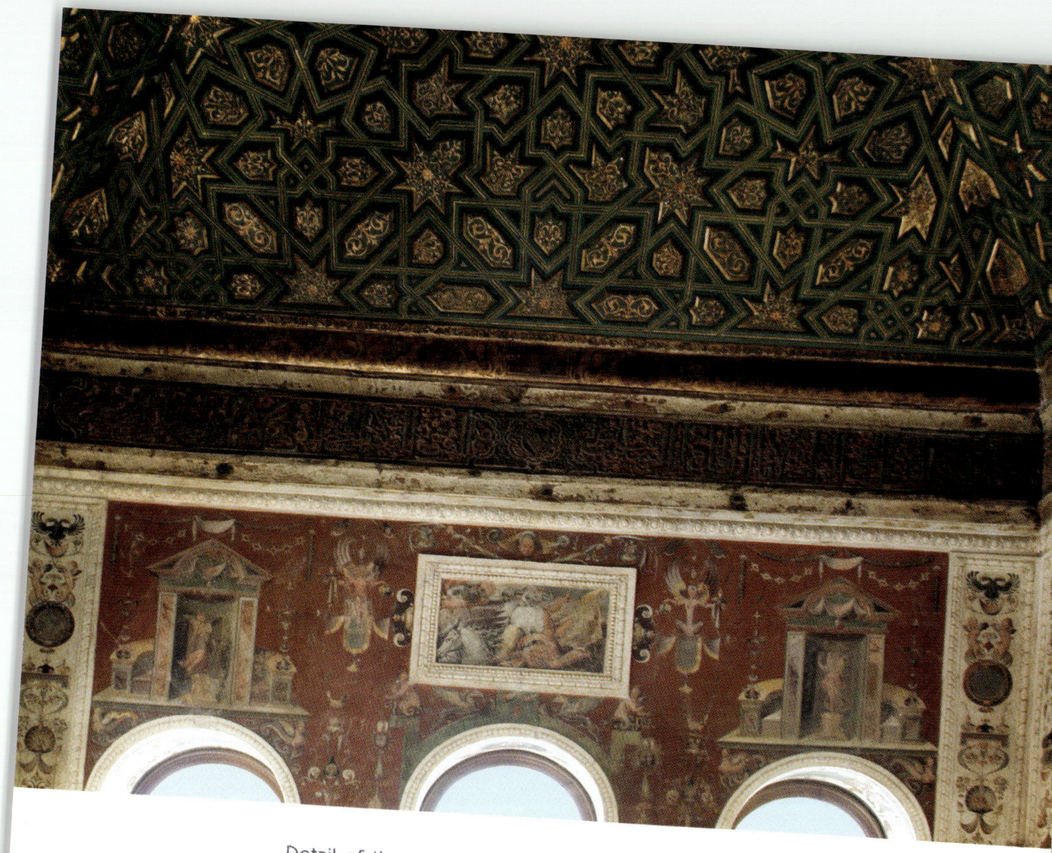

Detail of the mural depicting mythological themes in the Peinador de la Reina

heated space, reserved, or even perfumed by burning aromatic substances. It has a clear relationship with the Roman examples in the presence of the loggia or viewing point with the covered gallery and above all the painted decoration.

This small space is of enormous interest from the point of view of the wall decorations. First, a sequence of eight paintings represent Charles V's conquest of Tunisia in 1535. From the departure of the imperial fleet from Cagliari to the victorious return to Trapani, faithful to the notes taken by the painter Vermeyen. In a second hall, a series of four small paintings, framed in stucco, tell the story of Phaeton, covering the rest of the wall surfaces, including the intrados of the arches, with an ornamental repertory of grotesques, putti, architectural features and garlands. Finally, an outer gallery surrounds this central nucleus, connected with the entrance gallery; it opens to the landscape through basket handle arches resting on Nasrid columns. The walls were decorated in the same style as on the inside but logically, are more worn as they are in the open air, and have lost a large part of the paint and only ornamental series and the figure of one the Virtues (Moderation) remain. The authors were Julio Aquilis and Alejandro Mayner between 1539 and 1544.

Patio de la Reja and Patio de Lindaraja

Name: The name Patio de la Reja was given to this court because of the wrought iron balcony made between 1654 and 1655.
Date: 16th-17th cent.
Monarchy: Fundamentally Charles V (1516-1556)
Note: The great intimacy that this space achieves.

FROM THE LAST of Charles V's rooms to be visited, you arrive at a wide corridor with splendid views towards the Albaicín. This marks the northern boundary of the small Patio de la Reja. The sixteenth-century plans indicate this corridor was "made on the command of His Majesty" Charles V, and is of interest because it takes advantage of remnants of Nasrid columns and capitals, although some of the more valuable pieces are now on display in the Museum of the Alhambra.

The Patio de la Reja came into being when Charles V's appartments were built joining up with the Palacio de los Leones. This intermediate space then appeared between the rooms and the Torreón de Comares. The court features in some most incredible, unlikely legends about is use. It has been variously suggested that it was the prison of a sultana, or of Queen Joan I of Castile; it has also been said to have been where the Christian kings kept their crown jewels.

On the western side you see the basements that coincide with the Sala de la Barca and which from the seventeenth century were known as the Sala de las Ninfas after some classical sculptures kept there. The vaulted ceilings in these basements and, especially, the fact that at some points they provide quick access to other parts of the

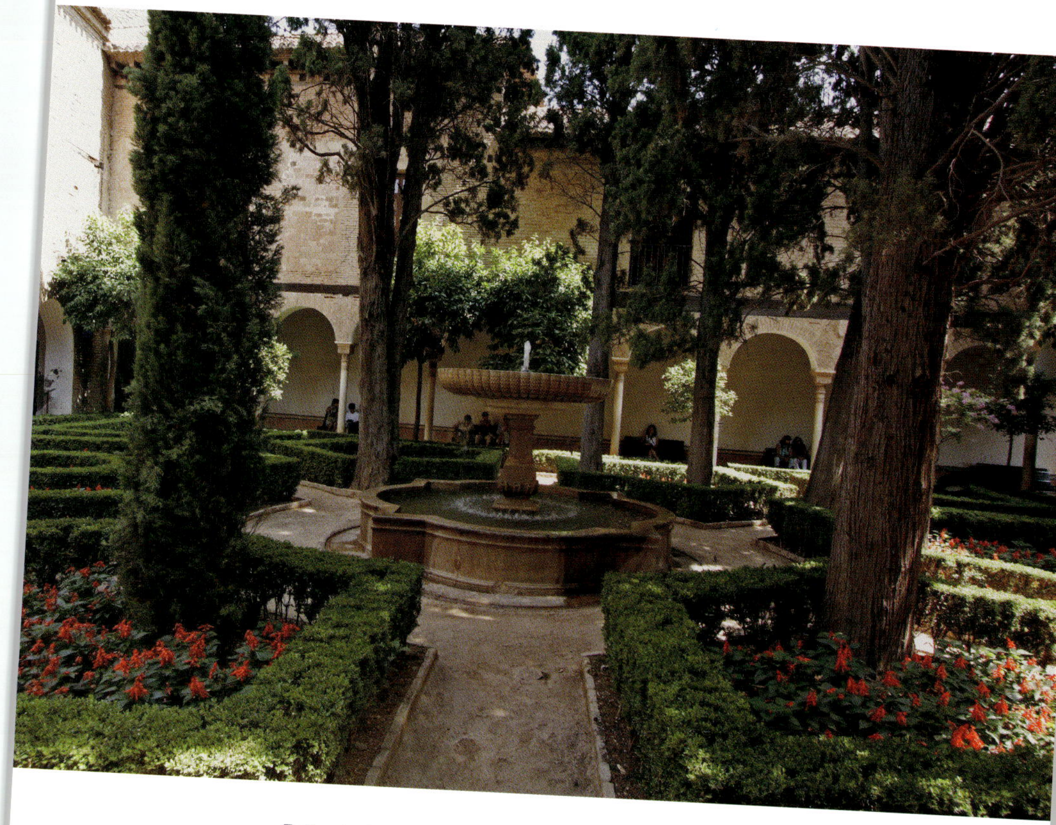

Patio de Lindaraja

Alhambra such as a direct link with the Cuarto Dorado, is of interest.

Crossing the Patio de la Reja, you move towards the adjacent Patio de Lindaraja where you find the fountain dated in 1626 and made by taking advantage of a very large Nasrid basin – today replaced by a replica – that is believed to have come from the Patio del Cuarto Dorado. To the right, you have a view of the Baño Real de Comares.

Baño Real de Comares

Name: Baño Real de Comares
Date and sultanate: Some researchers consider the baths already existed in the period of Ismāʿīl I (1314-1325) due to the archaic nature of the columns in the warm room. If that is the case, under Yūsuf I (1333-1354) what happened was that it was renovated fundamentally by adding the lantern, or *qubba*, in the rest room, some capitals, the inscriptions and the stucco in the massage room upper galleries.
Note: The architectural structure and decoration of the Baño Real de Comares are outstanding as it is a royal space. The tiles are especially interesting and some writers believe they are sixteenth-century whereas others point to their possible Islamic origin.

Leaving the Patio de la Reja, to the right you can look out through a small door to view part of the Sala de las Camas hall in the Banos de Comares. In reality, the original entrance is found on the east side of the Patio de Comares, but this is closed to ordinary visits as the space is not suitable for large numbers of people.

This chamber, traditionally named Sala de las Camas, is the *bayt al-maslaj* or dressing, massage and rest room. It was here that the architect Rafael Contreras made his greatest intervention between 1848 and 1866, rebuilding large part of the room and of the original conserving only the columns, paving and part of the tiling. The view does not enable you to see the following room, which would be the *bayt al-bārid*, the cold or transit room.

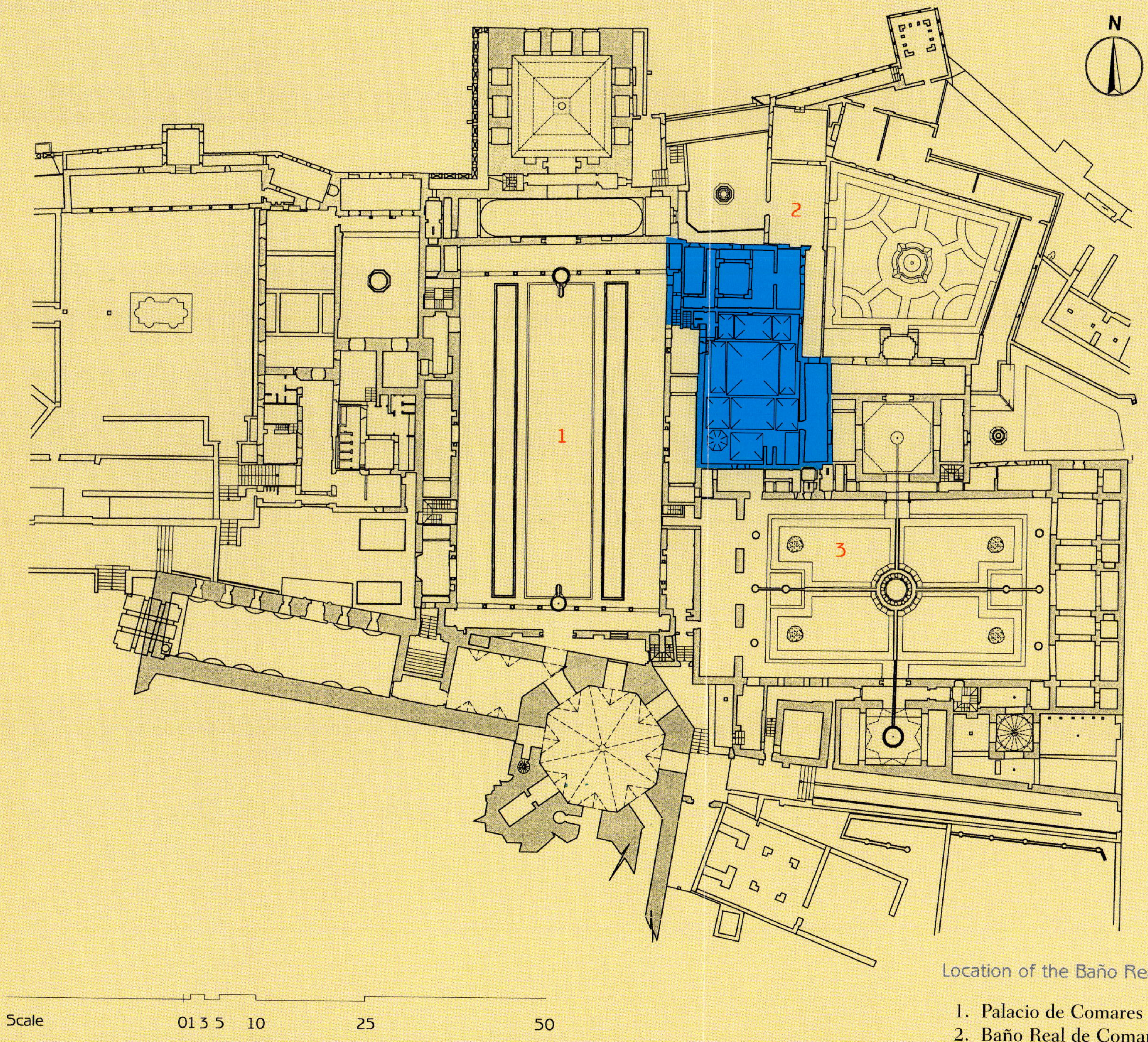

Location of the Baño Real de Comares

1. Palacio de Comares
2. Baño Real de Comares
3. Palacio de los Leones

Palacio de Comares and Palacio de los Leones with the Baños de Comares. Basement: current state (according to A. Orihuela Uzal, Casas y Palacios Nazaríes. Siglos XIII-XV, 1996, p. 97, based on the plan by L. Torres Balbás, Arch. Planos Alhambra, n.° 862, 1927).

1. Sala de las Camas (*bayt al-maslaj*)
2. Warm room (*al-bayt al-wasṭānī*)
3. Hot water room (*al-bayt al-sajūn*)
4. Boiler room

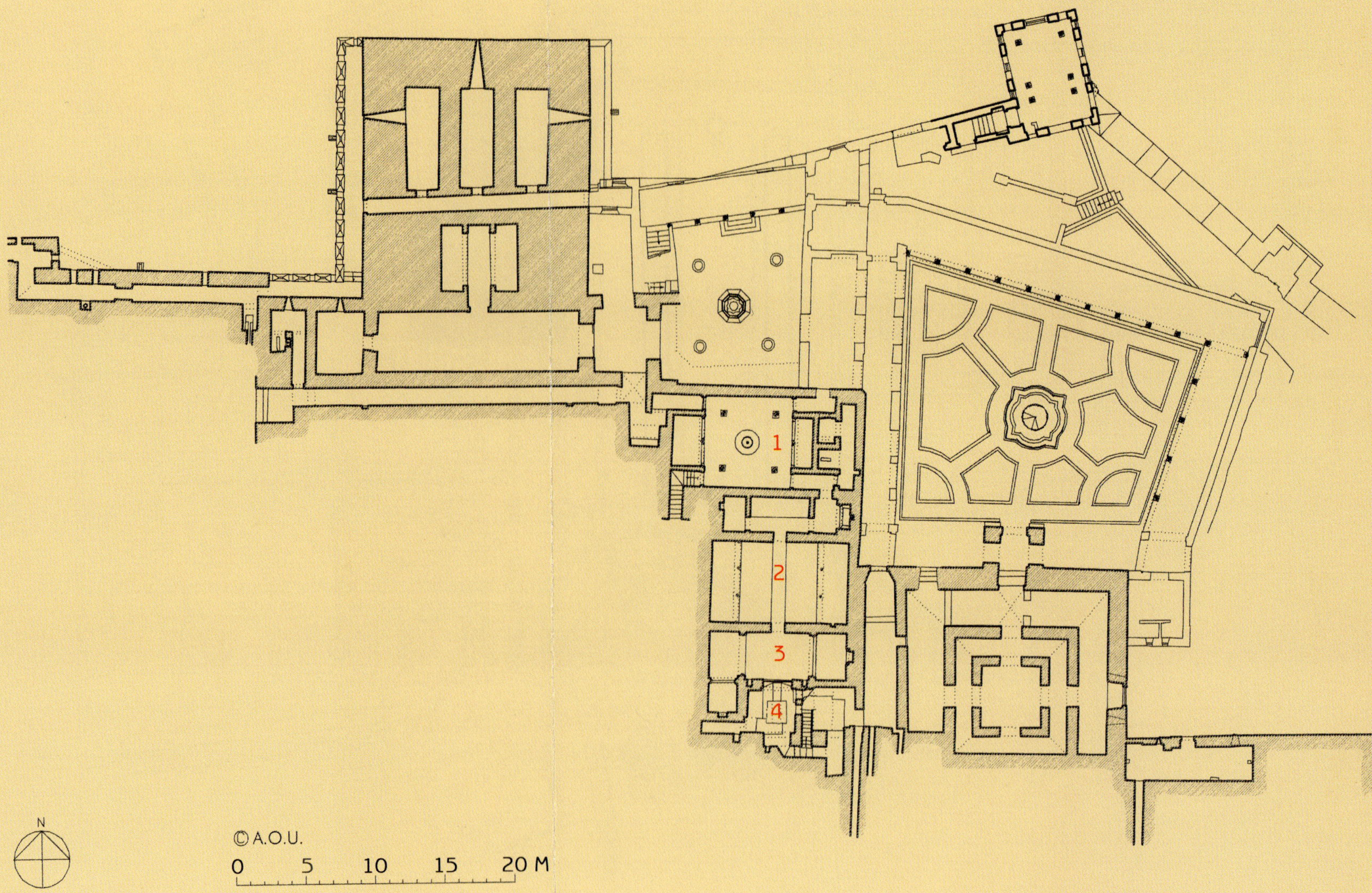

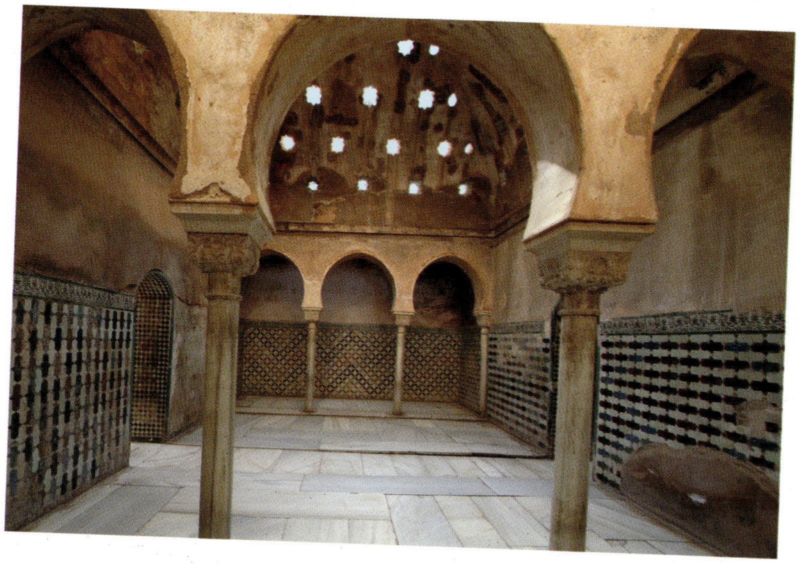

The warm room or *bayt al-waṣṭānī* is the largest room and has noteworthy spaces at the side with horseshoe arches on marble columns.

If you go on through the Patio de Lindaraja, you can see the *bayt al-waṣṭānī*, the warm room, where the outstandingly beautiful skylights that were opened or closed as necessary to control the steam in the baths. Next to this and behind it, is the *bayt al-sajūn*, the hot water room. To the south, after the hot water room, were the boiler and wood store, from where firewood would be taken along what was known as the Woodcutters' alley (today the west gallery of the Patio de Lindaraja). The hot air circulated through the hypocaust that ran below the hot water room and part of the warm room.

Although on first sight you might think this type of Islamic bath, *ḥammām* clearly derived from the Roman hot baths – and effectively there may be such a relationship – there does not seem to have been a simple transfer of the Roman hot baths to the Islamic baths. The traditional succession of apodyterium, frigidarium, tepidarium and caldarium of the Roman hot baths does not have the same proportions or relationship because the frigidarium of the Roman hot baths has little in common with the room of transition in the Islamic baths. In these, it does not maintain the large proportions of the Roman hot baths nor, especially, infrastructure like the swimming pools and gymnasiums.

The series of rooms that lie to the left of the Bath and close off the Patio de Lindaraja comprise some of the woodcutters' rooms and their access to the boiler, whereas the rest are those be-

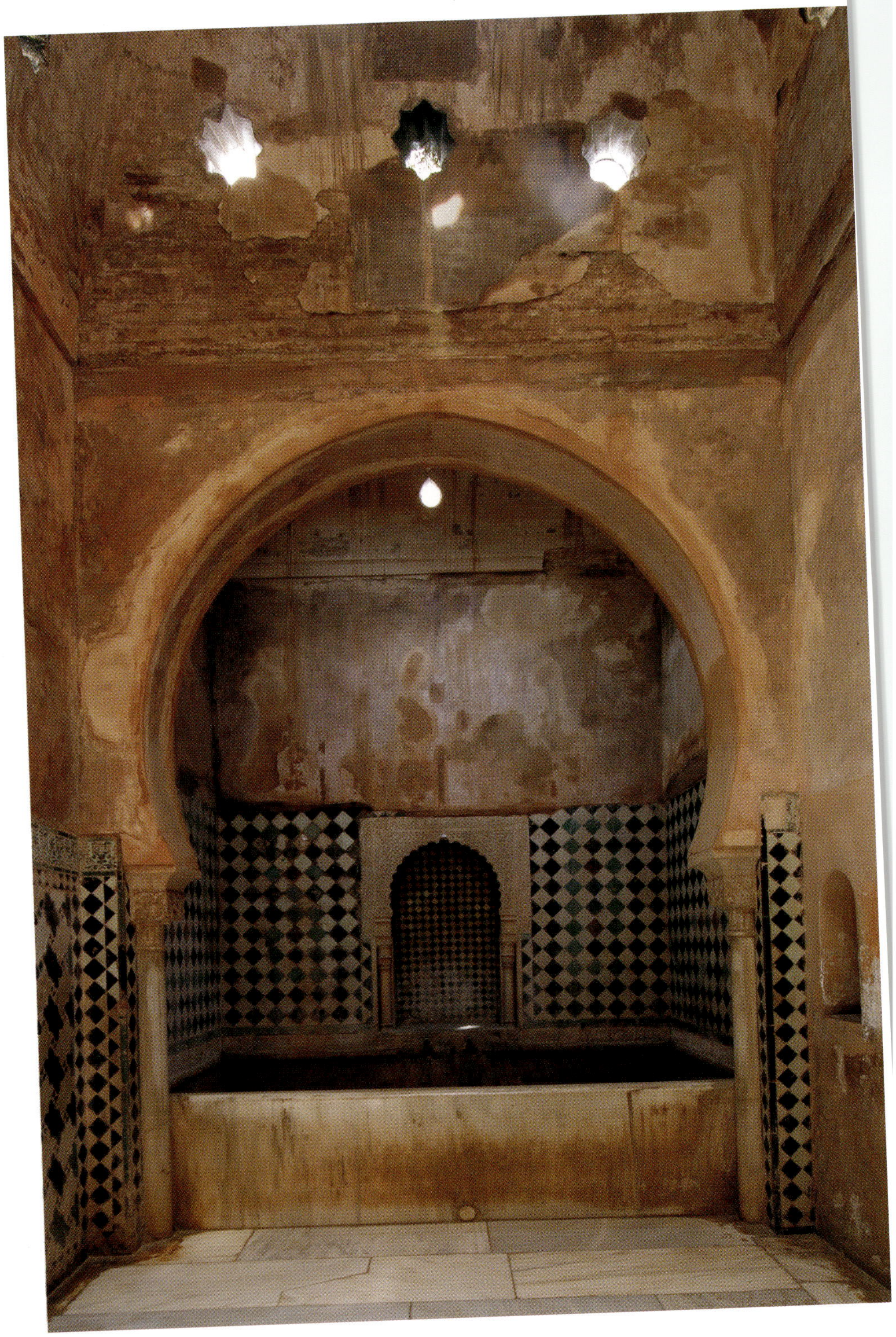

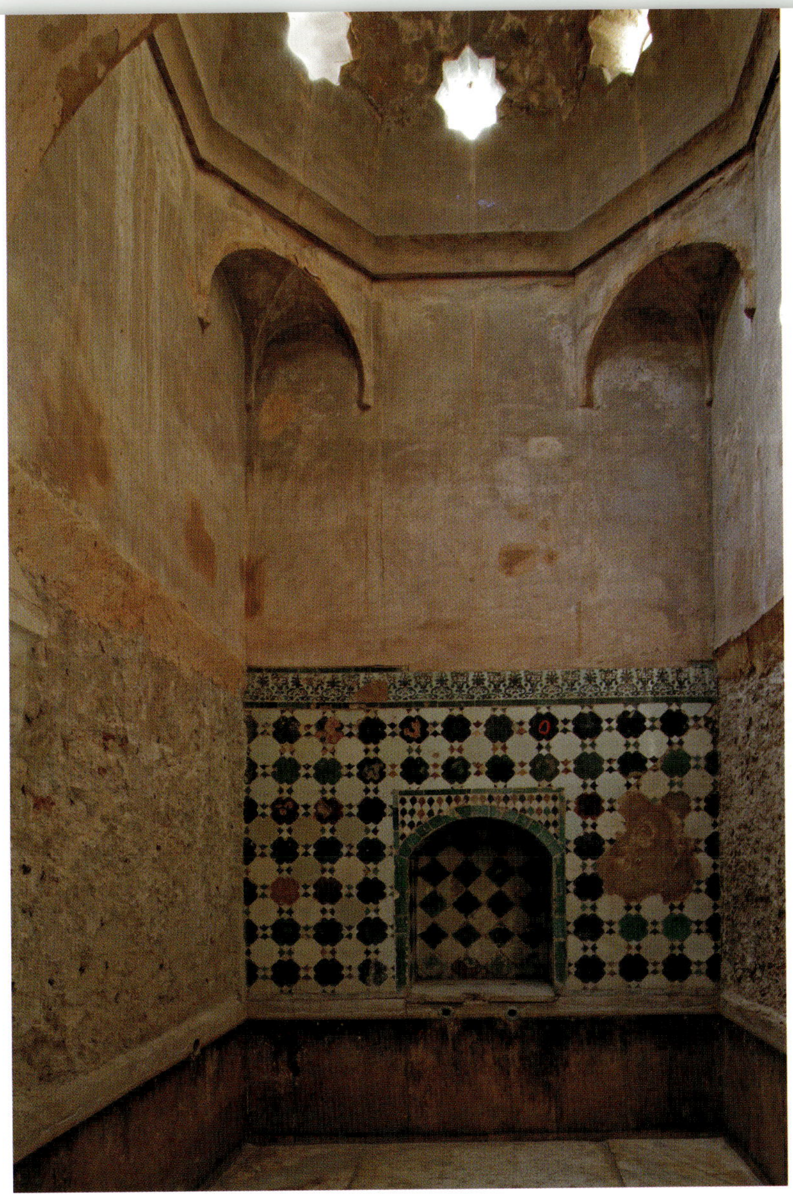

The hot water room or *al-bayt al-sajūn* has two immersion pools set out without the characteristic symmetry of other baths.

neath the Sala de Dos Hermanas that serve to insulate from damp, as well as the stores. The vaults of these rooms are original although much rebuilt in later periods. Among these vaulted rooms, the central one, known as the Sala de los Secretos, stands out for its resonance, now lost as a result of the sail vaulting.

El Partal

El Partal

Name: Palace and oratory of El Partal, Torre de las Damas
Date: 1302-1309
Sultanate: Muḥammad III (1302-1309)
Note: Leisure palace and viewing point; it is the oldest in the palace area with reasonably visible structures, predating the type of the Palacio de Comares. Its light and apparently fragile structure houses handsome wooden frames.

ON LEAVING the Patio de Lindaraja you find yourself in a wide open garden space known as the Jardines de El Partal due to the location there of a palace of the same name. In Arabic, El Partal means "the Portico". Gardens are set out in a series of plots of land or steps, and there are corners where at every step you are surprised by a series of ponds, low walls and a labyrinth of staircases. In reality, the entire space, which is considerably large, is now as pleasant as it is distant from its original appearance. Here, there once stood a series of palaces and houses meaning that this had to be considered an urban space. The ruin of many of these constructions meant it was impossible to recover its original appearance and it was decided, with criteria appropriate to another time, to create these gardens.

In order to gain a better view, you should stand to the north of the large pond. From there you can appreciate a series of buildings mounted literally on the wall. These constructions, unequal in

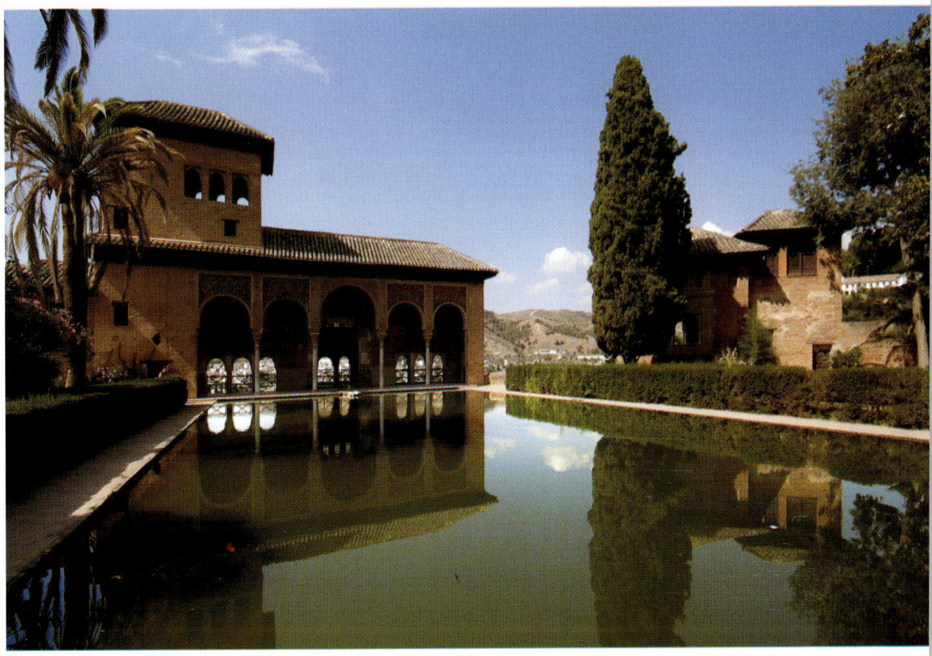

Palacio de El Partal

The little house in El Partal

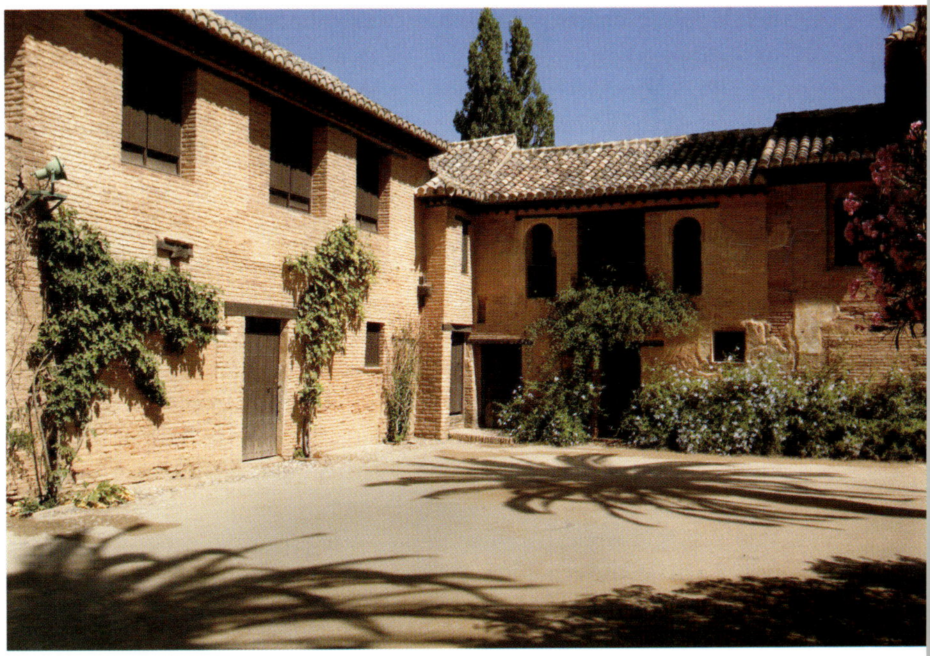

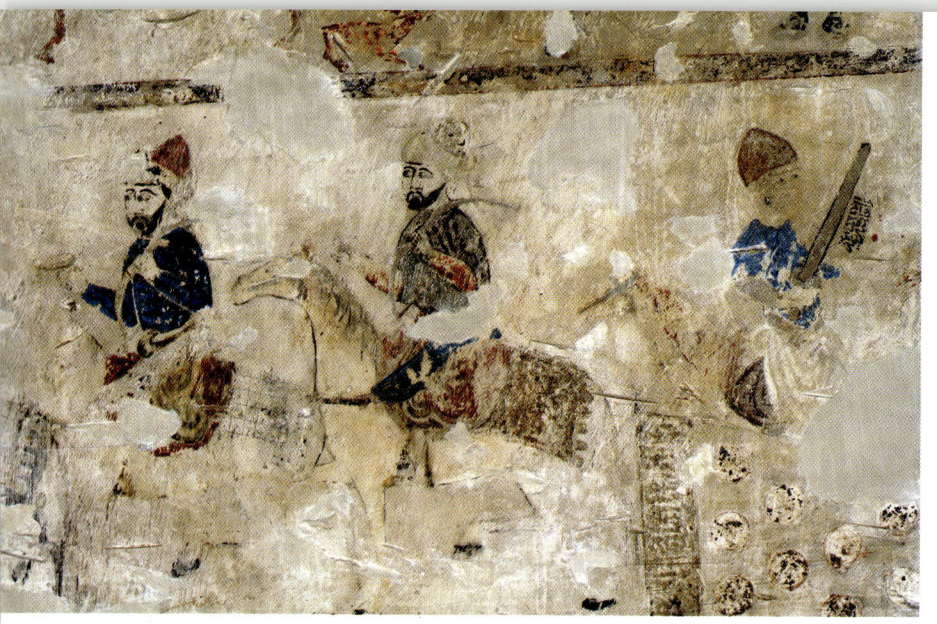

Details of the Nasrid paintings in the little houses in El Partal

appearance, are some little houses forming a corner, a wide portico and a small oratory built onto another dwelling. In spite of the difference in volume and complexity with respect to the palaces visited before it constitutes a series of buildings of great interest.

The oldest construction is the Palacio de El Partal, whose ornamental elements lead us to date it as the work of the sultan Muḥammad III, being the first reasonably well-conserved palace of those built in the Alhambra. With the loss of the wall and buildings that surrounded and closed off this palace, only one tower is conserved. This holds the *qubba*, or main hall, the arched portico and a pond of considerable size that fixes the compositional axis of the whole space.

To the west of the Palacio de El Partal, and built up against it, we find a small house known as the house of the Prince which, like the Oratory, was built by Yūsuf I. On the inside are remnants of stucco decorations, a most beautiful structure and some mural paintings in a courtly style that constitute the only conserved example of Nasrid painting (if we assume that the paintings in the Salas de los Reyes were the work of Christians). On the walls of the houses adjacent to this palace remains have been conserved of the red-painted plaster, imitating brick, and bands of inscriptions that go some way to confirming that the walls of these palaces were decorated like this. Visits are restricted to specific dates.

In the west wing of the portico, a small tower-viewing point known as the Torre de las Damas creates a strange lack of

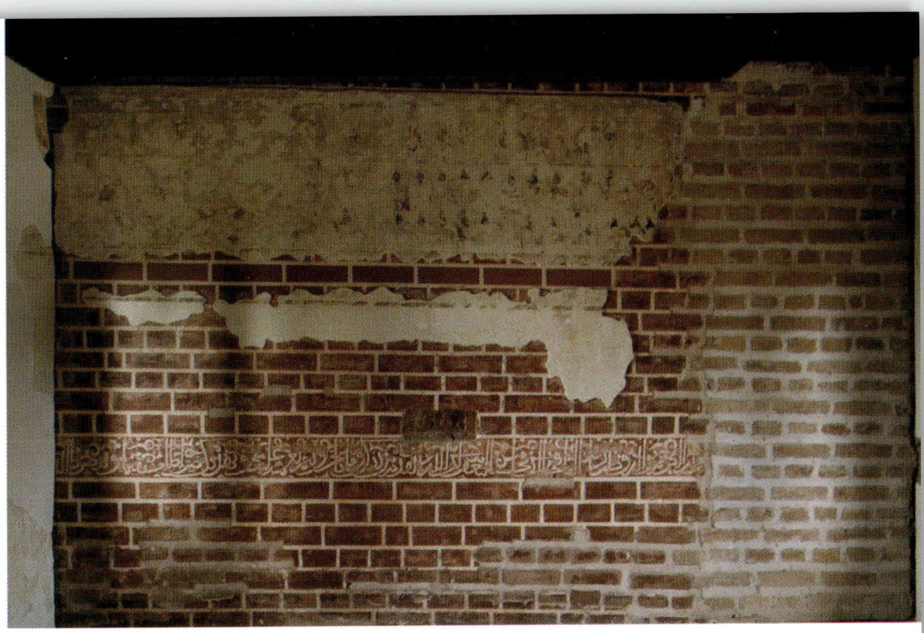

Remains of a wall with imitation brick and inscriptions in the little house in El Partal

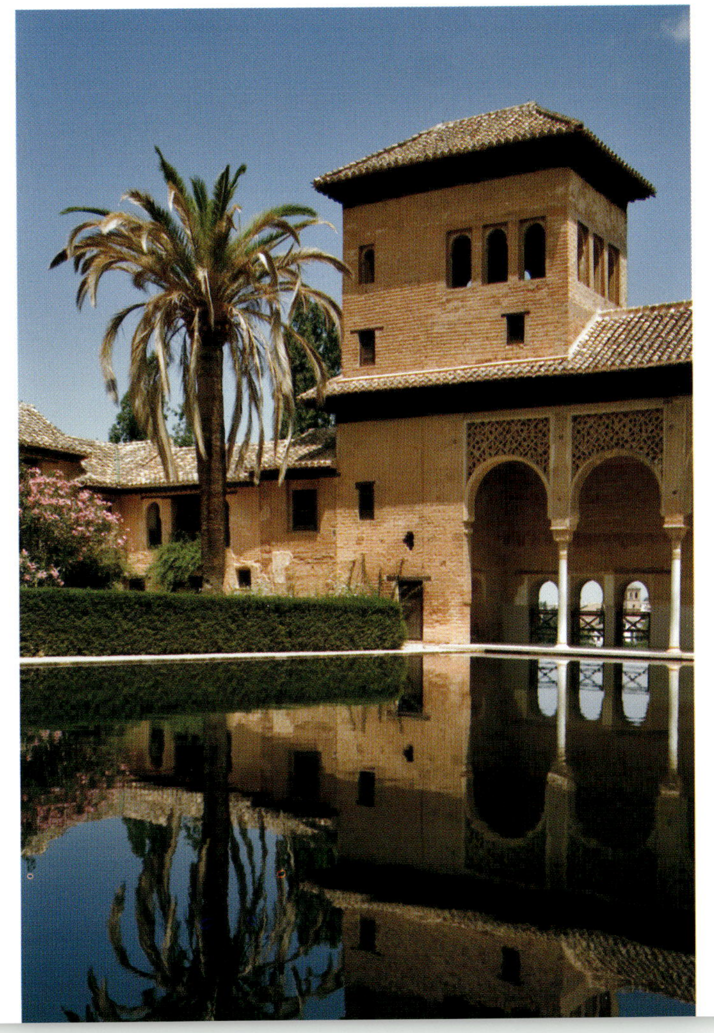

Tower of the Palacio de El Partal

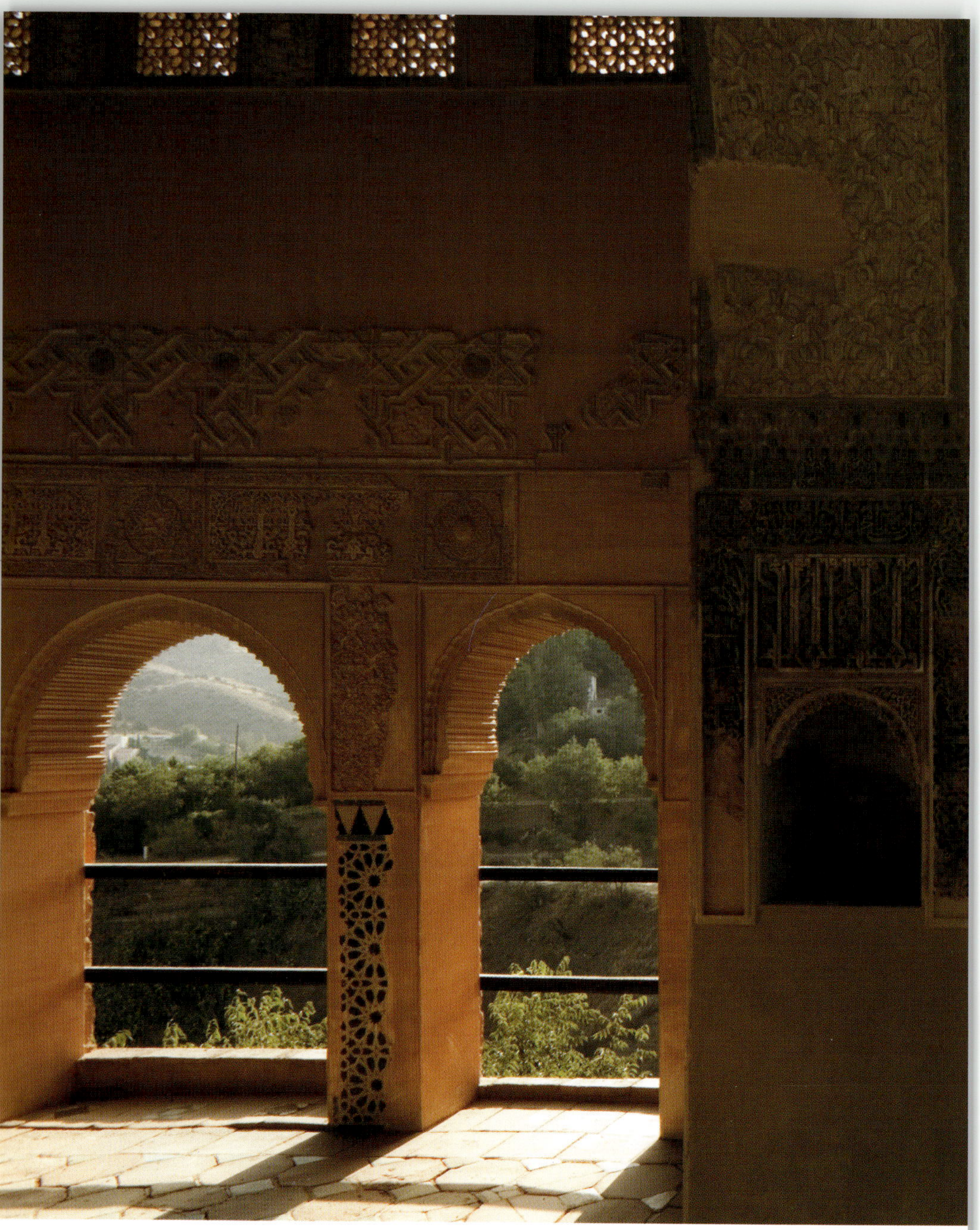

architectural, symmetry to beautiful effect. The desire for pure contemplation is accentuated as the viewing point is superimposed on the portico, which you enter by a door and staircase today closed to visitors due to its extreme narrowness.

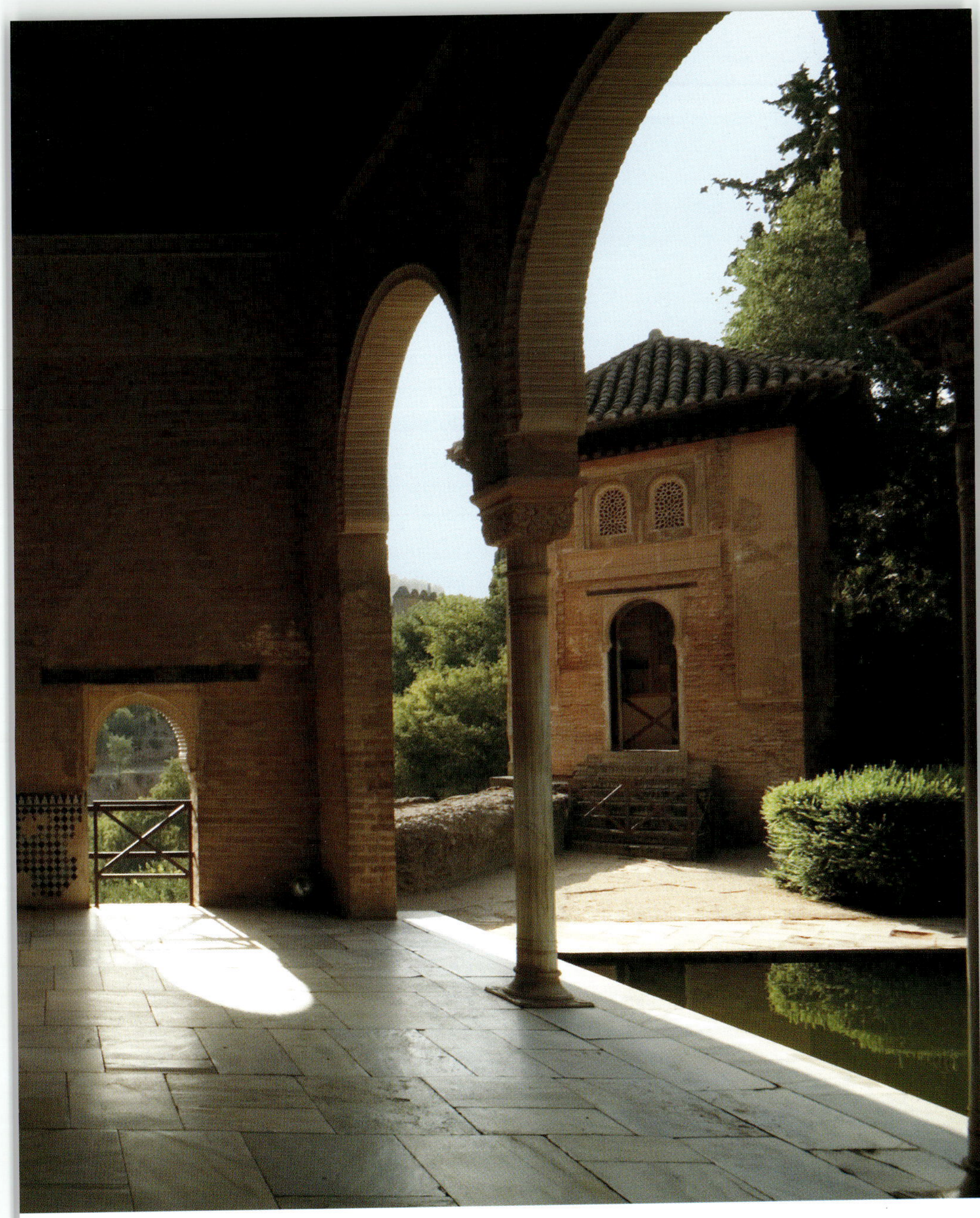

Viewing point of the Portico de El Partal

The series of arches and the portico miraculously conserve some remains of the original ornamentation, as in the nineteenth century it was converted into a private residence. The restoration of the portico is considered one of the most respectful interventions of

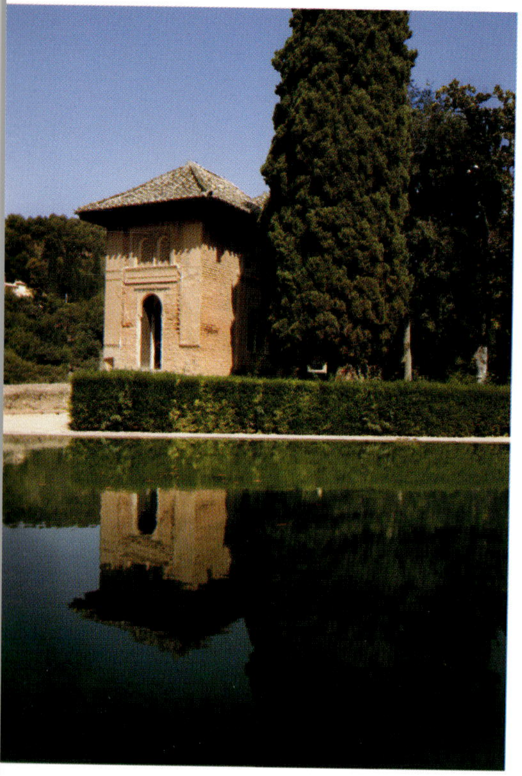

Oratory in El Partal

the period and was undertaken by Leopoldo Torres Balbás who reintegrated the panels of *sebka* in the side arches, the central one being the only one that is original. Instead of recreating the diamond-shaped decorations, fragments of plaster with holes punched in them were used. From a distance, they would give the impression and image of the former design but close up could be seen not to be original. The portico columns are also modern.

The principal chamber has a dado tiled in cold colours (blue, green, white) which confirm its antiquity, and remains of stucco decorations which stand out for the originality of some designs and the expressive force of the *ataurique* and inscriptions. Admirable in its originality is the wooden *alfarje* that covers the portico, whose domes and most delicate design play with the light reflected by the water in the pond; also admirable are the eaves of the viewing point, some of the few original ones to have been preserved.

In reality, this building is a pavilion where the windows open onto its walls, forming a subtle screen that filters and frames the dazzling vision of the Albaicín and Sacromonte districts.

To the right of the palace and also on the wall we find a small oratory, a true jewel of Nasrid art. Its tiny door with a pointed horseshoe arch is facing the *mihrab*, pointing in the direction of prayer. Thanks to its restoration in 1932, you are able to contemplate its beautiful, original stucco adornments and discover the specific values of an expansive liturgical concept perfectly in tune with a landscape created by God, in contrast with so many introverted Christian chapels that are closed to outer contemplation.

Going around the edge of the pond and climbing up the staircase with three arches of ivy, to the right of the second platform you reach the Rauda Real.

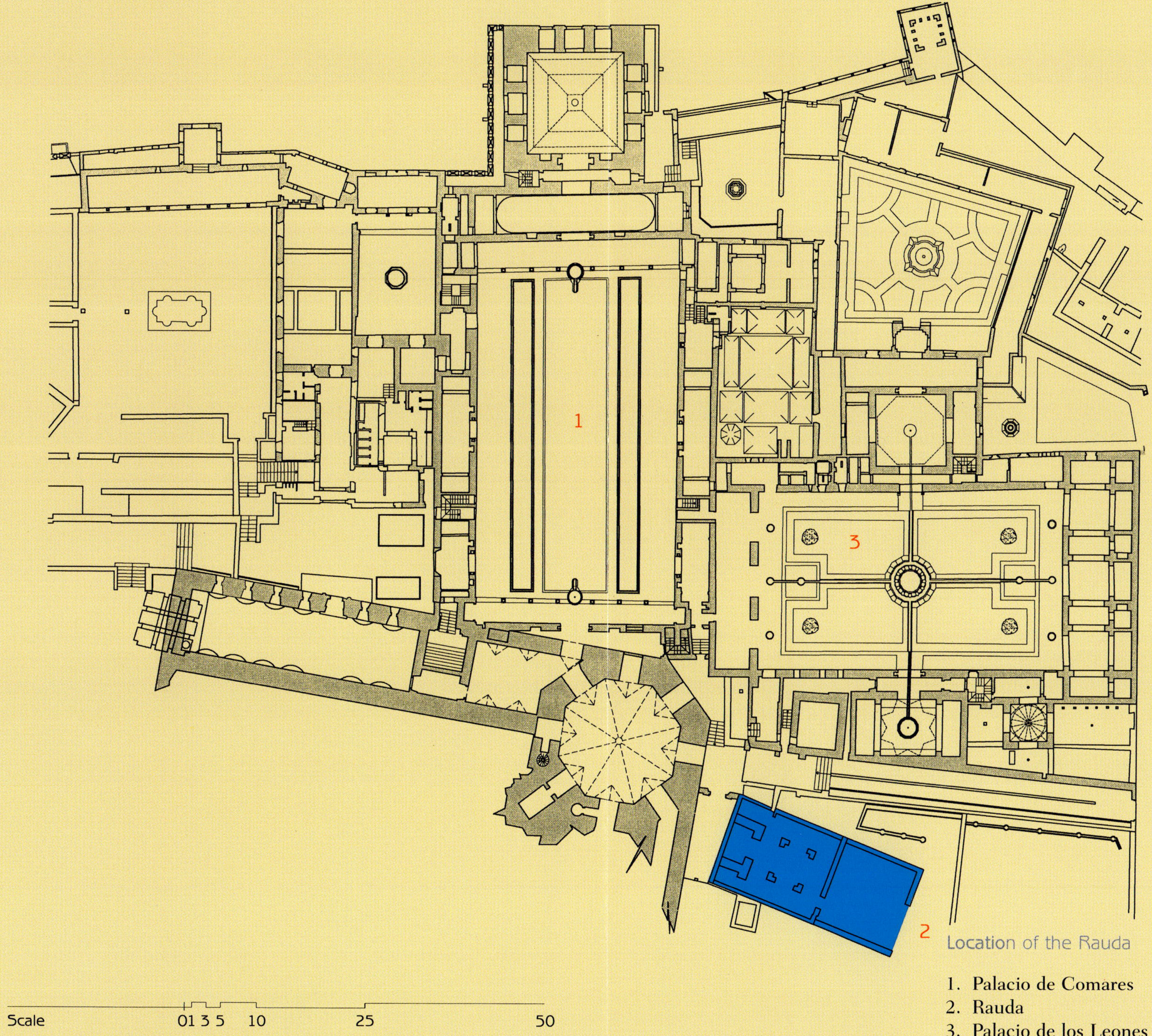

Location of the Rauda

1. Palacio de Comares
2. Rauda
3. Palacio de los Leones

Rauda Real

Name: Rauda
Date: 1314-1325 (problematic date)
Sultanate: Ismāʿīl I (1314-1325)
Note: Cemetery of the sultans of the Alhambra after Muḥammad III (1302-1309). In spite of the destruction suffered in the Christian period and its current state, this is an interesting structure as no similar mausoleums are known in al-Andalus.

WHERE THE PALACIO DE CARLOS V and the Palacio de los Leones converge you can contemplate the original entrance to Leones, and if you raise your eyes you glimpse something called the Patio del Harén. At this point you can appreciate part of the tour of the ancient Calle Real Baja that, coming from the main square giving access to the palaces, ran outside the wall of the Nasrid palaces and here continued towards the area of the Upper Alhambra and El Secano. Its route is very much changed today with the construction of the Palacio de Carlos V.

Starting in the street and passing through a door opened up on the southern side, you enter the Rauda, the Nasrid royal cemetery. This is formed by an originally domed, central pavilion, surrounded by a platform and three other small rooms to the northwest. You can see excavations or signs on the pavement of the tombs that served to house the bodies of the king and his family, always wrapped in a shroud and lain on their sides looking towards Mecca, so the building also required the appropriate orientation for the Muslim. Some of its ornamental elements, like the inscribed marble tombstones, are to be found in the Museum of the Alhambra.

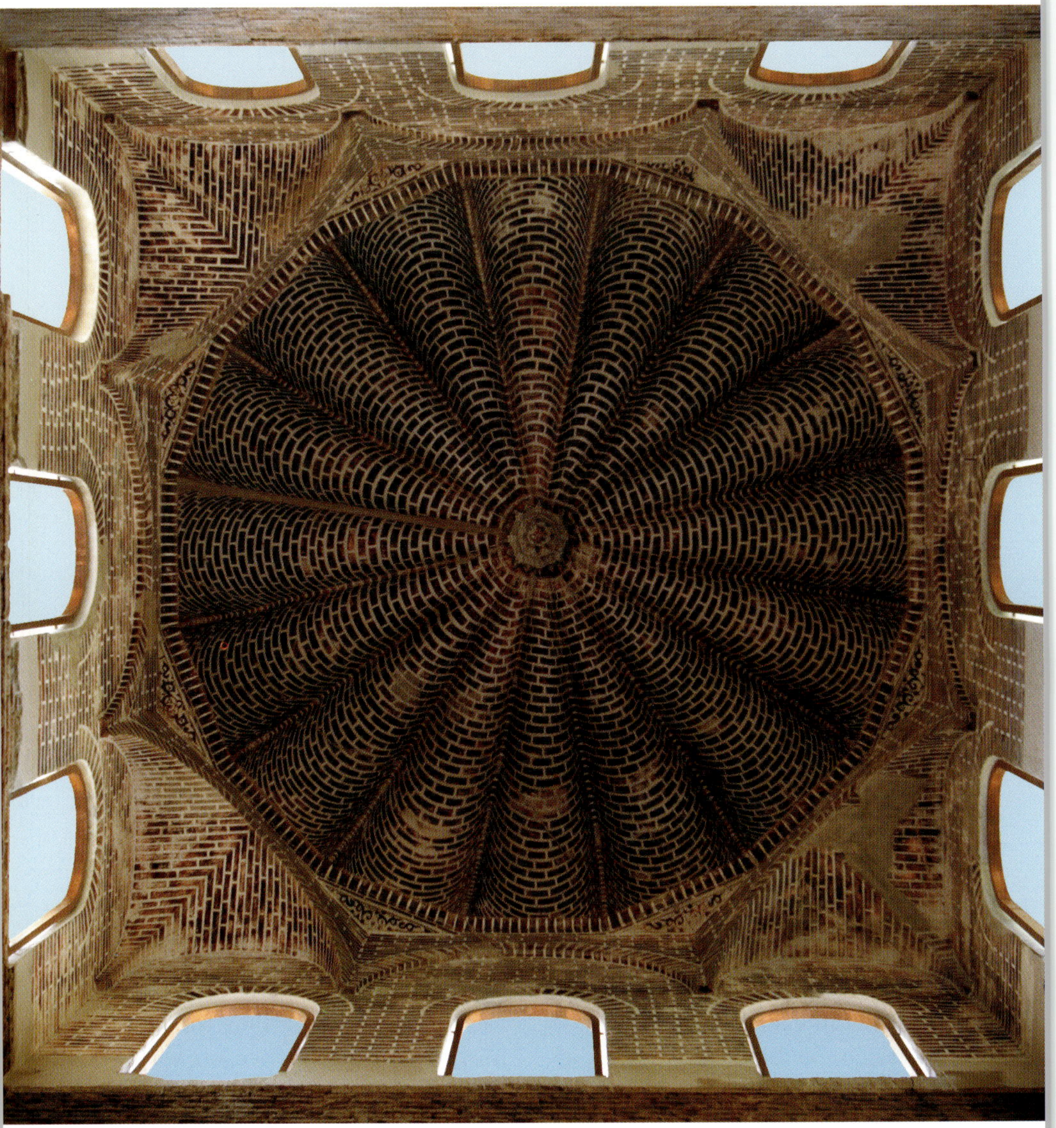

Inner wiew of the dome of a pavilion some authors suggest is part of the remnants of the Palace of Ismā'īl.

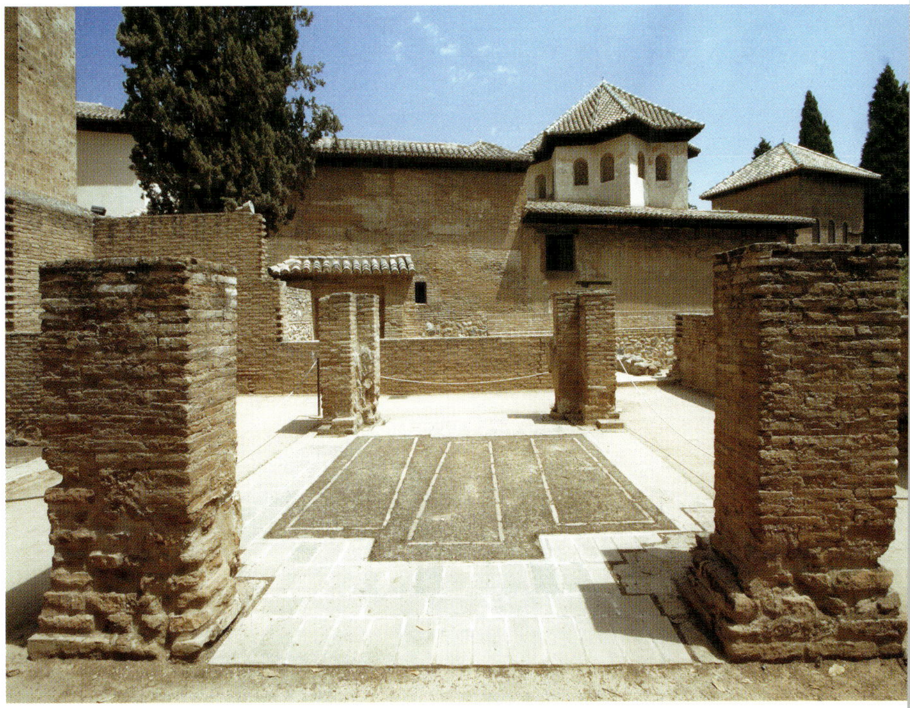

Remains of the Rauda Real

This place is of special importance for its historic evocation and respect for the legacy of those who left us such a rich inheritance.

Leaving the Rauda and going down some stairs you can look out onto a pavilion or open kiosk through four horseshoe arches. It has an admirable dome of interlinked vaults around a circular base in the Byzantine tradition, and repeats the model used in the Puerta de las Armas, as does the painted decoration simulating regular brick shapes. The building now appears to be out of context, if you recall that it is one of the remnants of the palace of Ismā'īl, mutilated when the palaces of Comares and de los Leones were built.

Jardines de El Partal and Paseo de las Torres

Name: Jardines de El Partal
Date: 13th-15th cent. Excavations, remodelling and landscaping 20th cent.
Sultanate: Various sultans and the Christian period
Note: These lush gardens, with pleasant corners and a multitude of staircases, plots, ponds and flower beds, was originally an urban zone occupied by several palaces and houses belonging to the Nasrid nobility and senior functionaries, the remains of which come to the surface in the form of high and low walls all over this space.

FROM THE RAUDA you can take two routes. If you have not yet visited the Alcazaba or the Palacio de Carlos V, and want to, you can leave the precinct through an iron railing next to the palace. If you want to continue to the Generalife or are looking for the entrance pavilion and car park, continue to the left through the gardens that stretch from El Partal to El Secano.

If you decide to continue to the left you will be surprised by a terrace with a modern kiosk where you can see the pond of what may have been a house. From here you pass the wall and pond of another house belonging to this urban area to finally reach the Palacio de Yūsuf III.

The palace is the most important building that has been identified in this area and you can see its central pond, the remains of a typical tower to the north, and to the east the remains of the bath that served the palace. In spite of the name it has been given it seems that this palace was constructed by

Palace of Yūsuf III and terraced houses to the west. Ground floor: partial hypothesis of its initial state (according to A. Orihuela Uzal, *Casas y palacios nazaríes. Siglos XIII-XV*, 1996, p. 122).

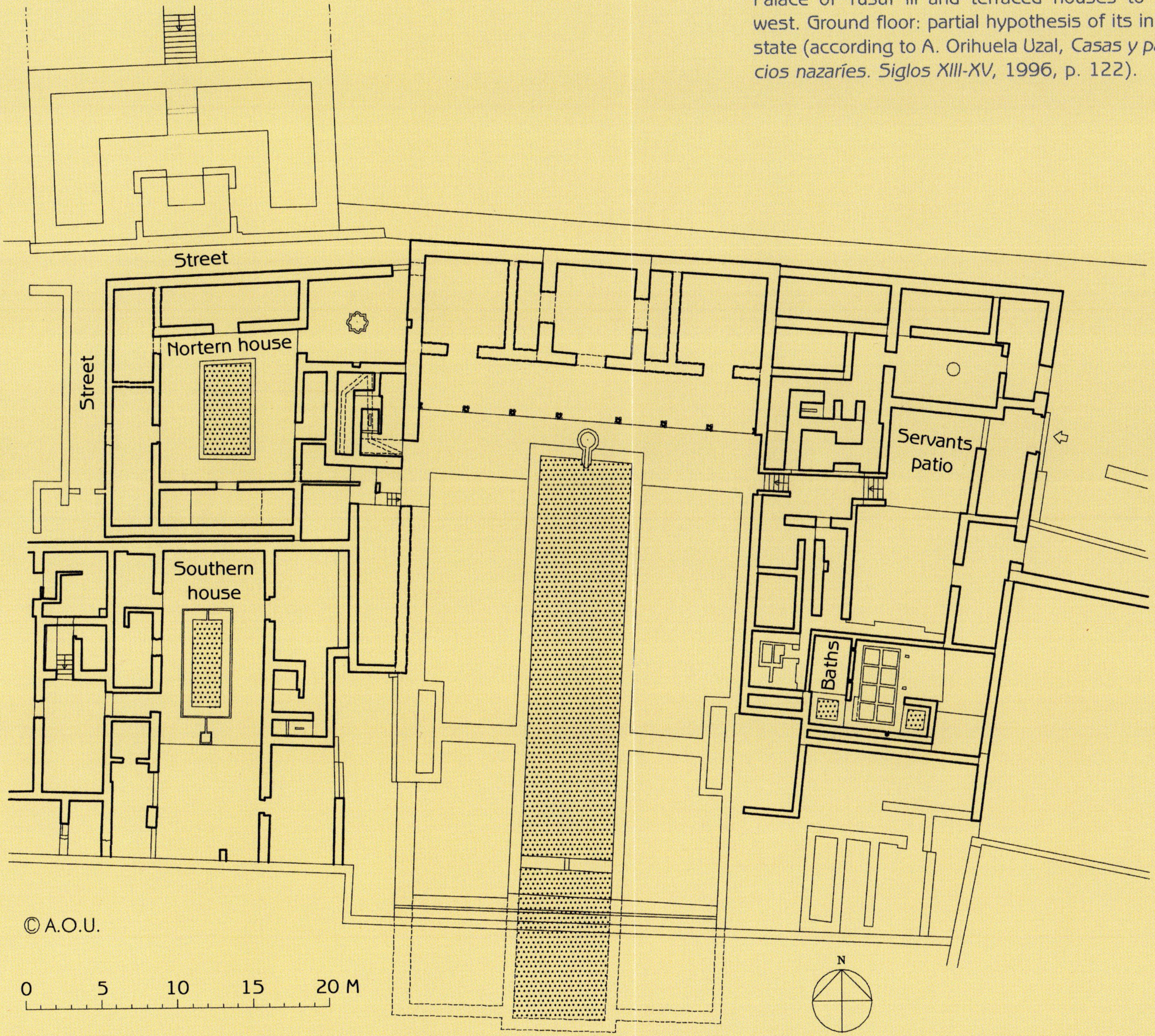

Muḥammad II (1273-1302) and remodelled by Yūsuf III (1408-1417). In the Christian period, it was the residence of the Counts of Tendilla, governors of the Alhambra, but their fall from power with the War of Succession (1700-1712) brought with it the destruction of the palace.

All this area was half devastated and disfigured by modern additions so in 1928 an archaeological criterion used during the excavation was to restore order, leaving visible traces of the foundations and distribution of the houses and completing this by landscaping the entire route to create a space that has led many to believe it was in its day an Islamic garden.

From this palace you can look out and contemplate to the north the possible continuation of the Calle Real Baja towards the Torre de los Picos. Moreover, you see the U-shaped pond with a pavilion and ceramic remains in the paving as well as a magnificent view of the urban landscape with the tower of the Palacio de El Partal to the left and to the right a view of the Generalife with the vegetable gardens.

One street to the east of the palace joined the Torre de los Picos to the Calle Real Alta. Following this path you can see the Torre de los Picos.

Torre de los Picos

Name: Torre de los Picos
Date: 14th-15th cent.
Sultanate: Muḥammad II (1273-1302) but with possible interventions under Muḥammad V (1354-1359;1362-1391)
Note: The tower that protects the Puerta del Arrabal and reinforces the wall. This tower is structurally one of the strangest and most original in the Alhambra. The stone-carved windows, a ribbed vault in the main chamber and the stone projections you can see in the upper body are clearly different to other Nasrid constructions.

THE TORRE DE LOS PICOS is one of the strangest and most original in the Alhambra and Christian builders may possibly have intervened. It was named after the cantilever projections in the upper body that permit better protection of the base of the tower and the gate located next to it. This gate, Puerta del Arrabal, is one of four in the city wall and connects it with the Generalife.

On the inside of the tower are two rooms, one above the other, and a terrace with the unusual feature of a traditional, Gothic ribbed vault with geometric figures of Islamic origin. The tower can only be visited when it is opened as "space of the month".

From here you can see the important vegetable gardens of the Generalife estate. Some have kept their original names, like the "Huerta Colorá" and the "Huerta de la Mercería". This was considered the "pantry to the Alhambra" for the role it played in supplying fruit and vegetables. Bounded by a mud wall and terraced plant beds, according to the tradition of Islamic agriculture still applied on Andalusia's Mediterranean coast, they still offer a faithful image of a medieval landscape cultivated in the same way and of enormous cultural value.

Next you find the Torre del Cadí or del Candil. This had a strictly military function and was a point of special importance in controlling access to the Generalife, with the entrance street and gate just in front of the tower.

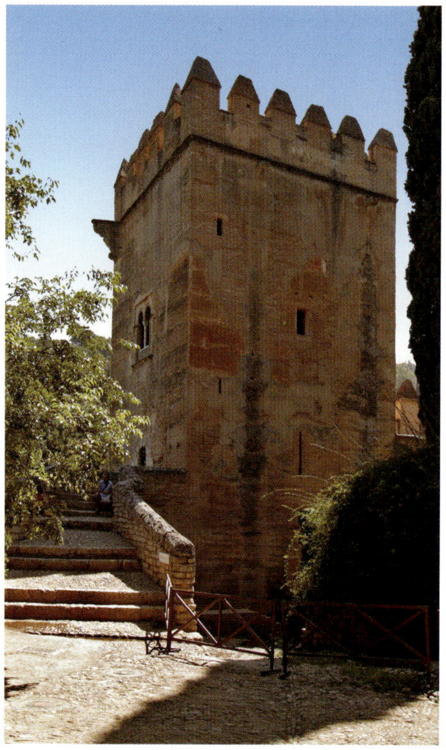

Torre de los Picos

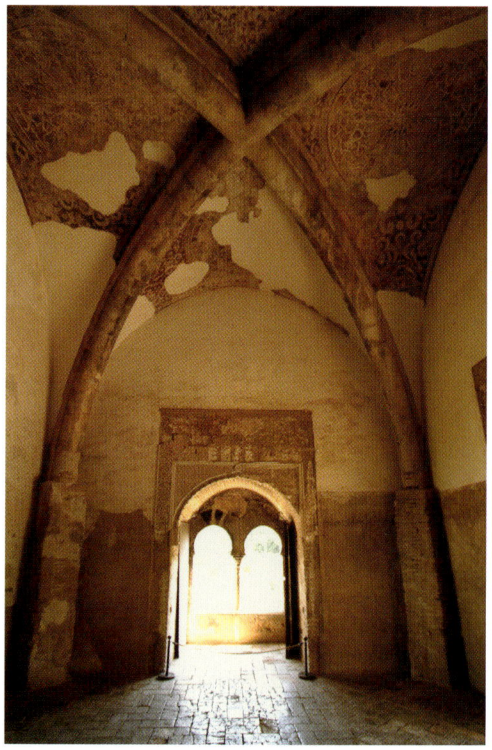

Detail of the vaulted ceiling with painted mural in the Torre de los Picos

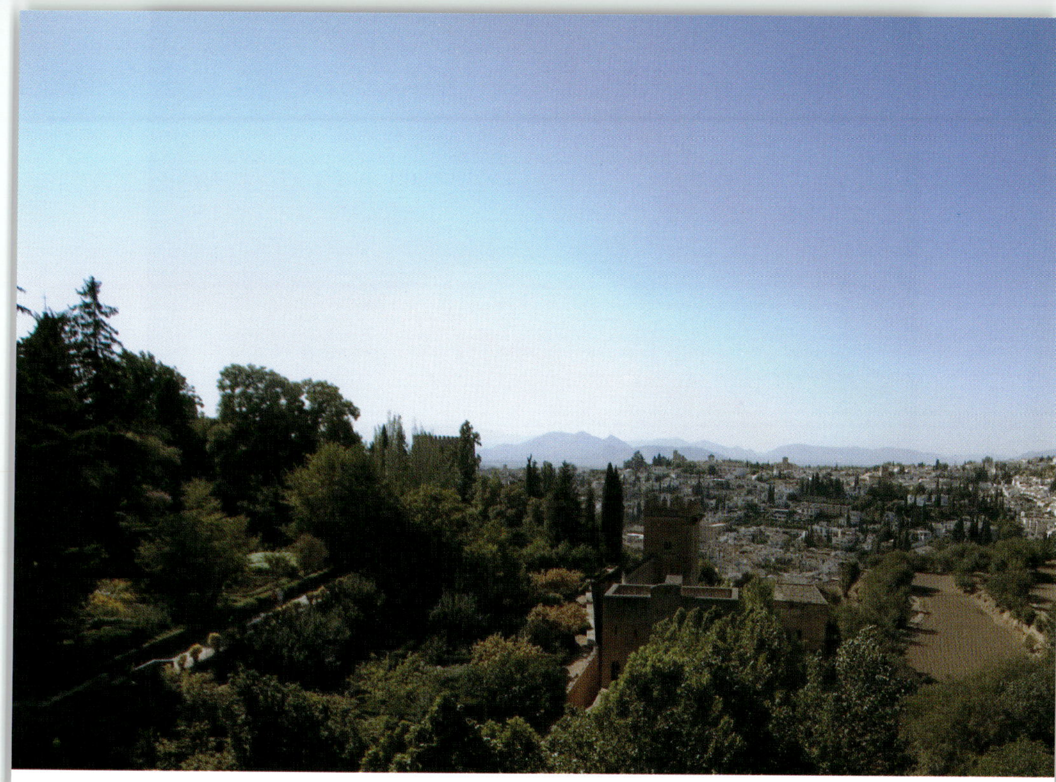

El Generalife estate

Torre de la Cautiva

Name: Torre de la Cautiva
Date: 1333-1354
Sultanate: Yūsuf I (1333-1354)
Note: Tower palace or *calahorra*. Surprising novelty in the type of Andalusian towers as it incorporates within a single, apparently defensive tower, a palace of minimal proportions, with painstaking decoration of stucco, tiling and texts written by the poet-vizier Ibn al-Ŷayyāb.

THE PATH THAT YOU FOLLOW on the visit gradually approaches the wall, bordered by parterres, to lead onto an esplanade in front of the Torre de la Cautiva. Both this tower and the following one along the line of the wall are works of most special interest in the constructive and artistic context of the Alhambra and of the art of al-Andalus. The poet-vizier Ibn al-Jaṭīb referred to them and praised them as *calahorra*. Visits are restricted to special times and circumstances.

Veritable fortresses on the outside, with their clean, straight volumes that scarcely differ from the

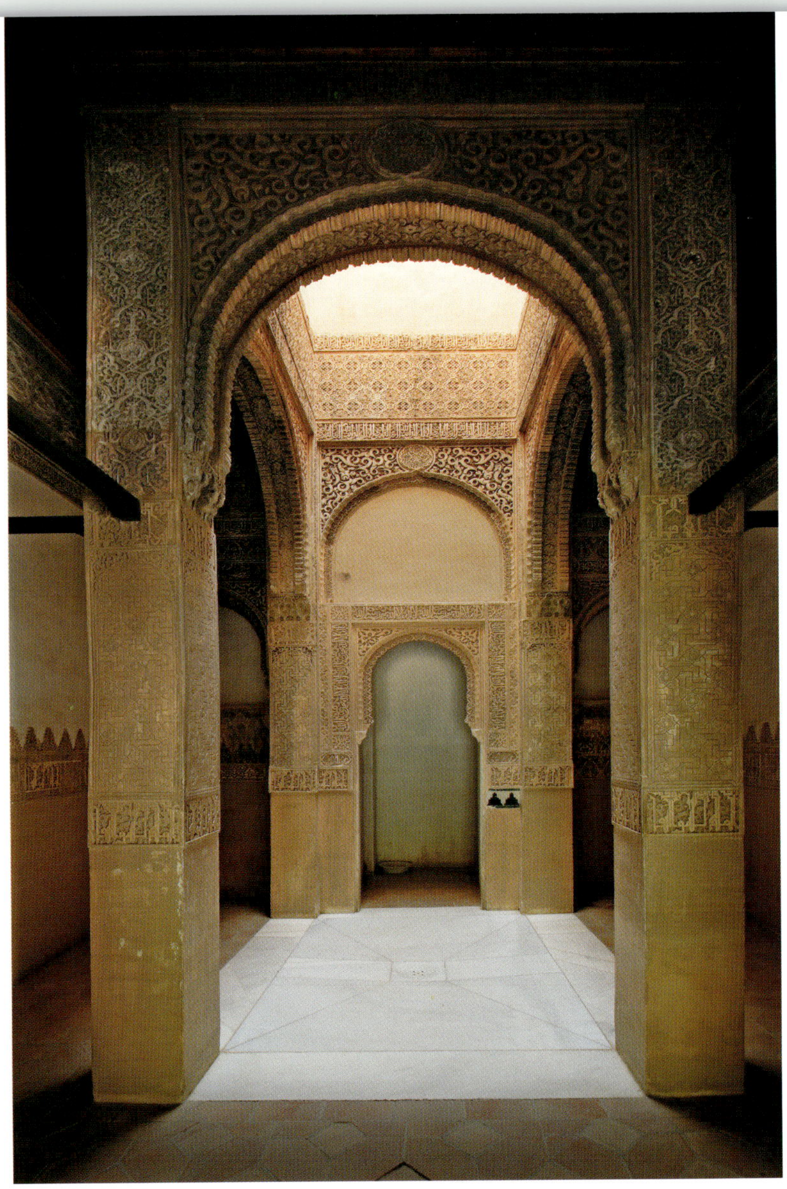

Interior of the Torre de la Cautiva

others in the precinct, on the inside they house delicate palaces in miniature, decorated whimsically and with a distribution difficult to guess from the outside.

The Torre de la Cautiva is to a certain extent the minimum expression of a Nasrid palace, enclosing within it all the elements necessary and typical in the *alcázares* of Granada, except the latrine of which not a trace remains. This is shown by its access with a crooked entry, after which it leads into a patio of barely two metres square, porticado on three sides with arches on pillars, and in the background the central chamber with bed chambers open to the countryside.

To a certain extent this hall is a first taste, a masterful trial of the symbolic, political and ornamental concept of the Salón de Comares. The dado is covered by beautiful tiling, finished off by friezes with Koranic inscriptions of complex manufacture and a perfect curvature of the pieces that adapt themselves to the half columns of the bed chambers. Above the dado are stucco adornments in addition to some epigraphs that record poems created by Ibn al-Ŷayyāb.

Unfortunately the paving, which must have been of tiles, and the original wooden structure have been lost. All the other lower rooms in arches, *tacas*, doorjambs, record with true obsession, epigraphs of religious content with continuous references to God and the benefits received from His especial protection. They also mention Yūsuf I as the builder.

The strictly military towers, like the Torre del Candil, that is located below the Torre de la Cautiva, are separated from the urban precinct by the Camino de Ronda, so that the parapet walk, the *adarve*, runs along the wall without possible communication with the city. In contrast, the Torre de la Cautiva crossed the street that passed below over a bridge or arch; the *adarve* passes similarly through a lower tunnel at the level of the main floor of the towers. In this way, the guards who patrolled the *adarve* passed below the tower-palace without disturbing the inhabitants of this tower, whereas in the military area, most of the *adarve* had to pass obligatorily through the interior room from which the passing of the guard was controlled.

Torre de las Infantas

Name: Torre de las Infantas
Date: 1392-1408
Sultanate: Muḥammad VII (1392-1408)
Note: Tower-palace or *calahorra*. This is the last construction that can be dated in the Nasrid Alhambra and in spite of presenting a less virtuous decoration than the other preceding palaces, the structural solution is highly original offering spatial richness.

If our knowledge of the Alhambra always provides us with admirable contrasts and surprises, in the Torre de las Infantas we have an eminent example. The smooth surfaces of

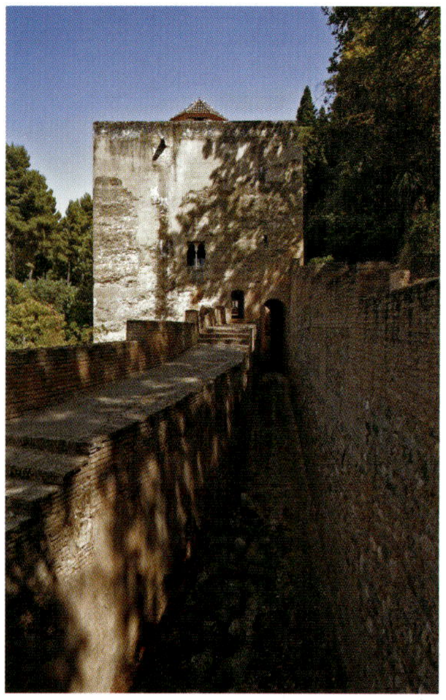

Torre de las Infantas with the parapet walk, or *adarve*, and Camino de Ronda

Torre de las Infantas

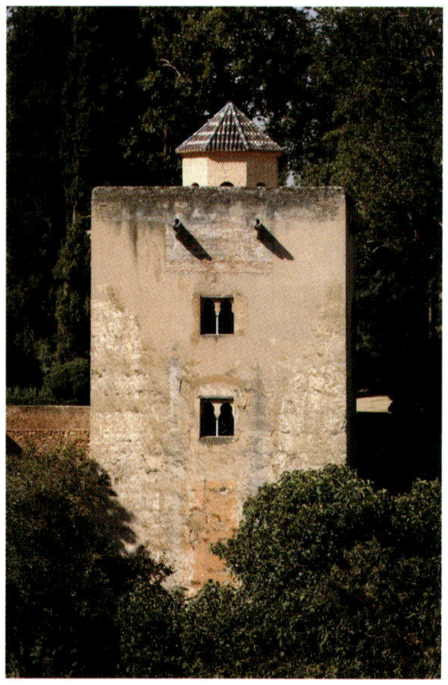

its façades, barely interrupted by recesses opened for the geminated windows formerly closed by thick window screens, would never lead you to suspect the structural complexity of the palace residence enclosed within. Its architectural merit has been increased by the suggestion in Washington Irving's tale of the three princesses that this was the origin of its name.

It is the last building of recognized importance to be built in the Alhambra, around 1393-1394, and even so the skills deployed in the layout of so small a palace continue to surprise. If in the previous tower, the adaptation was carried out on a complete palace, with its patio and portico included, here it adopts the structure of a royal hall, none other than the great Sala de Dos Hermanas, whose layout it repeats, adding to it the obligatory crooked entry passage.

Following the path that continues along the Camino de Ronda you reach another tower, the Torre del Cabo de la Carrera. As its name suggests, this was the end of this stretch of the wall and the parapet walk, the *adarve*, and also constitutes the end of the visit to the Alhambra before heading up the path towards the Generalife.

Leaving the Paseo de las Torres, you find yourself back at the modern bridge that you crossed at the beginning of the tour. Passing over the bridge

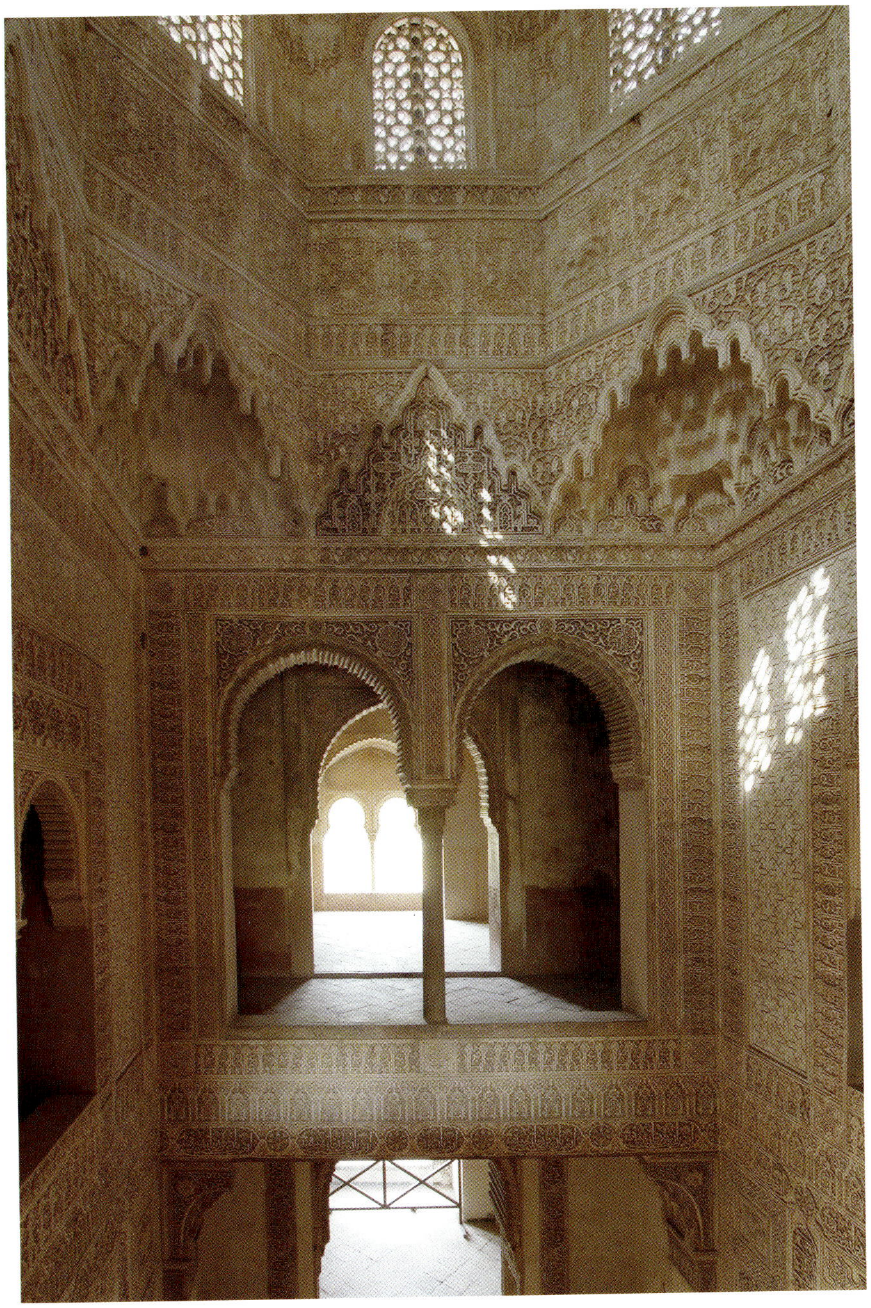

and to the right you head towards the entrance/exit pavilion, but to the left you enter the Generalife.

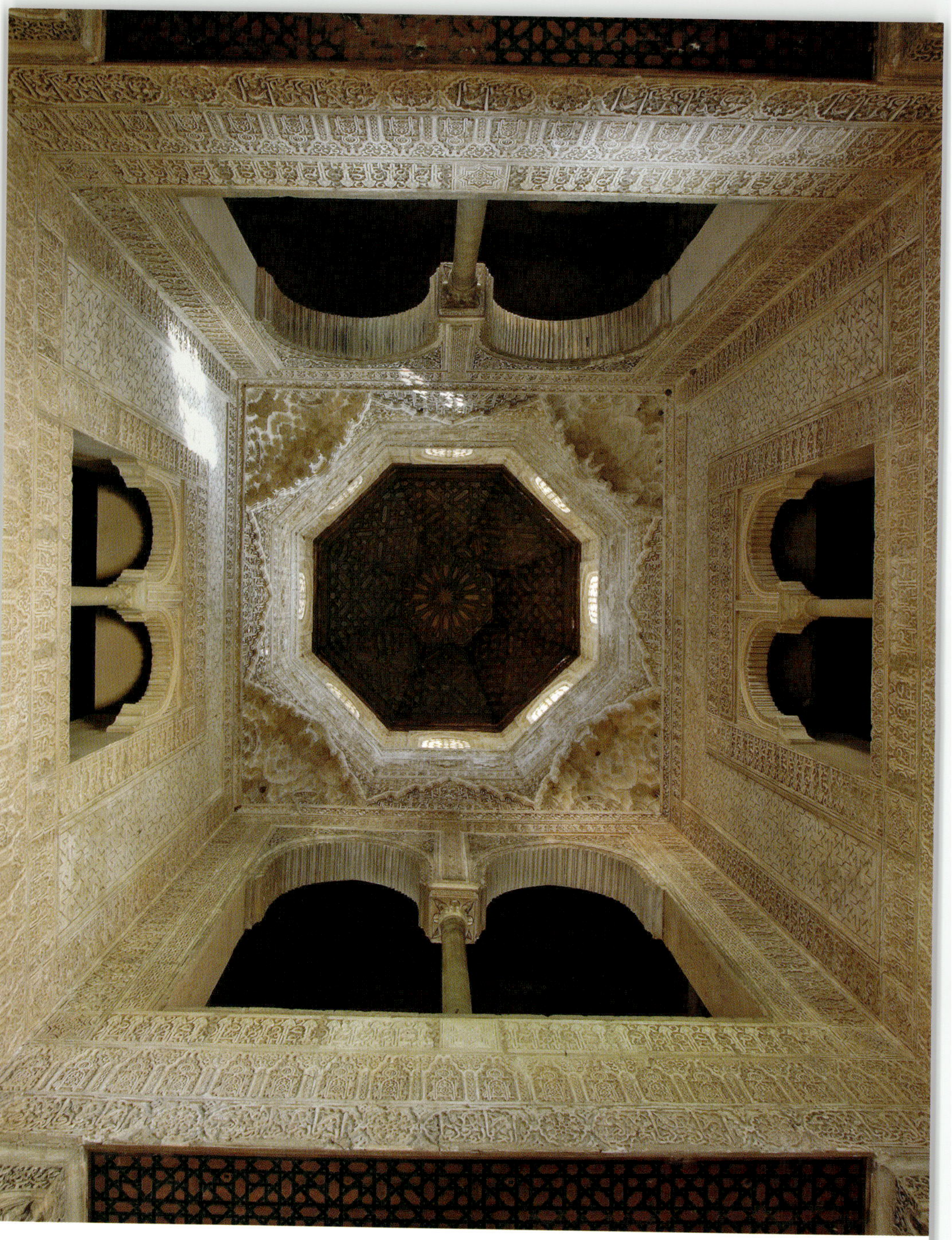

These pages show the inside of the tower, or *calahorra*, of Muḥammad VII (Torre de las Infantas), in its prodigious expression of contrasts between its closed and austere outer appearance and the organizationally and ornamentally rich interior. It is an example of the decline of the best century of Nasrid architecture.

El Generalife

Name: Generalife ("Garden", with several significant attributes)
Date: 13th-17th cent.; some gardens and Auditorium 20th cent.
Note: The gardens and hydraulic system

IN FRONT OF THE WALLS of the Alhambra, on the northeast side, stretching up the hillside of the Cerro del Sol, the *almunia*, the recreational estate of the Nasrid sultans, occupies a wide surface area that goes from the dip towards the River Darro valley to the current entrance pavilion to the Alhambra complex. Its name, Generalife (Ŷinān al-'arīf), holds a meaning about which various interpretations exist ("Jardin del zambrero"; "Jardin del citarista"; "Jardin del arquitecto"; "La Huerta Excelsa"; "Casa o mansion del Placer"), all of which revolve around the common concept of garden or *huerta* and its pleasant purpose. That, along with is exploitation for farming is why Nature becomes the essential element even though it includes equally palatial residences of an antiquity surpassing some in the Alhambra.

The historic vicissitudes the Generalife has suffered have above all punished the buildings, which show signs of the numerous alterations but, even so, maintain the greater part of their structure and more than enough elements of interest. Following the conquest in 1492, the estate was handed over to the noble *Comendador* Juan de Hinestrosa who with it assumed the role of mayor. It quickly changed hands many times until finally *don* Pedro Venegas, a knight belonging to a noble family of Granada, and his descendents, the marquises of Campotéjar, who from the seventeenth century held the title of keeper in perpetuity. Possession

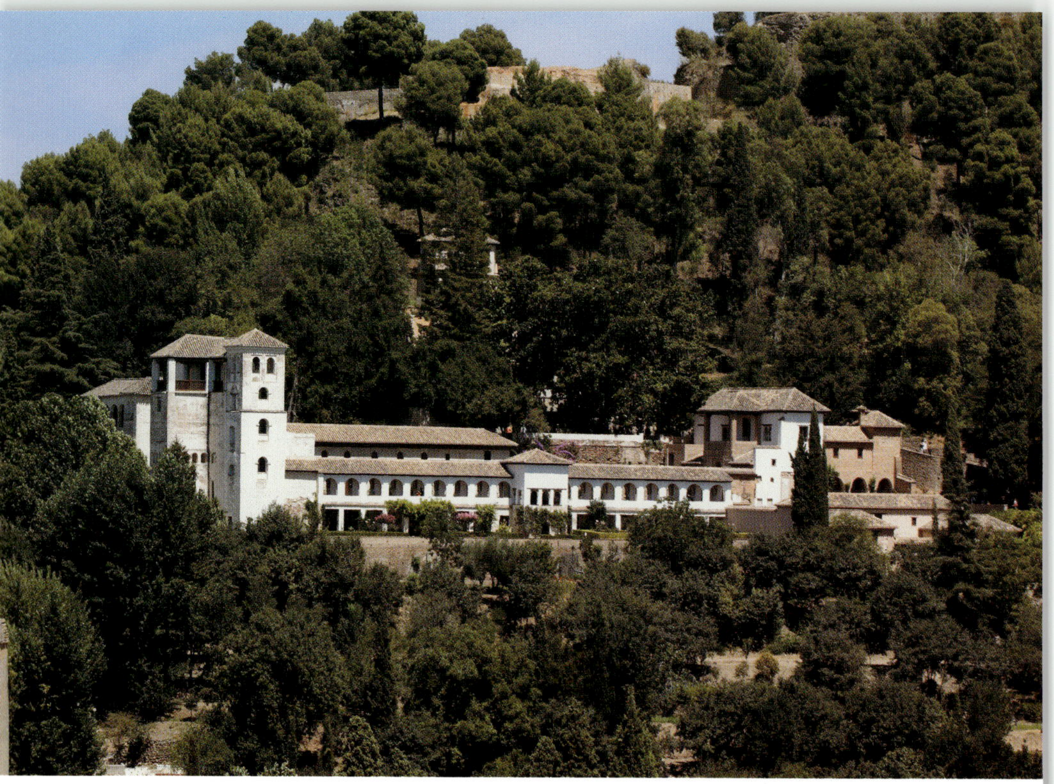

The Generalife

of the property was confused with the title and long legal battles ensued until in 1921 the Italian branch of the family, the Pallavicini, returned it to the Spanish state, integrating it into the wealth of the Alhambra, the complex of which historically it always was a part.

Access to the Generalife

There were three routes of access to the estate, at least originally: one directly from the Alhambra, the *camino real*, reserved for the sultan and his entourage, ascending through the vegetable gardens from the ravine of the Rey Chico through a small gate in front of the Torre del Candil; another, to the southeast end, near to the current entrance pavilion, and another to the north, in the upper part, through the so-called "Postigo de los Carneros". Currently the tourist visit is directed along the Paseo de los Cipreses and through the modern or "new" gardens that occupy the ancient Huerta de Fuente Peña and part of the Huerta Grande, linked with the entrance patios by the *camino real*.

One of the first constructions that attracts your attention is the Auditorium, the open-air theatre inaugurated in 1954, reformed between 2005 and 2006 and intended fundamentally for ballet performances in Granada's annual Festival of Music and Dance. From here you can stroll through the lower or new gardens, begun in 1931 and planned by the architect Francisco Prieto Moreno. First, the tour takes you through the second phase (finished in 1951) where the gardens are dominated by plants and jets of water that evoke Granada and whose principal design is based on four watercourses that form a cross. After these gardens begins the first phase, that comprises the sector touching the Nasrid construction and draws labyrinths. It is worth the trouble stopping to contemplate the views of the Alhambra and the city from here.

These gardens, although in general they conform to a formalization in line with modern western tastes, incorporate the richness of scented plants, shrubs and fruit-bearing trees connected with the tradition of Granada. Similarly, that the ground along the central path should be of smooth pebblestones and the hedges and "ars toparia" of sober geometric forms insert it into the Renaissance tradition.

Having crossed the gardens you approach the Generalife, access to which is through two entrance patios that have the structural simplicity of a workhouse, although it would not be so marked then when it conserved the plastered outer face of the wall, today lost. The first patio, called the "Apeadero" or "Descabalgamiento" as there is a bench built up against the end wall for riders to dismount, has buildings at the side intended to be used as stables.

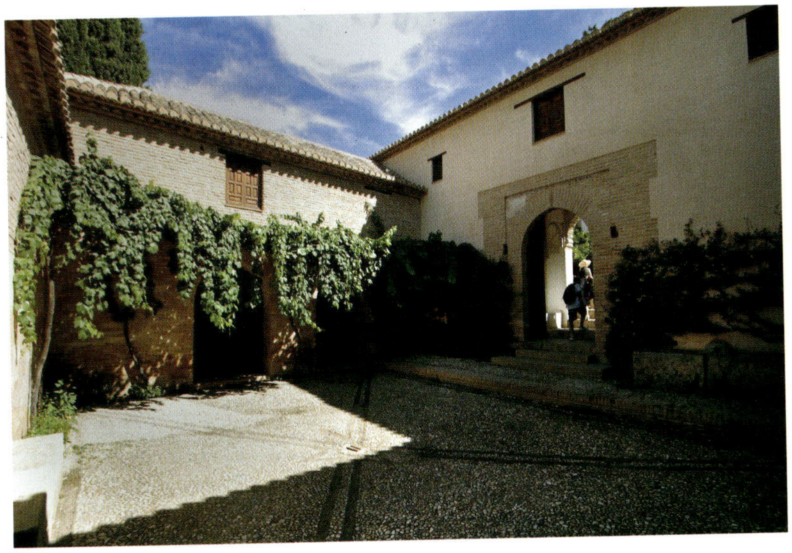

Patio de Descabalgamiento in the Generalife

The second, higher, patio to which you climb up a staircase after passing through a door that is in line with the first one and above which appear the same symbols of the hand and the key seen in the Puerta de la Explanada (or de la Justicia), also had galleries of arches at the sides but these have been lost today. Similarly, what is outstanding here is the lintel arched door which you climb up some steps to, as if it were a podium, with an interesting ceramic decoration in the lintel and the symbolic key, too. After the door and up some steep stairs you step out into a corner of the famous Patio de la Acequia, inside the palace-residence. A corner view of this enclosed garden was the correct one demanded by the aesthetic sensitivities of the times.

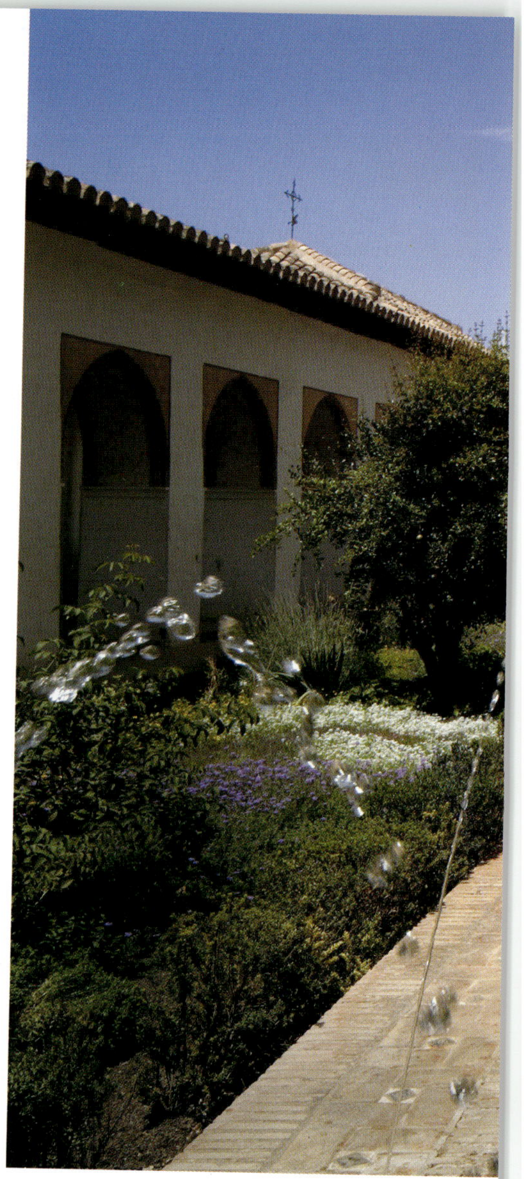

The residential centre of the Generalife

Name: Palacio del Generalife
Date: Fundamentally, the Nasrid construction lasted from 1275 to 1325 but substantial reforms would take place after the Christian conquest and especially in the 16th cent.
Sultanate: Muḥammad II (1273-1302); Muḥammad III (1303-1309); Ismā'īl I (1314-1325)
Note: The crossing with its elongated parterres and the watercourse that shapes the patio itself.

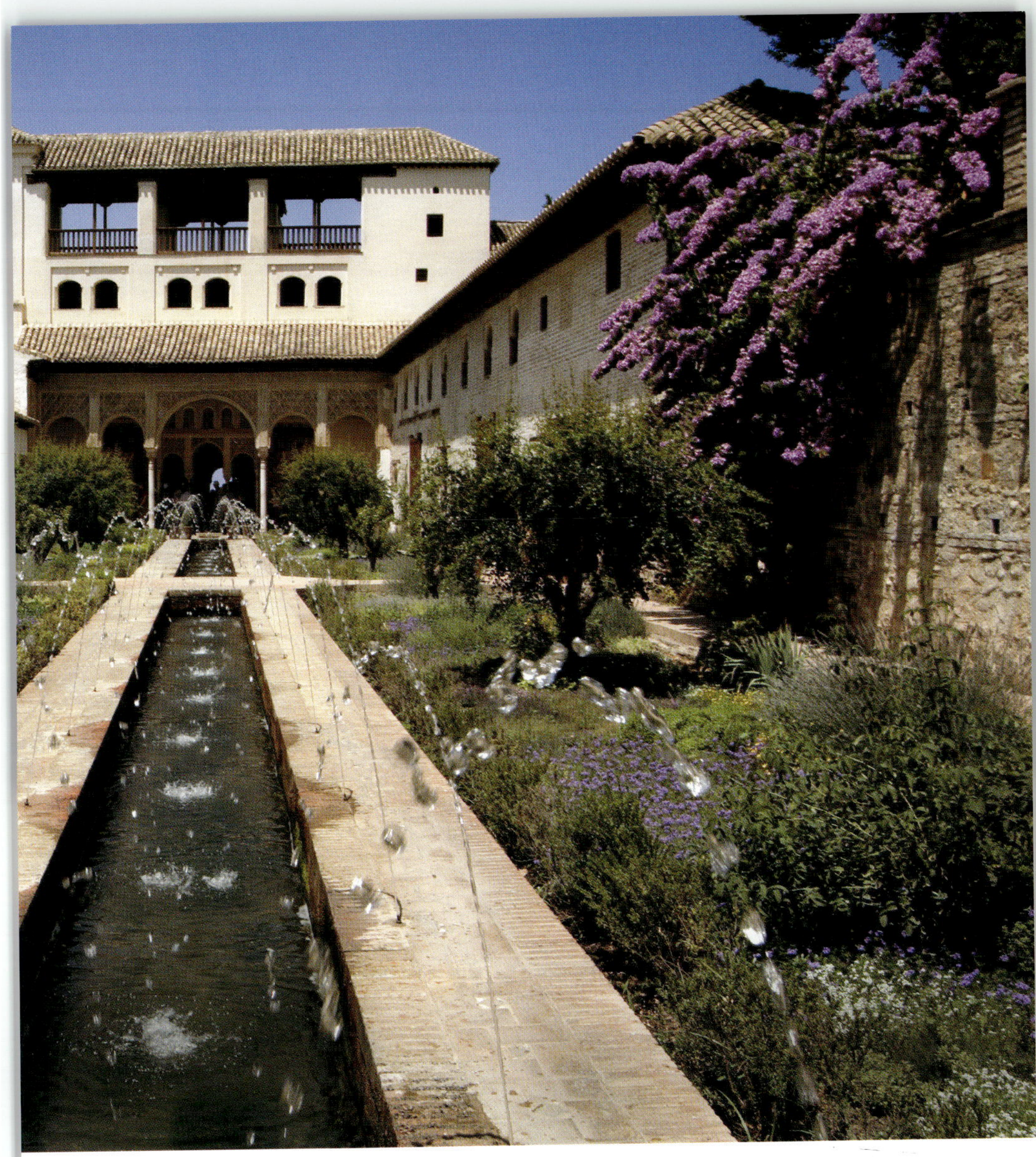

Patio del Palacio del Generalife (or Patio de la Acequia)

The Residence consists of two pavilions, north and south, joined by a long, water–course; in clear anticipation of the narrow structure of El Partal and the Comares palace. It was altered in 1319 by Ismā'īl which indicates that it must originally date from the second half of the thirteenth century. Both pavilions have been quite substantially altered having lost, moreover, almost all the side buildings that closed off the patio. However, its structure is perceptible and the galleries of decorative arches in front of the pavilions confirm this,

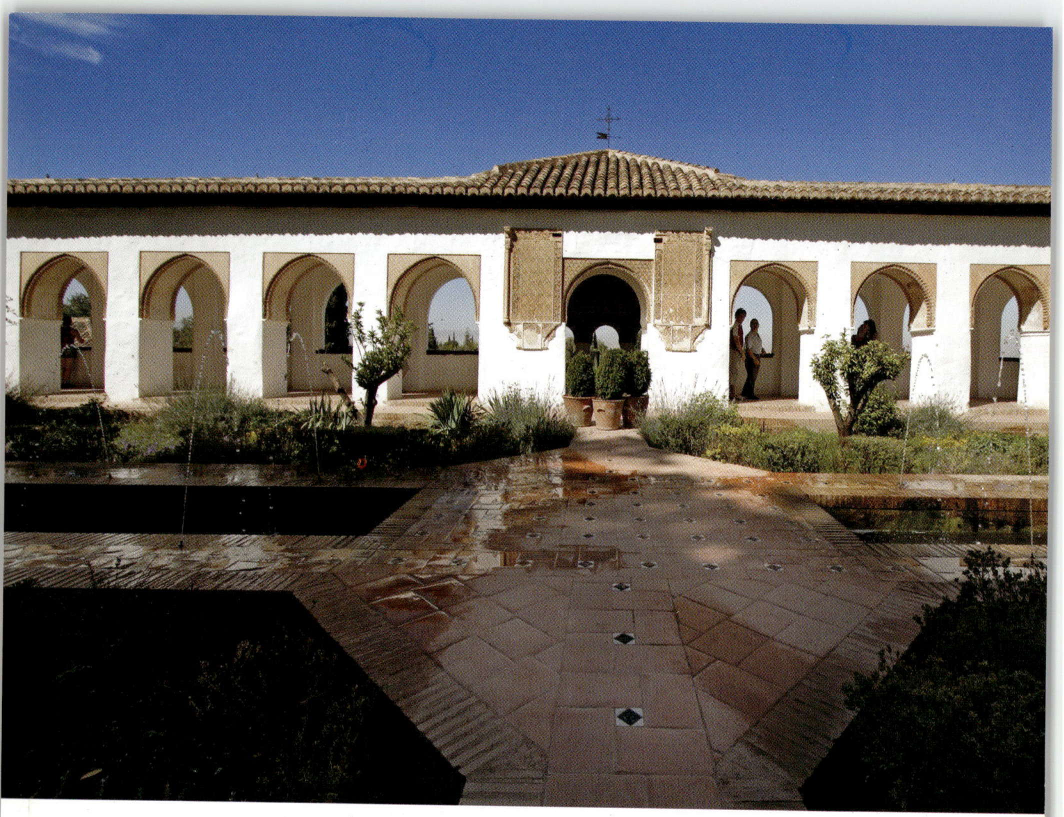

Detail of the place that would have been occupied by the pavilion in the centre of the Patio de la Acequia

above all in the north gallery where the roofing is continued with the little houses at the side that have survived.

For some, the south pavilion could have been intended as rooms for concubines and eunuchs, a "feminine" domain. This type of construction must have had two floors and a viewing point above the patio on the upper floor, although the current distribution of the space is much different. The remains of a staircase to the east permits access to the upper floor.

However, without doubt what attracts your attention is the Patio de la Acequia. The most spectacular element is the *acequia* itself, the central canal through which runs the already tranquil water of the Acequia Real. From the top of the mountain, the water comes down with great force to continue on its route to water vegetable and flower gardens. This long, narrow canal crosses in the centre through a platform, thus outlining a crossing, similar to that in the Palacio de los Leones and other earlier palaces in al-Andalus and in the Orient, but contrasting with the typically elongated type so often found. Each of the four parterres is octagonal in shape and since the intervention undertaken in 2003, they have been lowered to their original level. The

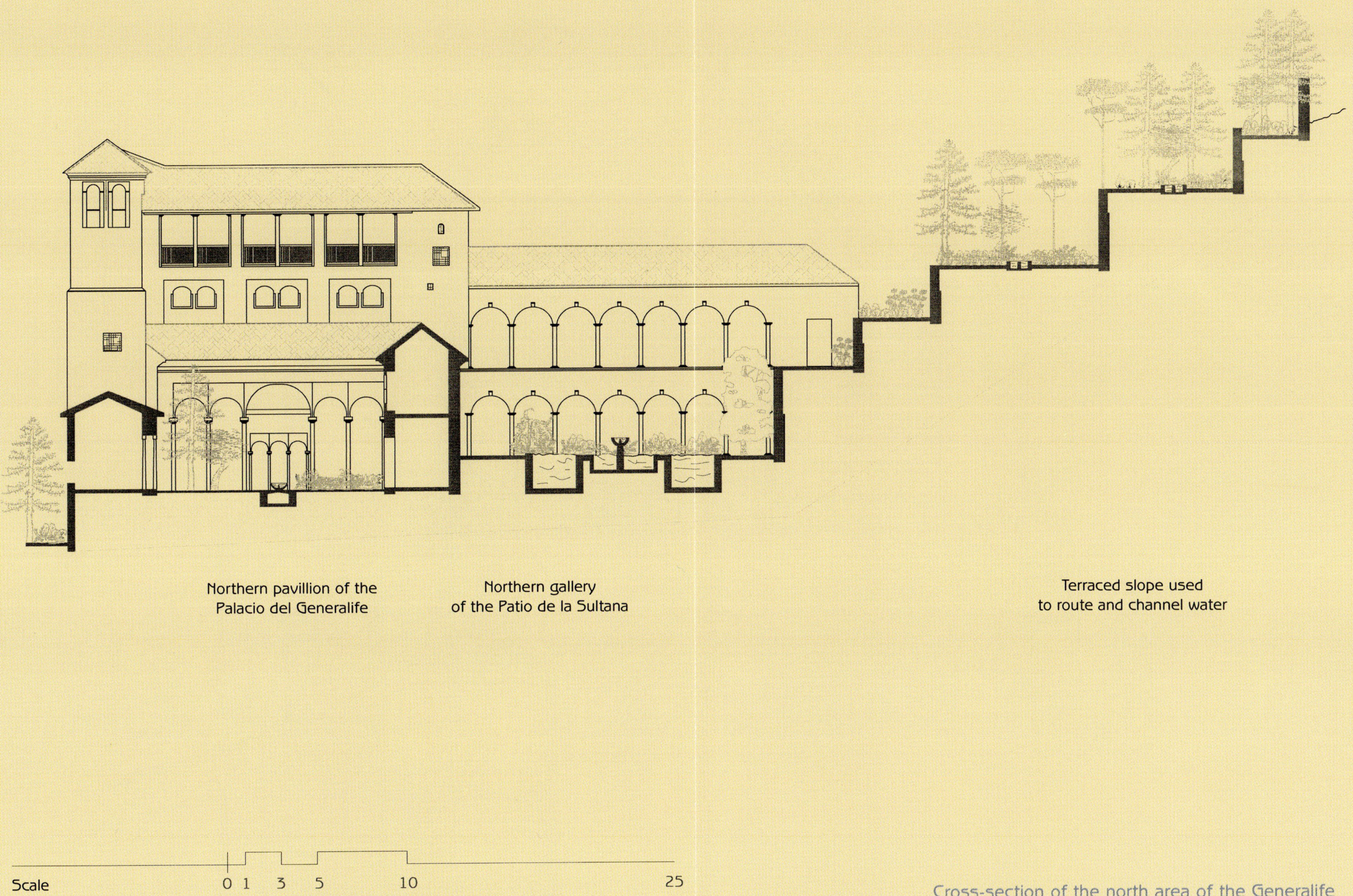

Cross-section of the north area of the Generalife

The Generalife

1. Patio de Descabalgamientos
2. Patio
3. Patio de la Acequia
4. Patio de la Sultana
5. Escalera de Leones
6. Jardines Altos
7. Escalera del Agua
8. Mirador Romántico
9. Casa de los Amigos

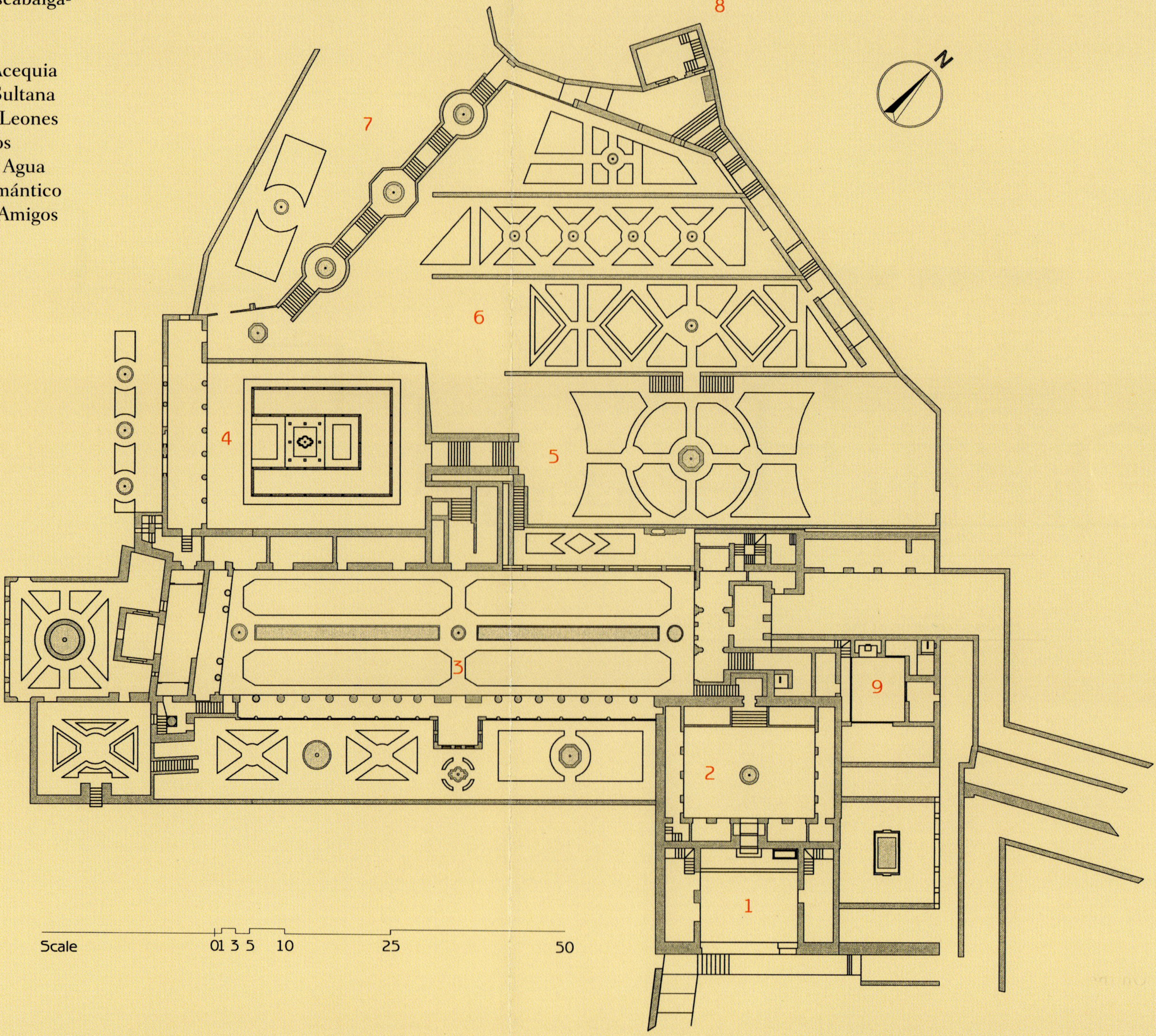

crossing itself, the point of intersection of the two axes, draws an octagonal structure in which would have stood a *cenador*, a pavilion surrounded by planted flowers and low shrubs similar to the flora of the Nasrid period. Of course, it did not count on the lines of high jets of water that have made this patio so popular but which date from the early nineteenth century and are a clearly romantic conception. To capture the crucial value of this central structure it is wise to bear in mind a text by a fourteenth-century Hispano-Arabic writer, Ibn Luyūn, who in his treatise on Agriculture describes an ideal *almunia* in these terms:

There should be a pavilion in the centre of the garden for
those who rest in it, who look at all the surroundings, in such
a way that he who enters should not hear what is said there, nor
anyone arrive unnoticed. The pavilion should be surrounded
with climbing roses and myrtle and of all the plants
that adorn a garden. This will be longer than it is wide
so that the view may talk at length in its contemplation...

(English version based on a translation from Arabic into Spanish by Joaquina Eguaras)

On the east side you find remains of some individual houses which are the few witnesses to have survived the fire of 1958. On the opposite side a long Christian gallery opens up conserving painted ornamental elements of the Catholic Kings. Originally, the wall was higher with the only opening in the centre, corresponding to the current viewing point projecting out over the lower garden. This space, square, still has remains of stucco from the time of Ismāʿīl on top of other even older ones from the beginnings of the sixteenth century.

Finally, the northern pavilion offers us the regal part with a lower and an upper floor, although the upper one is a wide-ranging late sixteenth-century Christian alteration that modifies the original proportions. The ground floor would house the throne room, as in Comares, which can be deduced from certain verses that adorn the central arch and which refer to the "dais" as being handsome as "the bride who appears bedecked...". In spite of being a recreational estate, guests came and in addition, affairs of state requiring urgent attention would be resolved here. A more intimate part would be provided by the tower viewing point on the western edge, fruit of the reforms of Ismāʿīl, about which the poetic inscriptions also inform us.

From the hall in the north pavilion you go up to the natural terrace occupied on its north edge by a body with a double Renaissance gallery. Before this, a patio known as the Patio del Ciprés de la Sultana opens up.

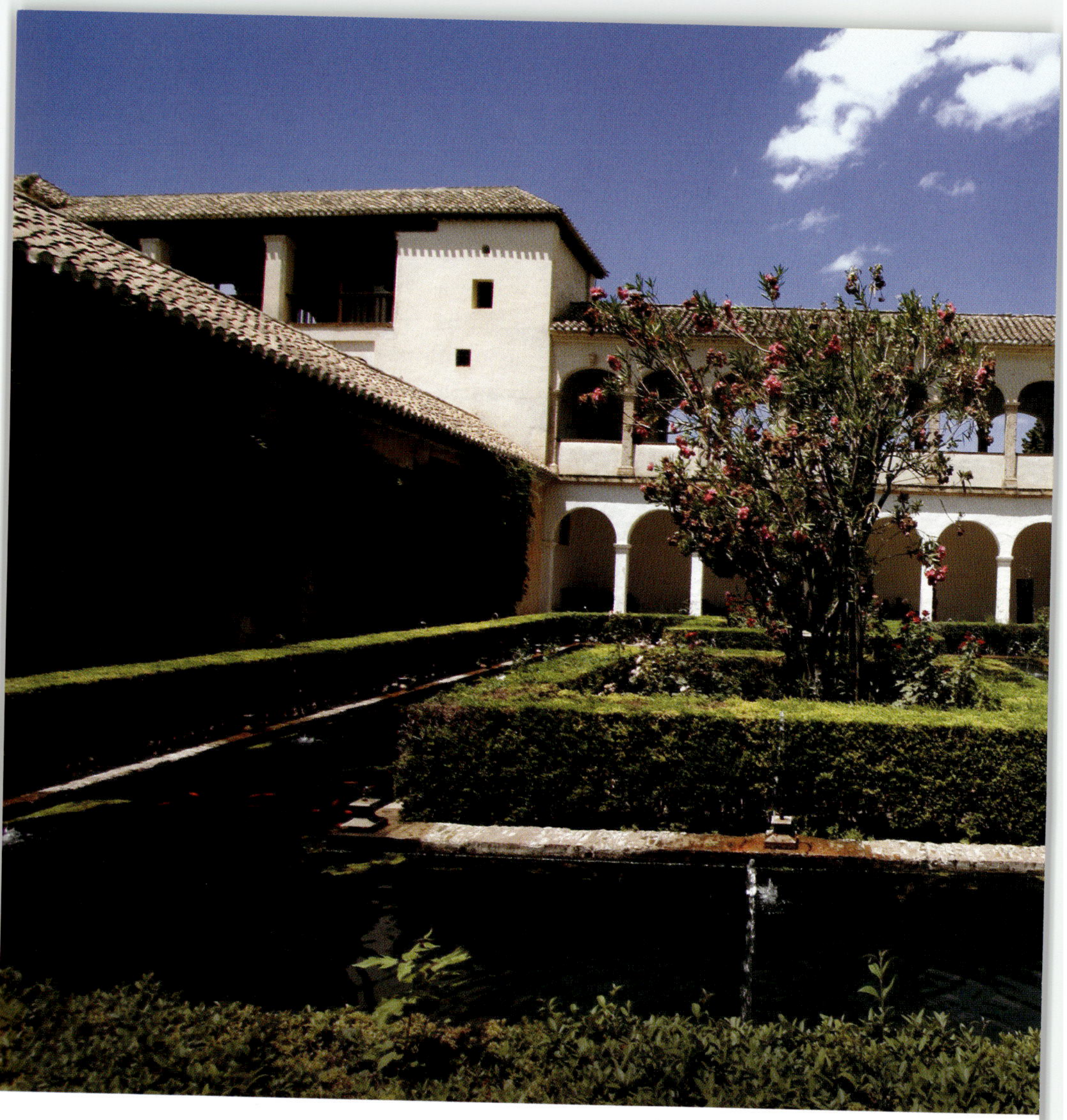

Patio del Ciprés de la Sultana and Jardines Altos

Name: Patio del Ciprés de la Sultana, after the enormous cypress tree at the foot of which, according to the legend narrated by Ginés Pérez de Hita, Boabdil's wife met with a member of the Abencerrajes clan, related to the sultan.
Date: Both the Patio del Ciprés de la Sultana and the Escalera del Agua are dated between 1275 and 1525.

THE 1958 FIRE that affected all of this part left clear signs of the existence of baths below this patio. In front of the garden of the

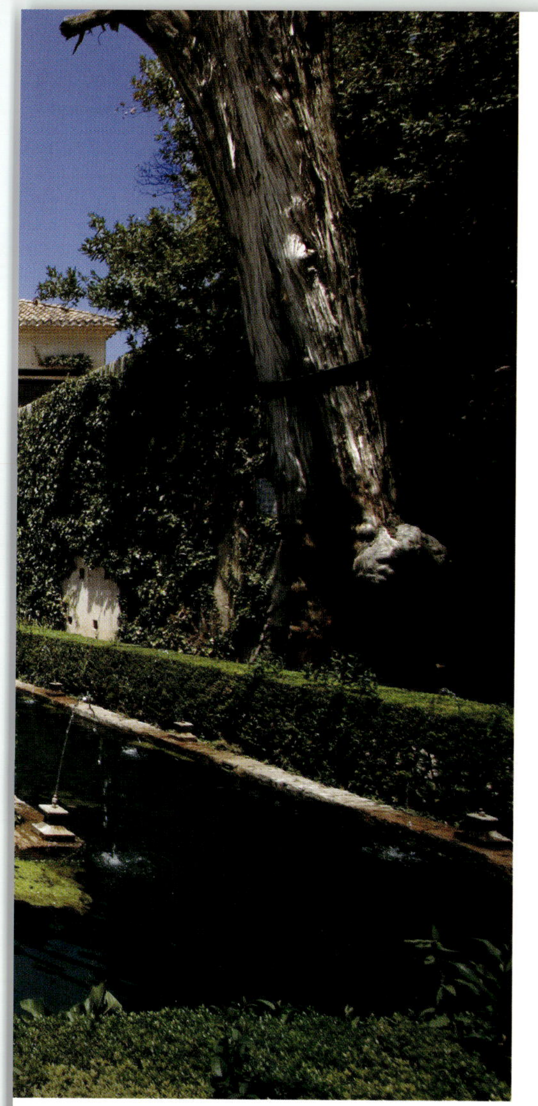

Patio de la Sultana

Patio de la Acequia in the Generalife, the Patio del Ciprés de la Sultana recalls the forms of a Baroque garden although it is dated later. On the eastern side of the patio you can see part of the Acequia Real as well as the cypress tree that gives it its name.

Above this space you find the upper gardens which you reach via the stairs de los Leones, named after the two, glazed ceramic figures that crown the entrance door. These are modern–built gardens and have a great variety of species of trees together with the flowers and jets of water. A plaque recalls the meeting between the ambassador of the Republic of Venice, the poet Andrea Navagero, and Garcilaso de la Vega during the summer of 1526 in the course of which the Venetian encouraged the Spaniard to introduce Italian metre in his poetry and, thus, into Spanish literature. Having read the plaque and climbed the stairs to the left you arrive at the Escalera del Agua, the water stairs. Perhaps the most spectacular in the Generalife together with the Patio de la Acequia. To Navagero, we owe a magnificent description of the sixteenth-century Generalife gardens and, above all, of these stairs that ascend to the higher part where the torrent of water that supplied the Acequia Real makes its entry. The watercourse is divided into three stretches with intermediate mesetas due to the steep slope. The water descends dizzily via the handrail and leaps in cascades, as well as along the channel that goes down the centre of the steps. Covered by a vault of bay trees, romantically but faithful to the tastes of the Nasrid sultans, it evokes the sensuality of water with all its connotations of fertility and purification. The path may have been

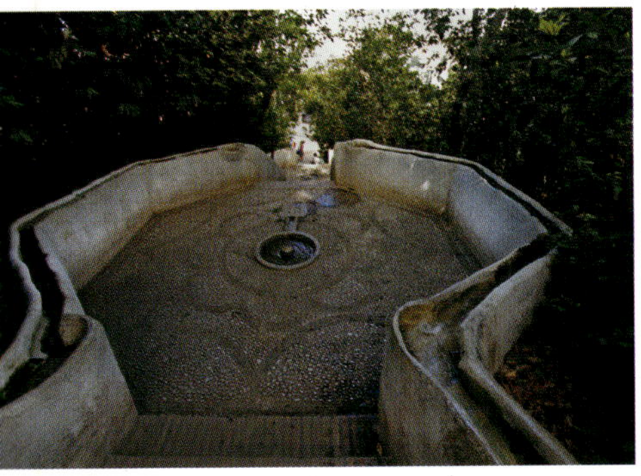

Detail of the Escalera del Agua with the handrail flowing with water

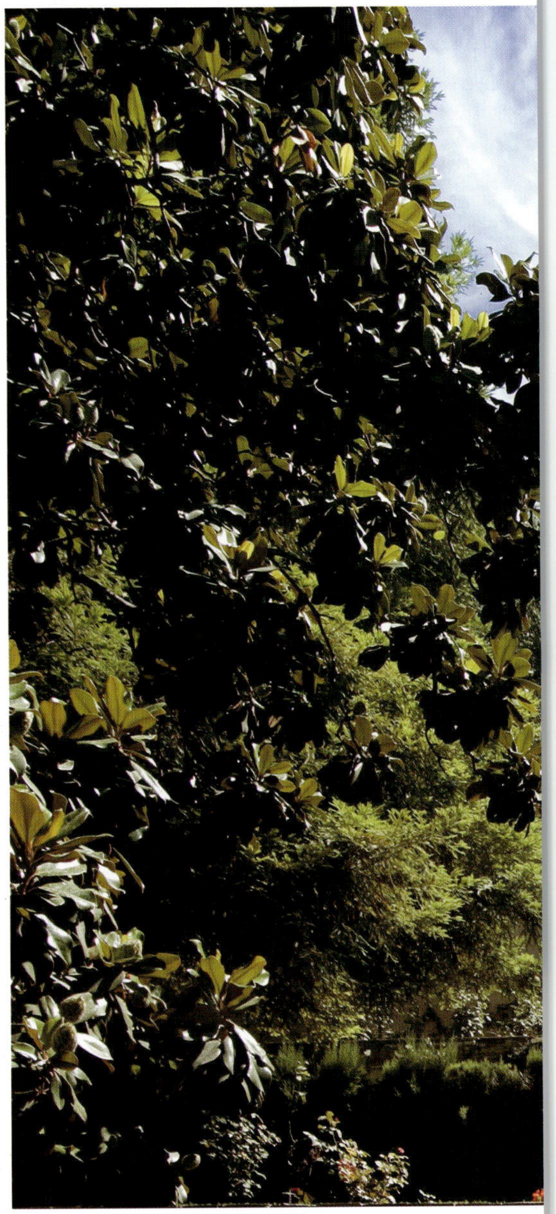

understood thus because, it is believed that once it led you up to an oratory which may in turn have been that referred to in 1836 by the administrator of the Generalife when constructing the Neogothic pavilion known as the Mirador Romántico.

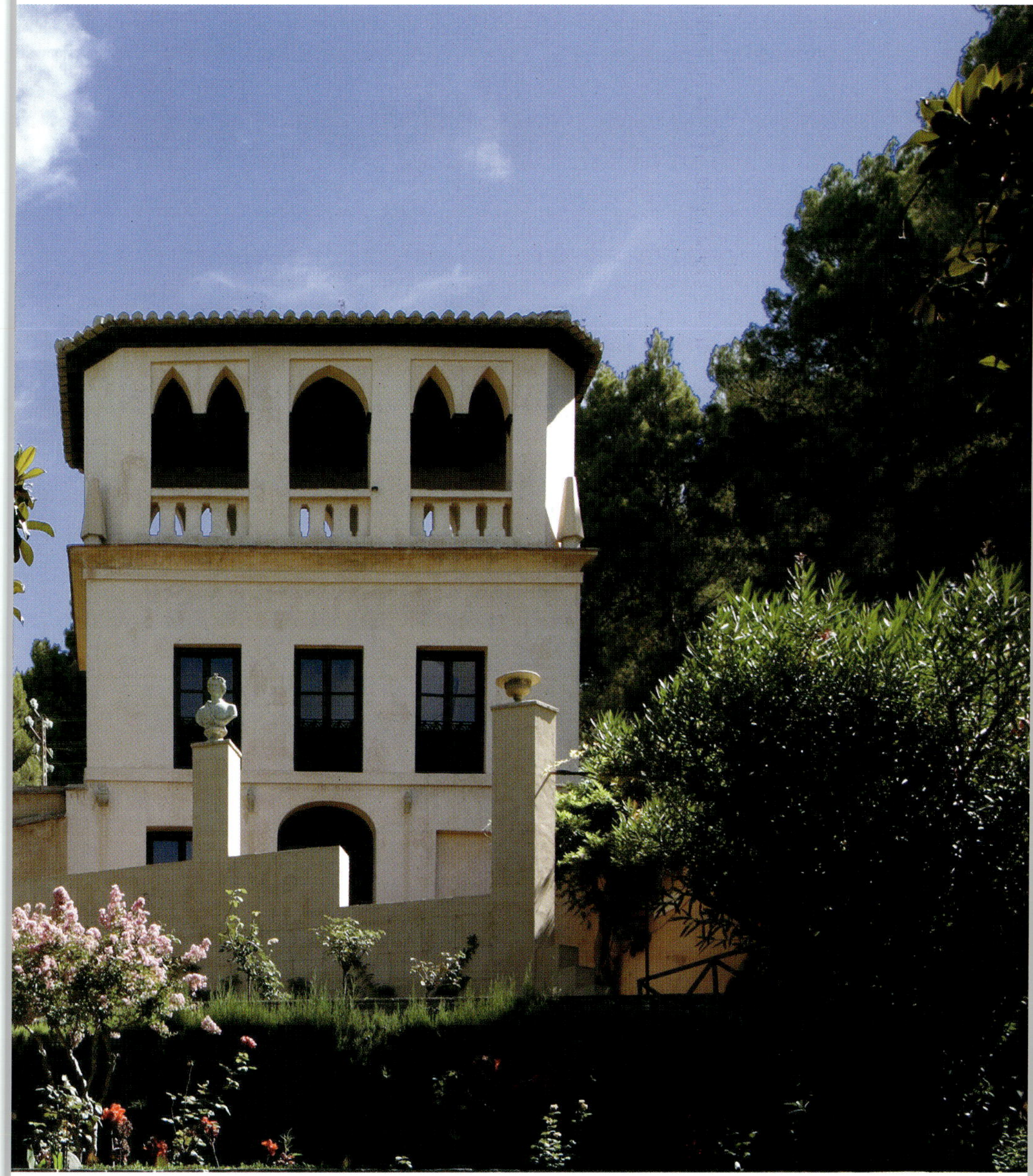

Mirador Romántico

Leaving by the so-called Postigo de los Carneros you walk down towards the Casa de los Amigos. Anyone who does not want to climb up to the Mirador Romántico should follow a straight line there from the Patio del Ciprés de la Sultana.

Casa de los Amigos

Name: The name Casa de los Amigos, the house of friends, comes from the supposition that it is the guest residence.
Date: Uncertain; some suggest it is post-15th-16th cent. although it is generally accepted as being one of the oldest constructions in the Alhambra and therefore would be dated 12th cent.
Note: While being an area that depends on the Palacio del Generalife, it has its own independent identity as a residential building.

THE BUILDING, behind the south pavilion of the Patio de la Acequia, was the guest residence that the much-quoted Ibn Luyūn recommends an *almunia* should have:

In the lower part of the garden there will be a dwelling
with its door, for a guest or friend of the owner,
that may have a pond surrounded by trees, that hide it
from those who live in the upper part.

(English version based on a translation from Arabic into Spanish by Joaquina Eguaras)

The remains conserved today, and which are only open on specific days of the year, permit us to deduce that the house had a square patio at its centre, around which the rooms were set out. On the south side, from where we currently enter, would be the hall. On the east side, closest to the Acequia Real, is the fountain or basin. On the south-east side is a latrine. On the north side would be the kitchen, while the stairs that we find on the northeast side may indicate that it had a second floor although the only thing that is certain is that the staircase was used at a later time as a link with the Palacio del Generalife.

You leave the Generalife along the Paseo de las Adelfas, parallel to the avenue on which you entered but at a higher level. In fact it is a path that edges along the wall of the Huerta de la Mercería until it links up with an avenue of cypresses opened in the second half of the nineteenth century for the visit of Isabella II. To the left, you leave behind the Albercones, the cisterns, with all the water-collecting system for the Alhambra which is described in the water tour. Descending, and to the right, you find the bridge over the Rey Chico ravine across which you enter the Alhambra precinct, a route recommended for those who have not previously seen this part of the visit; those who have, if you continue for a few metres more, you will find the entrance/exit pavilion and the car park.

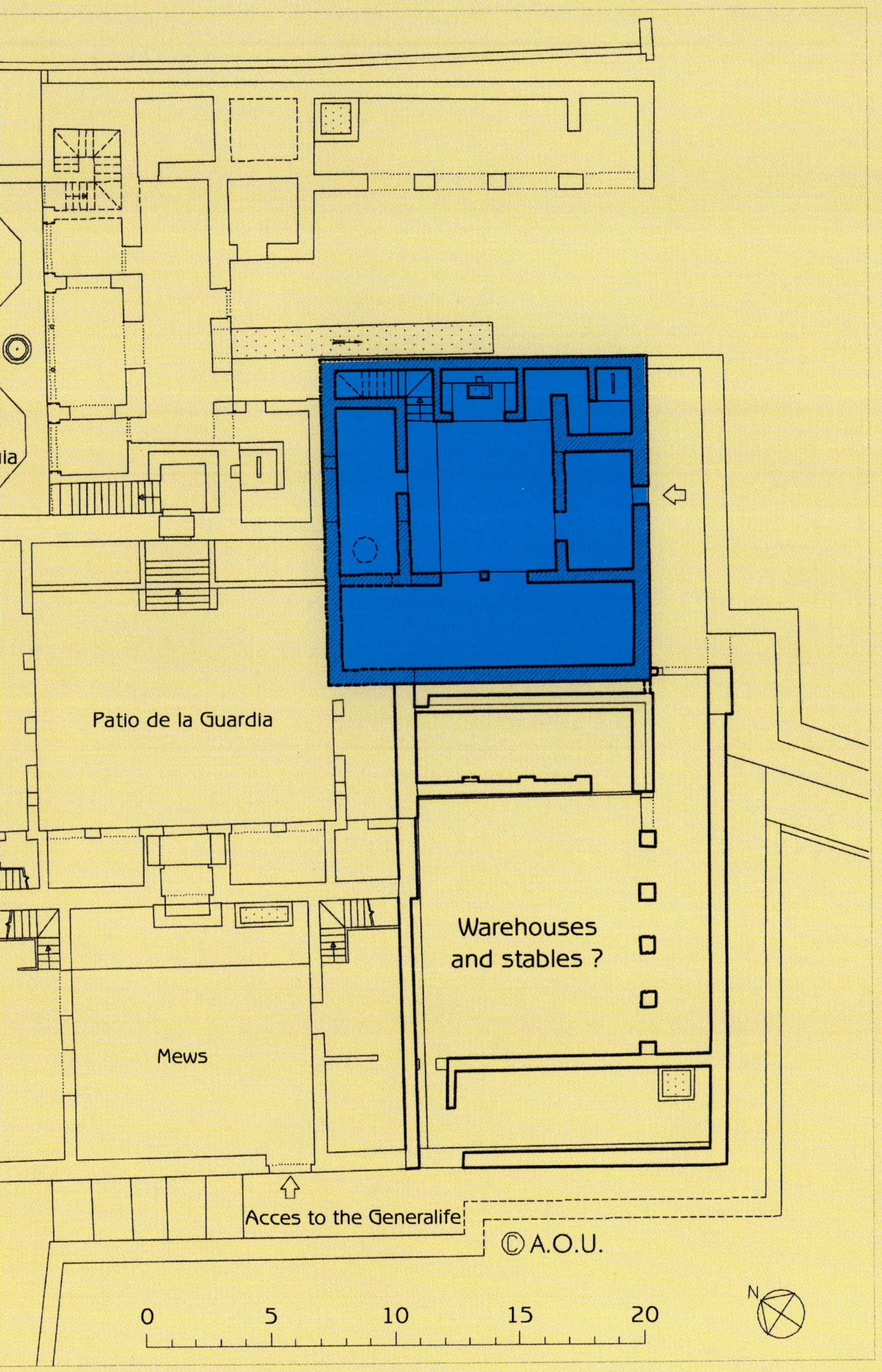

Casa de los Amigos. Hypothetical initial state (According to A. Orihuela Uzal, *Casas y palacios nazaríes. Siglos XIII-XV*, 1996, p. 216).

OTHER ITINERARIES

The Alhambra can be visited from a multitude of perspectives. As well as the itinerary proposed, there are many alternative ways to get to know the Alhambra from other points of view. The differences perceived by viewing the same space at different times of the day would surprise you.

The Alhambra is not just the fortified precinct as all its surroundings offer us an intense history. To enter from the city via the Cuesta de los Chinos recreating what was one of the Nasrid accesses, to stroll up the Cuesta de Gomérez appreciating not only the Nasrid remains but sixteenth- and contemporary nineteenth- and twentieth-century architecture, to go round the surroundings of the Alhambra to cover the water tour discovering how water arrived here and was stored to supply the palaces and the *medina*, to lose yourself in the gardens, follow some of the hikers' routes appreciating Nasrid remains in intimate communion with Nature, are some of the suggestions that help you understand that the Alhambra is the history of a whole territory with an appreciable, varied landscape.

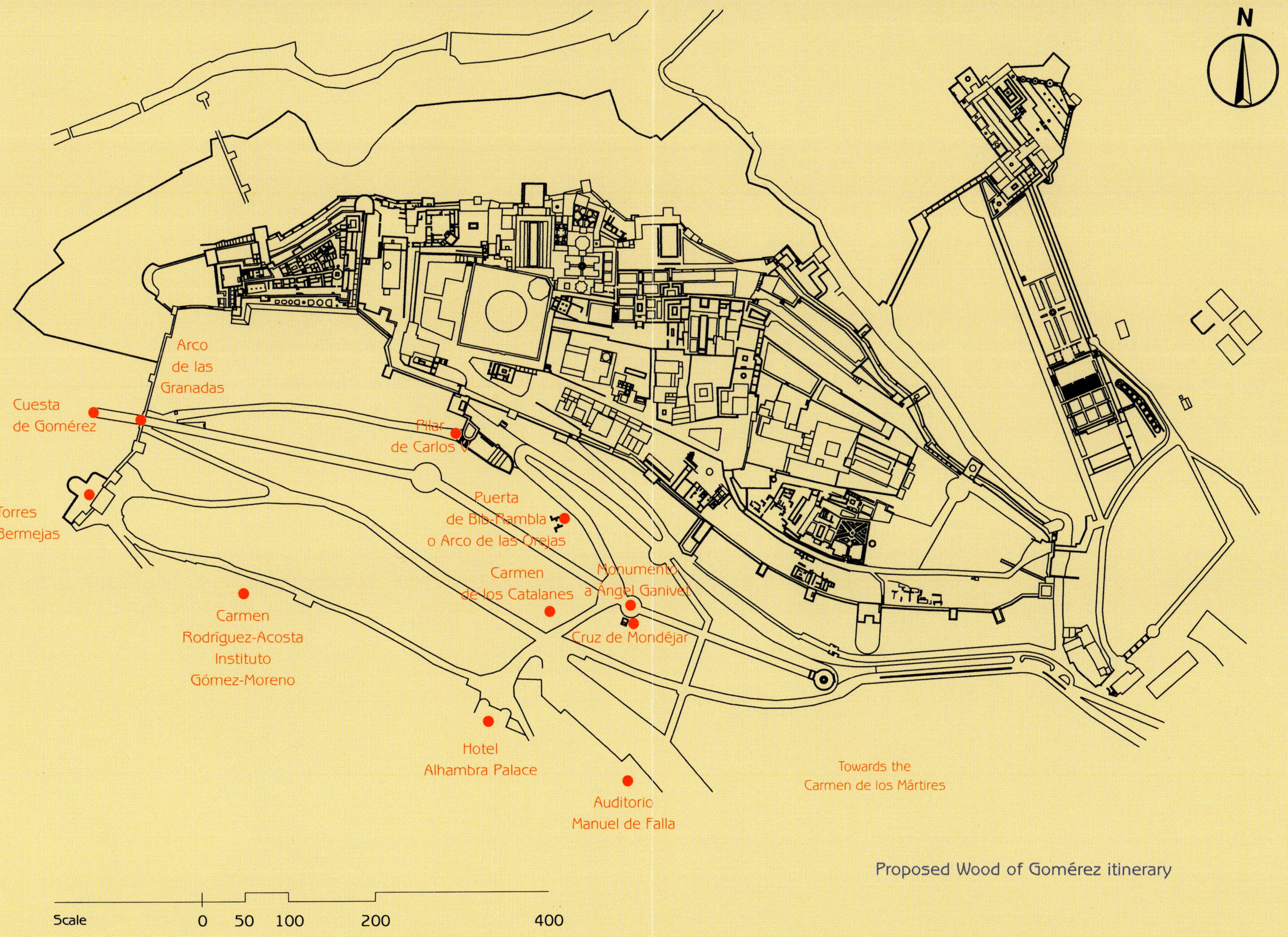

Proposed Wood of Gomérez itinerary

A stroll through the woods: the Bosque de Gomérez

LEAVING FROM Plaza Nueva, we start to ascend the hill of La Sabīka via the Cuesta de Gomérez. Even in Nasrid times this street existed and was widened and reformed in the period of Charles V. The street stretches between two hills, that of the Mauror which lies to the right and that of La Sabīka to the left.

The Cuesta Gomérez surprises you with the Puerta de las Granadas, dated in the second half of the sixteenth century, strengthening this access to the Alhambra with a Renaissance design in consonance with Italian models and, above all, with the Palacio de Carlos V. Near the Puerta de las Granadas and to the right rose up the Bāb al-Jandaq (Puerta del Foso) What is left are the remains of an arch.

The Puerta de las Granadas that today welcomes the majority of the visitors who enter the Alhambra from the city has a structure with three openings, evocative of the triumphal arches of Antiquity and very close to designs by Giulio Romano for another in the city of Mantua. It is associated with the Palacio de Carlos V, with which it shares the extensive use of pillow-shaped stone blocks. However, critics have pointed out that the blocks used in the gate are, in general, more crudely made than those in the palace. Together with other motifs, this distances the date of execution of the gate from that of the palace.

The composition seems somewhat crude and unbalanced by the overwhelming difference between the small side arches and the central one. The central body is overbearing, also in part because today it lacks some figures: the allegories of Peace and Plenty, that until the nineteenth century were over the pediment. Only the enormous pomegranates that give their name to the gate remain.

There seems to be no doubt that the outlines of the project must have been the work of Pedro Machuca, but at the end of his life, that is, around 1550. Two years later, Juan de Orea made the imperial eagle of the tympanum, but it is possible that the pillow-shaped blocks, above all those at the sides, were made at the end of the century.

Having passed through the Puerta de las Granadas, you find yourself facing three paths that fork out in the shape of a trident and lead us to different points of the Gomérez woods. That on the left leads towards the Pilar de Carlos V fountain and the Puerta de la Explanada, the central road ends at the Puerta de la Alberca and the entrance/exit pavilion to the monu-ment precinct, and the third path leads to the Carmen de los Mártires, although a side path takes you to the Torres Bermejas.

If you choose the path on the left, at your feet stands a marble cross erected in 1599 by an artilleryman of the Alhambra, Leandro de Palencia, and a small font, reconstructed in the first half of the nineteenth century. This path takes us to the Pilar de Carlos V, next to the Puerta de la Explanada.

The Pilar de Carlos V has been known as such since the eighteenth century – until then it was called "de las Trompetas" – and is dated in the sixteenth century (c.1545; the plans and designs date from the early 1540s) although it has undergone later reforms. The engineering design and interior hydraulic structure of the basin are outstanding as are the architectural design by Pedro de Machuca and the efforts of sculptors Nicolao da Corte and Alonso de Mena. This fountain has to be understood in its relationship with the Palacio de Carlos V as well as with the Puerta de las Granadas, it is another Renaissance element to complete the sweeping proposal of the Emperor's intervention in the Alhambra complex.

The fountain is abutted to a defensive bastion of the Puerta de la Explanada and takes advantage of the slope of the access ramp to the gate to construct a solid wall, inside which is the water tank with its piping and distribution system for the fountain.

At the same time, the wall conditions the architectural type of the fountain: a trough-like basin built against the wall. The basin itself measures some twelve metres, is built of marble, with its corresponding canopy in which are lodged significant iconographic motifs in a composition in two bodies, the lower one with the water spouts which some authors suggest are allegories of the rivers of Granada (Darro, Genil and Beiro), and others associated with three season (Spring, Summer, Autumn). These alternate with fleshy pomegranates in

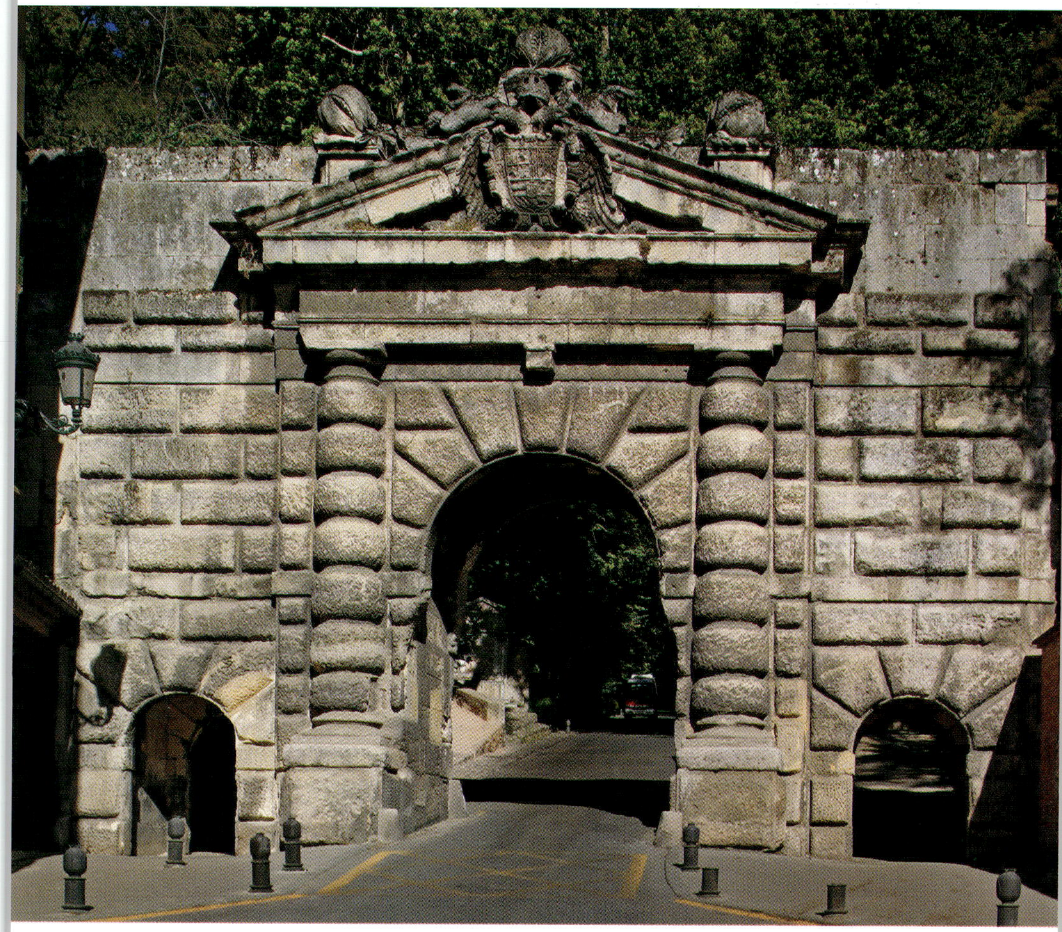

Puerta de las Granadas

relief and the shields of the Mendoza family at the two ends. The second body, a kind of small retable, bears a marble cartouche in the centre with the text: *Imperatori caesari Karolo quinto Hispaniarum regi*, flanked by the emblems of the Plus Ultra and the cross of St. Andrew, crowning the frontispiece with a half-point arch inside which the two-headed imperial eagle spreads its wings. Some children or putti embrace a pair of dolphins to the side of the shield, and another two with water jugs at the ends of the lower body, all pouring water, complete the repertory of images.

The wall against which the fountain is constructed is of sandstone and appears to be marked by Doric pilasters with four discs in relief located in the intercolumns showing now barely perceptible mythological themes that represent, from left to right:

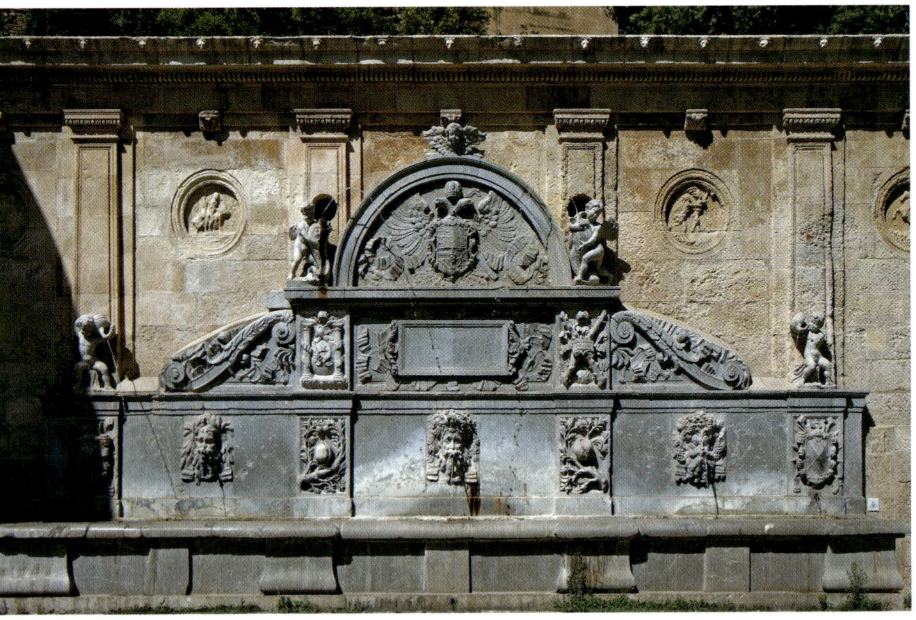

Pilar de Carlos V. On the following page a detail of the fountain.

Hercules slaying the Hydra of Lerna; Phrixus and Helle on the Golden Fleece; Apollo and Daphne and finally Alexander on his horse Bucephalus.

The sculptures correspond to Nicolao da Corte, according to a contract dated 1545, who possibly added the motifs not indicated by Machuca. Whatever the case may be, the deterioration caused by the harsh climate of Granada and the nature of the materials greatly affected this work and in 1624, on the occasion of the visit of Philip IV, many of the figures had to be restored, all those in the lower body, part of those in the upper one and even the mythological reliefs on the wall, work for which the sculptor Alonso de Mena was commissioned.

If you pass through the Puerta de las Granadas and chose the central cobbled path you will be able to appreciate a few metres further on the reconstruction of the so-called Puerta de las Orejas or de Bibarrambla, which corresponded to one of the gates of the Plaza Bibarrambla and was demolished in the second half of the nineteenth century. Some of the stone blocks of the original gate have been conserved but the rest is a reconstruction. Continuing straight ahead you arrive at a series of small squares with the popular fountains known as the Fuente del Tomate and Fuente del Pimiento. In one of these squares

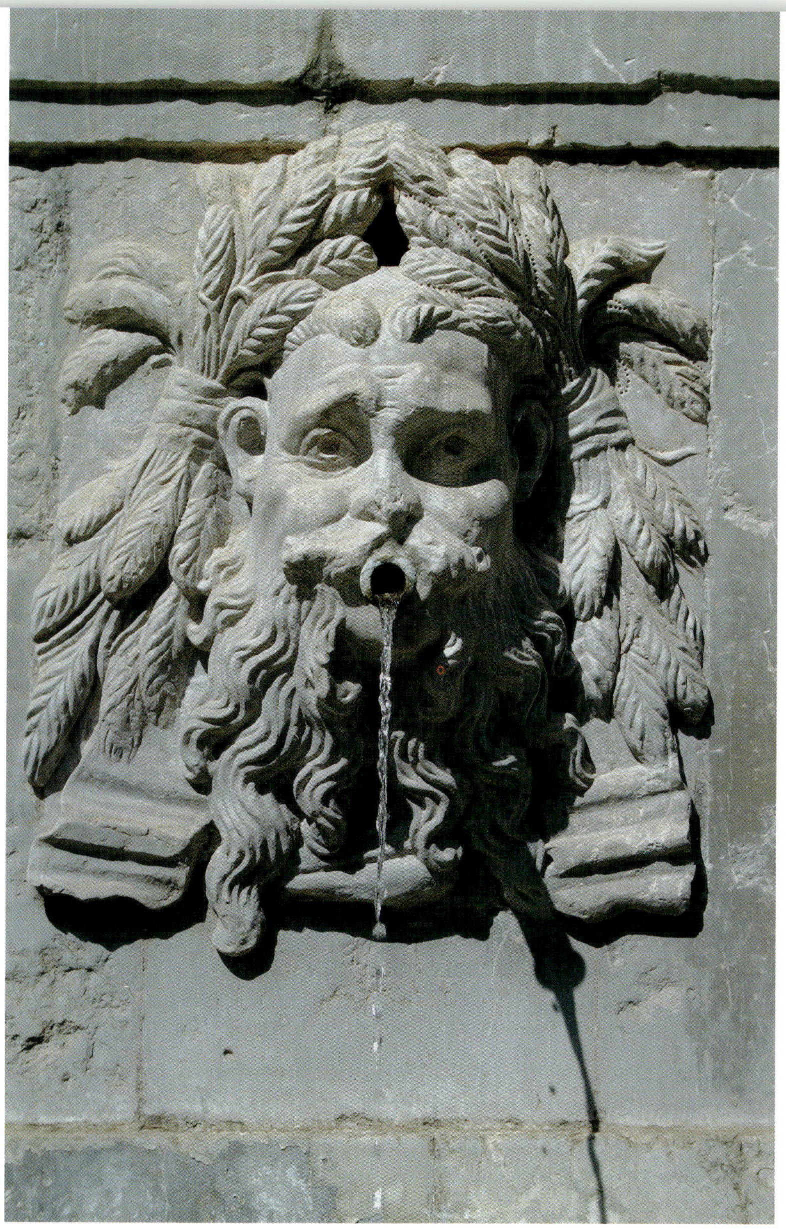

you will find the 1921 monument to Ángel Ganivet, the work of Juan Cristóbal and the cross erected by the Marquis of Mondéjar in 1641 atop a traditional Nasrid column. Crossing these squares you arrive again at the cobbled path where, in front of the Hotel Washington Irving, you can contemplate the Puerta de la Alberca (or de los Siete Suelos), that was immortalized in the engravings of the nineteenth-century Romantics who visited Granada.

If, on the contrary, when you pass through the Puerta de las Granadas you take the path to the right you arrive via a side path on the right at the Torres Bermejas. From there you can start an attractive route via a series of buildings of historic and artistic interest that mainly correspond to the nineteenth and twentieth centuries. This complex of buildings constitutes a small living catalogue of the contemporary architecture of Granada.

The Torres Bermejas are one the defensive elements of the Alhambra. The name comes from the red colour of the walls. There are three towers oriented towards the former Jewish quarter. Some have suggested they have elements of the original eleventh-century construction, with substantial Christian alterations such as the bastion. From the Torres Bermejas one stretch of wall connects directly with the Alcazaba and another descends towards the city. From this point you will be surprised by the magnificent views of the Torre de la Vela in the Alcazaba.

Near to the Torres Bermejas is the Callejón del Niño del Rollo, the narrow street where you find the Carmen Rodríguez-Acosta, a construction that belonged to the painter José María Rodríguez Acosta (1878-1941) and which critics consider one of the buildings that best encapsulates architecture between the wars. Under the direction of the painter himself the building was constructed fundamentally by the architect Teodoro Anasagasti in 1920. Currently it is the seat of the Rodríguez-Acosta Foundation, especially dedicated to the promotion of the arts. In the 1970s it was extended to accommodate the Gómez-Moreno Institute, under the tutelage of the Foundation, whose objectives are to provide incentives for research based on the valuable legacy of this family of intellectuals and to hold exhibitions of its collection. Outstanding works in the Gómez-Moreno collection include *La piedad*, attributed to Hugo Van der Goes (*c.*1480), and *La Virgin niña rezando* by Francisco de Zurbarán (*c.*1660) as well as an interesting collection of ceramics, glassware and Greek vases.

Parallel to the Callejón del Niño del Rollo runs the wall of the Carmen de los Catalanes, acquired some years ago by the regional government department of Culture through the Alhambra and Generalife trust. This is a large estate centred by a villa or *carmen* dating from the early 1900s, which seems to take advantage of an ancient defensive turret. The estate is protected to the south by a wall, parallel to the Callejón del Niño del Rollo, that could correspond to an old defensive wall that ran from the Torres Bermejas. The appearance of dungeons near to this line of defence suggests the idea of a prolongation of the wall towards today's Carmen de los Mártires, thus closing all the southern flank of the outer urban area of the Alhambra. Remains of Romantic

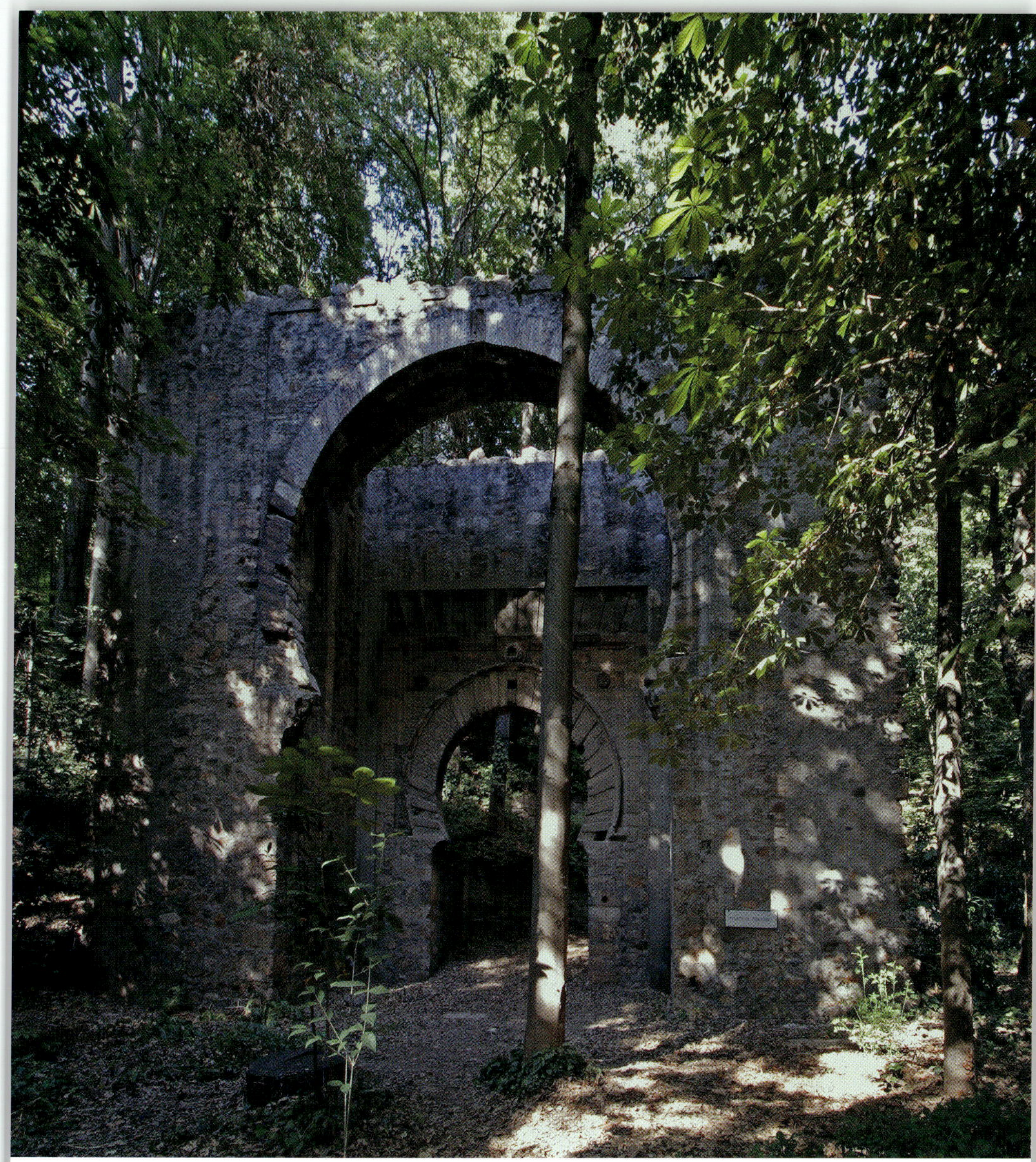

Puerta de las Orejas or de Bibarrambla

gardens in the interior of the *carmen* add a landscape and recreational value to this protective band around the Alhambra.

On this route your attention is caught by the Alhambra Palace Hotel, finished in 1910 by Modesto Cendoya who was at that time architect-curator of the Alhambra. The building constitutes a living example of the historicist tendencies and eclecticism that during the nineteenth and early twentieth centuries spread across part of Europe and that in Spain was most authentically represented in the Neoarabic and in *Neomudéjar*. In the case

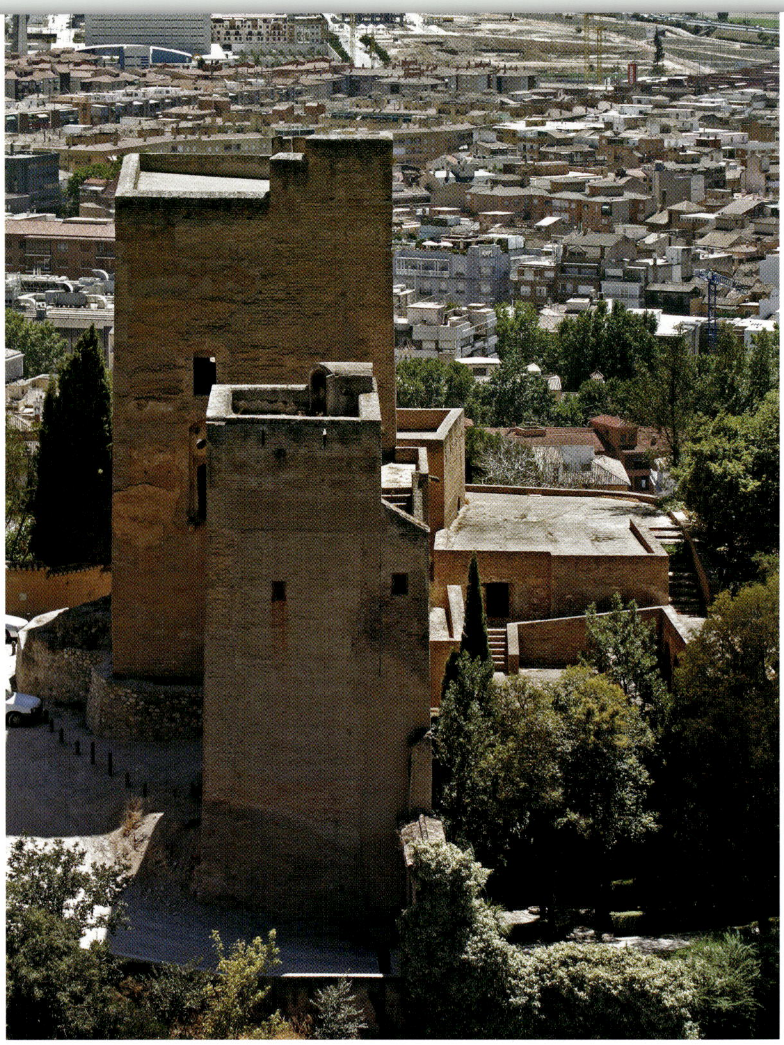

Torres Bermejas

From the Alcazaba a wall leads to the Torres Bermejas

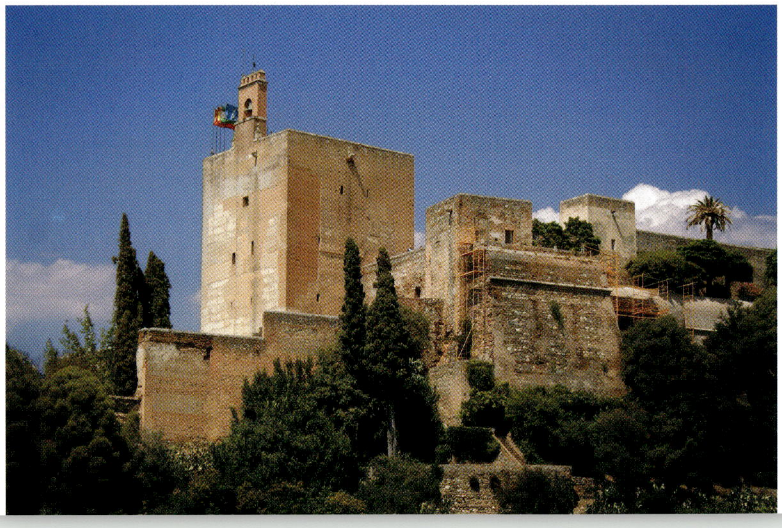

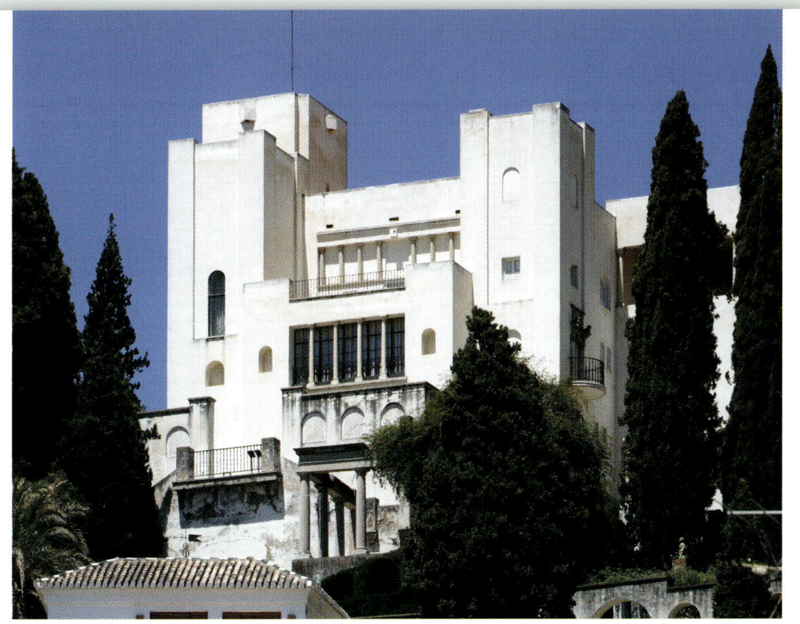

Carmen Rodríguez-Acosta

of the Alhambra Palace, here is a building that depicts an omnipresent trend in Spanish architecture that has been baptized with the name of *alhambrismo*. The interior of the hotel recreates the architecture of the Alhambra especially in the use of specific formal elements such as stucco.

Very close by and to the left of the Alhambra Palace Hotel, you find the Manuel de Falla music centre and the Manuel de Falla House and Museum, a tribute to one of the great musicians and composers of the first half of the twentieth century. The house where he composed some of his most important works can be seen during visiting hours and you can see some of his souvenirs exhibited there. You can also see a typical Granada house, whose architecture and garden are rooted in the Islamic tradition. Next to this is the Manuel de Falla Auditorium, by the architect José María García Paredes, which was constructed in 1978 making use of specific materials in order to integrate it into the countryside.

Finally, we should mention the Carmen de los Mártires, that ends the climb to the left of the Alhambra Palace Hotel. Located where Nasrid dungeons were found, according to the Christian travellers who saw them no sooner than the Christian conquest had taken place. On this site, the long–gone convent of Discalced Carmelites stood, where St. John of the Cross once was prior. It is believed this may have been where he wrote the *Cántico Espiritual*. The current building was constructed as a private house in the second half of the nineteenth century, and is

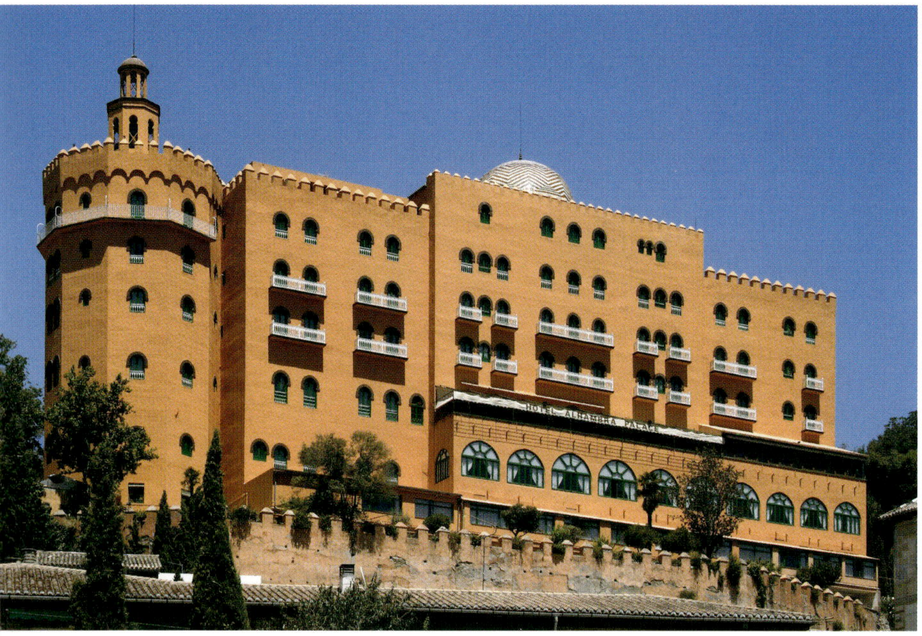

Alhambra Palace

Manuel de Falla Centre and Auditorium

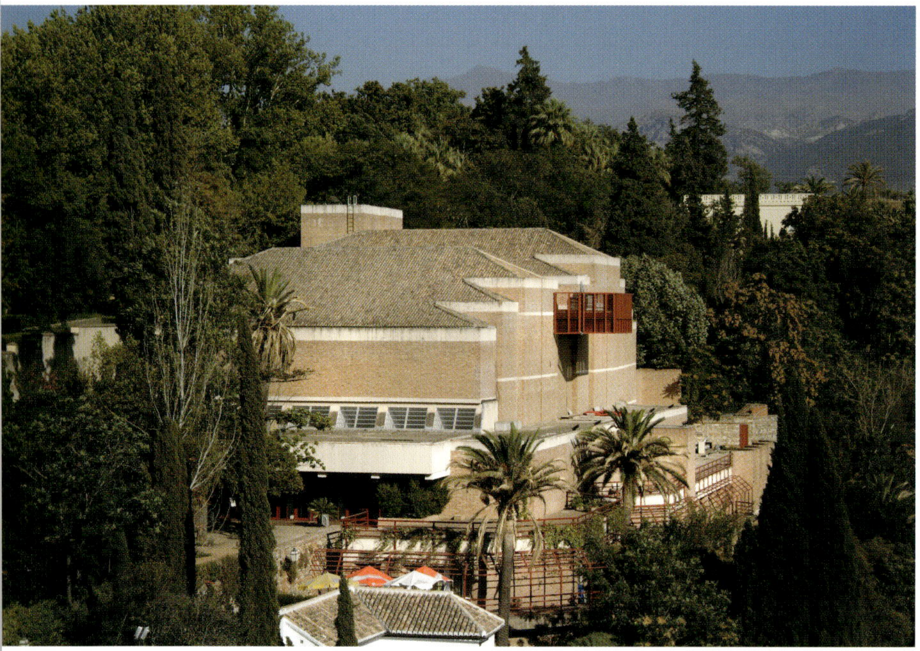

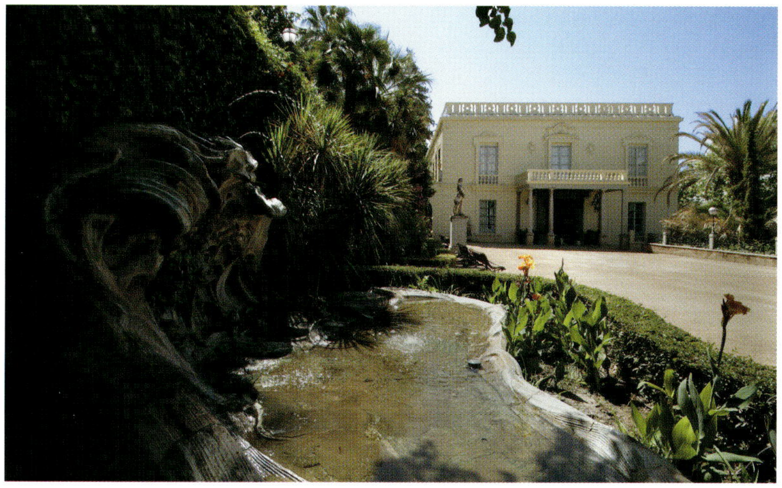

Carmen de los Mártires

Detail of the gardens of the Carmen de los Mártires

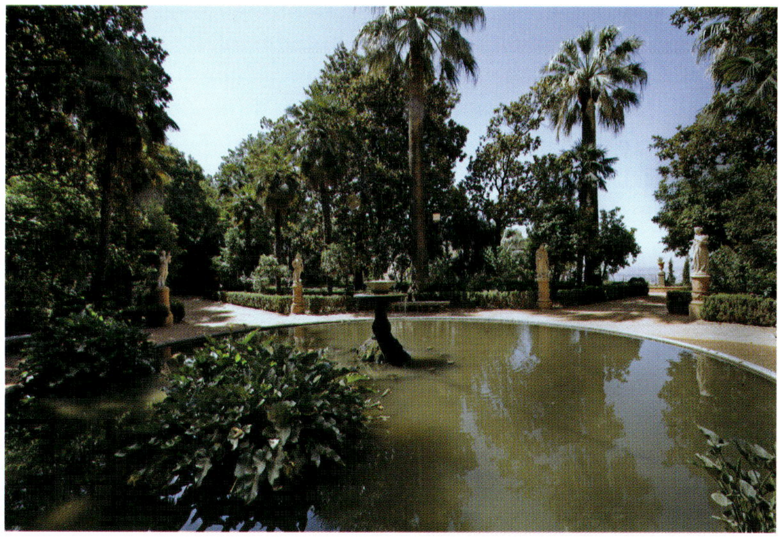

now municipal property, with its outstanding historic garden.

All along this route you delight in the Gomérez woods, that begin at the Puerta de las Granadas and ends at the official entrance to the precinct, giving it an extension of approximately some 8 hectares. There are nearly 1400 examples of full-grown trees and substantial numbers of younger ones. Among the most numerous species are elms and other species like horse chestnuts and plantains.

Along the Cuesta de los Chinos

FROM PLAZA NUEVA you can see a splendid view of the Torre de la Vela, that rises majestically over the hill, enabling you to appreciate the sensation of vigilance and defence of the Nasrid city that this tower must have transmitted. Crossing the Carrera del Darro and in front of the Bañuelo are remains of the Puerta de los Tableros, the ill-named Puente del Cadí. Little has been conserved on the south side of a horseshoe arch built up against a tower. It formed part of an adjacent wall that joined the Alhambra with the ancient Alcazaba in the Albaicín over which you crossed the river. Through the Puerta de los Tableros, the river Darro entered the city and it stood at the end of a defensive scarp that ensured the supply of water bringing it from the Darro to the Alhambra. Constructed with small finely–worked stone blocks it has verticals slits for the portcullis and floodgates which could close off the river channel.

The foot of the Alhambra startles you with the approximately of 5 hectares of the wood of San Pedro reaching from the Cuesta de los Chinos to the Cuesta Gomérez and the slope below the Torre de la Vela. It includes nearly 650 examples of mature trees of which more than half are elms. Other species are robinia, ash and plantains.

Following the Carrera del Darro, you are going to be seeing the different images of the Alhambra until arriving at the Paseo de los Tristes that has maintained throughout its history a playful, festive character. At the end of this walk you arrive at a crossroads that on the left leads to the Cuesta del Chapiz and on the right the Cuesta de los Chinos begins. From this point, the view of the Alhambra is spectacular, taking in practically all the north of the monumental precinct, from

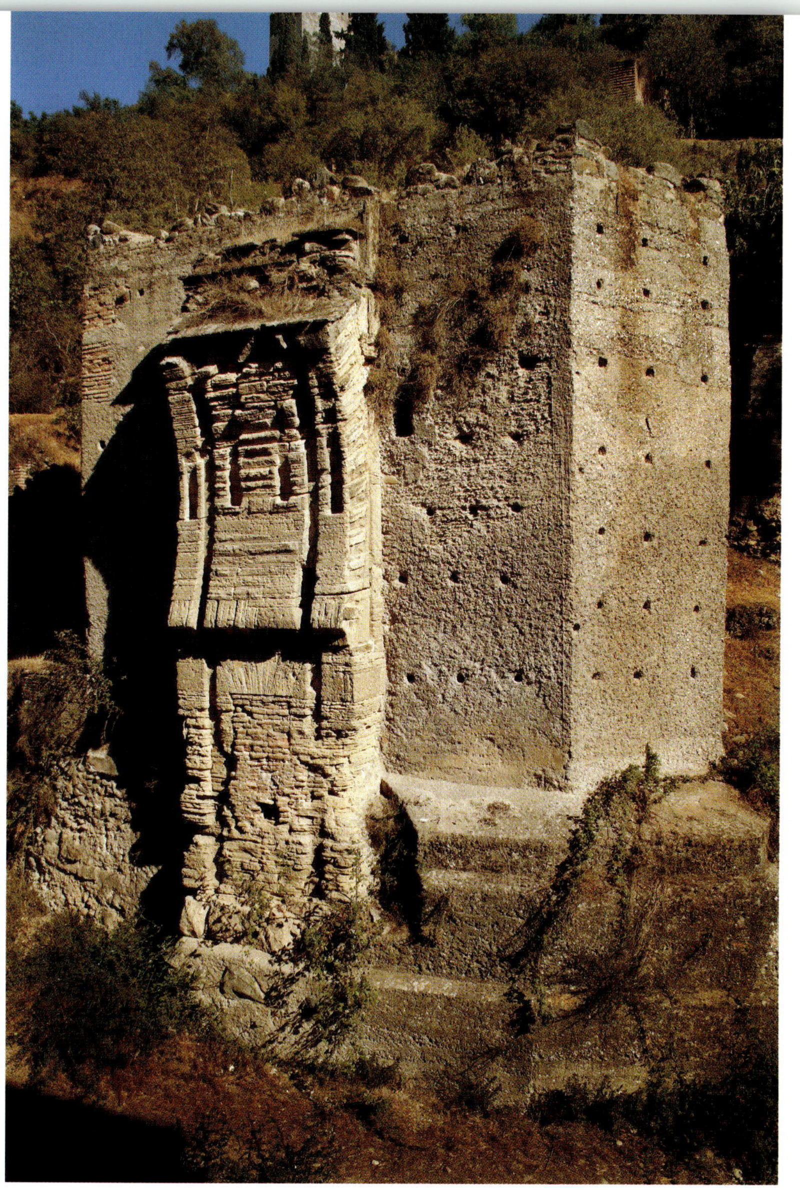

Puerta de los Tableros

the Torre del Homenaje in the Alcazaba, passing through the Torreón de Comares, Peinador de la Reina, and El Partal, to the Generalife. Without doubt, you can gain an idea of how the citizens of the lower Albaicín felt the presence of the Nasrid palace precinct.

We arrive at the Puente del Aljibillo or del Rey Chico, where the Cuesta de los Chinos begins. This bridge is one of the few that has been conserved and is quoted by Arabic sources, although most of it corresponds to a sixteenth-century reconstruction. Crossing the bridge

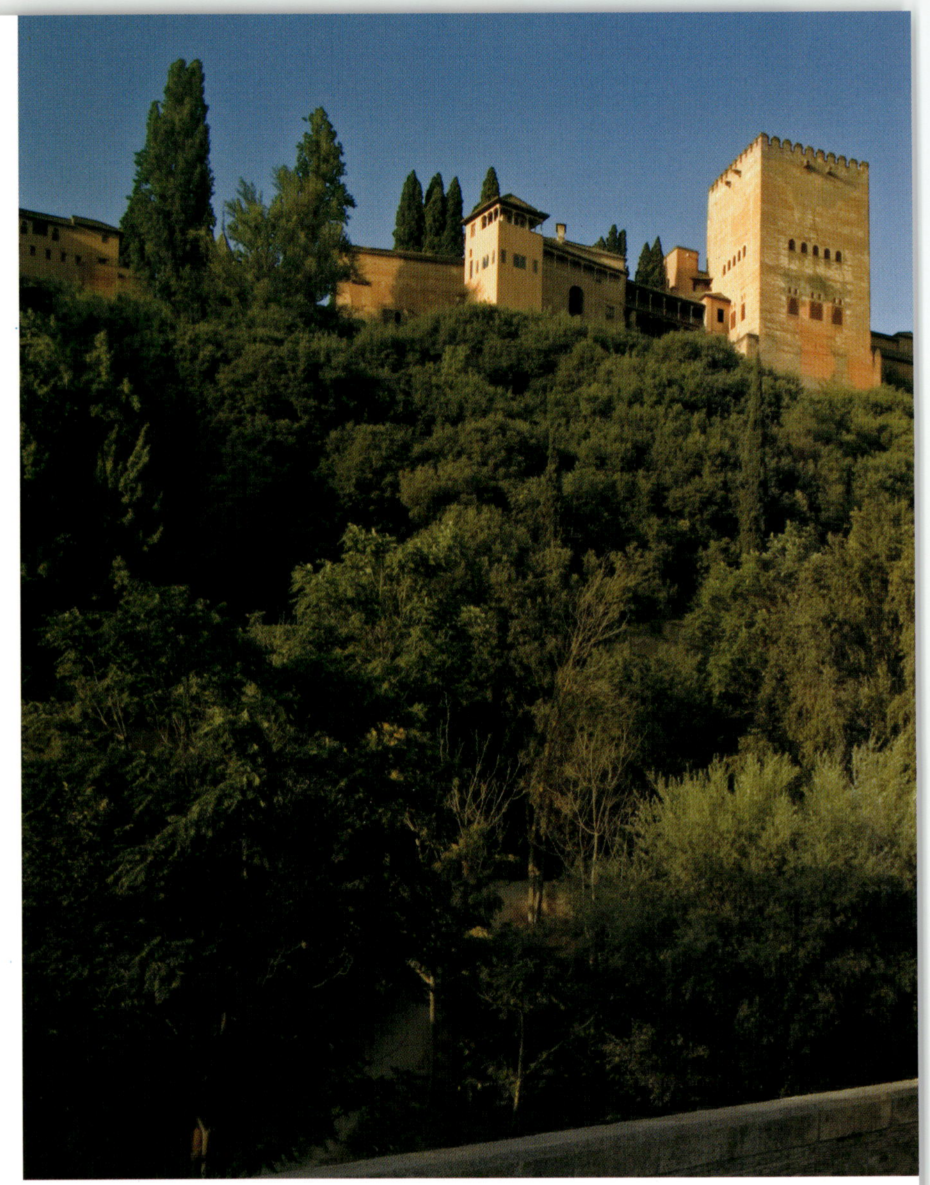

and to the right, the Rey Chico building catches your eye. This replaced an older dance hall and was projected as a building for leisure purposes. The construction of the present building at the foot of the Alhambra caused such controversy that it actually brought work to a halt. After much debate, the volume of the building was reduced and it was converted into a public theatre.

Crossing over the bridge and to the left you are led to the Fuente del Avellano, where the "Cofradía del Avellano" met presided over by the writer Ángel Ganivet. Its current appearance corresponds to the nineteenth

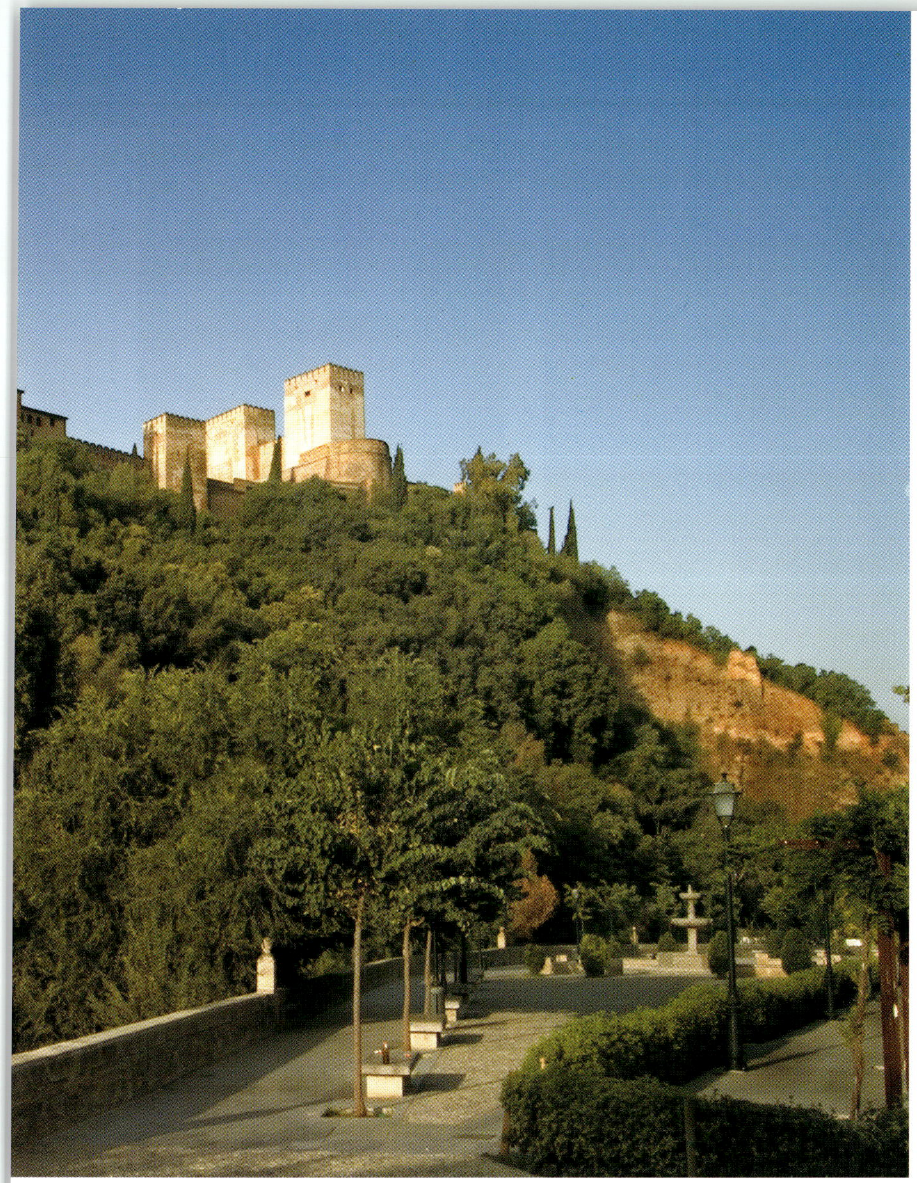

The Alhambra from the Cuesta de los Chinos

century. Further on you find the Fuente de la Salud and the Fuente de la Agrilla, both currently dry, which run around the edge of the Generalife.

In this area you also find interesting buildings like the Carmen de los Chapiteles. Known in the sixteenth century as the Casa del Moro Rico, it was the property of the Gran Capitán, whose coat of arms is displayed on the building.

The Cuesta de los Chinos separates the two hills of the Alhambra and the Generalife and leads around the edge of the Alhambra towers to the Puerta del Arrabal below the Torre de los Picos and from there to the

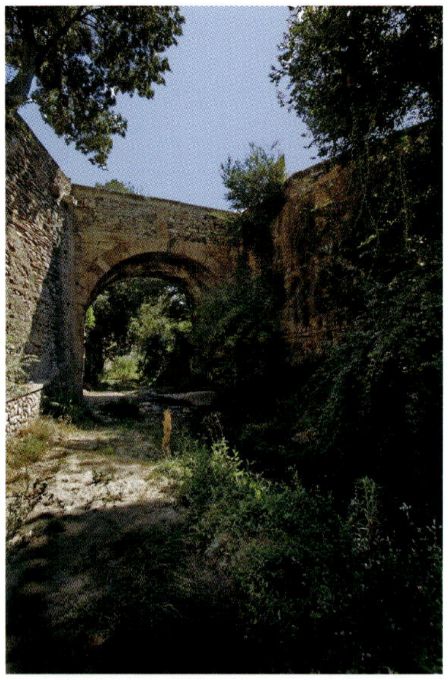

Puente del Aljibillo

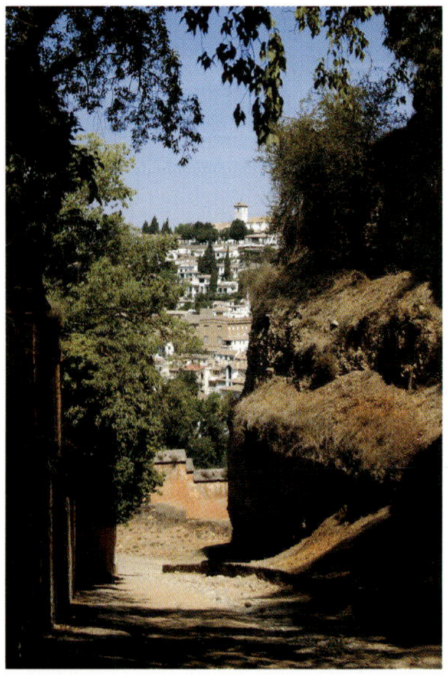

Cuesta de los Chinos

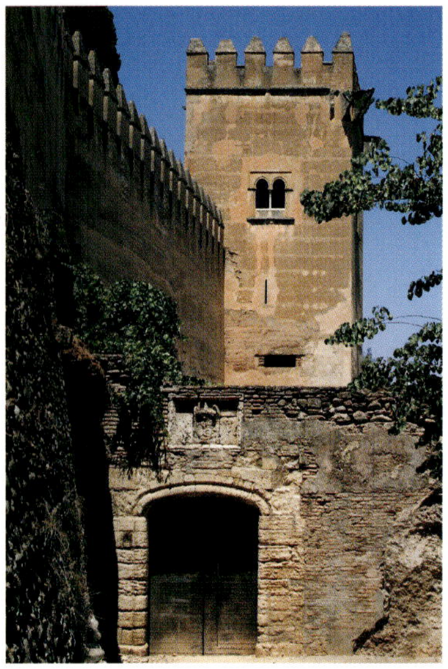

Torre de los Picos with the Puerta del Arrabal at its feet

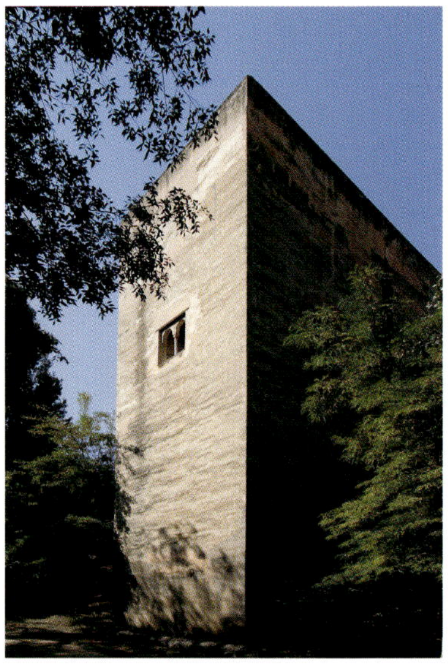

Cuesta de los Chinos with the Torre del Candil

Generalife. Thus, it connects Sacromonte and the Albaicín, and the lower Albaicín with the Alhambra. It was also known as the Cuesta de los Muertos as the municipal cemetery – in use until the early twentieth century – ended here.

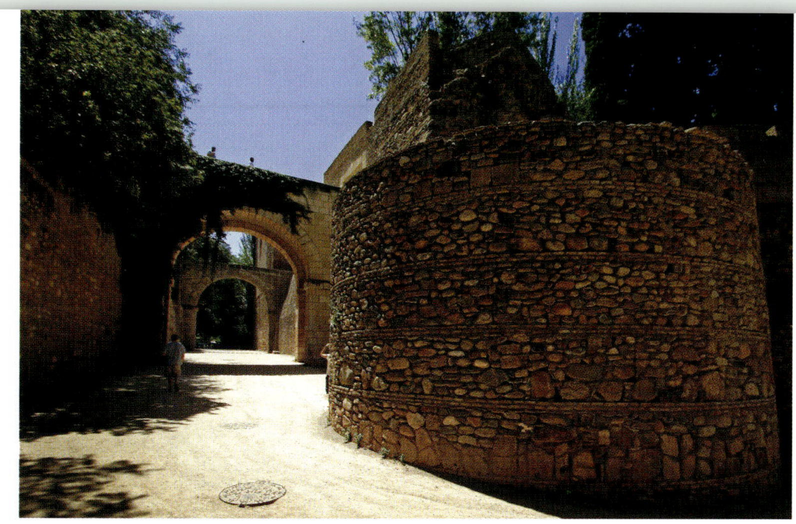

Torre del Cabo de la Carrera with the modern bridge and the aqueduct in the background

In spite of the steep slope, the walk that starts here is really pleasant. You can see the ruins of an ancient mill as well as the remains of an aqueduct and especially unusual views of the Torreón de Comares. As you gradually climb higher you can look behind to witness at some points a panorama of the Albaicín with the church of San Nicolás, raised up on the site of an ancient mosque, presiding over the hill in the foreground.

The Torre de los Picos is quickly recognized due to the pointed stone projections you can see in the upper body that permit better defence. This tower defended the Puerta del Arrabal, one of the gates open to the city that connected with the Generalife, altered in the reign of the Catholic Kings as the shield with the symbols of the yoke and arrows bears witness.

The next tower you find is the Torre del Candil. A strategic location, in front of it you find the path by which the sultan and his entourage entered the vegetable gardens and the Generalife, which you can see through wrought iron railings. As you continue, you find the Torre de la Cautiva and the Torre de las Infantas. Your perception of these towers differs greatly by comparison with when you saw them before from the inside the precinct as you begin to appreciate their overwhelming height.

Coming around the circular bastion of the Torre del Cabo de la Carrera, dated 1502 and identified by a commemorative plaque, you are surprised by the modern bridge that was built to make it easier for visitors to move between the Generalife and the Alhambra. After this bridge you can still appreciate the remains of an arch of the aqueduct that entered the Torre del Agua and transported water from the Acequia Real to introduce it into the Alhambra.

Tour of the Gardens

THE ALHAMBRA CANNOT BE UNDERSTOOD without the intimate relationship between architecture and Nature and the latter as a perennial garden of water and vegetation. The garden attached to and integrated into the house is part of a long tradition in the Ancient world. It is inherent to the Mediterranean climate and culture where Islam, seated on the edge of the sea, would adopt and adapt it to a previously unknown level of intensity and refinement. This is easy to understand if you think that the first Muslims came from the desert and consequently water was the most precious, economic, poetic, psychological and, of course, religious commodity. In the Koran, the Holy Book, the image of paradise could not be conceived of other than as a "flower and fruit garden which streams run through...".

You can follow this image of paradise manifest in the garden in all the architecture of al-Andalus, from the Caliphate to Nasrid Granada. However, it is here that it reached its climax. No one until this moment had described an interior space, a hall, like the Sala de Dos Hermanas in the Alhambra, in terms like those used by the courtly poet Ibn Zamrak: "I am the garden that beauty adorns...". The comparison would become ambivalent: if the house was like a garden, the garden was also seen as a house, in the most intense overlapping between architecture and Nature known. The importance of this relationship has lead to various interpretations, among which one of the most interesting ones sees in the development of Islamic Andalusian agriculture a representation of the garden. Agriculture entailed

On the following page, the Gardens of San Francisco

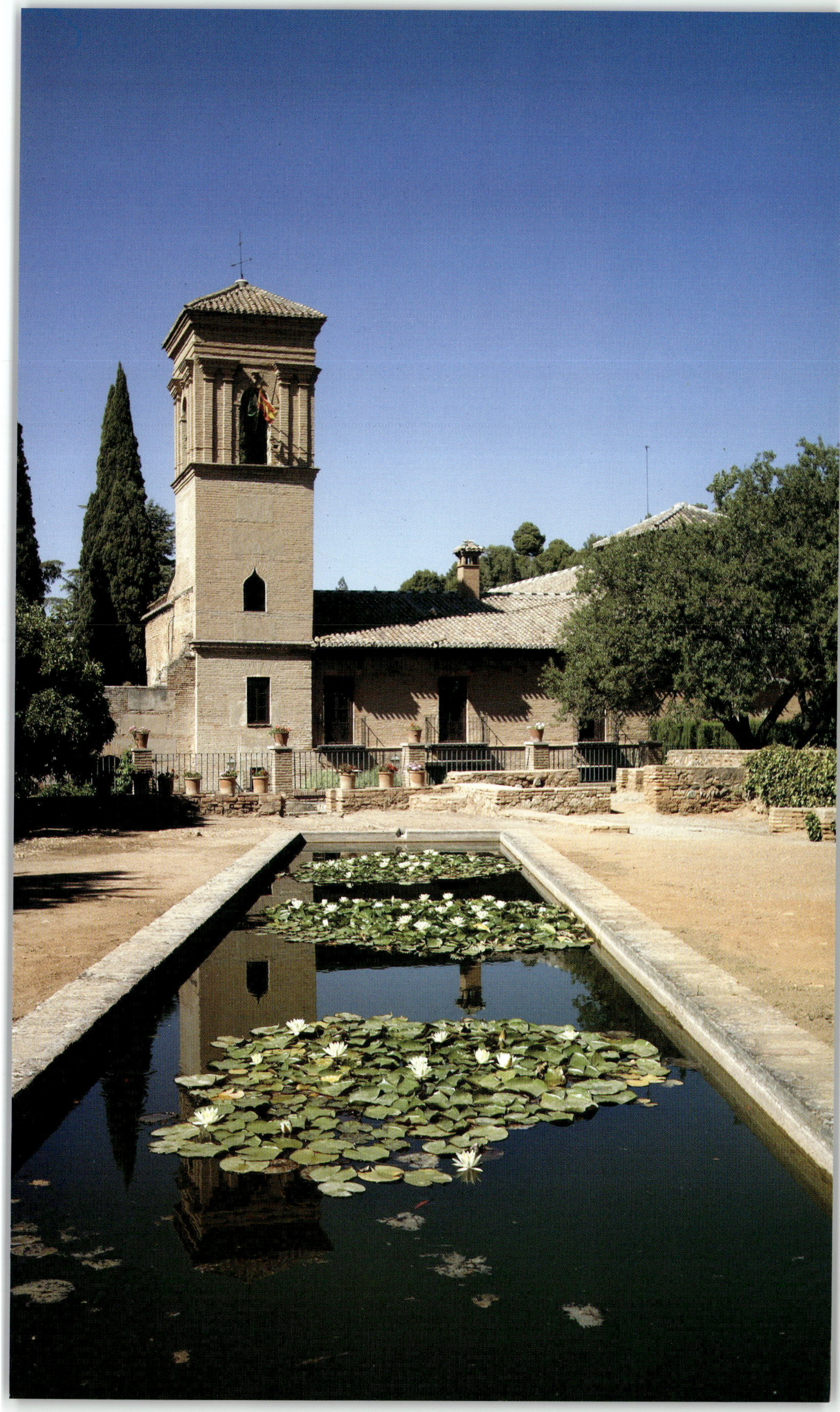

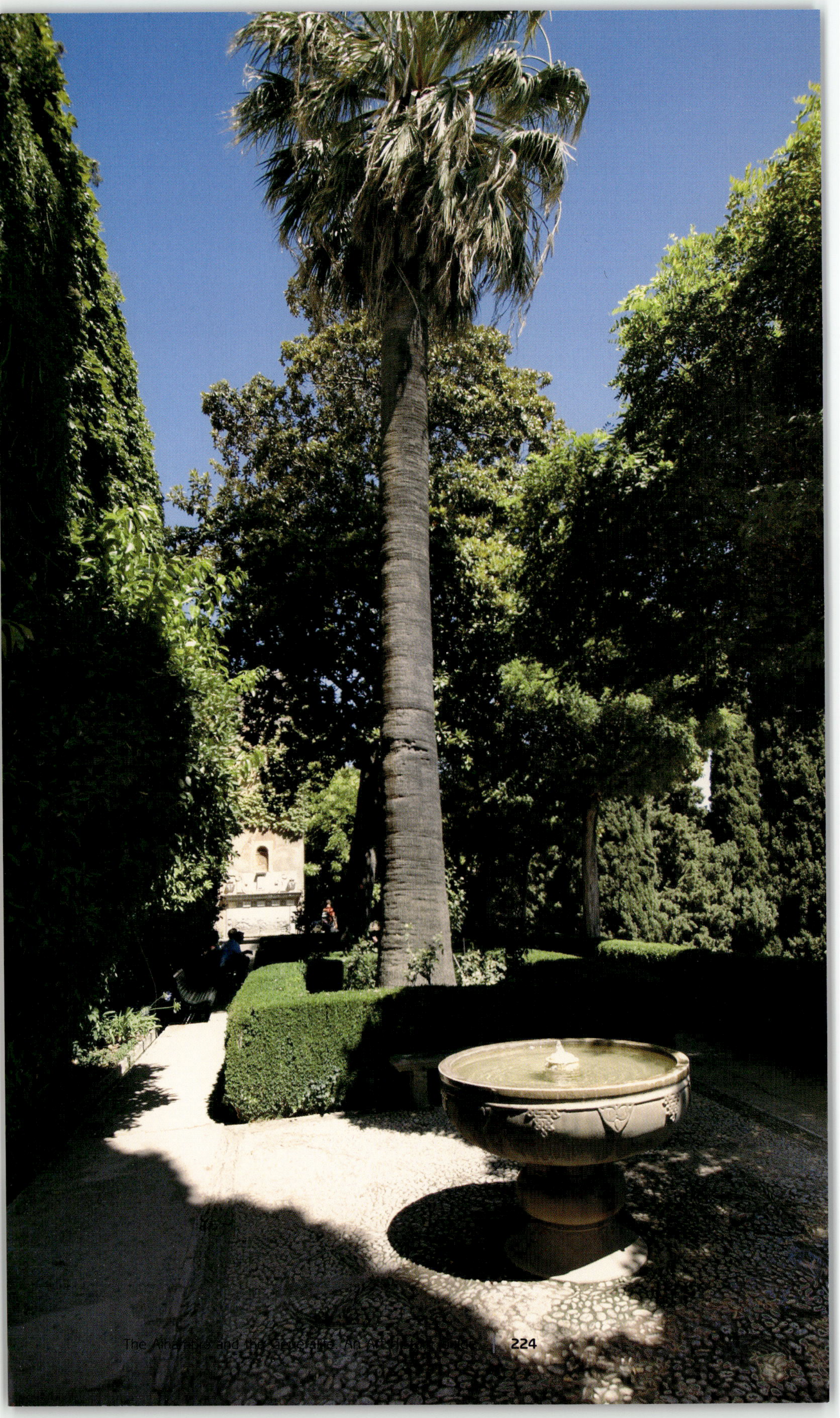

On the previous page, Jardín del Adarve

converting an often inhospitable, dry territory into a flower and fruit garden, an authentic prodigy of fertility.

And as fertility is water, "water is the mysterious life of the Alhambra", wrote Titus Burckhardt, it will always be present in the garden and if this is mere architectural space there it will occupy a central position, explicitly, bursting forth like a reviving spring and gliding silently like the river of paradise. Water, calm or in movement, registers all the poetic effects playing with the ambiguity of its flowing, liquid nature and the solid appearance of the silvery surface in the backwaters, so well-expressed by the poet Ibn Zamrak in reference to the fountain of the Patio de los Leones.

The tour of the gardens begins in the Paseo de los Cipreses and crossing the bridge, from where you arrive at an area known as El Secano, the ancient Nasrid *medina*. In the sixteenth

Paseo de las Torres with the Generalife in the background

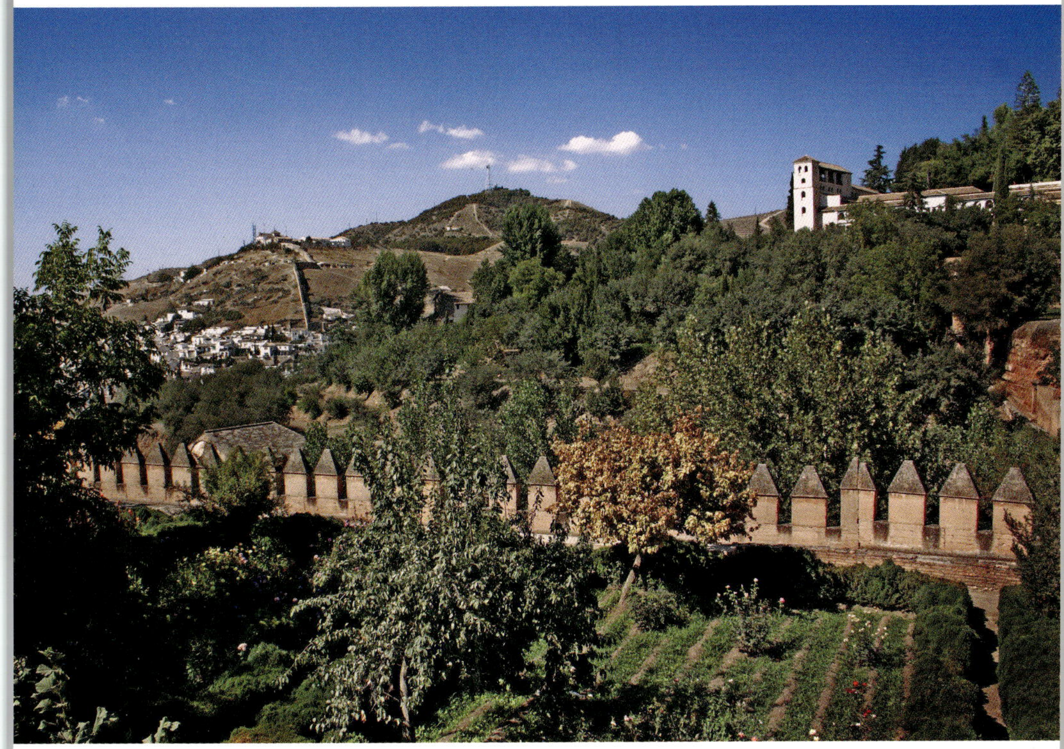

century, the water conduits that supplied the place were destroyed. From that time on, this space was converted into a plain, devoid of vegetation, and came to be known as "el secano". In Nasrid times the population of the *medina* lived here, generating everything necessary to supply and develop life in the Court. Currently this area is largely gardens, conserving remains of a palace pond and some tanneries in the proximity of the former convent of San Francisco, which you can see from here, built over the remains of an ancient Nasrid palace.

The Jardin de los Adarves in the Alcazaba constitutes the next point of interest. This is a raised terrace where you can contemplate a beautiful view. Dated in the seventeenth century, it was created on the initiative of the Marquis of Mondéjar as a Renaissance "belvedere". At the ends you find built against the wall two classically designed fountains and in the centre they have reused a white marble Nasrid fountain. A stroll around the Alcazaba enables you to contemplate the grove that descends to the city from the Torre de la Vela to contemplate the wood of San Pedro in the north and the Gomérez woods in the south.

On leaving the Alcazaba you head towards the gardens of El

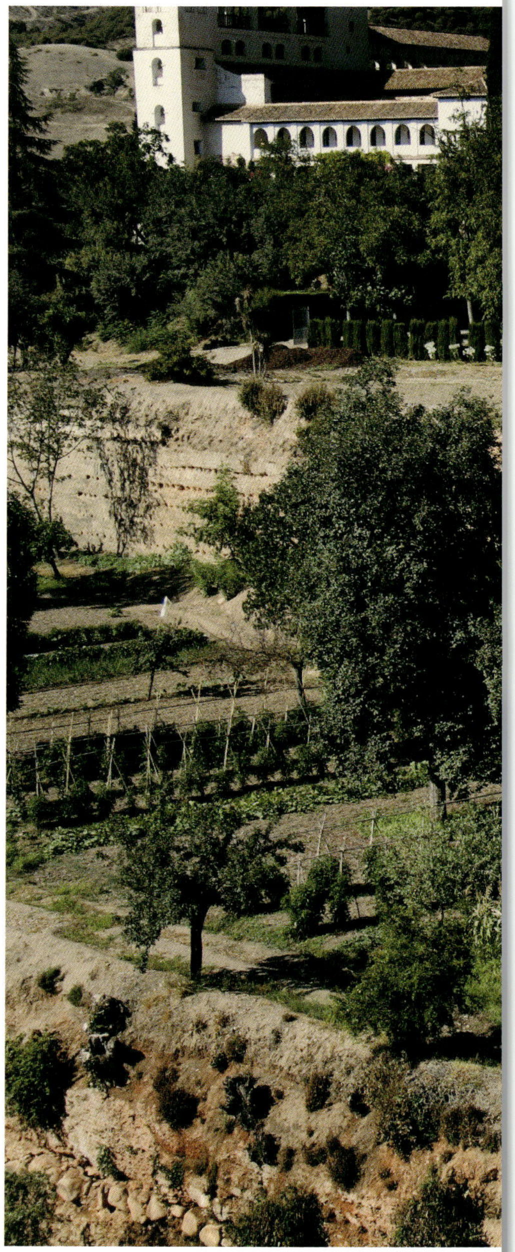

Huertas del Generalife

Partal, behind the Palacio de Carlos V. These gardens were created around 1920,

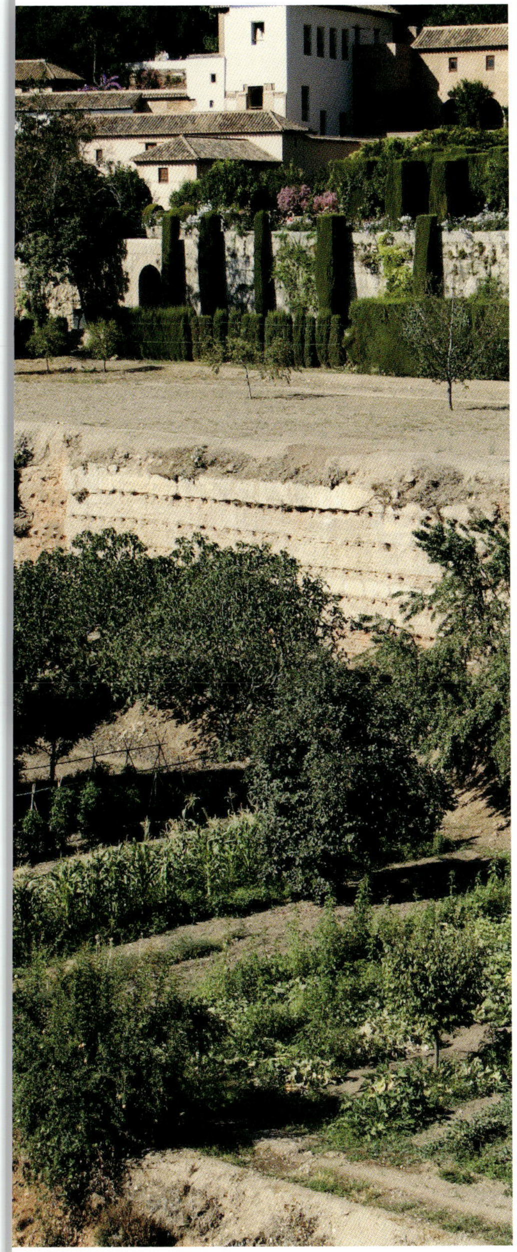

integrating archaeological and architectural remains in a single landscaped countryside. You can approach the portico gallery that precedes the main chamber, the tower of the Palacio de El Partal. Climbing the stairs you reach the Calle Real Baja and visit the Rauda, the cemetery of the sultans. Continuing along this street you come to the archaeological remains of the palace named after Yūsuf III, with gardens that correspond to Leopoldo Torres Balbás' time as architect.

You can continue the tour via the Paseo de las Torres. Along this route you contemplate the vegetable gardens and the Generalife. The Generalife vegetable gardens are organized in separate terraced beds with a wall that bounds the vegetable and fruit gardens. This terraced structure creates the drop in level necessary to water the crops from the irrigation channels. The principle vegetable gardens were the Huerta Colorada in front of the Generalife palace, Huerta Grande and Huerta de la Mercería to one and the other side of the gardens of the Generalife, and Huerta Fuente Peña in the area of the current Auditorium in the Generalife. These gardens provided the fruit trees and vegetables needed to supply the Alhambra.

Without doubt, the most attractive gardens are those of the Generalife. Since 1931 the area between the Generalife and the Alhambra has been cultivated, creating a garden-labyrinth

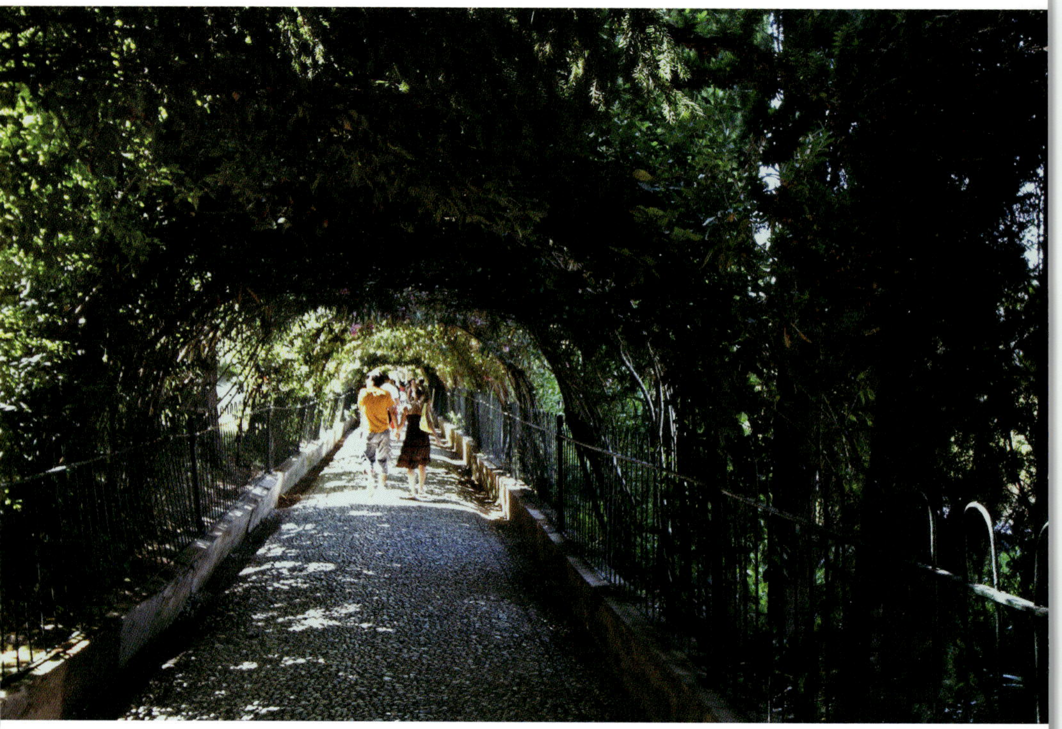

Overhead archways of oleander in the Jardines del Generalife

in what was the ancient Huerta de Fuente Peña and part of Huerta Grande.

Along a path covered by vaults of oleander you reach the upper gardens that recreate a typical Granada *carmen*. From here you arrive at the Escalera del Agua, the water stair where water, vegetation and architecture join together in perfect harmony.

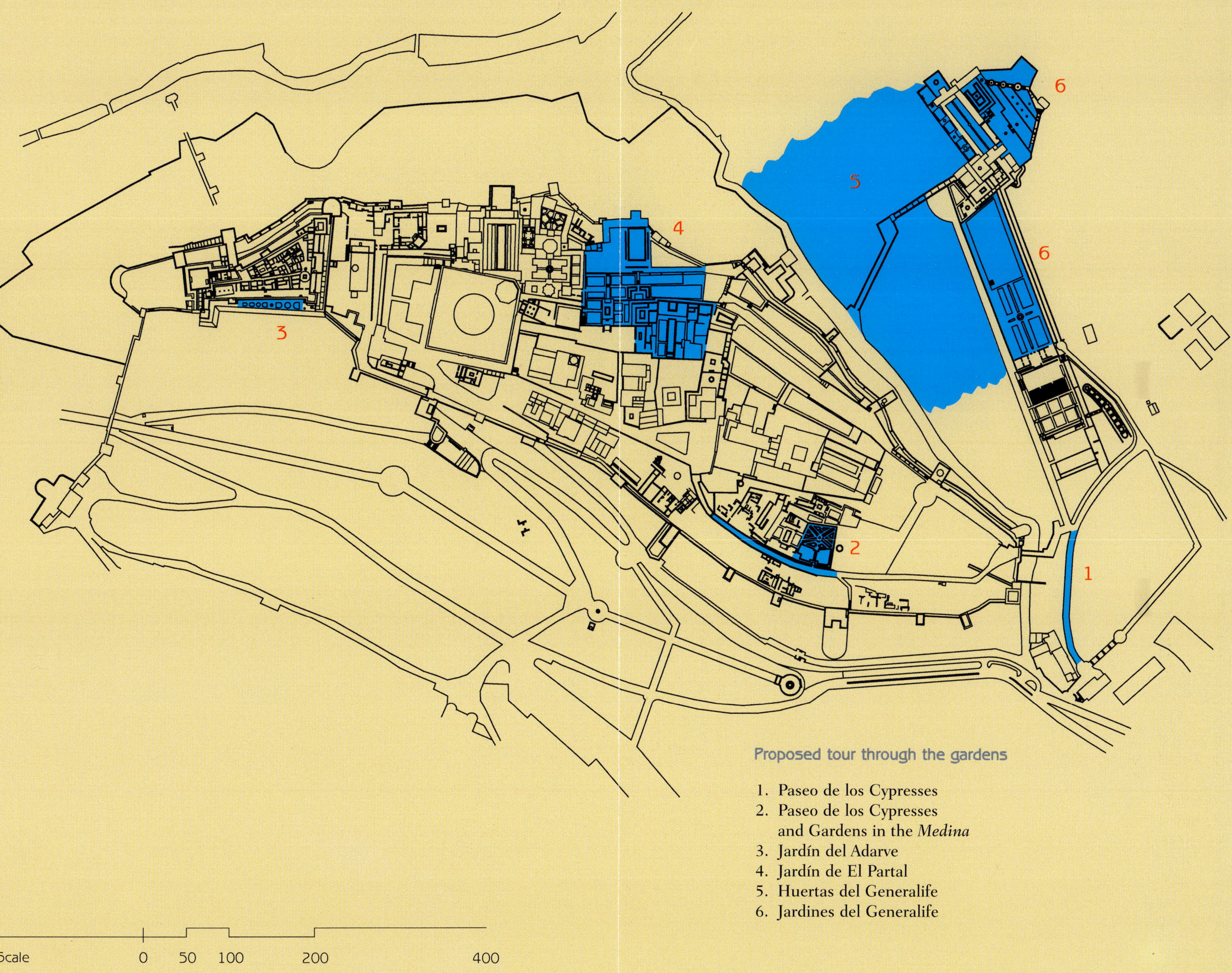

Proposed tour through the gardens

1. Paseo de los Cypresses
2. Paseo de los Cypresses and Gardens in the *Medina*
3. Jardín del Adarve
4. Jardín de El Partal
5. Huertas del Generalife
6. Jardines del Generalife

Tour by Water

ARAB SOURCES HIGHLIGHT the inclusion of water in Islamic architecture, especially in the palaces of al-Andalus. Think of the conduits in the Nasrid palaces of the Alhambra where, through a vast underground layer of lead piping, water flowed to the fountains and ponds. This union of architecture with water is constantly present in the Alhambra, either through the poetry that presents water as a gift of the sultan, or in the vases with water that are located in the *tacas* in the palaces, and to which the poetic inscriptions refer. Given the purifying nature of water, its greatest symbol in the Alhambra is perhaps the water stair, the Escalera del Agua in the Generalife.

But together with the religious symbolism we should point to its use in daily life that makes it necessary to store and channel it. The Alhambra is a good example of architecture dedicated to the supply and channelling of water. The perfection in Islamic buildings and constructions for the storage and distribution of water is an element unanimously emphasized by the Christians. *Aljibes*, water conduits, watercourses and garden fountains are common elements that attract the attention of the Christian travellers in the lands of al-Andalus and especially in the Alhambra.

In addition to the possibility of following a route through the inside of the precinct following its fountains, watercourses and *aljibes*, the Alhambra offers you an interesting tour on the trail of the water as it arrived and was stored, the water that was needed in the palaces, *medina* and baths.

The water the Alhambra receives comes from the river Darro, which rises to the east of the city. The river basin is situated to the northeast of the capital forming a small depression surrounded by mountains in the national parkland of the Sierra de Huétor mountains, and covers nearly 49 kilometres. On its way to the city, the Darro gathers water from many springs and brooks.

The Presa Real, located in a place known as Jesús del Valle, directs water from the Darro to the Alhambra. The current infrastructure corresponds to the twentieth century, but in the thirteenth century Muḥammad I must have intervened here to construct the royal watercourse, the Acequia Real, to adapt the hill to the new settlement in the Alhambra. The *acequia* runs along the north of the hill and splits into two branches: one becomes the Acequia del Tercio, so named because it takes a third of the flood from the Acequia Real, and the other is Acequia Real itself.

Before entering into the Generalife, the Acequia del Tercio follows a route that is extremely interesting because of its ingenuity, however the danger it entails means you should only take it as part of a programmed visit. The *acequia* canal slopes slightly to permit the water to flow while at the same time it produces clay sedimentation which favours the growth of vegetation along the riverbank in the form of overhanging greenery that prevents evaporation. At the same time, the vegetation in the *acequia* acts as a filter and decants the water. Several small Islamic bridges saved the *acequia* from hillside erosion that might have dragged vegetation and earth into it causing an obstruction. Following the original route along part of the upper stretch of the Nasrid *acequia*, the water is piped through an underground gallery, constructed in the 1950s.

The Acequia del Tercio enters the Alhambra and Generalife precinct in the area of the Mirador Romántico. From here its rustic appearance changes and the water channels are ornamented. From the Mirador Romántico the water flows down the water stair, the Escalera del Agua. In the Patio del Ciprés de la Sultana it rejoins the Acequia Real which enters the precinct via the north pavilion of the Generalife.

From the Patio de la Sultana the *acequia* continues to run via the Patio de la Acequia, descending through the south pavilion of the Generalife. Near the overhanging oleanders, the *acequia* continues through modern underground piping but following its original route. Through a gallery in the Paseo de los Cipreses, the water is raised with waterwheels in order to supply the area of the pools.

Here, you first see two ventilation wells, before the water reached the tower for the waterwheel and the pool known as the Albercón de las Damas.

The Nasrid Albercón de las Damas was established to extend the cultivated land in the *almunia*

On the following page, water in the Alhambra.

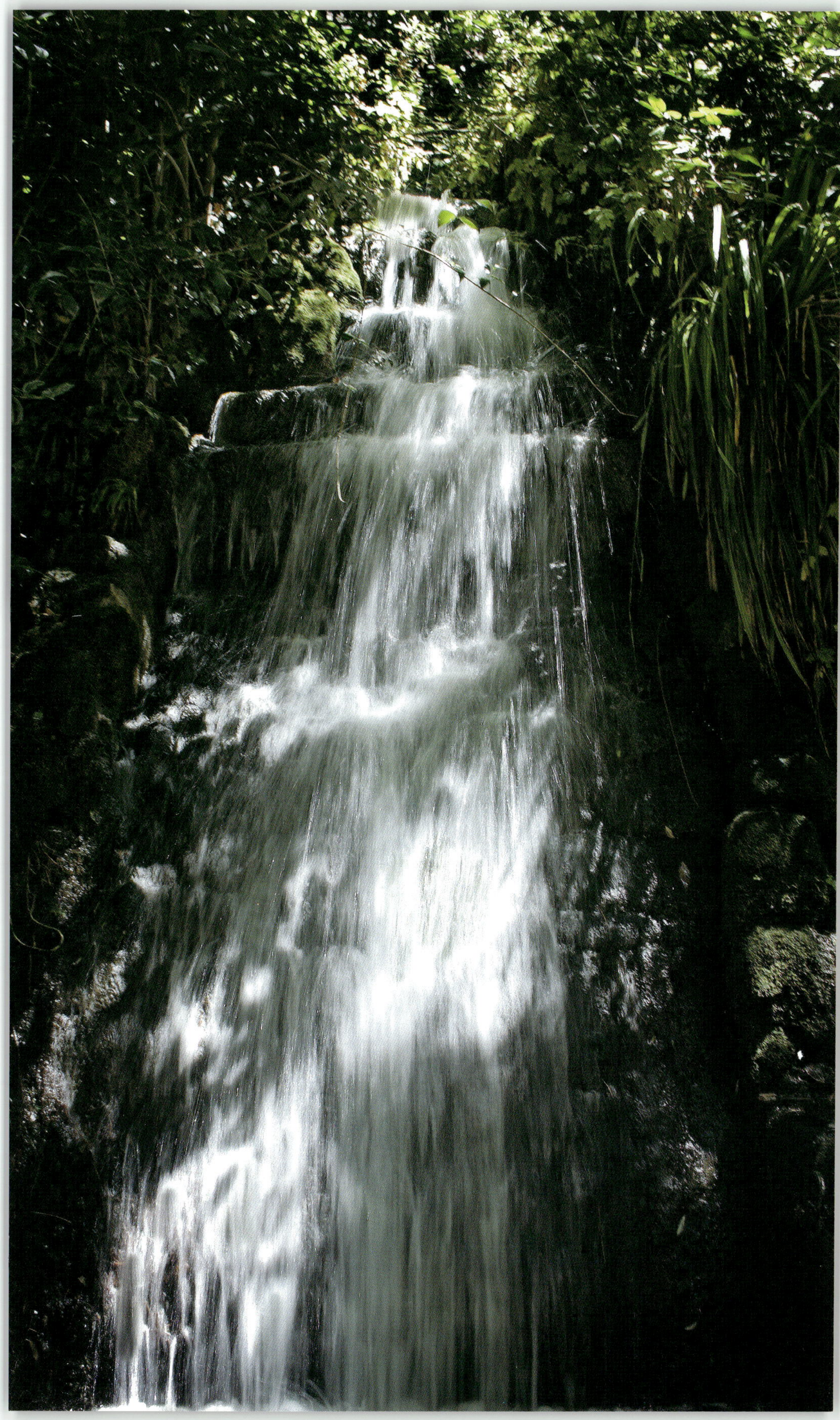

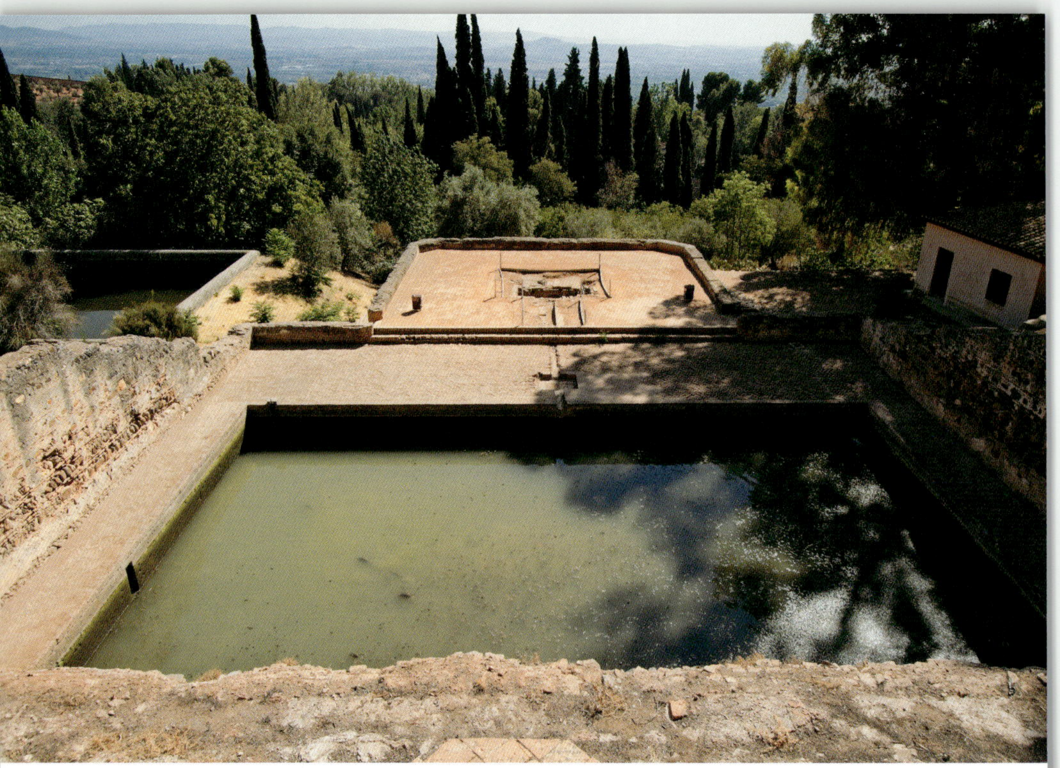

Albercón de las Damas

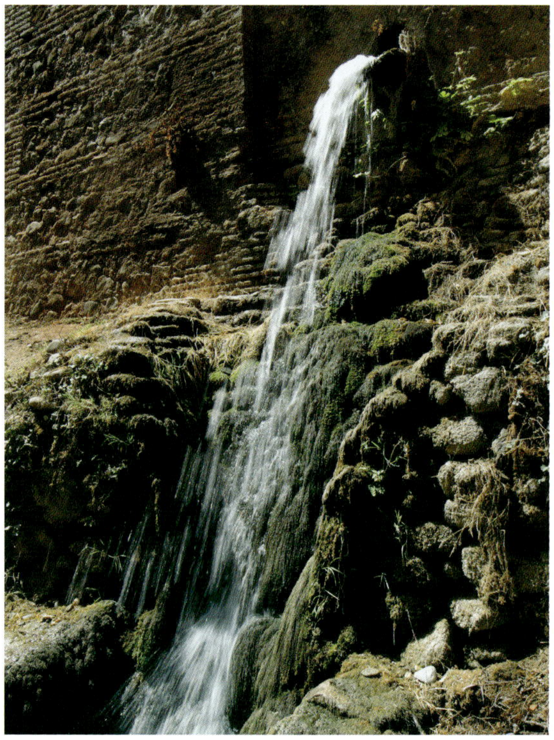

Spillway in the Alhambra

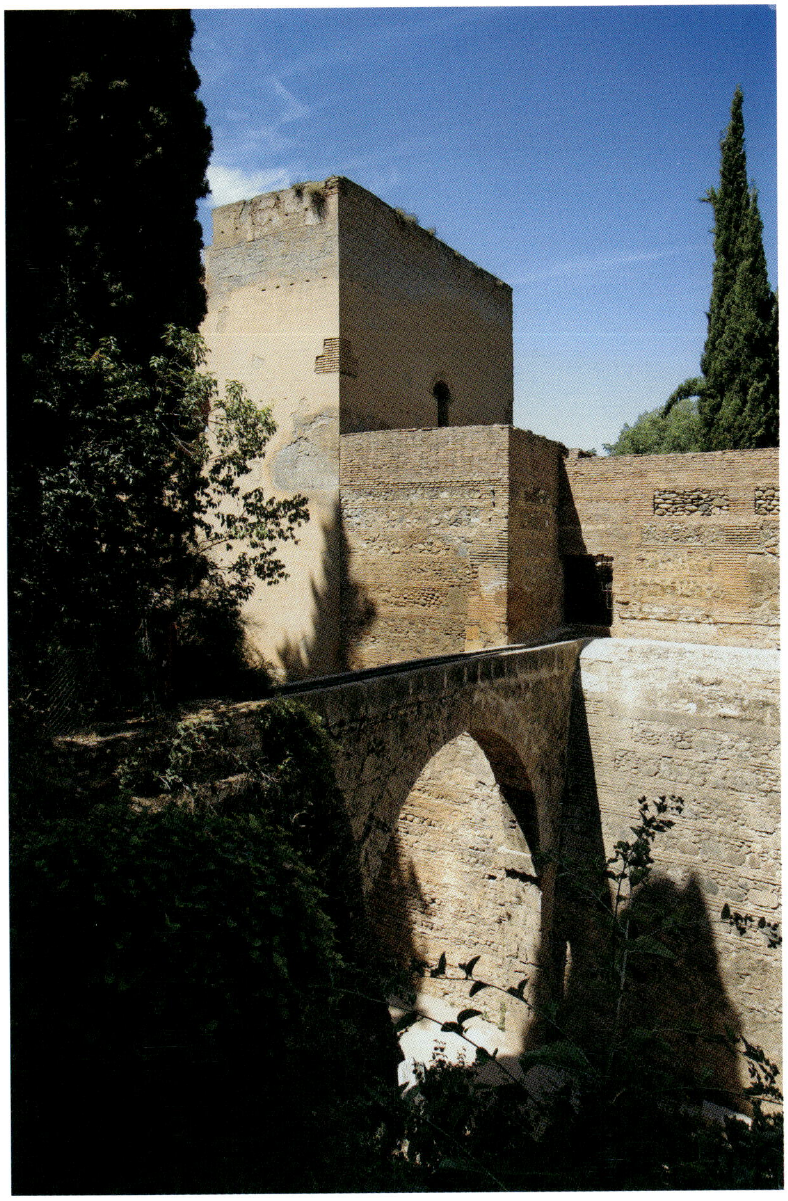

Aqueduct towards the Torre del Agua

of the Generalife and was fed by the Acequia Real where, although at a lower level, water was raised by an animal-powered water-wheel. That is, the water was directed through galleries to a well and from there it was raised with the water-wheel to pour it into the pool. Nearby another two pools were built in the twentieth century, the work of Leopoldo Torres Balbás and Francisco Prieto Moreno.

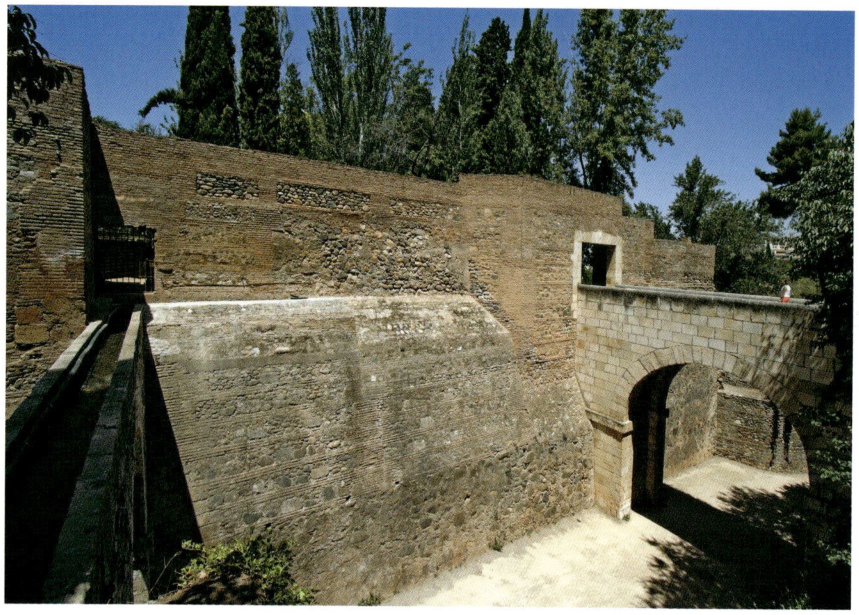

Detail of water entering in the direction of the *medina alta*

The *acequia* continues along the route that leads towards the new museums and here divides into two branches again: one goes to the area of the Carmen de los Mártires and the other continues entering into the Alhambra and arriving at the Torre del Agua, from there continuing towards the *medina*. Before it reaches the bridge there are several distribution channels that take water to all the *cármenes* in the area of the Mauror and the Antequeruela. Once it enters the Alhambra there is a series of spillways that regulate excess water, forming small cascades one of which you can see to the right of the modern bridge.

The *acequia*, now running underground, crosses what was the site of workshops and tanneries in the *medina* and today is El Secano, to the Parador de San Francisco. It continues along the Calle Real Alta and from the Callejón del Guindo the water is piped to El Partal on the one hand and the Patio de los Leones on the other.

The *acequia* passes through the Museum of the Alhambra, the *aljibe* in the Sala de Presentación, the Aljibe de Tendilla (closed to visits) and the Aljibe de la Alcazaba. It continues on its route towards the Puerta de la Explanada (or de la Justicia) and the Pilar de Carlos V. Near the gate and at the entrance to the Puerta de los Carros a spillway cascading water from the Calle Real attracts the attention. Further on, in the Torre del Capitán, you encounter yet another.

The Dehesa del Generalife and the hikers' paths

ANOTHER ENTICING alternative to learn more about the Alhambra is to travel across the unspoilt terrain of the outer urban park of the Dehesa del Generalife, officially named as such in 1995 and legally protected since then. As well as offering sports facilities, the park is especially indicated for hikers and mountain bikers. A tour around the area shows you the vast extent and variety of landscapes, materials, vegetation and animals that make it up. In this

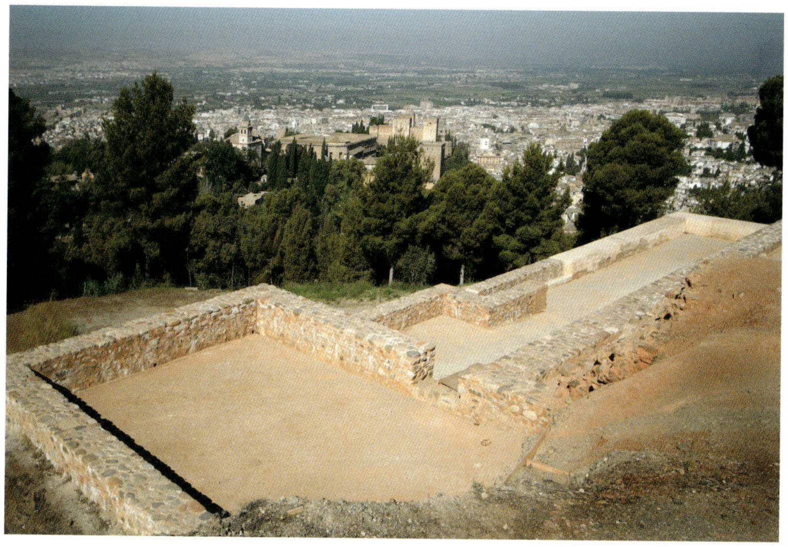

Remains of the castle of Santa Elena (or Silla del Moro).

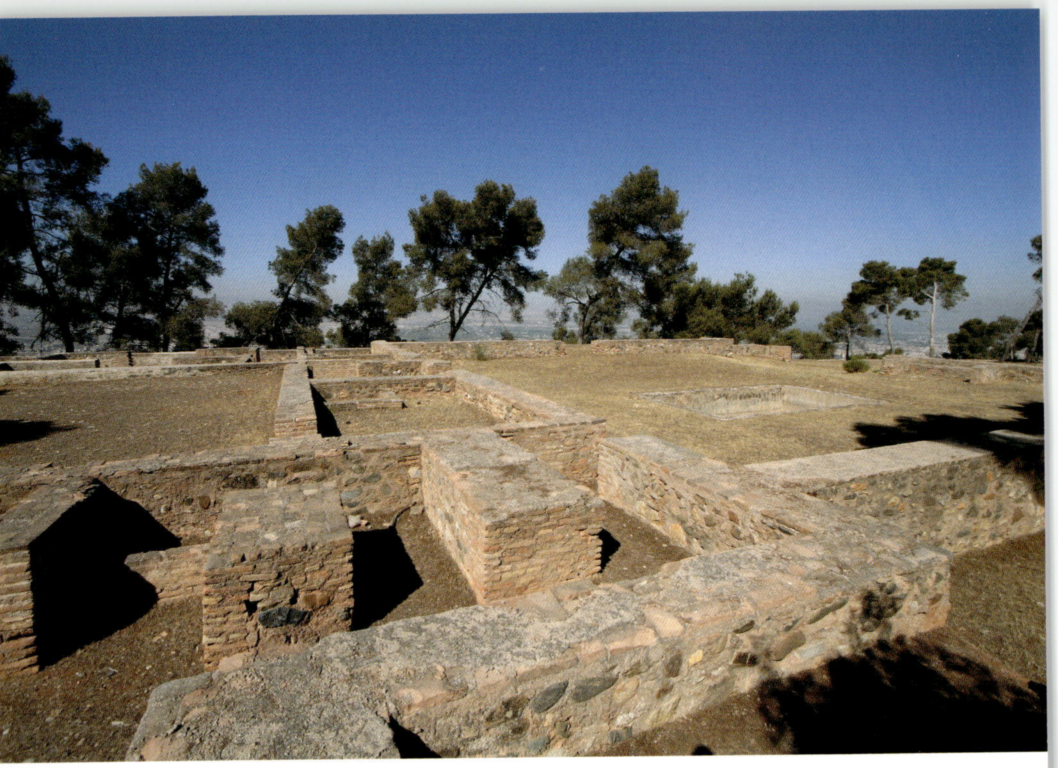

Remains of the Palacio de Dār al-'Arūsa

outer urban park, Cerro del Sol and Llano de la Perdiz stand out for their altitude and flatness, converting them into splendid viewing points over the city. Moreover, the park houses important, conserved Nasrid remains such as the Palacio de Dār al-'Arūsa, the Aljibe de la Lluvia and the Albercón del Negro.

On foot, you can start the tour along a pedestrian footpath, closed to traffic, near the car parks and above the new museums.

The first point of interest is the place known popularly as the Silla del Moro: the ancient ruins of the castle of Santa Elena which, according to seventeenth-century sources, was a favourite destination for pilgrims arriving in Granada for the first time. It is one of the buildings that suffered most during the 1810-12 Napoleonic invasion because of its strategic location. Below, the Albercón de las Damas water deposit, mentioned earlier, stretches out before you.

On the top of this same Cerro del Sol hill, a few metres from the Silla del Moro, you can follow a path, passing a fence that close off access by vehicles but not pedestrians, and turning right towards the ruins of Dār al-'Arūsa (visits are restricted to special timetables). As far as we know, this is the highest of the Nasrid palaces. The name means the house of the newly-wed or bride. In all, the buildings include three patios with a bath outside the

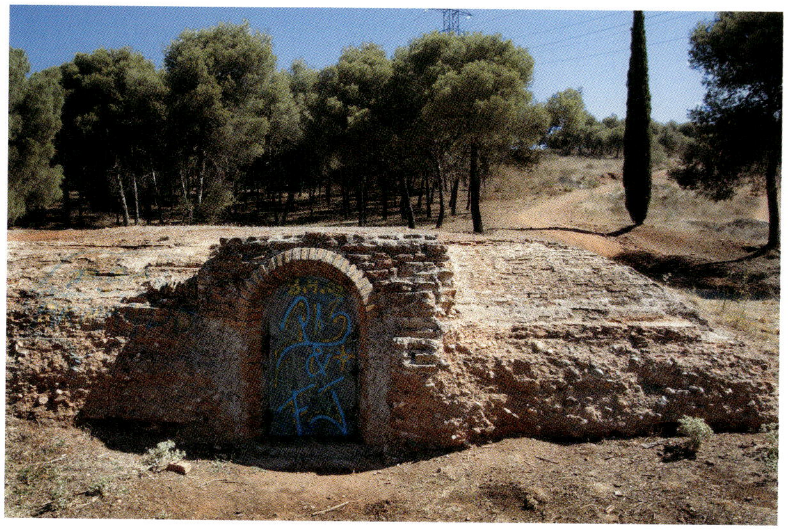

Aljibe de la Lluvia

palace, and on the north you find the remains of a water-wheel, an *aljibe* and a water trough–fountain.

From the Palacio de Dār al-'Arūsa and along the ridge of the hill, at a distance of some 900 metres, you reach another point of interest: the Aljibe de la Lluvia. The inside of this ancient Nasrid cistern includes different structures with vaulted roofs and a central rectangle where the rainwater enters. We do not know where this water was distributed to. Near the *aljibe*, a large *alberca* has been conserved which, some sources suggest was used to wash the gold-bearing sands found in the area.

Close to the Aljibe de la Lluvia, the water-wheel of a Nasrid well has been conserved. It was used to raise water to irrigate crops in the area. The remains of another large *alberca*, the Albercón del Cerro del Sol, identifies where this water was deposited. From here, you can enjoy the priceless views of the Sacromonte quarter.

On the way down, some 950 metres away, you arrive at another water deposit, the Albercón del Negro, in front of the space known as the Muslim cemetery. Dating from Nasrid times, the water deposit is spectacularly large and would apparently have served to take water to the Palacio de los Alijares. Only scattered remains of the palace are left in the surroundings of the municipal cemetery of San José. A few meters from the Albercón del Negro the mouth of the gallery that would have reached all the way to the palace, has been preserved.

The Alhambra from the city of Granada

THE ALHAMBRA AND GRANADA may seem inseparable but visitors down the years and citizens of Nasrid Granada above all, always perceive them as separate entities. This is logical in the medieval Islamic world from the functional point of view: power was isolated and raised itself above the city in defence and also as an expression of distance demanded by protocol. In this case, what is peculiar about the place of settlement chosen on a craggy height, in the last foothills of the Sierra Nevada mountains, cut out by the valleys formed by the river Darro and La Sabīka hill, gives a special value in terms of landscape to the magnificent complex and this in turn alters this same landscape, so that it glimpses a vision from "below", from the city, to the same extent as from "above", from the Alhambra. Granada and its surroundings are dominated.

In Nasrid times the effect of isolation and height must have been even stronger as the dense wood that today surrounds it did not exist and the bare whitewashed walls and towers were on open display. Thus, at least, it appeared to the Christians who besieged it in the image of the romance of Abenamar in which the towers are described as "high" and "shining", when seen from the open plain, the *vega*. Since then no traveller has been able to steal themselves away from the impression of height and dominion over the city, whether it be in the precise drawings of Antón Van der Wyngaerden or the picturesque views of Joris Hoefnagle, both sixteenth-century illustrators, to the distorted slenderness seen by their Romantic successors.

Today, more than five centuries have passed since the original inhabitants abandoned it, with all the interventions of the Christian monarchs, testimony

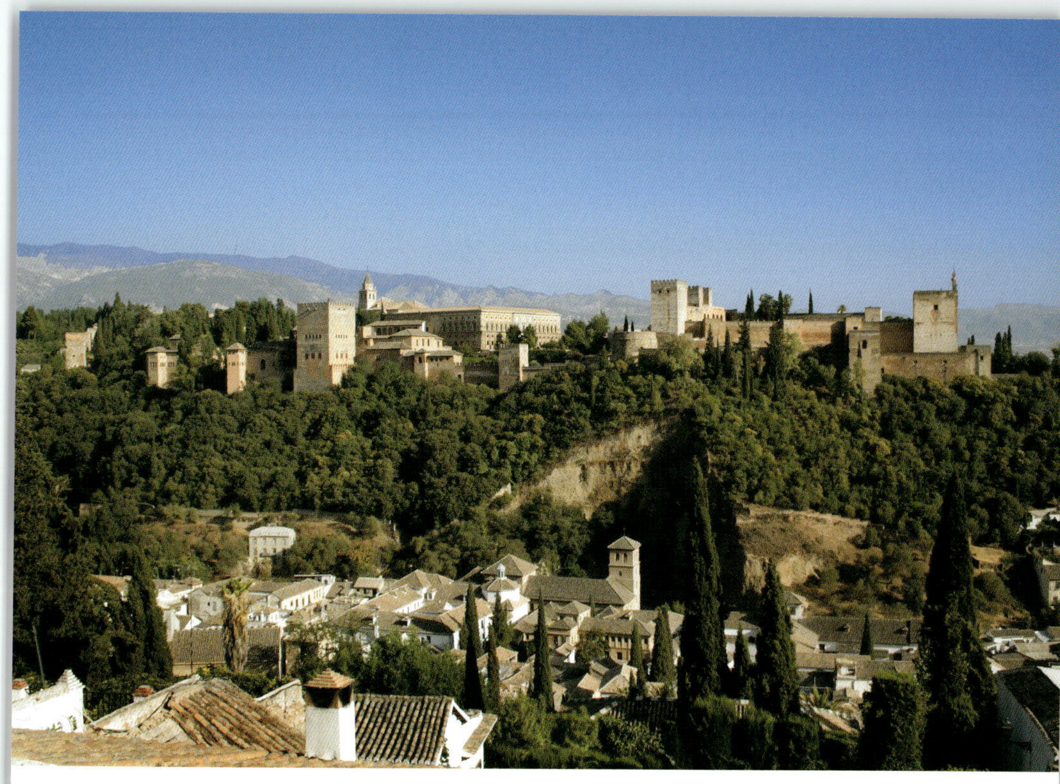

View of the Alhambra from the Mirador de San Nicolás in the Albaicín

nonetheless to their admiration and insistence on conserving this valuable monument, the Alhambra represents an architectural jewel perfectly incrusted on the promontory of La Sabīka hilltop, with the harsh roughness of the escarpment worn smooth, so useful in defence then. With the wood of elms and other species with which it was reforested following the conquest; a green band that highlights and enhances it above the city, cutting it out against the backdrop of Sierra Nevada in one of the most fascinating spectacles of shapes and colours that can occur in the world when you watch a sunset from the Albaicín.

Perhaps it is from the Albaicín where you can gain the best perspective to understand the singularity of the place, this meeting point of mountain and plain bounded by water, but also by the force and animation of the architecture over the place. In the long line that runs from the Torre de la Vela to the Generalife and the Silla del Moro the spectator can appreciate the succession of such different bodies and spaces from the military citadel at its western extreme to the pleasure villa in the Generalife that, though joined by the wall, allow you to see through the breaks and in the interior spaces the change

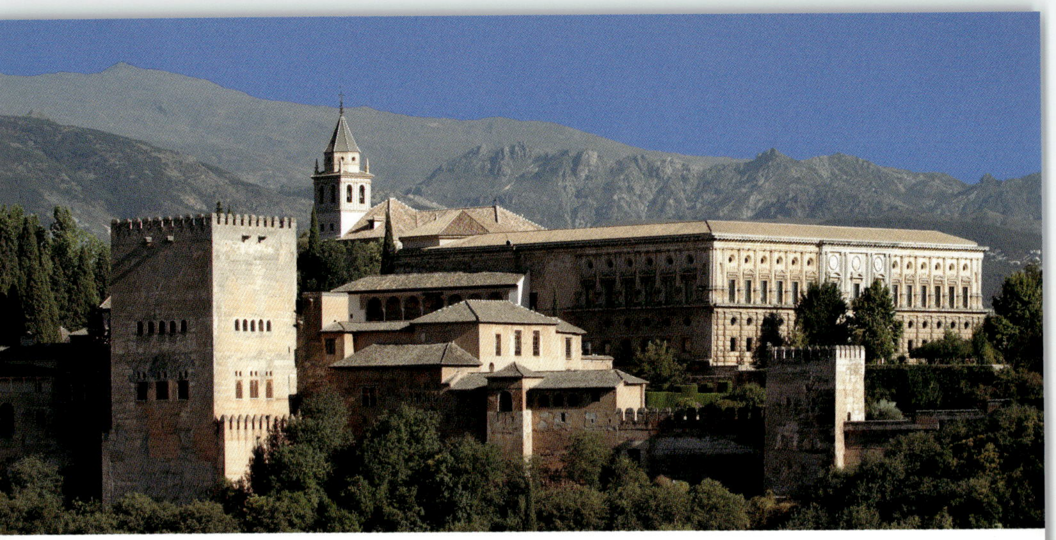

The Alhambra from the city

of scenery from the military to the palatial, subtly marked by the vegetation of the inner garden until ending in the wonderful agricultural "architecture" of the terraced beds that surround the Generalife. Each corner of the Albaicín offers us a different image of the Alhambra.

But from other points of the city we continue to contemplate the magnitude of the Alhambra, with views from Plaza Nueva or from the Sacromonte quarter where the changing light of the city surprises us with new sensations about the palace precinct.

As well as the walls and gates of the Islamic city, other Islamic monuments in the city also help us understand the singularity of Nasrid art in the Alhambra. A tour through the eleventh-century Zirid Bañuelo, the ancient Nasrid *alhóndiga* or Corral del Carbón, the Cuarto Real de Santo Domingo, the Madraza, and the Alcázar Genil among others, help us increase our understanding of Islamic art and its relationship with the Alhambra.

Appendices

Historical chronicle

WHAT IS AL-ANDALUS?

Name

The etymology of al-Andalus is not clear. A hypothetical derivation from *Vándalos* has been rejected and it is suggested that the interpretation of the toponym as derived from the myth of the Atlantes and applied to a compound toponym including the Atlas mountains and the Atlantic Ocean. However, it is hard to believe that the Islamic military forces who entered the Iberian Peninsular would know of this myth.

Date

Al-Andalus comprises the territory dominated by the Muslims in the Iberian Peninsular, including part of Portugal, from 711 to the conquest of the Kingdom of Granada in 1492. Given the context, this process was known as the "Reconquest" as it described the advance of the Christian kingdoms into the realms of al-Andalus, though in fact the term is debatable as in the Middles Ages no real intention of uniting Spain existed.

Principle periods

— Emirate (756-912) During the years following the entrance of the Muslims, and until the Umayyad dynasty, a succession of governors or *valíes* named indirectly by the Caliph of Damascus ruled. Disputes between Berbers and Arabs in the Iberian Peninsular facilitated the defeat and assassination of the Umayyads by the Abbasids in Bagdad. One of the fleeing Umayyads ('Abd al-Raḥmān I), was exiled and invited by his blood relatives to move to the Iberian Peninsular, where the caliphate of the Umayyads would be installed.

— Caliphate (912-1099), 'Abd al-Raḥmān III adopted the title of Caliph and Emir cutting links with the Abbasid dynasty in Bagdad. The Umayyad caliphate had its capital in Córdoba, where the Aljama mosque and the Madīnat al-Zahrā' became the two great symbols of Umayyad power.

— Civil war or *Fitna* (1009-1031)

— The kingdom of Taifas (1031-1091). The civil war put an end to the caliphate. After several years of confrontations, there was a dismembering and sharing out of the lands of al-Andalus among some fifty states or *taifas*. Seville was one of the most important of these, especially when ruled by al-Mu'taḍid of Seville, as was the *taifa* of Zaragoza. Another *taifa* was that of the Zirids who were installed in Granada around 1013.

— Almoravids (*c*.1066-1150). The Almoravids came from those followers of Islam who at the beginning of the eleventh century had propagated their faith south of the Sahara founding convent-fortresses. They had been called upon on various occasions by some of the *taifa* states and thus entered al-Andalus.

— Almohads (*c*.1150-1233). The Almohads professed a series of doctrines intended to purify Islam of innovations that had been being introduced into it. This was the period of the architectural splendour of Seville, personified by the Aljama mosque and the Giralda.

— The Nasrids (1232-1492). One last taifa, Muḥammad b. al-Aḥmar b. Naṣr, managed to gain control of the Kingdom of Granada around 1231, proclaiming himself sultan in Arjona in 1232, installing himself in Granada in 1237, and declaring himself a vassal of the Castilians. In 1492, the Nasrid kingdom succumbed to the conquest of Granada by the Catholic Kings through a pact or capitulation. Their maximum urban, architectural expression is the Alhambra.

PATRONAGE AND PRINCIPAL BUILDINGS IN THE ALHAMBRA

(From the Nasrid period until the expulsion of the Moriscos. The dates refer to the periods of mandate. The dates listed are those most widely accepted although there is debate and diverging opinions about the attributions and periods of some buildings so these should be taken as approximations.)

Nasrid period

Muḥammad I (1237-1273)

Acequia Real
Alcazaba
Possible start on the fortified precinct

Muḥammad II (1273-1302)

Generalife (some authors date this in the reign of Muḥammad III)
The palace known as Palacio de Yūsuf III
Torre de los Picos (first building)
Palace in the current Parador de San Francisco

Muḥammad III (1303-1309)

El Partal and the Torre de las Damas
Mezquita Real
Baño de la Mezquita

Puerta del Vino
Alterations to the Generalife

Ismā'īl I (1314-1325)
The Mexuar
Puerta de las Armas
Baño Real
Rauda Real (some authors date this in the reign of Muḥammad II)
Alterations to the Generalife

Yūsuf I (1333-1354)
Torre del Cadí
Torre de la Cautiva
Torreón de Comares
Puerta de la Explanada (or de la Justicia)
Oratory in El Partal
Alterations to the Baño Real
Alterations to the Mexuar
Torre Quebrada
Puerto de la Alberca (or de los Siete Suelos)

Muḥammad V (1354-1359) and (1362-1391)
Palacio de Comares (except the tower)
Palacio de los Leones
Alterations to the Mexuar
Alterations to the Puerta del Vino
Torre de Abū l-Ḥaŷŷāŷ (in the Peinador de la Reina)

Muḥammad VII (1392-1408)
Torre de las Infantas

Christian period

Catholic Kings (in the Alhambra from 1492 to 1516)
The great *aljibe* in the Plaza de los Aljibes
Conversion of a Nasrid palace into the convent of San Francisco
Restoration to wall faces
Alterations in the Generalife
First Christian alterations in the Mexuar and the Cuarto Dorado

Charles I of Spain and V of Germany (1516-1556)
Palacio de Carlos V

Arco de las Granadas
Pilar de Carlos V
Charles V's appartments (or Washington Irving's appartments)
Peinador de la Reina
Building work in the Cuarto Dorado and the Patio de Machuca
Building work in the Baño Real de Comares

Philip II (1556-1598)
Continuation of the building work in the Palacio de Carlos V
Church of Santa María de la Alhambra

Philip III (1598-1621)
Repair and restoration of roofs and towers
Late Renaissance vaulting commissioned for the Sala de Mocárabes
Construction of the church of Santa María de la Alhambra completed

MAJOR EVENTS IN THE CONSERVATION OF THE ALHAMBRA. (19th and 20th cent.)

1779. Henry Swinburne published *Travels through Spain in the Years 1775 and 1776* making the Alhambra fashionable in England and France and beginning a period in which the Romantics would give their particular vision of the Alhambra.

1787. Part one of José Hermosilla's *Las Antigüedades árabes de España* is published. In his drawings and plans he brings together the first serious studies of the Alhambra.

1837. Owen Jones and Jules Goury's *Plans, elevations, sections and details from the Alhambra* is published. Both authors made drawings of the Alhambra in 1834 although Owen Jones returned in 1837 to make more drawings that would complete the work. It is considered one of the most serious attempts at a scientific approach to the subject although they are clearly guided by Romantic enthusiasm.

1843. The architect Rafael Contreras carried out the restoration of the Sala de las Camas in the Baño Real, rebuilding a large part of the hall and of the original conserving only the columns, within the Romantic historicist tradition that he belonged to.

1870. The Alhambra was first declared a National Historic and Artistic Monument.

1923. Leopoldo Torres Balbás is named Architect-Curator of the Alhambra introducing a new policy consisting of respecting the original buildings as much as possible and intervening solely in cases calling for great urgency.

1979. Important delimitation of the precinct, with the substantial extension of the area through the inclusion of the Palacio del Generalife and all of the archaeological remains situated in the area surrounding Cerro del Sol.

1984. The Alhambra and the Generalife were included in the UNESCO World Heritage site list.

1989. New limits to the perimeter of the Alhambra were established and the process of declaring it an historic complex and of officially recognizing it as of cultural interest was begun.

1992. The planned restoration of the Palacio de Carlos V was begun.

2002. A protective perimeter was established around the complex, including a substantial area within that defined as being of cultural interest on the basis of the architecture and countryside.

Gallery of historical figures

TABLE OF SULTANS AND CHRISTIAN MONARCHS PRIOR TO THE CATHOLIC KINGS

Granada

1232-1273	(629-671 AH)	Muḥammad I, *al-Gālib bi-llāh*
1273-1302	(671-701 AH)	Muḥammad II, *al-Faqīh*
1302-1309	(701-708 AH)	Muḥammad III, *al-Majlū'*
1309-1314	(708-713 AH)	Naṣr
1314-1325	(713-725 AH)	Ismā'īl I, *Abū I-Walīd*
1325-1333	(725-733 AH)	Muḥammad IV
1333-1354	(733-755 AH)	Yūsuf I, *Abū l-Ḥaŷŷāŷ*
1354-1359	(755-760 AH)	Muḥammad V, *al-Ganī bi-llāh* [1st reign]
1359	(760-761 AH)	Ismā'īl II
1360-1362	(761-763 AH)	Muḥammad VI, *el Bermejo*, the Red.
1362-1391	(763-793 AH)	Muḥammad V, *al-Ganī bi-llāh* [2nd reign]
1391	(793-794 AH)	Yūsuf II
1392-1408	(794-810 AH)	Muḥammad VII, *al-Musta'īn bi-llāh*
1408-1417	(810-820 AH)	Yūsuf III
1417-1419		Muḥammad VIII, *el Pequeño,* the Small [1st reign]
1419-1427		Muḥammad IX al-Aysar, *el Zurdo,* the Left-handed, or *el Izquierdo*, the Left [1st reign]
1427-1430		Muḥammad VIII, *el Pequeño*, the Small [2nd reign]
1430-1432		Muḥammad IX al-Aysar, *el Zurdo*, the Left-handed, or *el Izquierdo*, the Left [2nd reign]
1432		Yūsuf IV, *Abenalmao*

1432-1445	Muḥammad IX al-Aysar [3rd reign]
1445 (849-849 AH)	Yūsuf V, *el Cojo*, the Lame
1446 (849-851 AH)	Ismā‘īl III
1447-1453 (851-857 AH)	Muḥammad IX al-Aysar [4th reign]
1453	Muḥammad X, *el Chiquito*, the Little One [1st reign]
1454	Sa‘d, *Ciriza* or *Muley Zad* [1st reign]
1455	Muḥammad X, *el Chiquito*, the Little One
1455-1462	Sa‘d [2nd reign]
1462	Ismā‘īl IV
1463	Sa‘d, *Ciriza* or *Muley Zad* [3rd reign]
1464-1482 (869-887 AH)	Abū l-Ḥasan ‘Alī, *Muley Hacén* [1st reign]
1482 (887-888 AH)	Muḥammad XI, *Boabdil* [1st reign]
1483-1484 (888-890 AH)	Abū l-Ḥasan ‘Alī, *Muley Hacén* [2nd reign]
1485-1486 (890-892 AH)	Muḥammad XII, *al-Zagal*
1487-1492 (892-897 AH)	Muḥammad XI, *Boabdil* [2nd reign]

(Dates in parentheses are *anno hegirae*, AH, in the year of the Hegira, the Muslim era as recorded in Arabic sources. Nicknames attributed to rulers are taken from *Historia de España* by Menéndez Pidal).

Kingdoms of Castile and León

1217-1252 Ferdinand III, the Saint
1252-1284 Alfonso X, the Wise
1284-1295 Sancho IV, the Brave
1295-1312 Ferdinand IV, the Summoned
1312-1350 Alfonso XI
1350-1369 Peter I, the Cruel
1369-1379 Henry II Trastámara
1379-1390 John I
1390-1406 Henry III, the Infirm
1406-1454 John II
1454-1474 Henry IV, the Impotent
1475-1479 Civil war
1476-1504 Isabella I *la Católica*, the Catholic Queen, (married in 1469 to Ferdinand II of Aragón who in 1479 inherited the Kingdom of Aragón bringing about the dynastic union of the crowns of Castile and Aragón).

Kingdom of Aragón

1213-1276 James I
1276-1285 Peter III, the Great
1285-1291 Alfonso III, the Liberal
1291-1327 James II, the Just
1327-1336 Alfonso IV, the Benign
1336-1387 Peter IV, the Ceremonious
1387-1396 John I of Aragón
1396-1410 Martin I, the Humanist
1410-1412 Interregnum
1412-1416 Ferdinand I, from Antequera
1416-1458 Alfonso V, the Magnanimous
1458-1479 John II
1479-1516 Ferdinand II *el Católico*, the Catholic King (married in 1469 to Isabella I of Castile. In 1479, on inheriting the Kingdom of Aragón the dynastic union of the crowns of Castile and Aragón came about.)

PRINCIPAL POETS IN THE NASRID ALHAMBRA

Ibn al-Ŷayyāb (1274-1349). b. Granada. Formed part of the *Dīwān al-inšā' al-naṣrī* (commissioned to take down correspondence and official documents and also, it seems, to compose poems in honour of the dynasty). He would become first minister, or vizier, in the reign of Yūsuf I. He remained in the Nasrid court for over fifty years, from Muḥammad II to Yūsuf I, until his death as a victim of the black plague. His first poems inscribed in the Alhambra seem to have been those in El Partal. He is confidently acknowledged as author of the poems on the *tacas* of the north portico of the Generalife as well as the poems in the Torre de la Cautiva. Other poems that are not found inscribed *in situ* are those in a *qubba* of Yūsuf I and a poem for the door of a royal baths in the Alhambra.

Ibn al-Jaṭīb (1313- 1374). b. Loja (Granada). Like his master Ibn al-Ŷayyāb formed part of the *Dīwān al-inšā' al-naṣrī.* He entered the service of Yūsuf I in 1349. He was first minister or vizier until 1359 when Muḥammad V lost the throne. When in 1362 Muḥammad V recovered the throne, he took up his former position which he held until his murder in 1374. A historian with important works about Granada such as *al-Iḥāṭa*, attributes to him the poems that frame the arches of the *tacas* situated to the right and left of the entrance of the Salón de Comares, as well as the poem in the Sala de Dos Hermanas that was later replaced by another poem by Ibn Zamrak.

Ibn Zamrak (1333-1393). b. Granada. Disciple of Ibn al-Jaṭīb, formed part of the list of candidates of the *Dīwān al-inšā' al-naṣrī.* He was named first minister or vizier under Muḥammad V. He was murdered in his home in 1393. Of his poems engraved on the walls of the Alhambra, the most notable are on the Fuente de los Leones, the poem in the Sala de Dos Hermanas (replacing that written by Ibn al-Jaṭīb), the poem on the entrance arch to the Mirador de Lindaraja, and that in the window screens of the *ajimeces*, of the viewing point there.

IMPORTANT FIGURES IN THE SIXTEENTH-CENTURY ALHAMBRA

Counts of Tendilla. From this family we have to highlight Íñigo López de Mendoza (1442-1515), second count of Tendilla and first Marquis of Mondéjar. He fought in the War of Granada from the start and was named Captain General of Granada and *alcaide* of the Alhambra. The Catholic Kings ceded to the family the palace named after Yūsuf III where the family lived until the eighteenth century when they were stripped of the title of *alcaidía* and lost their rights to live in the palace. The second count of Tendilla promoted the building of the Palacio de Carlos V, which was continued by his son Luis Hurtado de Mendoza, third count of Tendilla and second Marquis of Mondéjar, who assumed his father's role in 1515. Generally, the counts of Tendilla maintained a policy of great sensitivity and care for the Islamic Alhambra.

Master Fernando de las Maderas. He is the most important representative of the *Mudéjar* tradition in the Alhambra. A Muslim master craftsman known before his conversion as Master Avrán de las Maderas. Records exist of his work in the Alhambra from 1492 and throughout the reign of the Catholic Kings. Essentially he worked as master craftsman, adapting and repairing the Palacio de los Leones, Palacio de Comares and the chapel de los Baños.

Pedro Machuca (b. Toledo?–d. 1550 Granada). Painter and architect trained in Rome, where he worked in the workshop of Rafael de Sanzio. On returning to Spain, around 1519, he came to the Alhambra in the service of the count of Tendilla as a trusty squire, relied upon to handle administrative affairs and above all responsible for the construction of the new Palacio de Carlos V, which he directed until his death. However, his fine reputation comes from his painting.

Julio Aquiles and Alejandro Mayner. Both painters, who in collaboration with others of the Granada school, decorated, from 1537, the Sala de las Frutas, the parapet walk, or *adarve*, and the upper rooms of the Peinador de la Reina. Aquiles, qualified as an expert decorator, was from Rome and had been trained in Italy in the circle of the great Rafael and Juan de Udine, specializing in grotesques. In Spain he appears from 1533, decorating the palace of Francisco de los Cobos and a chapel in San Pablo de Úbeda, but the paintings in the Alhambra are his most important work, carried out between 1537 and 1545 after which no record remains. Mayner, is of unknown origins although it is conjectured that he was Flemish. He appears in Spain towards 1535 and no documentation of his work exists except for his intervention in the Alhambra. He is considered the author of the more narrative paintings, such as those of the conquest of Tunis, but his exclusive participation in the portrayal of the scenes from the fable of Phaeton and the motifs of the virtues has not been clearly established.

MOST IMPORTANT ARCHITECT-CURATORS OF THE ALHAMBRA

Rafael Contreras. The saga of the Contreras was inaugurated in 1828 when José Contreras was given responsibility for the safety of the Alhambra, assigning then an annual amount for the conservation of the monument. Although he was linked to the monument previously, in 1847 he was named as "restorer-adorner" Rafael Contreras, which he truly was in interventions in places such as the Sala de las Camas in the Baño Real. In these restorations of ornaments he sought extreme, unreal colourist effects, although at the time it was believed his work was authentic. In 1869 he was named Director and Curator of the Alhambra. In spite of these decorative restorations, without doubt he fostered greater respect for the monument. On the death of Rafael Contreras, his son, Mariano Contreras, took over the direction of works in the Alhambra from 1888 to 1907, being characterized by a policy of compulsory purchases of properties in order to recover the unity of the possessions that made up the Alhambra.

Modesto Cendoya. He replaced Rafael Contreras as Architect Director of Works from 1907 to 1923 when he was dismissed. Under his direction an important stage in the consolidation of structures began. He was responsible for interventions in the Torre de Comares and other works especially with regard to the underground drainage system. Following this first stage he began a second phase of restorations, not without controversy. His guiding principle was to recover the original Nasrid state of the Alhambra and hence his interest in the elimination of later interventions that he considered impeded a vision of the Nasrid complex. Among his discoveries stands that of the paintings in the Casas de El Partal.

Leopoldo Torres Balbás. Architect-Curator of the Alhambra from 1923 to 1936. He stands out for his conservative approach to the historic buildings as his basis for intervening was derived from the conservation of the buildings as they had been inherited, avoiding their ruin and consolidating them, but never completing them or re-building existing parts. His rigour and scientific knowledge led him to leave written records of all his interventions in the works diaries and plans in such minute detail that today we can reconstruct the history of his interventions. One of his most controversial interventions in the period was the roofing in 1934 of the eastern pavilion of the Palacio de los Leones, replacing the glazed dome of 1859.

Francisco Prieto Moreno. Architect who replaced Leopoldo Torres Balbás in 1936. He stands out for interventions in the spaces surrounding the fortified precinct with the clear intention of clearing the precinct situated behind the walls in an attempt to give the protected monument a certain degree of isolation. Another of the fundamental aspects of his work are the excavations he promoted in the surroundings of the Generalife (Silla del Moro, Palacio de Dār al-'Arūsa...) trying to recover what would be the archaeological park of the Alhambra.

MAIN ACADEMICS WHO BROUGHT THE ALHAMBRA TO WIDESPREAD PUBLIC NOTICE

Washington Irving (1783-1859). North American writer who is considered the first North American hispanist. The author of the *Tales of the Alhambra*, published in 1832 and which spread the name of the Nasrid complex worldwide. He lived in the Alhambra in 1829, the year when the Alhambra Autograph Book was begun in an attempt to stop visitors from leaving their signatures on the palace walls. During his stay he lived in the rooms that were constructed for Charles V near to the Sala de Dos Hermanas, and in his memory the name and memory of these rooms has been maintained as Washington Irving's appartments.

Manuel Gómez-Moreno González (1834-1918). Painter who towards 1866 began his activity as a researcher into the art of Granada, from then on becoming one of the most knowledgeable people about Granada and the province. He travelled with his son, also Manuel, to different villages in the province taking notes, making drawings and consulting archives. In 1892 he published the *Guía de Granada*, with a seriousness and rigour that were astonishing for their time and that continue to be a reference today. In his guide there is an entire tour of the Alhambra, filled with news taken from archive documentation and of suggestions of great value such as the consideration that the walls of the Alhambra were white and not red, or indicating for the first time the little importance of the part eliminated by the Palacio de Carlos V. In addition to other important publications about the Alhambra, like his study of the paintings in the Peinador de la Reina, his relationship with the monument was marked by his criticisms of the decorative interventions of Rafael Contreras.

Manuel Gómez-Moreno Martínez (1870-1970). Son of Manuel Gómez-Moreno González with whom he collaborated closely gathering the material for the *Guía de Granada*. He undertook important studies of the *mozárabe* churches between 1912 and 1918, worked on the *Mudéjar* of Toledo, studies into Islamic art in Spain, and specifically about the Alhambra with several publications on the Nasrid complex in general, as well as publications about the convent of San Francisco, Generalife, Torre de las Damas or the mural paintings in the Casas de El Partal.

Antonio Gallego y Burín (1895-1961). Professor, and one time dean of the Faculty of Humanities of the University of Granada. Mayor of Granada from 1938 to 1951, a period in which he undertook an important reform and inner urbanization of the city. One of his best known books is *Granada*. This art history guide to the city was edited in the 1930s and, as he himself said, constituted an updating of data based on the *Guía de Granada* by Manuel Gómez-Moreno. In addition to other publications related with the city, he wrote his reflections on the Alhambra making an evaluation of the monument complex and a description of its artistic elements, constituting a living testimony of what the Alhambra was like around 1940. In 1945 he was named Vice President of the Alhambra and Generalife trust until 1951, when he became Director General of Fine Arts, planning from Madrid the holding of the Festival of Music and Dance in Granada.

Emilio García Gómez (1905-1995). He was Director of the Spanish Royal Academy of History, founder of Spain's national science research council School of Arab Studies in Granada, and its first director in 1932. He held the Chair in Arabic and was especially sensitive and caring about Arabic poetry with a multitude of publications in the field of Arab Studies. Specifically, in the case of the Alhambra his notable works were such as *Ibn Zamrak, el poeta de la Alhambra* (1975); *Poemas árabes en los muros y en las fuentes de la Alhambra* (1985); *Foco de antigua luz sobre la Alhambra* (1988). In these works he translated several poems about the Alhambra and the Generalife that led him to interesting and much debated hypotheses about its function, use and the periods of the rooms in the Alhambra.

Jesús Bermúdez Pareja (1908-1986). Professor of Art history in the Faculty of Humanities of Granada. He also taught in the School of Arab Studies as professor of art and archaeology. He was to be director of the Museum of Archaeology of the Alhambra and of the National Museum of Hispano-Muslim Art. His research work is mainly centred on the Alhambra. Among his publications are *Pinturas sobre piel en la Alhambra de Granada*, dedicated to the paintings in the Sala de los Reyes in the Palacio de los Leones, or articles such as that on the Baño de Comares published in *Cuadernos de la Alhambra*.

Darío Cabanelas Rodríguez (1916-1992). In 1933 he entered the Franciscan Order, becoming a priest in 1940. Professor in the Faculty of Humanities of the University of Granada, he collaborated in the founding of the journal *Cuadernos de la Alhambra* of which he would later become the editor. He was the director of the School of Arab Studies in Granada. He has several publications especially related to the inscriptions such as one of his first studies on Alonso del Castillo, interpreter of Philip II and translator of the inscriptions in the Alhambra. He has also published on Islamic buildings like the Madraza and the Casa del Chapiz and especially about the Alhambra, focussing on questions of epigraphy in El Partal, the façade of Comares and the Fuente de los Leones. But special mention is deserved for his book *El techo del Salón de Comares en la Alhambra* where he makes a magnificent study of the decoration and symbolism of the ceiling and whose analysis has been recognized and accepted by the scientific community. To recreate the painted ceiling, he drew on the help of the painter Manuel Maldonado.

Henri Terrasse. Professor and French researcher who stands out for his vision of Hispano-Muslim art. In his well-known work *L'Espagne du Moyen Age* published in Paris in 1956, he introduced a chapter dedicated to Nasrid art with an analysis and reflections on the Alhambra that traditionally had been forgotten and left to one side in studies of the Medieval period on the Iberian peninsular.

Georges Marçais. French researcher. In 1938 he published "Remarques sur l'esthétique musulmane" where in a few pages he raised the complicated axes of the symmetry of the Patio de los Leones; to Marçais we also owe the view, made public in 1954, that the Casa Real of the Alhambra should be seen as two Islamic palaces, as two different creations and not as a single palace in which Comares had been explained as being the *serrallo* and the Palacio de los Leones as the *harén*.

Basic bibliography

AA.VV. *Arte islámico en Granada. Propuesta para un Museo en la Alhambra*. Granada, Junta de Andalucía-Comares, 1995.

AA. VV. *Carlos V y la Alhambra*. Granada: Patronato de la Alhambra-Consejería de Cultura de la Junta de Andalucía, 2000. Catálogo de la Exposición (al cuidado de Pedro Galera Andreu).

AA. VV. *El Palacio de Carlos V. Un siglo para la recuperación de un Monumento*. Granada, Comares, 1995.

AA. VV. *Les jardins de l'Islam*. París, ICOMOS,1976.

AA. VV. *Manifiesto de la Alhambra*, Madrid, 1953, (Granada: Fundación Rodríguez-Acosta–Colegio de Arquitectos de Andalucía Oriental, 1993).

ALMAGRO CÁRDENAS, Antonio. *Estudio sobre las inscripciones árabes de Granada*. Granada. Imprenta de Ventura Sabatel, 1879.

ÁLVAREZ LOPERA, José. La Alhambra entre la conservación y la restauración (1905-1915). Número monográfico de *Cuadernos de Arte de la Universidad de Granada*, XIV, 1977.

ARIÉ, Rachel. *El reino nasrí de Granada*, Madrid, Mapfre, 1992.

BARGEBUHR, F. *The Alhambra. A cycle of studies on the Eleventh Century in Moorish Spain*, Berlín, 1968.

BERMÚDEZ LÓPEZ, Jesús y GALERA ANDREU, Pedro, *La Alhambra y el Generalife. Guía oficial de visita al conjunto monumental*, Granada, Comares, 1998.

BERMÚDEZ PAREJA, Jesús. *Alcazaba y torres de la Alhambra*, Cuadernos «Temas de nuestra Andalucía» n.º 10, Granada, Obra Cultural de la Caja de Ahorros y Monte de Piedad de Granada, 1972.

BERMÚDEZ PAREJA, Jesús. *Palacios de Comares y Leones*. Cuadernos «Temas de nuestra Andalucía» nº 12, Granada, Obra Cultural de la Caja de Ahorros y Monte de Piedad de Granada, 1972.

—, *El Generalife*. Cuadernos «Temas de nuestra Andalucía» n.º 30, Grana-da, Obra Cultural de la Caja de Ahorros y Monte de Piedad de Granada, 1974.

—, *El Partal y la Alhambra alta*. Cuadernos «Temas de nuestra Andalucía» n.º 46, Granada, Obra Cultural de la Caja de Ahorros y Monte de Piedad de Granada, 1977.

—, *Pinturas sobre piel en la Alhambra*, Granada, Patronato de la Alhambra, 1987.

BORRÁS GUALIS, Gonzalo, *La Alhambra y el Generalife*, Madrid, Anaya, 1989.

BURCKHARDT, Titus, *La civilización hispano-árabe*, Madrid, Alianza, 1977.

CABANELAS RODRÍGUEZ, Darío, ofm. *El techo del salón de Comares en la Alhambra. Decoración, Policromía, Simbolismo y Etimología*, Granada, Patronato de la Alhambra, 1988.

CABANELAS RODRÍGUEZ, Darío, ofm. y FERNÁNDEZ PUERTAS, Antonio, «Inscripciones del Partal y Fachada de Comares», *Cuadernos de la Alhambra*, n.º 10-11, 1965, pp. 117-199.

—, «El poema de la fuente de Los Leones», *Cuadernos de la Alhambra*, n.º 15-17, 1979-1981, pp. 3-88.

DÍEZ JORGE, M.ª Elena. *El palacio islámico de la Alhambra: propuestas para una lectura multicultural*, Granada, Universidad, 1998.

DOMÍNGUEZ CASAS, Rafael, *Arte y etiqueta de los Reyes Católicos. Artistas, residencias, jardines y bosques*, Madrid, Alpuerto, 1993.

EGUARAS IBÁÑEZ, Joaquina, *Ibn Luyūn: Tratado de Agricultura*, Granada, Patronato de la Alhambra, 1988.

FERNÁNDEZ PUERTAS, Antonio. *La fachada de Comares. I. Situación, función y génesis*. I. Granada, Patronato de la Alhambra, 1980.

—, *The Alhambra*, Vol. I. Londres, Al Saqi Books, 1997.

—, «El arte», en *Historia de España de Menéndez Pidal*, T.º VIII****, Madrid, Espasa Calpe, 2000, pp. 193-284.

GALERA ANDREU, Pedro A. *La imagen romántica de la*

Alhambra, Granada, Patronato de la Alhambra-El Viso, 1992.

GALLEGO BURÍN, Antonio, *La Alhambra*, Granada, Patronato de la Alhambra, 1963.

GARCÍA GÓMEZ, Emilio. *Ibn Zamrak, el poeta de la Alhambra*, Granada, Patronato de la Alhambra, 1975.

—, *Poemas árabes en los muros y en las fuentes de la Alhambra*, Madrid, Instituto Egipcio de Estudios Islámicos, 1985.

—, *Foco de antigua luz sobre la Alhambra*. Madrid: Instituto Egipcio de Estudios Islámicos, 1988.

GÓMEZ-MORENO GONZÁLEZ, Manuel. *Guía de Granada*, Granada, Imprenta de Indalecio Ventura, 1892, 4.ª ed. facsímil Granada, Universidad-Instituto Gómez-Moreno de la Fundación Rodríguez-Acosta, 1998.

—, «Palacio de Carlos V», *Revista de España*, XVIII, 1985, pp. 191-225.

GÓMEZ-MORENO MARTÍNEZ, Manuel. «Granada en el siglo XIII», *Cuadernos de la Alhambra,* n.º 2, 1966, pp. 3-41.

GONZÁLEZ ALCANTUD, José Antonio; MALPICA, Antonio (eds.). *Pensar la Alhambra*. Granada, Diputación Provincial-Anthropos, 2001.

GRABAR, Oleg, *La Alhambra: iconografía, formas y valores*, Madrid, Alianza, 1980.

JACOBS, Michael, *La Alhambra*, Palma de Mallorca, Cartago, 2000.

LADERO QUESADA, Miguel Ángel, *Granada. Historia de un país islámico (1232-1571)*, Madrid, Gredos, 1969.

LEVÍ PROVENÇAL, E. y GARCÍA GÓMEZ, Emilio, *El siglo XI en 1.ª persona. Memorias de 'Abd-Allāh, último rey zirí de Granada, destronado por los almorávides (1090)*, Madrid, Alianza, 1980.

MALPICA CUELLO, Antonio, *La Alhambra de Granada, un estudio arqueológico*. Granada, Universidad-Junta de Andalucía, 2002.

MANZANO, Rafael, *La Alhambra. El universo mágico de la Granada islámica*, Madrid, Anaya, 1992.

NYKL, Alois Richard, Inscripciones árabes de la Alhambra y el Generalife. *Al-Andalus*, IV, 1936-39, pp. 174-194.

ORIHUELA UZAL, Antonio. *Casas y palacios nazaríes. Siglos XIII-XV*, Barcelona-Granada, Lunwerg-Legado Andalusí, 1995.

PAVÓN MALDONADO, Basilio. *Estudios sobre la Alhambra. Anejos de Cuadernos de la Alhambra*. 2 volumes.

Granada, Patronato de la Alhambra, 1975-77.
PUERTA VÍLCHEZ, José Miguel. *Los códigos de utopía de la Alhambra*, Granada, Diputación, 1990.
RODRÍGUEZ RUIZ, Delfín. *La memoria frágil, José de Hermosilla y las Antigüedades Árabes de España*, Madrid, COAM, 1992.
ROSENTHAL, Earl. *El Palacio de Carlos V en Granada*, Madrid, Alianza, 1990.
RUBIERA MATA, M.ª Jesús. *La arquitectura en la literatura árabe. Datos para una estética de placer*, Madrid, Editora Nacional, 1981.
—, *Ibn al-Ŷayyāb. El otro poeta de la Alhambra*. Madrid-Granada, Patronato de la Alhambra-Instituto Hispano-Árabe de Cultura, 1982.
SALMERÓN ESCOBAR, Pedro. *La Alhambra, estructura y paisaje*, Granada, Ayuntamiento, 1997.
STIERLIN, Henri; STIERLIN, Anne, *Alhambra*, Barcelona, Taschen, 1992.
TORRES BALBÁS, Leopoldo. *La Alhambra y el Generalife*, Madrid, Plus Ultra, 1953.
—, *Obra Dispersa*. Madrid, Instituto de España, 1981-85. (Recopilación de los artículos publicados por este investigador, con especial dedicación a la Alhambra).
VERNET, Juan, *Lo que Europa debe al Islam de España*, Barcelona, El Acantilado, 1999.
VIGUERA MOLINS, M.ª Jesús (Coord.). *El reino nazarí de Granada (1232-1492). Política, instituciones y economía*, Vol VIII***; *Sociedad, vida y cultura*, Vol. VIII****, «Historia de España de Menéndez Pidal». Madrid, Espasa-Calpe, 2000.
VÍLCHEZ VÍLCHEZ, Carlos. *El Generalife*, Granada, Proyecto Sur, 1991.
VIÑES MILLET, Cristina. *La Alhambra de Granada. Tres siglos de historia*. Córdoba, Monte de Piedad y Caja de Ahorros, 1982.

As far as journals are concerned, it is impossible to ignore the *Cuadernos de la Alhambra*, which have been published by the Alhambra and Generalife trust since 1965 and which have channelled research into the Alhambra into more than forty published volumes.

Glossary of words and terms

(and. ar. = Andalusian Arabic / cla. ar. = Classical Arabic / nort. ar. = North-African Arabic).

acequia: (and. ar. *as-sáqya* < cla. ar. *as-sāqiya*) Canal or ditch to carry water.

adarve: (and. ar. *ad-dárb* < cla. ar. *ad-darb*) Parapet walk. An open or covered walkway along the top of the wall that runs behind the battlements. It is also used to refer to a private street with a dead end.

agallonado: Used to describe an arch, vault or dome that has *gallones* which are umbrella–like, interlinked, concave, recessed adornments, which tend to end in a point, similar to a segment of an orange; in silversmithing the *gallón* is usually convex.

ajimez: (and. ar. *aš-šamís*) Window or balcony closed by a wooden window screen and occasionally overhanging the street; it enables you to see out without being seen.

alacena: (and. ar. *al-jazána* < cla. ar. *al-jizāna*) A wooden cupboard built into the wall, normally with doors and shelves, to store several objects.

al-Andalus: Name given in the Arab chronicles to the Iberian Peninsular dominated by the Muslims; Islamic Spain.

albanega: (and. ar. *al-baníqa* < cla. ar. *al-banīqa*) pediment. Triangular space between the extrados of the arch and the *alfiz* in Islamic architecture.

alberca: (and. ar. *al-bírka* < cla. ar. *al-birka*) pool or pond.

alcaide: (and. ar. *al-qáyid* < cla. ar. *al-qā'id*) The person responsible for guarding and defending a fortress.

alcazaba: (and. ar. *al-qaṣába* < cla. ar. *al-qaṣaba*) By definition it is the walled precinct or citadel which in Islamic cities defended the Caliph's, sultan's or governor's palace, and his elite guards. In the case of the

Alhambra, some authors defend the idea that the entire precinct was a single *alcazaba*, but traditionally the name has been given to the castle that stands at its western extreme.

alcázar: (and. ar. *al-qáṣr* < cla. ar. *al-qaṣr*) Royal palace.

alcoba: (and. ar. *al-qúbba* < cla. ar. *al-qubba*) Alcove or recess. In Hispano-Muslim architecture it is a side room that opens onto a main hall through an arch.

alfarje: (and. ar. *al-fárš* < cla. ar. *al-farš*) Flat wooden ceiling, generally decorated, consisting of boards on beams; mostly it is used to support a floor on a higher storey.

alféizar: (and. ar. *al-ḥáyyiz* < cla. ar. *al-ḥayyiz*) Wall that constitutes the sill of a window or door; the inner surface of an opening. Popularly used for the window sill.

alfiz: (and. ar. *al-ḥíz* < cla. ar. *al-ḥayyiz*) The mould or box consisting of two vertical parts topped by a horizontal closure that delimits or frames the Muslim arch. It may rise from the impost or from ground level.

algorfa: (and. ar. *al-gúrfa* < cla. ar. *al-gurfa*) Upper room in a house.

alhamares: Nasrid. *Alhamares* is a derivative of al-Aḥmar, they are the descendents of the first Nasrid sultan Muḥammad b. al-Aḥmar b. Naṣr.

alhanía: (and. ar. *al-ḥaníyya* < cla. ar. *al-ḥaniyya*) Bed chambers or small rooms at the back of the porches and of palace rooms, to be able to withdraw to. Etymologically it means "the arch", "the dome-covered chamber", and effectively it is usually marked by its entrance via an arch. It is confused with the term *alhamí* (rest or low bench).

alicatado: (alicatar, and. ar. *al-qáṭ'* [= the cut] < cla. ar. *al-qaṭ'* [= the cut]) Panel or work made with small pieces of ceramic of different colours, cut and joined together forming extensive panels. It should not be confused with the *azulejo*, which is a larger, regular-shaped piece, nor with the mosaic, which is made from *teselas*, pieces that are more or less the same and that are all very small.

aljibe: (and. ar. *al-ŷuíbb* < cla. ar. *al-ŷubb*) Cistern; normally underground construction to store water.

almizate: Central and highest panel in the structures in *artesa* or of domes.

almohade: (and. ar. *al-muwaḥḥád* < cla. ar. *al-muwaḥḥid*) Name of the dynasty that governed al-Andalus and the north of Africa in the twelfth and early thirteenth centuries; art of this period.

almunia: (and. ar. *al-múnya*) < cla. ar. *al-munya*) Estate or house with a market garden or typical rural farm.

aparejo mixto: Wall made with different materials and systems (stone, mud, brick, etc.).

apeinazado: In some structures, windows or window screens, geometric forms that arise due to the jointing or assembly of the main timbers with other smaller ones called *peinazos*, which may be structural or decorative.

armadura: Cover or wooden ceiling.

arrocabe: (and. ar. *ar-rukkáb* < cla. ar. *ar-rukkāb*) Like a cornice, it is a wooden or superimposed, decorated freize that runs around the upper wall of rooms and marks the boundary between the wall and the frame structure.

artesonado: Vault or decorated wooden ceiling with coffers or boxes. It is typical in classical and Renaissance architecture. It is also incorrectly applied to any type of structure or wooden ceiling.

ataujerado: Delicate, interlaced decoration in wood that does not go as deep as the structure; applied to gates and roofing.

ataurique: (ar. *at-tawríq* < cla. ar. *at-tawrīq*) Name given to the decorative plant-forms found in Islamic art.

áulica: connected with the Court or the palace; of a royal nature.

azulejo: (and. ar. *az-zulláyŷ* < cla. ar. *az-zulayŷ*) Brick or small tile of various colours used to cover floors, or walls or as a decoration.

azulejo de arista: Literally, edged tile. A pattern is made by pressing a mould onto the still wet surface of the ceramic tile creating rough edges and some small compartments (dips) onto which colours are poured. Normally, various *azulejos* are used (typically two or four) to make up a single figure. It was a characteristic technique at the end of the fifteenth and in the sixteenth centuries for architectural cladding.

***bayt*:** Hall or room.

barbacana: (and. ar. *báb albaqára* < cla. ar. *bāb al-baqara*) Fortification or low wall that precedes the main fortress and is separated from it by a lists or a pit.

beréber: (from the Northern Arabic *berber* < cla. ar. *barbar*) Berber. Term, considered inappropriate and derogatory, to refer to a people originating in the area of the Atlas mountains and in general the ancient Maghrib, many of whom entered the Iberian Peninsular with the Arabs and eastern Muslims.

buharda, buhedera: Opening in the front of some gates to harass the enemy from above; similar to a machicolation but in the face of the wall rather than overhead.

calahorra: Tower, apparently defensive from the outside, that protects a palace or sumptuous dwelling on the inside.

califal: Belonging to Islamic Spain in the tenth century, the height of the artistic and cultural boom of al-Andalus, with the mosque in Córdoba and the palace of Medina Zahara its greatest artistic creations.

can or canes: Pieces that jut out from a plane and serve to support the eaves.

carmen: (and. ar. *kárm* < cla. ar. *karm*) House with vegetable and flower gardens, in an urban setting and normally on different levels and closed in on itself by walls, traditional in Granada.

cenador: Bower or small pavillion, generally round, usually found in gardens, surrounded and sheltered by climbing plants or trees. In Granada *cenador* is also used for the open gallery on the ground floor near to a patio.

clave: The keystone, the stone that closes an arch or vault at its highest point.

coracha: Scarp. Wall with a parapet walk or interior tunnel that links an isolated tower with the main fortified precinct.

crucero: See *patio de crucero.*

dintel adovelado: Lintel or horizontal stone resting above a door or arch where you can see the arch-stones alternating in decoration, with a clearly ornamental intention; this inversion, of the arch below and the arch-stone lintel above, is characteristic of Islamic architecture in Granada.

epigrafía cúfica: Inscription in Arabic, with a markedly ornamental character, formed by angular letters that end in curious geometric plant-shapes. It is named after the city of Kufa (Iraq) where it originated.

epigrafía nasjí (*nasjī*) or cursive: Arabic inscription that reproduces the forms of traditional writing. Writing as an ornamental form has great importance and is widespread in Islamic art as it takes the role fulfilled in western architecture by images and figurative decoration.

faldón: Each side of a panel structure, going from the *almizate* to the *arrocabe*.

gorronera: upper door jamb. Specific, and to a certain extent popular name given to the frame, the *quicialera* of a door, formed by a cantilever or small beam, normally wooden.

gramiles: Parallel lines gauged into wooden timbers; it is an adornment found on gates, windows and structures.

grutesco: Decoration formed by whimsical shapes of animals, plants, fantastic creatures, textiles, metalwork and other motifs, which interlace creating bands or highly original friezes. It is a decoration typical of the Renaissance and is of Roman origin.

***ḥammām*:** Bath; place or location with hot or thermal water to perform hygienic and ritual functions. It is made up of a more or less constant series of rooms, *bayt* in Arabic, the most important are: *bayt al-maslaj* or hall of repose and waiting;

al-bayt al-bārid or the room where towels were given to the bathers; *al-bayt al-wasṭānī* or the warm room, normally the largest; *al-bayt al-sajūn* or the hot room; behind which was the hypocaust for the hot water and beneath it the oven that heated the floor.

harén: (via French, from the Turkish *harim* < ár. *ḥarīm*) Department or rooms in the house and Islamic palace destined for women. By extension it was also used to refer to all of the women living there.

hégira: (via French, from the Arabic *hiŷra*) Calendar of Islam which counts from the year 622 CE, the date on which Mahoma fled from Mecca to Medina.

jamuga: A folding chair with curved legs and a leather seat and back rest; it was more commonly used for formal ceremonial purposes than an ordinary, everyday piece of furniture. The richest chairs of this kind are decorated with crafted incrustations or marquetry.

lacería: Combination of geometric figures or bands made by crossing over the lines to form stars or polygonal shapes in the architectural ornamentation.

lazo: (see also *rueda de lazo*) Name given in Islamic art to the geometric decoration, normally in the form of circles or stars.

linterna: Lantern. An architectural structure with windows or skylight that stands out above the main body of the building to provide lighting.

lucernario: In Nasrid architecture, an upper opening of windows or small window screen set in a lantern or room, beneath the dome or structure, that admits light from overhead.

madraza: (and. ar. *madrása* < cla. ar. *madrasa*) Muslim school of higher education.

mampostería: Work made from medium-sized, irregular-shaped stones (*mampuestos*).

mazmorra: (and. ar. *maṭmúra* < cla. ar. *maṭmūra*). Dungeon, the underground prison. In the Alhambra there are several, above all in the Alcazaba, and occasionally they also served as silos or warehouses at one time. Also, on the nearby hill de los Mártires there were numerous dungeons from which many Christians were freed after the conquest of Granada.

medina: (and. ar. *madína* < cla. ar. *madīna*) City.

mexuar: (and. ar. *mašwár* < cla. ar. *mašwara*) Chamber where the viziers or ministers met in the medieval Islamic palaces.

mihrab: (*miḥrāb*) Niche in the oratory or Islamic mosque that signals the place to which prayers should be directed. The wall where it is located is called the *qibla*.

mocárabe: (and. ar. *al-muqárbas* < cla. ar. *al-muqarnas*) Ornamental motif formed by the combination of geometric elements, like small vaults or half vaults, presenting linked, stepped concave forms, like stalactites, that decorate cornices, corbels, arches, capitals or vaulted ceilings. Incorrectly also called *muqarnas*, which are works of the same type but with a pointed profile and typical of eastern Islamic art.

morisco: Term used to name Muslims obliged to convert to Christianity following the Reconquest; in earlier centuries they were also called "new Christians". Also some use *morisco* art to name the specific *Mudéjar* art of Granada that inherited some forms and structures from the Nasrid tradition.

mudéjar: (and. ar. *mudáŷŷan*) Name given to the Muslims who remained in Christian territory after the conquest, conserving their traditions, customs and religion. The *Morisco* would be a *Mudéjar* who had been baptized. By extension the term *Mudéjar* art is applied to that which developed in some regions of Christian Spain with aesthetic influences and/or techniques drawn from Islamic art. It is a wholly Hispanic art form and social phenomenon.

muladí: (and. ar. *muwalladín*, plural de *muwallád* < cla. ar. *muwallad*) Spanish Christians who converted to Islam.

***muṣallà*:** esplanade dedicated to ritual festivals and prayer.

nazarí: Derived from *naṣrī* and at the same time from Naṣr. The name of the dynasty that governed Granada from the thirteenth to the fifteenth centuries, descendents of Muḥammad b. al-Aḥmar b. Naṣr. Also applied to the works of art from this period.

Omeya: (and. ar. *umáyya* < cla. ar. *umayya*) Umayyad. The dynasty that governed al-Andalus from 711 until the early eleventh century.

parata: Bed or small terrace built on sloping ground and normally held up by a low wall.

patio de crucero: crossing. Layout peculiar to hispano-muslim and oriental architecture, consisting of a patio with central pathways forming a cross, where slender canals of water run, and a stone basin or fountain in the centre, whereas the parterres set out between them usually have a low garden.

***qubba*:** The translation would be "dome" in Arabic. By extension, this name is also given to the building or hall with a central floor and covered by a dome or lantern. It has both a structural and symbolic meaning. Examples of *Qubbas* in the Alhambra include the Salón de Comares, dos Hermanas, Abencerrajes, Sala de las Camas, Torre de El Partal.

quicialera: Name that traditionally in the studies of the Alhambra is given to the piece, normally of marble, with a hole in the centre, where the door frame is set.

rauda: (and. ar. *ráwḍa* < cla. ar. *rawḍa*) Royal cementery.

revellín: ravelin. Low wall that precedes and reinforces a fortification; in the Alhambra the name is given to the structures added in the Christian period to locate artillery pieces.

rueda de lazo: Name given to the interlaced geometric star design used in Islamic decoration. It is made up of different tiles, which include: the *sinos*, the central piece; *zafate*, each of the polygonal pieces that form the points of the wheel; bands, *almendrillas*, *candilejos*, etc. The number of points on the star determines the name of a particular *rueda de lazo*, with the most frequent being eight-, ten-, twelve-, or sixteen-pointed stars. They may appear to be linked the one to the other with different points forming combinations.

***šarī‘a*:** Open-air oratory or mosque. It is often confused with the *muṣallà*.

***sebka*:** Ornamental motif, originating with the Almohads, formed by linked rhombus with lobed or multilinear profiles.

sultán: (and. ar. *sulṭán* < cla. ar. *sulṭān*) Prince or governor of an Islamic territory.

taca: (and. ar. *ṭáqa* < cla. ar. *ṭāqa*) Small niche or alcove, with decorative outer arch, opened in the doorjamb or the bulk of the wall of a gate; it is peculiar to Nasrid architecture.

tapial: The name given to a wall of *tapias* or *tapial* to that formed by a mixture of earth, gravel and lime all dampened and flattened, that is built with wooden timbers; it was used systematically in the walls and towers of the Alhambra.

taracea: (and. ar. *at-tarṣí‘* < cla. ar. *at-tarṣī‘*) Handcraft made in wood by incrusting and assembling small pieces that can be of other woods, mother-of-pearl, metal, ivory, etc., creating figures with sharp colour contrasts. It is typical of the artisan tradition of Granada.

taujel: (and. ar. *tawšíḥ* < cla. ar. *tawšīḥ*) Flat decorated wooden ceiling in which the beams that support it remain hidden; it usually has holes in it.

techumbre: Name generally applied to wooden ceilings.

venera: Ornamental element shaped like a pilgrim's scallop shell.

visir: (and. ar. *al-wazír* < cla. ar. *al-wazīr*) vizier. Minister to a Muslim sovereign.

vitruviano: Referring to Vitruvius, the *c.*1 B.C. Roman architect who wrote the famous *Treatise on Architecture*.

zaguán: Vestibule at the entrance to a house or palace.

zapata: base. Wooden piece that is located on the right foot or wooden pillar.

zirí: zirid. Family of the kings or *taifas* in eleventh-century

Granada and by extension art in Granada in the same century.
zócalo: dado. The lower part of a face or wall intended to be decorated with tiles, glazed ceramics or painted.

Glossary of builgings and architectural features

Many of the buildings and architectural features of the Alhambra precinct have commonly used English translations whereas others are normally given in Spanish with literal translations to explain their meaning. Here is an alphabetical list of the most important of these structures.

Acequia Real: the Royal Watercourse

Arco de las Granadas: literally, the arch or archway of the pomegranates

Baño de la Mezquita: literally, the baths of the Mosque

Baño Real de Comares: literally, the royal baths in the Comares palace

Barrio castrense: the military quarter

Casa de los Amigos: literally, the house of friends, i.e. the guest house

Castillo del Moro: literally, the Moor's castle

Cuarto Dorado: the Golden Room

El "Harén": the Harem

El Museo de la Alhambra: the Museum of the Alhambra

El Palacio de Carlos V: the Palace of Charles V

El Partal: from the Arabic for "portico"

Jardines Altos: literally, the upper gardens

Jardines del Partal: literally, the gardens in El Partal

Mirador de Lindaraja: the Lindaraja viewing-point

Palacio de Abencerrajes: literally, the palace of the Abencerrajes, family

Palacio de Comares: the Comares palace

Palacio de los Leones: the Palace of the Lions

Palacios nazaríes: the Nasrid palaces

Patio de Comares: literally, the patio or court of the Comares palace

Patio de la Alberca; literally, the patio or court of the pool

Patio de la Reja: literally, the patio of the wrought-iron railing balcony

Patio de Lindaraja: literally, the Lindaraja patio or court

Patio de los Arrayanes: the patio or court of the myrtle bushes

Patio de los Leones: the patio or court of the Palace of the Lions

Patio del Ciprés de la Sultana: literally, the patio or court of the Sultana's cypress tree

Peinador de la Reina: the Queen's Dressing Room

Pilar de Carlos V: literally, Charles V's fountain

Puerta de la Explanada, or Puerta de la Justicia: Gate of the Esplanade, or Gate of Justice

Puerta de la Tahona: literally, the gate of the oven or of the mill, we do not known which the name refers to

Puerta de las Albercas, or Puerta de los Siete Suelos: the Gate of the Pools, also known as the Gate of the Seven Storeys

Puerta de las Albercas: literally, the gate of the pools

Puerta de las Granadas: the Gate of the Pomegranates

Puerta de los Carros: literally, the gate of the wagons, as its name suggests, a gate built to allow stone to be introduced into the Alhambra precinct during the building of the Palacio de Carlos V

Puerta de los Tableros: literally, the gate of the planks or timbers, constructed near to a wooden sluice gate over the River Darro

Puerta del Foso: literally, the gate of the pit

Puerta del Vino: the Wine Gate

Rauda Real: literally, the royal cemetery

Sala de Abencerrajes: Hall of the Abencerrajes, named after members of this Nasrid family supposedly murdered there

Sala de Dos Hermanas or Sala de las Losas: Hall of the Two Sisters or of the Flagstones, named because of the flooring

Sala de la Barca: literally, the hall of the Barca, possible a corruption of the Arabic for blessing

Sala de las Camas: literally, the hall of the beds

Sala de las Frutas: Hall of the Fruit, named as such because of the painted decoration

Sala de los Ajimeces: literally, hall of the *ajimeces*, named after the wooden screens that closed off the windows

Sala de los Mocárabes: Hall of the Mocárabes, named after the stalactite-like plaster decorations on the ceiling

Sala de los Reyes: Hall of the Kings

Sala de los Secretos: literally, the hall of the secrets, named as such because of the echoing resonance it once had

Silla del Moro: the Moor's Seat

Torre de la Cautiva: literally, the tower of the Captive Lady

Torre de la Ladrona: literally, the tower of the lady thief

Torre de la Pólvora: literally, the gunpowder tower, i.e. the arsenal

Torre de la Sultana: literally, the tower of the Sultana

Torre de la Vela: Watchtower. Earlier known as the Torre de la Campana, the bell tower, and the Torre del Sol, the tower of the sun

Torre de las Armas: literally, the tower of arms

Torre de las Cabezas: literally, the tower of the heads

Torre de las Damas: literally, the tower of the ladies

Torre de las Infantas: Tower of the Princesses

Torre de los Picos: literally, the spiked tower, named as such because of its defensive elements

Torre del Adarguero: literally, the tower of the (leather) shield bearer

Torre del Agua: the Water Tower

Torre del Cabo de la Carrera: literally, the tower at the end of the street

Torre del Homenaje: Tower of Homage

Torre Quebrada: literally, the broken tower, named as such because part of the upper structure caved in in the 19th century

Torreón de Comares: the tower of the Comares palace

Torres Bermejas: literally, the red towers, named as such because of their red stone walls